Monstrous Children
and Childish Monsters

Monstrous Children and Childish Monsters

Essays on Cinema's Holy Terrors

Edited by MARKUS P.J. BOHLMANN
and SEAN MORELAND

Forewords by Steven Bruhm and James R. Kincaid

*Afterwords by Kathryn Bond Stockton
and Harry M. Benshoff*

McFarland & Company, Inc., Publishers
Jefferson, North Carolina

LIBRARY OF CONGRESS CATALOGUING-IN-PUBLICATION DATA

Monstrous children and childish monsters : essays on cinema's holy terrors / edited by Markus P.J. Bohlmann and Sean Moreland ; forewords by Steven Bruhm and James R. Kincaid ; afterwords by Kathryn Bond Stockton and Harry M. Benshoff.
    p.   cm.
Includes bibliographical references and index.

ISBN 978-0-7864-9479-8 (softcover : acid free paper) ∞
ISBN 978-1-4766-1986-6 (ebook)

1. Children in motion pictures.   2. Horror films—History and criticism.   I. Bohlmann, Markus P.J., 1978– editor.   II. Moreland, Sean, 1975– editor.

PN1995.9.C45M77 2015
791.43'6523—dc23   2015004998

BRITISH LIBRARY CATALOGUING DATA ARE AVAILABLE

© 2015 Markus P.J. Bohlmann and Sean Moreland. All rights reserved

No part of this book may be reproduced or transmitted in any form or by any means, electronic or mechanical, including photocopying or recording, or by any information storage and retrieval system, without permission in writing from the publisher.

Front cover artwork © MANDEM (www.MythpunkArt.com)

Printed in the United States of America

McFarland & Company, Inc., Publishers
 Box 611, Jefferson, North Carolina 28640
  www.mcfarlandpub.com

Acknowledgments

We would both like to thank all of our contributors for their insightful work and patience, and particularly Steven Bruhm, James R. Kincaid, Kathryn Bond Stockton, and Harry M. Benshoff for their inspiring scholarship, generous encouragement, and critical comments. We would also like to thank Phil McKnight for his editorial eye and MANDEM for granting us permission to include their artwork as the cover image.

Markus P.J. Bohlmann wishes to express his gratitude to his friends and family, monstrous and otherwise, for their love and amity.

Sean Moreland would like to thank his wife Madeleine for her unflagging support and their cherished little monster Melodie for her odd, awesome insights.... And both for putting up with his frequent and much-needed retreats to his lair to work.

Table of Contents

Acknowledgments   v
Foreword   STEVEN BRUHM   1
Foreword: Sweet Demons—And Us   JAMES R. KINCAID   7
Introduction: Holy Terrors and Other Musings on Monstrous-Childness
    MARKUS P.J. BOHLMANN and SEAN MORELAND   9

PART I. LOOK WHO'S STALKING

Monstrous Newborns and the Mothers Who Love Them: Critiques of Intensive Mothering in Twenty-First-Century Horror Films
    KAREN J. RENNER   27
"She needs more": The Villainization of Infertile Women in Horror Films   BROOKE W. EDGE   42
When Procreation Becomes Perversion: Zombie Babies
    KRISTINE LARSEN   61

PART II. FRANKENSTEIN'S KINDERGARTEN

"My hideous cinematic progeny": *Rosemary's Baby*, *Eraserhead* and *Frankenstein*   SARAH LEVENTER   79
"Doesn't everyone want their parents dead?" Monstrous Children in the Films of Ridley Scott   COLIN YEO   96
Of Radioactive Sprites and Diminutive Tyrants: Hammer's Monstrous Children   REBECCA A. BROWN   107

Part III. The Adoption Papers (Adaptations)

What About Grendel's Son? Shades of Monstrosity in
  Beowulf and Grendel Danny Gorny 125
Bringing Out Henry James's Little Monsters: Two Film Approaches
  to *The Turn of the Screw* Fredrik Tydal 142
The Monstrous Child: Replacement and Repetition in *The Shining*
  Dustin Freeley 160

Part IV. Troubled Teens and In-Betweens

Demon Drugs or Demon Children: Take Your Pick
  Sharon Packer 173
Disability and Slasher Cinema's Unsung "Children"
  John Edgar Browning 177
Monstrous Mammies in Lee Daniels's *Precious* Debbie Olson 188
Violent Nymphs: Vampire and Vigilante Children in
  Contemporary Cinema Lisa Cunningham 206

Part V. Peek-a-boo: Future Monstrosities and Beyond

"Insects trapped in amber": The Mutant Child Seer in Contemporary
  Spanish Horror Film Jessica Balanzategui 225
Hanna: The Child as Monster Who Is Supposed to Believe
  Tamas Nagypal 245

Afterword: Monstrously Yours? Kathryn Bond Stockton 261
Afterword Harry M. Benshoff 267
About the Contributors 271
Index 275

Foreword

Steven Bruhm

When Markus P.J. Bohlmann and Sean Moreland told me they were assembling a collection of essays on monstrous children, and invited me to write a foreword, I thought, "What fun! How delightful!" This response is, to those who know me, rather predictable. As someone who has devoted his whole professional life—and more of his personal life than is perhaps healthy—to consuming horror and the gothic, I find the topic of monstrous children to hold intellectual possibilities that Bohlmann and Moreland's book invitingly taps. As someone who has taught children's literature and culture for many years, I find the topic to pull into high relief what so much children's literature—from folk and fairy tales to the contemporary stylings of Roald Dahl or the late lamented Maurice Sendak—already makes palpable to a reader who is not content merely to slap the anodyne "It's only a children's story" on some of the most gruesome and horrible of narrations. And as someone whose queer engagement with the world finds the current glorification of "The Child"—and its demand, literally or symbolically, for a new reification and glorification of "The Family"—to be emotionally tiresome and intellectually confounding, I greet the machinations (and worse) of monstrous children with a delicious glee. This is the emotion, I think, that most underlies my delight at being asked to contribute: a delight not at what the monstrous child *represents* so much as a delight in what it *destroys*.

Mine is a malicious delight, to be sure; it is, simply speaking, a *schadenfreude* that takes pleasure in observing the demise of what I take to be the most normal and normalizing impulses of contemporary Western culture. Any foray into the world of the gothic, horrible, or monstrous child will pretty quickly present its audience with an array of hapless parents who earnestly want to do well by their children, who believe they are doing well by their children, or who are willing to spend enormous resources (financial, emotive, self-sacrificial) to do better by children who, for whatever reason, do not rise to meet this generosity with gratitude or affection. Sure, there are the Chris MacNeils (of *The Exorcist*) and Rachel Kellers (*The Ring*) who may have "selfishly" put their feminist desires for a career ahead of what Karen J. Renner in this collection analyzes as "intensive mothering," but there are more commonly the Rosemary Woodhouses (*Rosemary's Baby*), Katherine Thorns (*The Omen*), and Kate Colemans (*Orphan*) who desperately want children, who will do anything to (accede to the cultural imperative to) have children, and who will congratulate themselves for having achieved the dream of a nuclear family, only to be rewarded with spawns of Satan, malignant murderers, or space aliens bent on taking over the planet. And so if my *schadenfreude* is the property of a perverse and childless male academic, it is also the property of filmmakers and audiences at least since the 1950s (think *The Bad Seed* [1956] or *Village of the Damned* [1960]) and much earlier: as Sarah Leventer and Colin Yeo remind us in this collection, one of the earliest pieces of gothic fiction, Mary Shelley's 1818/1831 *Frankenstein*, delivers to us the pleasures of watching the monstrous child decimate his self-absorbed, wrong-headed, yet curiously well-meaning father. Each year we pay millions at the box office, the DVD store, iTunes, and pay-per-view to smack our lips at the destruction of the family we elsewhere invest enormous capital in propping up.

A number of the offerings in this collection recognize the *schadenfreude* inherent in the medium and give us fascinating analyses of it. Bohlmann and Moreland, drawing on Renner's earlier work, note how the current culture of "attachment parenting [...] clearly influence[s] the sustained popularity and pervasiveness of cinema's monstrous children," a pro-natalist drive that Brooke Edge, citing Lee Edelman and following Elaine Berland and Marilyn Wechter, calls a "fetal attraction." Be it in the intensive—and feminist-resonant— mothering model of the lioness protecting her (monstrous and malignant) cub, the perverse infertile woman on the outside of a family but looking jealously in, or, in Colin Yeo's analysis, the "tyrannical [paternal] characters possessed by hubris" for whom monstrous children then "serve as a rectifying force" or "counterbalance" to patriarchy (cue Victor Frankenstein and his Creature once more), the child-monster satisfies some of our most cherished political fantasies of punishment and restitution. Indeed, coming off Sarah Leventer's essay we might begin to wonder whether sexual reproduction is *always* an act of hubris. Hence one aspect of the *schadenfrohe* quality of monstrous children: they work to provide us with what John Portman has recently called, in *When Bad Things Happen to Other People*, a sense of the *appropriateness* of suffering in another person or group, a just desert for their sinful or misspent energies.¹ Monstrous destruction restores fairness to an unfair world. And as often as not, that deserved suffering and the *schadenfreude* it inspires is directed at ourselves—as parents or care-givers to young people, but also as the politically blighted "children" of noxious histories of slavery (for Debbie Olson), civil war (for Jessica Balanzategui), science and technology (Kristine Larsen, Rebecca A. Brown), or widespread misogyny (for Lisa Cunningham). To the degree that horror cinema implicates us in perpetuating tyrannies, *schadenfreude* can come to look little different from masochism, and we become both producer and object of the "child as a vehicle for sanctioned aggression," in Dustin Freeley's words. But at the same time, such *schadenfroher* masochism works to imagine social restitutions, alternative ways of being, histories lived otherwise.

That strangely salubrious version of the pleasure we take in infantile destructiveness offers for a number of contributors to this volume a more reparative horror genre than we sometimes imagine. Queer theorist (and erstwhile reader of the gothic) Eve Kosofsky Sedgwick has suggested that "reparative reading" might now be a welcome and fertile alternative to "paranoid models" in which the critic, smartly trained in the hermeneutic of suspicion, can detect with infinite reservoirs of satisfaction the hidden ideologies, the buried "isms" and "phobias," the noxious philosophies of any piece of fiction.² The reparative mode, conversely, may invite us to take the fragments of narration and reassemble them, Frankenstein-like, into a new, unexpected, yet suggestive gestalt, something offering affective engagements that do not depend for their value on the smugly condemning "we know what that means." Such is the mode of monstrous children, at least for some of the contributors here. Whether it's the filmic contextualizations of *Beowulf* that give us, in Danny Gorny's words, a "freak with a family," or the will-to-explanation back stories that John Edgar Browning analyzes in blockbuster franchises like *Halloween* and *Friday the 13th*, cinematic gothic often works to provide in mirror reflection that subjectivity of the monster that was denied Stoker's *Dracula* (but not Francis Ford Coppola's), or that was given to Mary Shelley's Creature while being completely misinterpreted by his maker. And this, I think, is one of this book's most delightful surprises: for all its invocation of *schadenfreude*, it also invites us to identify with or pity the monstrous child, and thus to pose the timely critical question: how might monstrosity, even malignancy, challenge the intellectually entrenched assumption that the only alternative to suspicious paranoia is irresponsible naivety or irrepressible sentimentality? Or to flip the question around: what role does the now ubiquitous back-story play in our pleasure at watching the monstrous child as the agent of a no-longer-pure-and-simple evil? In what ways does "trauma" inflect our *schadenfreude*?

It is from this ambivalence regarding the possible agencies of the evil child—and our possible responses to those agencies—that this book takes its best energy. Many of the essays here are informed by Lee Edelman's implacable argument in *No Future: Queer Theory and the Death Drive* that the figure of the Child is continually deployed to represent a future that can never be, but whose fantasy subtends a "reproductive futurism" that holds the child as the prop of a stultifying normalcy.[3] Following Edelman, the critics assembled here focus on the Child's alleged promises for a stable future, but they also detect in cinema's darker archive the rejoinder to these promises. For them, the gothic, horrifying, monstrous child is profoundly *anti*-futural in that such an uncanny child "troubles fixations on futurity through (re)activating the past," as Balanzategui writes, "while simultaneously functioning as incubator for a future which will never eventuate." That past, as Fredrik Tydal reminds us, is as much phylogenetic as ontogenetic, given that the monstrous child appears to be the product of a late Victorian culture forced to pit child-idealization against theories of brutal primitivism, the anthropological assertion of "childhood as the savage state in human development" that would provide Freud with so much critical leverage. Such a child, at least for Tamas Nagypal, can then be nothing more than a kind of cypher for the power of belief, wonderment, and reparative innocence in a world given over to cynicism and hopelessness— a child that is supposed to believe in goodness precisely in order that we don't have to. But as Bohlmann and Moreland make clear from the outset, the "childness" of the cinematic monster is always something more than mere projection or disavowal: "childness"—the term that runs throughout this volume in unfixed and nonce-taxonomic ways—always speaks to "an elusive quiddity, a spectral essence," according to the editors, gesturing "both toward the discursive construction of 'the child' [...] and toward something extra-discursive, extra-linguistic, and even ineffable; some inaccessible *sine qua non* without which 'the child' could not be conceived."

The ineffable, inaccessible quality of childness takes futural form, but not in the ways of which Edelman is rightly suspicious. Rather, this quality is best captured in Jessica Balanzategui's gorgeous description of Ana from Victor Erice's film, *The Spirit of the Beehive*: "She appears like the mysterious spectres which haunt [...] horror films, standing on the threshold of, and *summoning*, a new, unpredictable situation" (emphasis original). This new, unpredictable situation may partake of the apocalyptic, it may partake of the reparative (or both, for aren't apocalypses often imagined as reparative?), or it may be something entirely other—a new form of cinema, a new definition of childhood, a new mode of cultural critique. The idea of the summoning both suggests urgent demand and forestalls its content, placing this collection on the cusp of something whose future it is exciting not to know. My thanks to Markus Bohlmann, Sean Moreland, and the contributors for this collection. Reading it was, is, and will have been a pleasure.

Notes

1. John Portman, *When Bad Things Happen to Other People* (New York: Routledge, 2000).
2. Eve Kosofsky Sedgwick, *Touching Feeling: Affect, Pedagogy, Performativity* (Durham: Duke University Press, 2003).
3. Lee Edelman, *No Future: Queer Theory and the Death Drive* (Durham: Duke University Press, 2004).

Steven Bruhm is the Robert and Ruth Lumsden Professor of English at Western University in London, Canada, and managing editor of the journal Horror Studies. *He is the author of* Gothic Bodies: The Politics of Pain in Romantic Fiction *and* Reflecting Narcissus: A Queer Aesthetic, *as well as numerous articles on the gothic, queer theory, and dance; he has also coedited, with Nat Hurley,* Curiouser: On the Queerness of Children.

Foreword

Sweet Demons—And Us

JAMES R. KINCAID

"Not in utter nakedness, but trailing clouds of glory...."
Yeah, sure. The romantic child was no sooner constructed than his demon shadow popped up: the Satanic child, the child we can resent, despise, beat on to our heart's content. This schizophrenic vision reminds one of the way marginalized people are often seen and forced to live, given choices that are no choices at all. Simone de Beauvoir long ago analyzed a similar situation for women: angels or monsters, but never human.

Women have made some headway in achieving humanity. Not so children.

This extraordinary collection of analyses does more than document this miserable situation; it offers a way out. Showing the great range and force of this demonizing, the way it controls our seeing and thinking, this collection suggests through the deep persuasiveness of its arguments that we can think and feel our way into different, kinder constructions.

I want to be both personal and honest and say bluntly and crudely that I enjoyed reading this collection enormously. I recognize that such a statement may sound flabby and self-indulgent, but I mean only to register how assured, sophisticated, and uniformly bold these essays are. You'd think they were addressing a safe, well-worn topic: Tennyson's metrics perhaps. How things have changed in the last twenty years: back then, works on children and sexuality, mine certainly included, tended to mark their entry into the field with a host of defensive strategies, not least endless qualifiers and circumlocutions. None of this is true of these essays, which go right for the heart of our cultural misappropriation of "the child," in this case as an object of horror, the monster hiding in the basement, evoked by our nightmares and our deepest needs.

The scholars represented here are well aware that the monster embodies attractions too dangerous to be faced head-on, that our long-standing and cowardly fascination with the child exists behind disguises we convince ourselves are still working. The adorable, passive, receptive child is certainly present in our cinema, as are the plots that deploy him or her for our uses. This empty child waiting for the adult to complete him is as needed now as in the days of Shirley Temple, Brandon DeWilde, Bridget Anderson, or Macaulay Culkin. Take a look at *A Perfect World* (1993) or the acclaimed *Mud* (2012), pedophilic dream narratives in the same old style.

The horrorshow child provides a cover for our aggressive needs but is not really different from the traditional cutesy figure, as several of the scholars here note: both are strangely without agency or motivation—all that is hogged up by the adults. The children, from Victor Frankenstein's little boy onward, are there to be acted upon, their power always really lodged in adult figures, in us.

We in the audience, devoted to looking, exercise our sadism in the dark, protected by a cultural and artistic tradition that never asks to be examined, only repeated. Whether we are reading of the latest school shootings, mobilizing more anti-predator/pornography/pedophile actions, or sitting in a theater, we manage the same maneuvers. The child, the object of our gaze, is given little to do but enact the same old roles for our pleasure: monster or unacknowledged victim.

We can see enactments of this voyeuristic displacement everywhere in our culture, in the mania for yammering on about the very rare school-kid crimes, for instance, most notably Columbine, but also available to us now and then at other random spots across the country. We know these are absurdist, random events—or a part of us does—but we can't let them alone, and we revel in our self-satisfied yammering. Kids are safer at school than anywhere else, certainly at home; but we so need these dramas-in-the-head that we ignore all that, pretending the dangers are external, not in any way connected to our needs.

This brilliant collection mounts a humane and layered analytical power, allowing us to see, in so many forms, the child we are maneuvering cruelly and selfishly. Essay after essay shows us this figure in monstrous forms, draws us into the mechanisms by which these cinematic images come into being. They are, we cannot help but see, figures drawn by our own needs, projections not from the booth but from our minds and libidos. As a result, this collection may do much more than show us what we're doing; it may allow us to do differently, do better.

Jim Kincaid has taught at Ohio State, Colorado, Berkeley, the University of Southern California and Pitt, generally in English but with stints in women's studies, cultural studies and honors colleges. He has published widely in Victorian literature, childhood studies, theory and constructions of sexuality.

Introduction

Holy Terrors and Other Musings on Monstrous-Childness

MARKUS P.J. BOHLMANN
and SEAN MORELAND

Holy Terrors

> *Wer darf das Kind beim rechten Namen nennen?*
> —(said by Faust to Wagner)
> Johann Wolfgang von Goethe, *Faust* Part I, 588–59

> *Ein jeder Engel ist schrecklich.*
> —Rainer Maria Rilke, *Duineser Elegien*

> *Sourtout, il fallait, coûte que coûte, revenir à cette réalité de l'enfance, réalité grave, héroïque, mystérieuse, que d'humbles détails aliment et dont l'interrogatoire des grandes personnes dérange brutalement la féerie.*
> —Jean Cocteau, *Les Enfants Terribles*

This book gathers together a number of essays concerning the relationship between monstrosity and childness (a term whose implications we explore below) as mediated by cinematic fictions since the 1950s. We are convinced that a collection of this sort is the ideal forum for addressing this topic, as it allows us to move beyond the problematic desire to find a single meta-narrative to account for this extremely varied and complex phenomenon. Instead, the assemblage of approaches offered here permits multiple, and at times even productively contradictory, explorations of the role of monstrous children in popular cinema. While various historical, social, and intellectual trends (including the lingering ideological specters of Puritanism, Romanticism, and

Victorianism, the abolishment of child labor, the post–World War II advent of attachment parenting, a growing generation gap, and many more) are factors which clearly influence the sustained popularity and pervasiveness of cinema's monstrous children, none of these factors is in and of itself sufficient to explain either the longevity or the variety of this fecund trope. Similarly, this collection makes no claims to be (and realistically could not be) exhaustive in its coverage of this topic. Its emphasis falls primarily on Euro-American, English-language cinema, and given the limited scope necessitated by its format, we were unable to include treatments of the monstrous-child trope in, for example, East Asian or South Asian cinema (although both make frequent and fascinating use of monstrous-childness; for example, a discussion of the prominence of the ghostly child in the *Yurei* of Japanese film and folklore alone could populate a volume unto itself). As each contributor to this volume is all too well aware, this collection represents merely the cracking open of a window into a vast conceptual and representational landscape, rather than a completed journey through the worlds made available by conceptions of monstrous-childness.

Thus, instead of making a bid for meta-narrative totality, each of the following essays respects the tremendous variety of intersections between monstrosity and childness in film, and each serves as a complement to the differing perspectives offered by the others. There are, however, certain theoretical and thematic underpinnings that unite the diverse approaches pursued in this collection. Many of these are, at least loosely, evoked by the title of this introduction, which bears some explanation.

The phrase "holy terror" may have entered the English language as early as the 14th century (making it as venerable as the word "monster" itself), but its idiomatic application to "a person of exasperating habits or manners" is much more recent. The *Oxford English Dictionary* cites the first written instances of this usage in the 1880s.[1] By the mid–20th century, the term became increasingly associated with unruly children, an association which led to its use in translating the title of Jean Cocteau's novel *Les Enfants Terrible* (1929) into English (1955). Jean-Pierre Melville's film adaptation (1950) of Cocteau's novel can be recognized retrospectively as a harbinger of the innumerable monstrous children of cinema that would follow. The film's meditation on childhood as a lyrical mingling of magic and menace, expressed through the secret game shared by the young protagonists, anticipates the uncanny portrayal of the children in Jack Clayton's *The Innocents* (1961; discussed at length by Fredrik Tydal's contribution to this volume). Both of these subtle explorations of monstrous-childness were a far cry from the overt monstrosity of the *Village of the Damned* (1960), *Rosemary's Baby* (1968; see Sarah Leventer's essay in this volume), and even more so from *The Exorcist* (1973) and the many films that followed in its slime-spattered wake. Nevertheless, the conflation of childhood and monstrosity that unites these diverse films means that much can be gained from seeing them as part of a continuum, one also occupied by the advancing legions of cinematic monstrous children which continue unabated today.[2]

The phrase "holy terrors" powerfully evokes the conflation of innocence and fear that defines our cultural conception of childhood. Over the course of modernity, the child has served as both repository and emblem of our aspirations and our fears, our dreams and our nightmares. Characterized alternately as angel or imp, image of the soul or base animal, our idea of the child is a locus both of all that is most esteemed in our humanity, and all that is most inhuman about us. Following Philippe Ariès, many writers have noted that "the child" in its modern sense is a fairly recent conception (a claim which is reconsidered by Danny Gorny's contribution to this volume). In Colin Heywood's words, "[o]nly in comparatively recent times has there been a feeling that children are special as well as different, and hence worth studying in their own right."[3]

It is doubtless that this exceptional status, this perceived difference, has insured the interconnectedness of the child and the monster in our cultural imaginary. Our use of the word "monster" is informed by the work of many writers and theoreticians, including Robin Wood, Jeffrey Jerome Cohen, and Judith Halberstam, who have drawn attention to the connections between monstrosity and the demonstration of difference. In the most basic psychological terms, as Wood pointed out three decades ago,[4] the alterity that separates them (children) from us (adults) makes them ideal candidates for the dubious distinction of being made monstrous.

The historical emergence of "holy terror" as a way of describing an unruly individual notably corresponds to the period when the child became radically reconfigured by Victorian society. According to Hays and Hiner, as

> the nineteenth century ended, attitudes about children—most children and not just those of the middle classes—began to shift. If children had been regarded as economic assets before—as cheap labor or social security for their parents in old age—they now came to be valued for themselves. That is, children became more valuable emotionally as they lost value economically.[5]

It was this trans-valuation of sentimentalized children and their childhoods that led to Ellen Key's prescient characterization of the twentieth century as "The Century of the Child," a phrase popularized by the title of the English translation (1909) of her *Barnets århundrade* (1900). Key's anthemic opening paragraphs powerfully metaphorized the dawning century as "a small naked child, descending upon the earth, but drawing himself back in terror at the sight of a world bristling with weapons."[6] Key's text both envisaged and demanded a new social organization for a new century; society should be oriented around the family, a social organization itself conceptually organized around the "holiness of generation," a holiness whose halo could be easily seen in the sanctified figure of the child, the cherubic center of her argument. Lee Edelman, more recently, has interrogated, and excoriated, the centrality of this rhetorical figure in *No Future: Queer Theory and the Death Drive* (in this volume, Tamas Nagypal incisively challenges some of Edelman's theoretical formulations).

It is also with the close of the nineteenth century that the discipline of psychoanalysis emerged. Adopting the child as a locus for its own intellectual structure, psychoanalysis has had a drastic effect on our tendency to view "the child" as a developmental stage in the journey toward a presumed adult telos, a stage wherein all manner of things may go monstrously awry. Virgina L. Blum has described how Freud's devotion to and theorizing of the adult patient may have nothing but the child in mind.[7] Yet, while psychoanalysis has had a great deal to say about the child, it has been largely concerned not with children per se, but with using the child as a way of explaining the adult. Just as "the child" has been the locus of virtually every ideological regime founded on the rhetoric of the family, from Freud to Lacan and beyond, "the child" has also been the foundation of the psychoanalytic enterprise. Blum therefore aptly observes that "[p]sychoanalysis [...] is the preeminent twentieth-century discourse about childhood, a discourse that [...] refuses to examine the inevitable aporias occurring when adult subjects treat as ultimately knowable a position they have both internalized and forsaken."[8]

The pervasive reorganization of both our social and psychological reality under the image of the child would intensify in the period following the Second World War, leading to the creation of an ideological world in which, in Lee Edelman's words, "the Child has come to embody for us the telos of the social order and come to be seen as the one for whom that order is held in perpetual trust."[9] For Edelman, this trust determines the political sphere where policy-making for "our" (innocent, angelic) children merely serves the adult purpose of extending normative conceptions into a future already pre-defined by adults.[10]

A comparable intensification of the child's figurative centrality occurred with the emergence of Lacanian psychoanalytic theory. Lacan's infamous mirror stage posits the child as the origin of identity, only to have it processed by a symbolic order on the basis of anxiety, taboo, and denial which are projected, in turn, back onto and into the child. It is notable that Lacan's psychoanalytic project, with its emphasis on a lack at the heart of all subjectivity, emerges alongside the first wave of cinematic monstrous-children after World War II. The proliferation of such figures in the post-war period leads Karen J. Renner to ponder, "[p]erhaps in an era so entirely child- and family-focused, resentment is being secretly harbored about the expectations that children require never-ending devotion and bring complete fulfillment, and perhaps these films are expressing it."[11] The evident co-dependency between "the child" of conservative ideology, "the child" of psychoanalysis, and the many monstrous children of cinema presents a fascinating entanglement, and one which has led to the concealment of both our real and imagined children under the totalizing, if contradictory, figure of "the child." Each of the essays in this collection is, in some way, concerned with exposing such concealments, and revealing the polymorphous childness that seethes beneath them.

Why Childness?

> *He ... with his varying child-nesse, cures in me Thoughts, that would thick my blood.*
> —(said by Polixenes of his son Florizel)
> William Shakespeare, *Winter's Tale* (1623) I. ii. 171

> *In all our stories, there is but one erotic child, and its name is Purity: without color, station, or gender.*
> —James R. Kincaid, *Erotic Innocence*

> *...the child was bound to be monstrous too, because it resulted from all sorts of shifting, slipping, dislocations, and hidden emissions that I really enjoyed.*
> —Gilles Deleuze, "Letter to a Harsh Critic"

There are two other important considerations that unite the essays in this collection. First, each is grounded in awareness that the film(s) it treats are not primarily "about" actual, or particular, children. Instead, the films considered are recognized as mediations of, and meditations on, our tendency to use images of children, and associations with childhood, as ways of approaching (or obscuring) other elements of our experience; in other words, our tendency to turn "the child" into a fetish that is too often confused with the real thing.

Second, the films considered here were not created, produced, and marketed specifically with child-audiences in mind. This is not, in other words, chiefly a collection concerned with children's cinema. Rather, the films considered here were primarily directed toward adult audiences. They are thus, in a certain sense, akin to adults speaking about (or perhaps above the heads of) children, and often saying things that they would be less likely to say while speaking with (or, more likely, to) children. Such films represent a repository of desires and anxieties given rise by the evident alterity that marks the identity of the child from the non-child point of view. As our title suggests, the films explored throughout this book are obsessed with forms of childness, forms which verge, in strikingly different ways, on the borders of monstrosity. As the following essays detail, these narratives offer incisive exposures of the cultural logic that already connects our conceptions of what constitutes monstrosity to our conceptions of what constitutes the child as an image or an ideal (one that is perhaps best to contemplate altogether independently of actual children).

Our decision to focus with this collection exclusively on film, as opposed to other media and forms of cultural expression, is informed partly by the historical connection between cinema's emergence as an art-form and the rise of this new ideology of the child. It is also informed by our sense that one of cinema's most powerful effects is its potential creation of a state of curious, wondering susceptibility in audiences (a suggestion that has previously been made, albeit with different inflections, by Stephen King and Robin Wood[12]), an effect that is as likely to be derided as infantilizing (i.e., making us "childish") as praised as imaginatively empowering (i.e., making us "child-like").

In light of these suggestions, there is a certain poetic, and compelling, logic about the fact that cinematic fictions have created so many revelations of childness through their unmaskings of "the child." Perhaps these suggestions intimate how it is that cinema can so potently operate on and liberate the affects and percepts that are condensed and compressed into the figure of the child and its childhood.

While many of the films examined in this book could be considered part of the horror genre, or at least as part of the broader category of *cinema fantastique*, our focus is not on horror as a cinematic genre, but on films, regardless of their genre or style, which reveal something generative and unsettling by (re)moving, at least momentarily, the two-faced mask (little devil, little angel) that the child in the popular imaginary is normally made to wear. Nevertheless, we are keenly aware of the prior connection that exists between *cinema fantastique* and children's perception, as well as our perception of children, all of which are tinted by a certain degree of otherworldliness. As Ian Wojik-Andrews points out, a "defining characteristic of children's films and children's culture in general is the presence of an alternative world,"[13] an alternative world that impinges multiply and vitally on this one, as suggested by the dangerous consequences of the game at the heart of *Les Enfants Terribles*. This alterworldliness within the world we have is evoked, we hope, by the phrase monstrous-childness itself, however ungainly its hyphenation might seem.

Given its near-obsolescence, our insistence on using the word "childness" throughout this introduction bears some explanation. To this end, it is useful to ask how its meanings differ from those of the more familiar "childhood." Childhood, defined as the "state or stage of life of a child; the time during which one is a child; the time from birth to puberty,"[14] is a term connoting membership in a group (children, as defined within a particular historical and cultural moment) and closely linked to a developmental periodization, one that has, admittedly, varied quite widely throughout the word's historical evolution, from its early references to the womb and infancy exclusively, to its later more class-specific use in describing a young servant, to its current flexible designation of everything from infancy to adolescence.

Childhood is understood as something one passes out of at a particular moment in one's life, or as something one must set aside in gaining maturity, as in Paul's ubiquitous formulation in 1 Corinthians, "When I was a child, I spake as a child, I understood as a child, I thought as a child: but when I became a man, I put away childish things."[15] "Childish things" must be cast off, cast out, abjected (a notion Lisa Cunningham's essay in this volume addresses). Adulthood is thus predicated on the abjection of the child one used to be, albeit in an imagined, idealized state, just as the Freudian conception of individuality is predicated on the abjection of the maternal, as Kristeva famously illustrated. This leads Steven Bruhm to emphasize

> the degree that the Freudian child is the very child who founded us in our status as adults, [yet] we can only recognize and continually repress the fact that that child is our father or our mother, and has taught us more about sexuality than we can endure. The sexual child, the Gothic child, is not the fallen child; rather, it is the open fault-line on the landscape of our fantasies, fantasies that must endow our (inner) children with a sexuality we need to constitute ourselves yet to destroy in our "children."[16]

With the recent eruption of childhood studies, the term childhood has seen something of a scholastic renaissance. The term "childness," on the other hand, has lain fairly fallow since its apparently infrequent use from the Elizabethan until the Victorian eras. Nevertheless, we are convinced that it is needed to fill what amounts to a semantic gap, for which related terms such as "childlike" and "childish" are ill-suited due to the particular connotative directions they have taken in modern usage.[17] We use the term "childness" to suggest both that the child is always defined through a kind of elusive quiddity, a spectral essence, and that, in Kincaid's words, the "child is functional, a malleable part of our discourse rather than a fixed stage; 'the child' is a product of ways of perceiving, not something that is *there*" (emphasis original).[18] The term childness gestures both toward the discursive construction of "the child," reminding us of the forms of perception and representation involved in creating this idea, and toward something extra-discursive, extra-linguistic and even ineffable; some inaccessible *sine non qua* without which "the child" could not be conceived. It suggests, in short, the without within so crucial to the alterity of children (and of the adult), while distancing itself from confusion with the reality of *actual* children.

The term allows us to engage critically with how our language forces conflation of our notions of the child, and our notional children, with the living reality of particular children as subjects unto themselves. To think for a moment in terms of the analogy of gender, how impoverished would our discourse be if we were unable to differentiate "the feminine" or "femininity" from the reality of particular women? Yet this is very close to the semantic vacuum we face where "the child" is concerned. Further, the relationship between "the child" and "the woman" is not merely analogical, but rather grounded in a common root, both etymologically and conceptually. Childness has long been closely linked with femininity; the word child was "originally always used in relation to the mother as the 'fruit of the womb,'" and was very early on associated exclusively with female children.[19] Given this shared history, it should come as no surprise that the monstrous-child is often closely associated with both the monstrous feminine (as Barbara Creed has defined it[20]) and the monstrous-queer. In Harry M. Benshoff's words, "the male homosexual or queer" is "monstrous precisely because he embodies characteristics of the feminine," which is "the source of the monstrous taint."[21]

By a similar logic, Kathryn Bond Stockton exposes an adult heterosexual order as monstrous in that it offers a radically distorted view of childhood (a)sexuality, given "the general cultural and political tendency to officially treat *all* children as straight, while continuing to deem them asexual."[22] This eclipse of queerness in children contaminates conceptions of the child, which is always, as Stockton points out, a little odd and queer to begin with.[23]

We suggest childness as a *point de depart* from the linguistic, conceptual, and perceptual limitations of "the child," a term which imposes, as Susan Honeyman argues, its own particularly insidious form of discrimination:

> The choice of definite article implies a universal or stereotype, revealing a deeper obstacle: in recognizing that we are presumptuous in our construction of childhood, we seem to excuse ourselves from the need to radically alter our rhetoric and

thought. Abstraction hides prejudice, enabling us to overlook the near bigotry revealed in readings of "the child," when it would be plenty obvious, not to mention offensive, if we constantly generalized representations of "*the* woman," "*the* black," or "*the* Hispanic" and in doing so dared to speak for all [emphases original].[24]

Moving away from the metonymic containment performed by the singular noun and definite article that posits an essential, and generally negative, stasis of meaning in which the subject becomes trapped entails a de*monstr*ation of the limits of our prior discourse of childness. Monstrous-childness thus re*monstr*ates against the bewitching assumptions imposed on us by habitual expression, and the received wisdom it propagates.

In the introduction to her earlier collection of essays, *The "Evil" Child in Literature, Film and Popular Culture*, Karen J. Renner, one of our contributors, points to the difficulty in defining both "evil" and "child." She claims that what constitutes "evil" is not only determined culturally, but also historically, by a certain *zeitgeist*, and that "this fact alone tells us much about the predominant ideologies and presumptions that prevent a more straightforward type of evil child from forming in the cultural imagination."[25] As the nested quotations in Renner's title suggest, talking about the "evil child" in itself reveals a profoundly problematic debt to a cultural heritage reaching back to the inception of the angelic child figure in the Romantic age, a figure whose effaced whiteness tends to blind us to the variable fluidities of childness.

This volume seeks to both further the work done by Renner's and other earlier studies, and also to go beyond them, resurrecting childness as a way of unsettling the petrified ideology held in place by the impoverished language of "the child." This monstrous-childness, and the monstrous-children which are here gathered around it, gives rise to unruly impulses as a form of radical protest against the artificial imprisonment created by a stifling discourse informed chiefly by a combination of repression and projection rather than creation and transformation.

The "monstrous" which has found its way into the title of this collection, and the "children" which have made their way into the essays it collects, should not be conflated with the moral principle of evil (although there is certainly, in many cases, some overlap between the two). Neither should it be confused with restrictive definitions of the monster such as that proposed by Noël Carroll in *The Philosophy of Horror* (although it certainly has many parallels with Carroll's conception, and many of the cinematic monsters considered in the following essays could well correspond to Carroll's classificatory system).

The concept of monstrosity which primarily concerns us is rather what

Gilles Deleuze, drawing from Nietzsche, describes as "the pure unformed."[26] Deleuze enlarges the definition of the monstrous by recognizing it as something generative, the form of which is never given. Monsters are monstrous because they always escape human comprehension; they demonstrate what we do not know, and remonstrate against our presumption to know. How like children are our monsters! Or, as Jeffrey Jerome Cohen has it, "monsters are our children," since they "ask us how we perceive the world, and how we have misrepresented what we have attempted to place. They ask us to reevaluate our cultural assumptions about race, gender, sexuality, our perception of difference, our tolerance toward its expression. They ask us why we have created them."[27]

Each comes to be *without* the normative adult socius, but nevertheless makes its appearance *within*. Each comes on like the fairy in Grimm's version of "Sleeping Beauty," who, despite having no invitation, inevitably crashes the birthday party, a party which was thrown for (and perhaps even *over*, but hardly *by*) Beauty, herself a testament to the virginal void which links "the feminine" to "the child" by a logic of evacuation. Each signals the unyielding presence and operation of a disruptive, displacing force we have termed monstrous-childness. Giving birth to monstrous-childness, then, makes room for dissidence, difference, and perhaps, if we allow ourselves a momentarily utopian mood, a means to transcend the pathological politics that have hitherto dominated adult-child relations.

Do You Fear (for) Your Child? Of Screening (and Screaming) Children

> *Fear isn't so difficult to understand. After all, weren't we all frightened as children? Nothing has changed since Little Red Riding Hood faced the big bad wolf. What frightens us today is exactly the same sort of thing that frightened us yesterday. It's just a different wolf.*
> —Alfred Hitchcock, *It's Only a Movie: Alfred Hitchcock: A Personal Biography*

> *These days, when you leave the theatre after a fright-movie, you can't go home again—not because you've lost your innocence, as the adage suggests, but because you're afraid that your child will kill you.*
> —Steven Bruhm, "Nightmare on Sesame Street"

> *[T]here has never been a more revolting sight than that of a generation of adults which, having destroyed all remaining possibilities of authentic experience, lays its own impoverishment at the door of a younger generation bereft of the capacity for experience.*
> —Giorgio Agamben, *Infancy & History*

Childhood is a threshold that is delineated (and arguably even experienced) retrospectively. Its discursive and narrative construction seems to have been indelibly colored by the Edenic myth, as a paradoxical paradise we can look back upon longingly, but can never re-enter once we've partaken of the knowledge that inaugurates us into adulthood. James R. Kincaid writes that behind our "obsessive-compulsive drive" to represent and control the image of the child is a "muddled confusion about our own lost childhoods, our fantasies and wishes, our cultural fables, all those pretty images, all those erotic dreams—and the real thing, which gets in the way, the child before us."[28] We are convinced that re-introducing the term childness is a useful strategy against the conflation of "the child" as an idea(l) with children as subjects whose struggles with the paradoxes of subjectivity are complicated by the fact that the terms used to convey that subjectivity are almost invariably given, and controlled, by those who are themselves no longer children. Our conception of monstrous-childness shares many affinities with Kathryn Bond Stockton's critique of teleological growth and the sideways maneuvers it denies.[29]

The organization of this book is thus meant as a parodic engagement with the teleological developmental assumptions that have bound childness to "the child." Each section loosely corresponds to a "stage" or "phase" in the life of a hypothetical monstrous child, from its (and it is rendered an *it*, rather than a *s/he*, by the discursive logic which both infuses and confuses our conceptions of monstrosity and childness) inception and fetal development to the troubled teen years that serve as an egress into adulthood, the point at which this "childish thing" must be put away, or put down, so that the adult may be "born."

This format is also a mocking reflection of the notion that the child is the "seed" of the adult-to-be, a notion that has predominated at least since the Romantic period. To take one famous instantiation of this notion, Wordsworth's "My Heart Leaps Up" suggests that childhood is a prelude to a being-yet-to-be, with its famous declaration that "the Child is father of the man." This conceit serves as one of the founding gestures of what Bruhm terms the discourse of "the child within," so predominant in our times: "Stemming from a romanticism inaugurated by Rousseau and William Wordsworth, 'the child within' has moved in the last few decades from a site of embarrassment (who before the 1980s would have pined to return to immaturity, to be psychologically infantilized?) to one of desire, even covetousness (the child within holding the privileged role of psychological insight, domestic bliss, even world peace)."[30]

Since this conceptual childhood's popularization in the early modern period, especially under the aegis of Romanticism, it has been inseparably linked to a powerful nostalgia. James R. Kincaid has written much about the dangerous role adult nostalgia plays in contemporary Western conceptions of the-child-as-innocent, conceptions that inform what he calls a "culture of child molestation."[31] Kincaid has therefore provocatively insisted that adult nostalgia is a major factor in the eroticization of the child (and woman) that centers on innocence and its annulments. He claims that

> [t]he constructions of modern "woman" and modern "child" are very largely evacuations, the ruthless distribution of eviction notices. Correspondingly, the instructions we receive on what to regard as sexually arousing tell us to look for (and often create) this emptiness, to discover the erotic in that which is most susceptible to inscription, the blank page.[32]

This climate both fosters and forbids child-loving while ignoring the actual child that is to embody the image of innocence adults so ardently long for. Our culture of child-loving stifles the actual children it alleges to love; its pedophilia comes with pedophobia, a fear of getting in touch with and too close to the actual child.[33]

Another form of child-loving, the discourse of the inner child becomes a way of symbolically retaining the child, while still performing its abjection as a gesture that permits entry into adulthood. It is, in other words, an introjection of the child, which is thereby saved, while at the same time being sacrificed, in the creation of this image. The discourse of the inner child is deeply entangled with psychoanalysis's dissection of the child into discrete developmental phases, each a potential pitfall that can corrupt or pervert the adult that the child is supposed to become. This sacrificial/preservational objectification of the child begins to look rather alarmingly like Nabokov's infamous monster-child, Lolita, who only exists for readers through the mediation of her narrator (the Dr. Frankenstein to her monster, if you will) Humbert Humbert, himself an adult whose monstrosity extends from his having been trapped in one of these fraught developmental stages.

In effect, Humbert's pedophilic ideal of those "chosen creatures," the "Nymphets," is a crystallization of exactly those insidious conceptual tendencies that writers including James R. Kincaid and Bruhm warn us against. Humbert's defining delusion is that certain girl-children between the ages of nine and fourteen have a "true nature which is not human, but nymphic (that is, demoniac)."[34] While Humbert's claim is disturbing, it also merely exaggerates the fetishistic tendencies already at work in the received wisdom about the inner child and the child-as-innocent.

As Bruhm states, "Innocence and corruption are not opposites; each makes the other possible ... childhood innocence exists 'prior' to corruption but corruption is the only means by which we can recognize and name that innocence. Thus, we attempt to recapture that innocence by 'healing' or eradicating the very corruption that structures it. To find our innocence we must destroy it; we return to the child within in order to kill it."[35] Killing "childhood," in the term's very ambiguity, becomes the concern of the contributions of this volume. Each essay turns to the screening of, and screaming of, monstrous children, chronicling our fear for and of children and their reckoning with an adult world through a cinematic lens.

"Look Who's Stalking" contains essays that focus on inception and infancy. Karen J. Renner's "Monstrous Newborns and the Mothers Who Love Them: Critiques of Intensive Mothering in Twenty-First-Century Horror Films" sets the stage by providing an interpretive framework for the monstrous infant, one which examines the relationship between the incidental physical monstrosity of monster-infants and the purported moral monstrosity of their mothers. Renner persuasively argues that these monstrous children are effects created by the demonization of certain maternal ideologies within the primarily male cinematic imaginary they inhabit.

Brooke W. Edge's "'She needs more': The Villainization of Infertile Women in Horror Films" turns to inception in the age of technological reproduction, disclosing the fears of technology, social surveillance, and abjection surrounding the "monstrous" infertile women and the children they are supposed (not) to have. Closing this section with an examination of a particularly pervasive trope of recent horror films, Kristine Larsen's "When Procreation Becomes Perversion: Zombie Babies" considers the popularity of the zombie infant in terms of women's fears of infertility, of pregnancies and births, and of not being able to love the child-invader feeding away inside their wombs.

"Frankenstein's Kindergarten" gathers together essays that deal with cinematic monstrous children whose creation is indebted, often quite directly, to Mary Shelley's techno–Gothic Ur-text, *Frankenstein*. These essays are further united in suggesting that a world of "adult" Enlightenment values resembles a frightful kindergarten run by Shelley's eponymous scientist. Sarah Leventer's "'My hideous cinematic progeny': *Rosemary's Baby, Eraserhead,* and *Frankenstein*" turns to *Frankenstein*'s central narrative and employs monstrous-childness to undermine the rational order personified by male-centered, Enlightenment logic, revealing the repository of sexual, familial, and ideological nightmares produced by such logic. Colin Yeo's "'Doesn't everyone want their parents dead?' Monstrous Children in the Films of Ridley Scott" reads the sci-fi/horror films of Scott's oeuvre as descendants of Shelley's novel, drawing on its philosophical concerns and ramifications, many of them mediated through figures of monstrous-childness. While being less directly concerned with *Frankenstein* as a pre-text, Rebecca A. Brown's "On Radioactive Sprites and Diminutive Tyrants: Hammer's Monstrous Children" considers a number of British films whose gothic children nonetheless stand in the shadow of Shelley's creation, and whose monstrosity both enables and reflects their survival strategies during the Cold War era.

"The Adoption Papers (Adaptations)" deals with cinematic adaptations of literary texts featuring monstrous children. Danny Gorny's "What About Grendel's Son? Shades of Monstrosity in *Beowulf and Grendel*" explores children as liminal figures that interrogate the boundaries between childhood and adulthood, humanity and monstrosity. Gorny further offers some thoughts on the ways the English language has evolved along with cultural conceptions of childhood, and discusses the relationship between tale-telling and reality, discovering monstrous potentialities that refuse to settle for one master discourse but spark continued narrations and adaptations.

The secret world of childhood is taken up by Fredrik Tydal's "Bringing Out Henry James's Little Monsters: Two Film Approaches to *The Turn of the Screw*," which locates the horror in these films as lying with the adult characters' barred access to an elusive childhood. Such inability to locate childhood is what makes for the monstrous in *The Turn of the Screw*, displacing monstrosity both from the governess and the children in whom these various interpreters of the novel have tried to re-locate it. In contrast, Dustin Freeley's "The Monstrous Child: Replacement and Repetition in *The Shining*" explores the anxieties between father and son, in which the latter acts as a reminder of the former's failures and incapacities amidst the pressures of the socio-symbolic order. Following Deleuze's concepts of difference and repetition, this essay aims to delink father and son from repeating the same generational programs, and to enjoin them in the production of differences whereby adoptions of the same become adaptations with a difference.

"Troubled Teens and In-Betweens" explores adolescent characters that find themselves not only in between the ageist realms of childhood and adulthood, but also in-between categories of race, gender, and the divide of the human/inhuman. Psychiatrist Sharon Packer's contribution, "Demon Drugs or Demon Children: Take Your Pick," mediates upon the fascinating, and troubling, discursive overlap between Hollywood portrayals of supernaturally monstrous children (especially that in Friedkin's seminal film *The Exorcist*) and the ongoing debates about the widespread prescription of psychiatric drugs to children and youths. John Edgar Browning's essay "Disability and Slasher Cinema's Unsung 'Children'" turns to slasher movies that give rise to "Adult Child" killers amidst disabling discourses on childhood and adulthood. Debbie Olson's "Monstrous Mammies in Lee Daniels's *Precious*" takes up the pathologies of Western culture's discourse on childhood as a predominantly white one that "others" black female children. In "Violent Nymphs: Vampire and Vigilante Children in Contemporary Cinema" Lisa Cunningham explores hyperbolic performances of helplessness and girlness by homicidal young female characters, framing them as facilitating moments that employ childness as a destabilizing force that allows for the integration of otherness within received discourses on both childhood and adulthood.

"Peek-A-Boo: Future Monstrosities and Beyond" looks forward to the future, or the death, of "the child," turning to the discourse of futurity and its politics *for,* but never *by,* children. Jessica Balanzategui's "'Insects trapped in amber': The Mutant Child Seer in Contemporary Spanish Horror Film" explores Spain's traumatic past and the nation's appeal to progress, which comes at the cost of its ghosted and entombed children. Yet these children come to thrive in trauma's spatio-temporal fissures, becoming Deleuzian "child seers" who peek beyond the narratives of linear progression that have previously tried to define them.

Critiquing Lee Edelman's futurity in *No Future* and its anti-social divide between a self-perpetuating social order and its queer disruptions, Tamas Nagypal's "*Hanna*: The Child as Monster Who Is Supposed to Believe" turns to *Hanna* as a film and character that complicates Edelman's binarizing positions of inclusion/exclusion, conformity/disruption, and domination/victimhood. Hanna's monstrosity shows in her refusal to settle into binarisms and in her occupation of a new mode of subjectivity called childness that unfolds along Lacan's concept of the supplement and Žižek's notion of the sublime. Closing out this volume on monstrous-childness, Nagypal's essay aligns itself with the others in their critiques of narratives *on* (both purporting to be about and founded in the name of) children, but never *by* them. It is an apt point of departure, with its illustration of how new discourses made possible by monstrous-childness can displace the figure of "the child," as well as deterritorialize the contested and congested conceptual space of childhood through childness.

Notes

1. See "holy, adj. and n.," *OED Online* (March 2013, Oxford University Press).
2. For a cursory summary of films involving strange and dangerous children, see Karen

J. Renner's introduction to *The "Evil Child" in Literature, Film and Popular Culture* (New York: Routledge, 2013).

3. Colin Heywood, *A History of Childhood: Children and Childhood in the West from Medieval to Modern Times* (Cambridge: Polity Press, 2001), 2.

4. Robin Wood, "The American Nightmare," *Hollywood from Vietnam to Reagan and Beyond* (New York: Columbia University Press, 2003).

5. Joseph M. Hawes and N. Ray Hiner, eds., *A Cultural History of Childhood and Family in the Modern Age* (Oxford: Berg, 2010), 4.

6. Ellen Key, *The Century of the Child*, trans. Marie Franzos (New York: Putnam, 1909), 1–2.

7. Virginia L. Blum, *Hide and Seek: The Child Between Psychoanalysis and Fiction* (Urbana: University of Illinois Press, 1995), 25.

8. Blum, *Hide and Seek*, 8.

9. Lee Edelman, *No Future: Queer Theory and the Death Drive* (Durham: Duke University Press, 2004), 11.

10. Edelman, *No Future*, 11.

11. Renner, *The "Evil Child,"* 21.

12. See, for example, Stephen King, *Danse Macabre* (New York: Berkeley Books, 1983), 99–100, Stephen King, "Why We Crave Horror Movies," in *Models for Writers: Short Essays for Composition*, eds. Alfred Rosa and Paul Eschholz (Boston: Bedford/St. Martin's, 2004), 460–463, and Robin Wood, "The American Nightmare," 63–84.

13. Ian Wojik-Andrews, ed., *Children's Films: History, Ideology, Pedagogy, Theory* (New York: Garland, 2000), 10.

14. See "childhood, n.," *OED Online*, (March 2013, Oxford University Press).

15. 1 Corinthians, 13:11, King James translation.

16. Bruhm, "Sesame Street," 110–1.

17. See, for example, the *OED* entry for each term. Childlike is used "almost always in a good sense, with reference to the innocence, meekness, etc., of children; opposed to childish, which is generally used in a bad sense." "childlike | child-like, adj. and adv.," *OED Online* (March 2013, Oxford University Press).

18. Kincaid, *Erotic Innocence*, 19.

19. "Child, n.," *OED Online* (March 2013, Oxford University Press).

20. Barbara Creed, *The Monstrous Feminine: Film, Feminism, Psychoanalysis* (New York: Routledge, 1993).

21. Harry Benshoff, *Monsters in the Closet: Homosexuality and the Horror Film* (Manchester: Manchester University Press, 1997), 6.

22. Kathryn Bond Stockton, "Eve's Queer Child," in *Regarding Sedgwick: Essays on Queer Culture and Critical Theory*, eds. Stephen Barber et al. (New York: Routledge, 2002), 185; emphasis original.

23. Harry Benshoff, *Monsters in the Closet: Homosexuality and the Horror Film* (Manchester: Manchester University Press, 1997), and Kathryn Bond Stockton, *The Queer Child, or Growing Sideways in the Twentieth Century* (Durham: Duke University Press, 2009). On the eclipse of queerness in children, see also Sedgwick, *Tendencies*, 154–164.

24. Susan Honeyman, *Elusive Childhood: Impossible Representations in Modern Fiction* (Columbus: Ohio State University Press, 2005), 10.

25. Renner, *The "Evil Child,"* 6.

26. Gilles Deleuze, *The Logic of Sense* (New York: Columbia University Press, 1990), 107.

27. Jeffrey Jerome Cohen, "Monster Culture (Seven Theses)," in *Monster Theory: Reading Culture*, ed. Jeffrey Jerome Cohen (Minneapolis: University of Minnesota Press, 1996), 20.

28. Kincaid, *Erotic Innocence*, 164.

29. Kathryn Bond Stockton, *The Queer Child, or Growing Sideways in the Twentieth Century* (Durham: Duke University Press, 2009).

30. Bruhm, "Sesame Street," 107–8.
31. James Kincaid, *Erotic Innocence: On the Culture of Child-Molesting* (Durham: Duke University Press, 1998), 140.
32. Kincaid, *Erotic Innocence*, 16.
33. Kincaid, *Erotic Innocence*, 14.
34. Vladimir Nabokov, *The Annotated Lolita*, ed. Alfred Appel, Jr. (New York: Vintage, 1991), 16.
35. Bruhm, "Sesame Street," 108.

PART I

Look Who's Stalking

Monstrous Newborns and the Mothers Who Love Them

Critiques of Intensive Mothering in Twenty-First-Century Horror Films

Karen J. Renner

In her 1996 book *The Cultural Contradictions of Motherhood,* Sharon Hays argued that contemporary American child-rearing had become dominated by an ideology she termed *intensive mothering*, which she claimed was defined by three mandates: first, that mothers should be the primary caretakers of their children; second, that proper caretaking required mothers to "[lavish] copious amounts of time, energy, and material resources" on their children; and, third, that mothers should regard mothering "as more important than [their] paid work."[1] Hays's concept of intensive mothering—and the ideology itself—has proven to be enduring: since the publication of Hays's book, scholars have continued to illustrate its pervasive and pernicious influence upon a variety of contemporary texts, including *Working Mother* magazine (Duqaine-Watson), examples of so-called mommylit (Parkins), baby manuals (Michaux and Dunlap), and even films about pregnant assassins (Goren).[2]

Significantly, most of the primary texts that have been shown to uphold this ideology are female-authored, intended for a female audience, and often both. This trend complicates the claim that the idealization of intensive mothering acts as a patriarchal backlash against women, designed to return them to the home and burden them with an impossible set of domestic standards. It is equally plausible that approving portrayals of intensive mothering validate a choice to return to more traditional realms and roles, a message that some women might want to hear. If texts show mothers as all-loving and self-sacrificing and demonstrate that this type of mother love is essential to a child's healthy development, then motherhood becomes a heroic undertaking rather than a retreat from career ambitions and professional advancement. The fact that motherhood itself has also become an active academic area suggests a desire to treat maternity itself as being worthy of professional study.[3]

If intensive mothering is deified in these female-authored and female-consumed arenas, the case is far different in the male-dominated genre of horror. In this genre, intensive mothers more often produce boogeymen than well-adjusted offspring, or act as the primary horrors themselves.[4] The subversion of intensive mothering within the horror genre further complicates the claim that this ideology is a patriarchal device designed to constrain female existence. Since horror films are still more often created by men and cater to what are assumed to be primarily male viewers, their negative treatment of intensive mothering suggests that this ideal is not upheld consistently across genres, between genders, or amongst different age groups. However, as we will see, the critique of intensive mothering in horror films is not necessarily an act of feminist liberation from domestic constraints.

Two recent horror films provide especially grotesque portrayals of intensive mothers: Joseph Rusnak's 2008 remake of Larry Cohen's 1974 film *It's Alive* and the 2009 movie *Grace*, directed by Paul Solet.[5] Both center on women, respectively named Lenore and Madeline, who give birth to babies who need to feed on blood rather than on their mother's milk. As the only ones aware of their babies' true natures, Lenore and Madeline devote themselves to secretly providing for and protecting their carnivorous infants. In doing so, they become completely isolated from the rest of the world, their lives revolving entirely around their babies' needs. They become, in other words, extreme examples of intensive mothering. Their plights momentarily generate sympathy; however, ultimately these films fiercely condemn these women as embodiments of a dangerous set of attitudes and practices.

Perhaps these male-authored films express sincere concerns about a rigid maternal ideal that proves damaging to women and those around them. In fact, their undermining of intensive mothering could suggest that men are just as uncomfortable with an ideology that devalues their own domestic contributions and dismisses their ability to serve as satisfactory caretakers and homemakers. These horror films might register male dissatisfaction with an ideology that ousts them from the home and views them as providers first and parents second. However, as we will see, they also script motherhood in equally problematic ways. Furthermore, both films portray the protagonists' espousal of intensive mothering as a personal choice rather than the result of social pressure, thus making the critique psychological rather than cultural in nature.

Defining the Monstrous Newborn Narrative

In their introduction to this collection, Sean Moreland and Markus Bohlmann importantly point out that treatments of "monstrous childness" are so diverse that they cannot be distilled down into a single master narrative. For this very reason, I have attempted elsewhere to distinguish between subtypes of "evil" child plots as they appear in a variety of cultural texts, including the possessed child, the feral child, and the antichrist-as-child narratives.[6] But even these subtypes are far from consistent ideological vehicles—including the one this essay focuses upon, the monstrous newborn narrative.

I focus on the monstrous newborn *narrative* because I agree with recent critics that the "monster" is determined less by a set of static characteristics than by its role within a larger narrative. Building off critics like Noël Carroll and Jeffrey Jerome Cohen, who approach the monster as an entity with certain features,[7] Matt Hills, for example, agrees that monsters typically "(1) violate cultural categories, (2) inspire revulsion and disgust, and (3) cue a sense of threat" but argues that they "only do so via the representation of narrative events such as the victim shrinking away from the monster."[8] A similar point has been made by Asa Simon Mittman, who claims that a monster is "not really known through observation" but rather "through its *effect*, its impact."[9]

Embedded within both Hills's and Mittman's discussions are two vying definitions of "monster": one is a label based on more immediately observable features while the second is an earned designation. The monstrous newborn narrative purposely contrasts these two definitions. It juxtaposes the child's observable monstrosity (i.e., its physical differences from the norm of "newborn-ness") with the moral monstrosity of adults (revealed as the plot unfurls) in order to make its thematic point: that the apparent monstrosity of the child is a reflection and effect of the moral monstrosity of the adult. While the child's monstrosity is inherent, an inevitable result of the conditions of its conception, the monstrosity of the adult is active and intentional, and therefore more blameworthy. The monstrous newborn may "violate cultural categories" of newborn-ness in appearance, ability, appetite, or affect. It may also "inspire revulsion" due to its differences from the typical newborn, and, if those differences allow it to harm others, then it may additionally "cue a sense of threat." But the newborn is still a newborn, after all. Having only recently emerged from the womb, it has had no time to "accrue" monstrous characteristics on its own but rather has been "born that way"; its lack of intentionality reduces its culpability. In addition, the monstrous newborn lacks a complete moral understanding of the consequences of its actions. Even if it is far more cognizant than the typical tot, its comprehension of the world is still inferior to the adults who surround it. Ironically, then, the monstrous newborn narrative actually preserves the Romantic image of childhood innocence by attributing apparent violations to corruption from the adult world.

The monstrous newborn narrative accomplishes its ideological agenda of tracing the incidental monstrosity of the child to the intentional monstrosity of the adult by manipulating three variable plot points: (1) the nature of the child's monstrosity and its consequences; (2) the cause of the child's monstrosity; and (3) the responses of the adults who are aware of the child's monstrosity. Monstrous newborn narratives do not highlight a singular form of adult corruption. Rather, the ways a particular text handles these variables determine its critique. Different monstrous newborn narratives perform different cultural work, and even the same text can support multiple interpretations.[10]

The first variable concerns what features of the newborn make it monstrous. In some cases, visible abnormalities—such as fangs and claws—mark the baby's difference and make it a viable threat. Other stories assign the newborn a "normal" appearance but advanced cognitive development and a more complex psychology—typically one that does not resemble the helpless, loving, and innocent nature we expect of an infant. What makes the newborn monstrous in these narratives, then, is partly its deviation from the norm in terms of appearance and/or mental capacities. But the consequences of these differences are important as well: if they result in harm to others and if the child intentionally inflicts that harm, then the child's monstrosity is made even more concrete.

However, to a large degree, the nature of the newborn's monstrosity is incidental because it is clearly not a reflection of the child's choice or will. Rather, these narratives typically allude to an external cause, which become the real "monster" of the story. In other words, the child's monstrous nature is merely a physical emblem of the moral monstrosity of the adult. In some stories, the etiology of the child's abnormality is a pollutant or other environmental toxin or a purposeful scientific manipulation, of which the child is an unwitting victim. These types of narratives mitigate the horror prompted by the child's monstrosity and instead direct our distaste at the true villains of the tale, such as irresponsible corporations that sell unsafe products or utilize dangerous manufacturing processes or maniacal scientists more interested in breaking scientific ground than in behaving ethically. When a cause is not definitively specified, the narrative prompts the viewer to interpret the story metaphorically. In many cases, the narrative points out flaws in either or both parents' personalities or reveals problems within their relationship or the larger family unit. Such narratives suggest that monstrous-childness is a result of the world without; they simply do so in a more dramatic, less literal fashion: if indulgent parents spawn a spoiled brat in real life, in horror films they produce an actual flesh-eating beast. In identifying external causes for the observable monstrosity of the child, these texts highlight the greater moral atrocities of adult society.

Equally important in shifting the label of "monster" from child to adult are the choices adults make in response to the appearance of the monstrous newborn. Again, the nature of the child's monstrosity proves important here only insofar as the extent to which it advertises itself. If the abnormality is visibly obvious, then obviously people will be instantly aware of it; if hidden, then only a select few may know. For example, in Larry Cohen's *It's Alive* (1974), a newborn armed with fangs and claws escapes from the hospital after killing off everyone in the delivery room except for his mother and becomes a public threat; the pharmaceutical executives who suspect they are responsible for the child's deformity simply want it eradicated, with no evidence left behind. In the sequel *It Lives Again* (1978), these mutant babies have become a nationwide epidemic, born to all manner of couples. By expanding the child's impact from the single family to society at large and by juxtaposing the community's condemnation with the compassion that enlightened adults exhibit, Cohen's films critique our tendency to revile those who violate norms; the babies become the victims of an unforgiving society, which in itself is the cause of their deviance.

In other films, when the adult's monstrosity is not physically manifested and thereby a secret known to few, the adult's actions become the subject of moral contemplation. Such is the case in the remake of *It's Alive* and *Grace*. Both films handle the key variables of the monstrous newborn narratives in ways that allow them to serve as critiques of intensive motherhood. First, in both stories, the children are monstrous on the "inside," their appearances suggesting nothing other than normal babies. As a result, only their mothers know their true natures. In *It's Alive*, Daniel's angelic appearance serves as an effective disguise for his carnivorous appetites and predatory abilities; he can apparently hide the fangs and claws he hunts with at will. Grace's appearance does not betray her hunger for blood either, but, unlike Daniel, she lacks the strength to provide for herself. Neither movie gives a clear reason for the children's revolting dietary predilections, leading viewers to seek more symbolic causes, the most viable of which are their mothers' problematic attitudes toward maternity. Finally, in both films, the mother chooses to remain the sole bearer of her baby's terrible secret and to protect and provide for her child even if it means hurting herself and others.

Together, these similarities yield narratives in which the newborn's incidental monstrous features merely serve to reveal, through the diegesis of the films, the more horrifying intentional and moral monstrosity of the intensive mother. The appearance of the monstrous newborn creates a set of narrative circumstances that allows for the ramifications of intensive mothering at its most extreme to be exposed. The "monsters" that these women birth are simply physical embodiments of their mothers' deviant maternal ideals. Specifically, the films cite these mothers for three "sins," all of which result from their adherence to the ideology of intensive mothering: (1) a readiness to entirely sacrifice themselves, body and soul, for their babies; (2) a willingness to sacrifice others, with or without their consent, for their infants' wellbeing; and (3) an utter lack of authentic interest in their partners unless proffering romantic or sexual attention helps them provide for their children. If the monster symbolically embodies the preoccupations of a particular cultural moment, as theorists like Cohen and Carroll have argued, the monstrous newborn is a secondary sort, a harbinger of a more threatening monster yet to be revealed.

It's Alive Yet Again: Rebirthing Cohen's Monstrous Infant

If acknowledged at all, Josef Ruznak's 2008 remake of *It's Alive* is almost consistently panned, described as an uncalled-for revisiting of a film of already questionable merit. Even Cohen himself has disowned it.[11] Certainly, the contemporary version has little in common with its predecessor aside from a shared title, a general similarity in premise, and a rough equivalency in the names and functions of the main characters. In Rusnak's remake, the central character, Lenore, is a graduate student whose academic ambitions are interrupted by an unexpected pregnancy. She leaves school in order to move in with the father of her child, Frank, and his younger disabled brother, Chris, intending to return to her studies once the child is born. The baby comes earlier than expected, and Lenore is rushed into the delivery room for an emergency C-section. She is later discovered, still anesthetized, with her newborn,

Daniel, sleeping nestled peacefully on her chest; around her lies the entire attending staff, brutally slaughtered. We know that the baby is responsible and Lenore seems to suspect as much as well, but everyone else in the film assumes that a passing psychopath stepped in to commit the murders, for nothing about Daniel's cherubic countenance suggests that he is out of the ordinary. While Cohen's original newborn announced its monstrosity in its appearance, Daniel's vampire-like ability to hide his claws and fangs when not on the hunt means that only his most intimate companion—his mother—becomes aware of his true nature. Lenore chooses to keep this knowledge to herself, a decision that forces her to constantly monitor and attend to her child in order to preserve their secret. Thus, a young woman, initially unsure she even wanted to keep her baby and far more focused on her career, chooses a life of intensive mothering.

Though the film is ambiguous as to what exactly Lenore's prenatal contributions to her child's monstrosity are, *It's Alive* leaves no doubt that Lenore's behavior once she has become a mother is reprehensible. Lenore forgives Daniel's carnivorous habits with bizarre haste, severing our sympathies with her just as quickly. Daniel uses his fangs to feast on Lenore's breasts, leaving them chewed up and bruised, yet she never complains. When she cannot sate his capacious hunger, he seeks other fare, including small vermin and the household cat. Although it takes some time for Lenore to find definitive proof that Daniel is a predator, once she does, she doesn't seem especially surprised or bothered. When Lenore first catches Daniel feeding on a bird, she simply scolds him, saying, "Do not ever ever ever eat this." Later on, Lenore finds Daniel feasting upon a jackrabbit in his crib; she gags but ultimately just disposes of the carcass. Lenore's unwavering love for her child in spite of his revolting eating habits makes her unconditional mother-love seem perverse rather than laudable.

Over the course of the film, Lenore's inadequate emotional responses to the deaths caused by her son and her continual refusal to take any action against him suggest that Daniel's physical monstrosity is merely a symbolic embodiment of his mother's monstrous ethics. Even after Daniel graduates to human prey, Lenore refuses to divulge his secret or take measures to control her savage son, resulting in further emotional distance between protagonist and viewer. At one point, Daniel viciously slaughters a psychiatrist solicited by the police to question Lenore regarding the delivery room murders. When Lenore discovers the man's mutilated corpse—and her son happily devouring his kill—she chokes back her nausea and routinely disposes of the car in a nearby lake. Even when Daniel kills two of her closest friends, Lenore just stashes their bodies in the basement. She grieves but is not so horrified by Daniel's behavior that she seeks to end his predatory reign, even when his victims are those nearest and dearest to her.

Lenore's maternal choices make her the true monster of the film. Her son is merely a tangible symbol of her willingness to allow others to be harmed in order for her son's needs to be met. At the end of the film, Daniel goes on a rampage, killing several more police officers and even attacking his own father. It is only then that Lenore takes matters into her own hands. Leaving Frank, the man she supposedly loves, with hardly a word—Frank is, incidentally, quite seriously wounded at the time—she carries Daniel back into the house, which, during the chaos, has caught on fire. The final scenes show Lenore in a rocking chair, singing to Daniel as the nursery goes up in flames around them. While we might appreciate that Lenore has finally accepted that Daniel is simply too dangerous to live, her self-sacrifice comes too late to redeem her, for her maternal devotion has allowed the deaths of five innocent people. Furthermore, the ending suggests that Lenore feels that she has no reason to live without Daniel: he may be an abomination, but he is *her* abomination. Here is the ideology of intensive mothering in its starkest terms, but it is hardly admirable.

If Lenore's unequivocal allegiance to Daniel at the expense of everyone else, including herself, is the most obvious way in which the film portrays intensive mothering as monstrous, Lenore's treatment of her partner, Frank, offers a complementary critique. Frank is, by all means, a loving and supportive boyfriend and a devoted father. However, even before Lenore is fully aware of Daniel's violent potential, she excludes him from fatherhood. When she finds him rocking the child, she immediately tells him that Daniel is swaddled too tightly and takes the child from him when Daniel starts to cry. She later asks Frank quite pointedly if he is going to work and secretly rolls her eyes when he declares that he likes staying home with her and his son. In these scenes, the film protests that the exclusion of men from parenthood is yet another problematic aspect of intensive mothering.

Although far less of a crime than hiding the remains of her son's slaughters, Lenore's manipulation and rejection of her partner suggests the extent to which motherhood is for her an all-consuming obsession. At one point, Frank asks Lenore to find a babysitter so that they can enjoy a night out together. Knowing the truth about Daniel, Lenore cannot agree to Frank's request and leave her son home alone, but she also knows that if she continues to behave so distantly, Frank's concern will only make him more likely to "interfere." That evening, she dons a little black dress and makes an elaborate dinner for Frank and Chris at home, claiming that it's time that she "pa[id] attention to the other men in [her] life." It is obvious that Lenore is only manipulating matters so that she can take better care of Daniel. Not only does her performance of devotion satisfy Frank's need for attention and allay any suspicions he has, it also allows Lenore to remain within arm's reach of Daniel, able to protect him should the need arise. Sexuality is a ruse, a means to an end, a ploy that allows Lenore to focus ultimately on her primary desire: mothering.

The film's title, a line appropriated from *Frankenstein* (1931), and its reference to a monstrous "it" would seem to suggest that the primary monster of this film is Daniel. However, as those familiar with that film and the novel that inspired it know, the creature is no more a monster than the man who made him. A horrid patchwork of body parts, the creature is a physical abomination, certainly; however, Dr. Frankenstein's decision to bring such a creature to life and then abandon it makes him equivalently monstrous in moral terms. *It's Alive* employs a similar set of ethics, ultimately demonstrating that Daniel's monstrosity is a result of Lenore's warped notions of motherhood (first, its irrelevance to her and then its supremacy above all else). She embraces the tenets of intensive mothering but in doing so becomes as grotesque as her flesh-eating son, and her death at the end of the film is as much of a relief as Daniel's.

Forsaking All Others But Child: *Grace*

Unlike Lenore, Madeline, the protagonist of *Grace*, has no doubts about being a mother. From the beginning, her happiness and selfhood depend entirely upon maternity. Indeed, aside from her strict vegan principles, motherhood seems to be the sole defining trait of Madeline's identity. So focused is she on becoming a parent that when her baby dies *in utero*, Madeline insists on carrying it to term. The baby is stillborn, but Madeline prays for her baby to live, and the infant inexplicably returns to life. Believing her to be a miracle, Madeline names her baby Grace.

But what initially appears to be a lovely testament to the power of mother love quickly becomes nightmarish, for Grace is no normal child. Rather, she appears to be some kind of a living corpse slowly decomposing right in front of Madeline's eyes. Her hair falls out in clumps when brushed gently, her skin seems to slough off during a bath, and she emits an awful smell and attracts flies by the dozen; so many, in fact, that Madeline must cover her crib with mesh and hang numerous strands of fly paper from the nursery ceiling. Madeline soon learns that Grace needs blood for sustenance, and Madeline initially tries to sustain her with her own supply. But Grace's appetite proves too great for Madeline to satisfy. Madeline becomes anemic, appearing deathly pale and almost bloodless. A mixture of vampire and zombie, Grace is the apparent monster of the story.

However, Grace's physical monstrosity quickly pales in comparison to her mother's monstrous behavior. Aware that she cannot appease Grace's appetite alone, Madeline seeks other sources of sustenance, even using methods that directly conflict with her most deeply cherished values. For much of the film, Madeline has declared herself a strict vegan and animal rights activist. During her daily chores, she watches a television station that continually broadcasts disturbing documentary footage displaying the atrocities of the meat industry, what she jokingly refers to as a "vegan horror movie." However, Madeline quickly sacrifices these ideals for Grace, buying up pounds of meat, in an attempt to wring out enough blood for Grace to drink. Grace's needs quickly override the principles that Madeline once held most dear, suggesting that her identity has become entirely dependent upon her role as mother. Not only does this choice mark her as a hypocrite, but her decision to waste pounds of animal flesh for a mere baby bottle's worth of blood seems a particularly repellant violation of her vegan philosophies.

Madeline does more than abandon her vegan code, for Grace, it turns out, is incapable of digesting animal blood. When a doctor insists on seeing Grace to verify her health, Madeline hits him over the head, inadvertently killing him. Rather than feeling shocked by the murder she has just committed, Madeline instead treats the event as a prime opportunity to provide for Grace: she cuts into the man's arm with scissors and drains his blood into one of Grace's bottles. In doing so, Madeline replicates a procedure displayed earlier in an animal rights video in which a pig was bled in a similar manner. The procedure is nauseating, and Madeline's ability to perform it with relatively little delay or disgust marks her as the true monster of the film. Later, when Madeline's mother-in-law, Vivian, comes investigating and discovers the body of the doctor, she and Madeline struggle, and Madeline eventually bites her in the throat. The symbolic logic of the film is clear: Madeline is as much a vampire as her daughter. Her life demands the "food" of motherhood. Grace is a personification of her mother's monstrous appetite for maternity. The conclusion shows Madeline on the run from the law for the murders she has committed, aided by her friend and midwife, Patricia. In the final scene, Patricia finds Madeline nursing in a pool of blood "She's begun to teethe," Madeline explains, opening her shirt to reveal breasts that have been literally chewed up by her child. The image is revolting and impossible to view as an acceptable sacrifice on Madeline's part. Furthermore, this new development raises questions about whether Madeline and Patricia will now seek out other human victims to satisfy Grace's hunger.

However, the focus in *Grace* is less on the human victims that pile up due to the monstrous newborn than on the ways that an all-consuming maternal desire leaves women unable to truly love anyone but their children. Like Lenore, Madeline seems to value her partner as little more than a sperm donor and future provider for her child. The opening scene depicts a passionless sex act entirely intended for procreation. During this scene, Madeline stares off into the distance, completely uninvolved emotionally or physically. Her husband is as anonymous to us as he apparently is to her: we see him only from behind, a body thrusting with machine-like precision. Once he climaxes, he moves off of Madeline and disappears without a word, leaving her to clutch her knees to her chest in a posture meant to increase the likelihood of conception.

At other points, Madeline actually seems disgusted by her husband. Although he is supportive of her vegan principles, he remains a meat eater and at one point asks Madeline—who appears to have been a stay-at-home wife before becoming a stay-at-home mom—to prepare liver for his dinner. Although she agrees, it is clear that doing so incites repulsion and disdain for her mate. She watches him eat the meal with a barely repressed look of disgust. And yet when Grace proves to be the ultimate carnivore—an eater of human flesh no less—Madeline expresses no revulsion. Maternal affection gives Madeline a forgiving perspective of her daughter that romantic love did not allow her to have for her husband. That Madeline merely tolerates her husband as a means to a maternal end is emphasized most prominently when the couple suffers a car accident. Though her husband is obviously dead, Madeline cares only about the wellbeing of her unborn child; the first thing she says to the Good Samaritan who arrives is that her baby "isn't moving." Indeed, we never witness Madeline mourning her husband at all. It is obvious that Madeline becomes a wife only so she can be a mother. As with Lenore, Madeline's insincere treatment of her partner reveals the distastefulness of a motherhood that trumps all other relationships.

What makes the message in *Grace* different from Rusnak's version of *It's Alive* is that Madeline is not the only woman shown to have such a distorted conception of the importance of motherhood. Madeline's mother-in-law, Vivian, is also afflicted by similar ideals. She, too, treats her husband with disdain, infantilizing and humiliating him over a sock he left lying in their bedroom. At another time, she pretends to initiate foreplay, when really all she wants is for him to orally stimulate her nipples. Partly, her behavior seems motivated by a desire to experience the pleasures of breast-feeding in the wake of losing her only child, whom she nursed until the age of three. But afterwards, when we see her locate her old breast pump and work on inducing lactation, we realize that she has plans to breastfeed her own granddaughter after she steals her away. By including Vivian in the film, Solet points out that perverted notions of motherhood are pervasive, not simply the warped conclusion reached by Madeline in response to Grace's peculiar needs. Solet constructs the maternal obsessiveness of these women as the natural outcome of motherhood rather than behavior solicited by cultural pressure; their warped actions are a sign of psychological defect rather than forced adherence to a problematic social script. Like Daniel, the flesh-eating Grace is the apparent monster of the film, but she serves only to reveal the true monster: a mother's perverse devotion.

Conclusion

Scholars like Carroll, Hills, sand Mittman argue that while certain characteristics are commonly shared by monsters, monstrosity is also largely an effect: we learn to fear and loathe a monster partly because the narrative teaches us to do so. One of the easiest ways narratives can instruct us in this manner is through the reactions of other respectable characters. When they respond with repulsion and fright, so should we. However, because *It's Alive* and *Grace* focus so intently on the solitary experiences of Lenore and Madeline, viewers cannot rely on these types of cues. Instead, these films partly launch their critique against these intensive mothers by linking their unwavering maternal devotion to a complete disregard for others. In addition, by formulating a symbolic connection between the form of the newborn's monstrosity (a vampiric nature) and their mother's decisions to "feed" off others, these movies suggest that their monstrous children are merely visible emblems of the dangerous monsters that lurk beneath a veneer of motherly love. In a sense, the pattern is a familiar one in creature features, from *Aliens* to *Arachnophobia*: characters battle noisome creatures only to discover that there is a far larger and more threatening "queen" to dispatch.

Although the remakes of *It's Alive* and *Grace* critique intensive mothering, not all monstrous newborn narratives function in this manner. After all, intensive mothering itself has not always existed as an ideal nor have evaluations of its merits and shortcomings remained consistent over time.¹² Both the remake of *It's Alive* and *Grace* respond directly to the recent idealization of the intensive mother, seemingly providing a healthy counterpoint to plaudits given to her in other arenas. These films show that intensive motherhood demands unreasonable sacrifices of the mother, jeopardizing her ability to have a balanced life that includes healthy adult relationships, especially with her romantic partners. In addition, the movies depict intensive mothering as causing suffering for others beyond the family as well; it may take a village, these films seem to suggest, but perhaps the village should be *asked* first. At first glance, then, these films seem to voice symbolically many of the problems with intensive mothering that feminists have cited and thus act as a welcome ally in the fight against this ideology.

But because the monstrosity of the intensive mother is partly due to her frigidness, these critiques might be merely masked attacks on mothers who "neglect" the romantic and sexual needs of their (male) partners. That motherhood and female desire are treated as mutually exclusive in these films is surprising, considering the recent attention given to so-called MILFs and "cougars" and the high visibility of sexy celebrity moms. On the one hand, this treatment of mothers as sexual creatures is a welcome recognition that motherhood does not necessarily fulfill all of a woman's needs nor does it erase her sexual identity. On the other, the elevation of the sexy and sexual mother could put even more pressure on women, for now they must make sure to satisfy their lovers' needs on top of taking care of their immense maternal responsibilities. As Addison, Goodwin-Kelly, and Roth put it, "[e]ven as they intersect[,] ... sexuality and maternity do not suggest increased freedom for mothers, but rather continued and perhaps even greater cultural and ideological scrutiny of their bodies and activities."¹³ The critique of intensive mothering in these two twenty-first-century horror films seems similarly problematic. In an era in which sexy mamas are all the rage, it is not surprising that women who would allow the demands of motherhood to interfere with their desirability would suffer rebuke.

Even more problematic are the ways the films entirely ignore the idea of intensive mothering as a social construct. They present intensive mothering as a self-ordained role rather than one that women feel compelled to take on due to societal pressure. Intensive mothering is thus treated as a delusion that individual mothers suffer rather than a broader social issue. Robin Wood has made a similar complaint about David Cronenberg's *The Brood* (1979), a movie about a woman who transforms her anger into tiny monsters who are birthed from sacs that hang outside of her body. Wood complains that "the terrible children are the physical embodiments of the woman's rage. But that rage is never seen as the logical product of woman's situation within patriarchal culture; it is blamed entirely on the woman's mother."[14] A similar criticism could be made of *It's Alive* and *Grace*, films made thirty years later. Even though they reveal the monstrous aspects of intensive mothering, they source these features to the psychological effects of motherhood rather than to its social construction, making the monstrous mother a convenient scapegoat for problematic cultural expectations.

Notes

1. Sharon Hays, *The Cultural Contradictions of Motherhood* (New Haven: Yale University Press, 1996), 8.

2. Jillian M. Duquaine-Watson, "All You Need Is Love: Representations of Maternal Emotion in *Working Mother* Magazine, 1995–1999," in *Mother Matters: Motherhood as Discourse and Practice. Essays from the Journal of the Association for Research on Mothering*, ed. Andrea O'Reilly (Toronto: Association for Research on Mothering, 2004), 125–38; Wendy Parkins, "Shall I Be Mother? Motherhood and Domesticity in Popular Culture," in *Feminism, Domesticity and Popular Culture,* eds. Stacy Gillis and Joanne Hollows (New York: Routledge, 2009), 65–78; Melissa Buis Michaux and Leslie Dunlap, "Baby Lit: Feminist Response to the Cult of True Motherhood," in *You've Come a Long Way, Baby: Women, Politics, and Popular Culture*, ed. Lilly J. Goren (Lexington: University Press of Kentucky, 2009), 137–58; Lilly J. Goren, "Supermom: The Age of the Pregnant Assassin," in *You've Come a Long Way, Baby: Women, Politics, and Popular Culture*, ed. Lilly J. Goren (Lexington: University Press of Kentucky, 2009), 159–75.

3. See, for example, Susan J. Douglas and Meredith W. Michaels, *The Mommy Myth: The Idealization of Motherhood and How It Has Undermined Women* (New York: Free Press, 2004); Janelle S. Taylor, Linda L. Layne, and Danielle F. Wozniak, *Consuming Motherhood* (New Brunswick: Rutgers University Press, 2004); Ann C. Hall and Mardi J. Bishop, *Mommy Angst: Motherhood in American Popular Culture* (Santa Barbara: Praeger, 2009); Heather Addison, Mary Kate Goodwin-Kelly, and Elaine Roth, eds., *Motherhood Misconceived: Representing the Maternal in U.S. Films* (Albany: State University of New York Press, 2009); Elizabeth Podnieks, ed., *Mediating Moms: Mothers in Popular Culture* (Montreal: McGill-Queen's University Press, 2012); and Rebecca Feasey, *From Happy Homemaker to Desperate Housewives: Motherhood and Popular Television* (London: Anthem Press, 2012).

4. One need only think of Mother Vorhees and her slasher son Jason of the *Friday the 13th* series or *Mother's Day* and its remake (1980, 2010). Anne Williams claims that the Male Gothic often traces its "gruesome physical materiality" back to "the otherness of the *mater*/mother who threatens to swallow or engulf." *Art of Darkness: A Poetics of Gothic* (Chicago: University of Chicago Press, 1995), 106.

5. *It's Alive*. Dir. Josef Ruznak. First Look Pictures, 2008. DVD. *Grace*. Dir. Paul Solet. Anchor Bay, 2009. DVD.

6. In the introduction to *The "Evil Child" in Literature, Film, and Popular Culture* (New York: Routledge, 2012), 1–27, I discuss the possessed child and the feral child. I also deal briefly with the antichrist-as-child in "The Apocalypse Begins at Home: The Antichrist-as-Child Film," *Frame: Journal of Literary Studies* 26.1 (2013): 47–59. In the book-length study I am currently working on, I also include chapters on vengeful child ghosts, "gifted" children, Lolitas and Nikitas, the serial-killer-as-child, and school shooters and other murderers.

7. In *The Philosophy of Horror, or Paradoxes of the Heart* (New York: Routledge, 1990),

Carroll acknowledges that what constitutes a monster is at least partly determined by "the affective responses of the positive human characters" in a text, which "provide a set of instructions ... about the way in which the audience is to respond" (17). However, he focuses mostly on criteria of monstrousness, such as formlessness, indescribability, category blending, and the conflation of species, all of which yield feelings of disgust and fear. Cohen's seven theses in the first chapter of *Monster Theory: Reading Culture* (Minneapolis: University of Minnesota Press, 1996), 3–25, provide necessary characteristics of monsters as well.

8. Matt Hills, "An Event-Based Definition of Art-Horror," in *Dark Thoughts: Philosophic Reflections on Cinematic Horror*, eds. Steven Jay Schneider and Daniel Shaw (Lanham, MD: Scarecrow Press, 2003), 142.

9. Asa Simon Mittman, "The Impact of Monsters and Monster Studies," introduction to *The Ashgate Research Companion to Monsters and the Monstrous*, eds. Asa Simon Mittman and Peter Dendle (Surrey: Ashgate, 2012), 6.

10. For other approaches to the monstrous child narrative, see Karen Valerius, "*Rosemary's Baby*, Gothic Pregnancy, and Fetal Subjects," *College Literature* 32.3 (2005): 116–35; Lucy Fischer, "Birth Traumas: Parturition and Horror in *Rosemary's Baby*," in *The Dread of Difference: Gender and the Horror Film*, ed. Barry Keith Grant (Austin: University of Texas Press, 1996), 412–31; A. Robin Hoffman, "How to See the Horror: The Hostile Fetus in *Rosemary's Baby* and *Alien*," in *The "Evil Child" in Literature, Film, and Popular Culture*, ed. Karen J. Renner (New York: Routledge, 2012), 150–72; Susan Yunis and Tammy Ostrander, "Tales Your Mother Never Told You: *Aliens* and the Horrors of Motherhood," *Journal of the Fantastic in the Arts* 14.1 (2003): 68–76; and Andrew Scahill, "Deviled Eggs: Teratogenesis and the Gynecological Gothic in the Cinema of Monstrous Birth," in *Demons of the Body and Mind: Essays on Disability in Gothic Literature*, ed. Ruth Bienstock Anolik (Jefferson, NC: McFarland, 2010), 197–216.

11. While one of its more generous reviewers, Gareth Jones, describes it as "unnecessary, yet entertaining" on the website *Dread Central* (http://www.dreadcentral.com/reviews/its-alive-2009#axzz2pYIVDuXK, accessed January 5, 2014), Britt Hayes, writer for the horror culture website *Brutal as Hell*, calls it "a cesspool of horror film offenses, bundled into 90 minutes of eye-gouge-inducing hell" (http://www.brutalashell.com/2010/02/dvd-review-its-alive-2008/, accessed January 5, 2014). Although credited as a screenwriter on the remake, Cohen describes it as "a terrible picture ... just beyond awful" and is careful to point out that his collaboration extended no further than selling the screenplay for a healthy profit. Bruce Layne, "Larry Cohen Interview," accessed January 5, 2014, http://69.195.124.61/~filmsinr/2009/12/21/larry-cohen-interview/.

12. Rebecca Plant, for example, notes that stay-at-home moms were degraded following World War II: "By stigmatizing 'idle' housewives, deriding female voluntary efforts, and pathologizing prolonged mother love, numerous commentators in the 1940s and 1950s undercut the ability of such women to construct a satisfying identity based on motherhood and homemaking." *Mom: The Transformation of Motherhood in Modern America* (Chicago: University of Chicago Press, 2010), 16.

13. Introduction to *Motherhood Misconceived: Representing the Maternal in U.S. Films* (Albany: State University of New York Press, 2009), 2.

14. Wood, "An Introduction to the American Horror Film," in *Planks of Reasons: Essays on the Horror Film*, eds. Barry Keith Grant and Christopher Sharrett (Lanham, MD: Scarecrow Press, 2004), 136. See also Wilson.

"She needs more"

The Villainization of Infertile Women in Horror Films

BROOKE W. EDGE

Infertility is a condition feared by women not just for the personal pain and hardship it brings, but also for the shame and stigma that society imposes on them insofar as women who are unable to conceive children fail to embody the socially presumed "purpose" of the female sex, which is to be mothers. While a demonization of clinical conditions appears callous and out-of-touch with today's seemingly medically sympathetic culture, consideration of infertility's representation in horror films reveals this prejudice against "barren" women to be frighteningly present underneath our society's veneer of compassion for childlessness. Depictions of infertile women as driven to desperate lengths in the pursuit of children—and children borne by those manic mothers figured as abnormal offspring—hamper advances in understanding infertility. This essay analyzes such representations in light of theories of social surveillance, abjection, and fears of technology to better understand "monstrous" infertile women and their children in contemporary horror film.

Infertility's representation in horror may be viewed as a "monstrous condition"—described by Harry Benshoff in *Monsters in the Closet* as internal, invisible, and lurking within seemingly "normal" individuals. While Benshoff focuses on cinematic depictions of homosexuality, he notes that "[s]ome people have always considered anything that opposes or lies outside the ideological status quo intrinsically monstrous and unnatural."[1] That fear of difference threatens the domestic sphere in Robin Wood's work on the horror film, where he argues that "normality" and "the family" are threatened by the monster. Monsters are "the projection on to the Other of what is repressed within the

Self in order that it can be discredited, disowned, and if possible annihilated."[2] But that dread does not reside only on the societal level. It is of note that individuals who suffer from infertility largely want to fit into the norm of parenthood but face a challenge from within themselves, an invisible monster—infertility—wreaking havoc inside by keeping them from having children. Infertility, unseen but interior, destroys dreams with every reproductive cycle. So for the infertile, monster-annihilation requires self-annihilation.

Employing the aforementioned paradigms of the monstrous, this paper frames the monstrosity of infertility as concealed, shameful, and stigmatized because the condition opposes hegemonic social constructions of gender norms and pro-natalism. Twofold in its terror, infertility is monstrous to the individual sufferer in its personally destructive nature, refusing to settle for the often long-held goals of having a child. In a larger, cultural sense, the social expectations that influence the gravity of the perceived personal failure of being infertile view infertility as being threatening to the self and society, requiring obliteration, or at least removal from acceptable discourse. Just as this volume in passim illustrates how monstrous children are cultural ramifications of repression and projections of fears, so these women who aspire to bear children, but who fall short of that "normal" ability, are made monstrous in an effort to obscure and obliterate a perceived threat to social and physical norms and expectations. When they defy stigmatization to build a family via science or adoption, that monstrosity is passed down to the resulting monstrous children.

Themes of traumatic birth and fear of the reproductive female body in cinematic horror have been well documented and analyzed.[3] Far fewer studies, however, have investigated the cinematic interpretation of a woman's struggle to achieve motherhood. This dearth of attention can be seen as a reflection of society at large, which has tended to sweep the topic of infertility under the conversational rug. Even women who bear the weight of infertility are often loath to admit it. Infertile women are seen as "others" in society, stigmatized as abnormalities in the human reproductive system and thereby positioned to be both pitied for their unfortunate burden and feared for the threat they potentially cause to the circle of life.[4] Their ailment, however, is increasingly subject to medical treatment and media coverage, and subsequently to open discussion. This greater cultural prominence aids those suffering from infertility, but it also makes them emotionally ripe for the horror genre's picking, as filmmakers have a legacy of drawing inspiration from both fears of physical failure as well as new (and often misunderstood) scientific developments (dis)regarding the body.

Portrayals of the female body—especially as monstrous in the horror film—are loaded with cultural meanings and messages. Infertility, as a condition with significant personal ramifications and yet weighed down by social stigma, is particularly ripe for depiction in an effort to convey values regarding its causes and handling, particularly in relation to the female sex and its reproductive (in)abilities. In *Managing the Monstrous Feminine*, Jane Ussher writes:

> There is no "natural" reproductive body that prefigures discourse. Indeed, it is discourse, and the enacting of femininity within a highly regulated framework, which produces notions of the "natural" reproductive body having particular effects, reifying the woman who is in control of the unruly reproductive body as a creature of substance; an ideal to which we, as women, should aspire.... The external gaze which pervades cultural discourse and institutional practices, and is taken up by significant others in our lives, can thus act to position us as mad, bad or dangerous[;] ... the fictions framed as facts that circulate around the fecund body are central to the definition and maintenance of social order.[5]

Infertility's depiction in cultural texts, then, is not merely something we observe in the cinema or on our television screens. Those representations invade personal lives and relationships, and how we see others and ourselves. As detailed by Ussher in the above consideration of "facts" about the female body, discursive frames in cultural works impose limits upon ways of speaking and thinking about a stigmatized condition such as infertility, and those parameters become naturalized as cultural truths. Cultural texts that work within such discursive frames serve to further reinforce stigma and stereotypes.

Analyzing works of recent decades' cinematic canon with an eye on infertility, ensuing medical meddling, and the terrifying children that result, from campy creep-outs like *It's Alive* (1974) and *Grace* (2009) to the more high-end horror of *The Ring* (2002), and the *Alien* series, brings the burgeoning incorporation of infertility in horror to the fore. Infertility stigmatized as monstrous and as producing monstrous offspring emerges through a consideration of Foucauldian bio-power, Julia Kristeva's notion of the horrific abject, and, combining both, fears of altering the human body with science and technology. Before delving into that analysis though, I would like to give a brief history of infertility and its stigmatization.

About Infertility

Two recurrent themes run through what little historiography of infertility exists: medicalization of the condition, and its social stigmatization.

Both facets play into infertility's depictions in horror films. In the twentieth century, the primary sources for infertility advice, counsel, and "miracle working" shifted from the church to the doctor's office, turning the cultural opinion of infertility from a state of being to a medical issue requiring resolution.[6] In sociological literature, Arthur Greil explains in *Not Yet Pregnant: Infertile Couples in Contemporary America*, "medicalization ... describe[s] the process by which certain behaviors come to be understood as questions of health and illness, subject to the authority of medical institutions."[7] Greil writes that this medicalization of infertility indicated larger cultural shifts in the twentieth century, as science and technology assumed greater prominence in American society at large. From correctional institutions and social work to management of the family home, Americans increasingly turned to scientific research to streamline and industrialize everyday life.[8]

According to the Center for Disease Control's National Survey of Family Growth, more than ten percent of the American reproductive-age population is infertile. Recent decades of work in the field of reproductive endocrinology—including hormone treatment and assisted reproductive technology (ART) (itself coldly scientific terminology evocative of science fiction)—have seen significant progress in assisting infertile women with conceiving and carrying a fetus to term.[9] Hereby, the 1920s and 1930s brought more understanding of endocrinology and hormonal effects to the medical field and, thereby, more information about the menstrual cycle. Only after that did medical intervention in most conception complications become more effective.[10]

Clomid and other ovulation-stimulating drugs were introduced in the 1960s, followed by the first successful *in-vitro* fertilization in 1978—the children born from this procedure were called "test-tube babies," a term conjuring depictions of abnormal laboratory conception and birth from science fiction and horror. At that same time in horror films, numerous monstrous medically-assisted mothers and their offspring began appearing on screen, including in texts to be discussed later in this essay.

These mid-twentieth-century breakthroughs in hormone therapy aided not just conception, but also pregnancy prevention.[11] As a result, more women first attempted to plan a pregnancy at a later age, which due to advanced maternal age sometimes necessitated medical assistance with fertility challenges. It is of note that while media in the late twentieth century reported an "epidemic" of infertility as numbers of women and men seeking treatment rose dramatically, infertility rates are not what changed. The shift occurred in the reporting about and technology of treatment for the condition, not the demographics of infertility itself.[12] Infertility became a prominent social issue due to concerns with "turning fertility on" after being able to control it more accurately in recent years thanks to better contraceptive methods, media attention to scientific advances in treating infertility and women emphasizing careers in tandem with (or instead of) motherhood, and obstetric expansion into treating infertility when birth numbers declined.[13] As Margaret Marsh details, the conflation of medicine and morals around fertility had existed for ages, including associating infertility with unfeminine behaviors, putting career or other "selfish" interests first to delay conception, and not truly desiring a child. These were amplified and exacerbated with increasing cultural concern over women in the workforce, the Pill, and medical intervention in conception.

This brief history of infertility informs stigmas and stereotypes that persist today: the infertile female as not a real woman, infertility caused by a woman's selfish pursuits or unstable emotions, and infertility as a dangerous opportunity for toying with nature. That these tropes still surface in contemporary popular culture is telling of present-day attitudes toward the condition of infertility and the women who suffer from it, informing how members of our society—including those who are infertile—think about infertility.

Stigma on Film

Infertility stigmas form the basis of the depiction of childless women in horror films, feeding into their demonized treatment in those films in particular as well as the popular media at large. In a pro-natalist society where female roles and identities are centered on reproduction, women who fail to reproduce successfully are not just worthless, but dangerous. The stigma of infertility delineates those who suffer with the condition as distinctly outside social acceptance. In the sociological theory of Erving Goffman, stigma "makes an individual or cultural form problematic."[14] Stigma tarnishes the image of an individual or group, therefore making stigmatized people somehow less desirable and of a lower quality than those Goffman refers to as "normals." Additionally, as Goffman posits that they are devised to distance the "normals" from the stigmatized, stereotypes are intertwined with creating and reinforcing stigma broadly through a culture. Portrayals of stereotypes and negative tropes in cultural texts, then, widely disseminate messages of normality and deviance.

Jeffrey Jerome Cohen, in his work on the figured monstrosity of teratology, writes of the cultural construction of what we fear and shun, enabling the exposure of stigma's relation to infertility. If something deviating from the social norm is detected—"[t]he monster is difference made flesh, come to dwell among us," he writes—those cultural constructions are called upon to set the monster apart. Cohen notes that monstrous difference originates from within us, because we as a community create the boundaries that define normality, as well as the stereotypes and stigmas that reinforce those cultural battle lines.[15] This dovetails with the aforementioned definition of "monstrosity" as something that is internal, lurking, and that requires annihilation to maintain "normalcy."

In addition, this menace merits stigmatization to guard against a perceived ultimate threat to society's very future existence. Monstrosity, Benshoff states, involves "fears about sex and death."[16] Infertility is sex without procreation—without life—and for many sufferers the end of their biological legacy and end of aspirations for a "normal" family. Lee Edelman extends the motherhood mandate to a reproductive one in his denunciation of "reproductive futurism," by which political discourses impose heteronormative imperatives through a focus on children, thereby positioning effective queer resistance outside the political domain, rendering it untenable. This concept "authenticate[s] social order" by framing political struggles for future children, and, Edelman asks, how can one argue against the future?[17] Social and political concerns, from healthcare and education to the environment and anti-drug campaigns, are shaped by discourses about coming generations, and our contemporary obligation to their survival. Figured in the context of queer theory, reproductive futurism negates any aspect of culture that does not support and work toward life in a future tense. Sex must therefore be framed as serving that future life, and it must be heterosexual and procreative. Sex without such reproductive potential is figured as meaningless. Infertile individuals, therefore, are outside such an "effective" culture and are essentially meaningless, made queer in the same way homosexuality is figured by Edelman as disruptive and unwelcome in a reproductive futurist ideological environment. The presence of infertile persons in the social order threatens "normal" reproduction, reinforcing their ascribed monstrosity and need for obliteration.

Damaging stereotypes of infertility that appear routinely in popular culture in general and in horror films in particular include the working woman who has waited too long, the infertile woman desperate to conceive, and the "barren" woman driven to infertility-induced mania. The infertile woman in media can be driven to desperation, as, for example, in sensational evening news tales of baby snatchers and even in-utero kidnappings.[18] On cinema screens, *The Hand That Rocks the Cradle* (1992) depicted an infertile woman insinuating herself in the lives of a happy family in order to care for, breastfeed, and ultimately take over another woman's baby. Cultural suspicion of fertility drugs resulted in the demon spawn of 1974's *It's Alive* and discomfort with "test-tube babies" informed techno-baby threats in *Alien: Resurrection* (1997) and *Splice* (2009) (and is manifested in recent media fascination with multiple births such as *Jon & Kate Plus 8* and "Octomom"). When fertility drugs fail, the inability to bear children leads to the trope of monstrous adopted children in horror films—*The Ring* (2002) and *Orphan* (2009), among others—the unnatural expansion of a family being the direct result of the female's failure to grow and nurture a "proper" family with her own biological offspring. As monstrous children on film are detailed throughout this volume as reflections of cultural fears, likewise these infertile women who exist outside the social norms of their sex and the motherhood mandate are demonized in an effort to do away with a perceived social and psychological threat. Ignoring that stigmatization by turning to adoption or science to achieve motherhood leads to monstrosity inherited by the younger generation.

Monsters, created by culture, "are essential to enable all of us to grapple with very basic human limitations and fears," explains Cynthia Freeland in *The Naked and the Undead*. They elicit emotional reactions and, as a result, provoke consideration of what we fear.[19] The horror films considered in this essay play on anxieties about women's reproductive abilities and medical treatments, which necessitates thoughtful study of the society in which infertile individuals operate and these films are made. The remainder of this essay will address various interpretations of those anxieties, as infertile women are depicted as obsessive, abject, and unnatural.

Self-Obsession and Infertility

Women whose self-interest—in the form of career or body obsession—causes infertility and ensuing lunacy exist as one mode of monster in horror films. Overly concerned with work outside the home or with the extreme regulation of their biological clocks, they are marked as manic threats to themselves and to their surrounding society's idealization of docile, maternal women. The cultural motherhood mandate that expects women to desire childbearing and rearing "can—and has—stigmatized those whose unions are involuntarily childless as well as those who choose not to have children. Historically, it has been invoked to valorize women's fertility and to castigate those with expectations for achievement beyond the confines of home and family."[20] Aberrations from that mandate, whether in the form of the woman who works or who is not relaxed and confident in her childbearing abilities, have traditionally been punished accordingly, not least by condemnation in cultural representations.

Women permeating the workforce in greater numbers in the later decades of the twentieth century, combined with the reproductive choices allowed by the Pill and legalized abortion, reinvigorated concerns of the non-maternal woman in social consciousness and rallied worries over women not fulfilling the purpose of their sex. If these women refused motherhood, or could not biologically become mothers, could they be classified as female? This "monstrous gender-bending"—recalling monstrosity's insidious anti-hegemonic qualities threatening pro-natalism and patriarchy—informed fears of female sexuality. As explained by Noël Carroll in *The Philosophy of Horror*, cinematic monsters "can raise categorical misgivings by virtue of being incomplete representations of their class ... categorically contradictory, incomplete, or formless."[21] This also enhanced anxiety around a perceived weakening of the traditional family structure, illustrated in a number of popular horror films in the 1970s and 80s that fixated on women's bodies and family homes turned horrific.[22]

If women blurring gender boundaries with career aspirations frightened many, removing the primary element of their womanhood—fertility—took them further into the realm of terrifying incompleteness. Elaine Berland and Marilyn Wechter studied cultural representations of female characters on film from 1930 to 1975, and found that early cinema often marked female professionals as masculine and business oriented rather than maternal. They explain that 1987's *Fatal Attraction* encapsulates the late-twentieth century consternation surrounding gender roles and the conflicting messages sent to women, benefiting from playing on the uneasiness of baby boom generation women trying to have it all: successful in the stereotypically male sphere of the workplace as well as in their traditional realm of the home. Jobs competed with biological clocks for equal, and simultaneous, attention. In this successful thriller, professional woman Alex becomes unhinged after a weekend affair with married Dan. Alex obsesses over her lover and a domestic life, and becomes monstrous in her seemingly unflagging drive to unseat his wife as mother and partner. Berland and Wechter posit that Alex suffers from a fatal attraction not to the protagonist, but to the longing to "have it all"—"career, sexuality, the man and the baby—the fetal attraction.... Her wish to integrate the various yearnings is seen as sufficiently dangerous to require that she be eliminated [at the hands of a woman who is both wife and mother] so that the traditional oppositions may be restored."[23] Alex becomes—or at least says she becomes—pregnant by him despite having been pronounced infertile due to a previous "bad" miscarriage. Driven to desperate lengths to win Dan, Alex murders his family pet, kidnaps his daughter, and attacks his wife, who ultimately shoots Alex to death. The infertile career woman threatens the home and is subsequently eradicated by the fertile stay-at-home mom, thereby restoring balance, normality, and the safety of the domestic sphere.

Notions of "real womanhood" are dominant narratives reinforced by cultural discourse, including popular culture texts such as *Fatal Attraction* and other films analyzed here. These notions instill in the female audience parameters of how they "should" be, what the norm is. Monstrosity refuses to respect those definitional boundaries. Monsters form the basis of horror because they are interstitial and impure, writes Carroll, "cross[ing] the boundaries of the deep categories of a culture's conceptual scheme."[24] The sullied, suspicious quality of infertility reinforces the need for regulation by society at large in order to police that state of being outside the desired norm.

Once women in film turn their minds from career to conception, their obsession with control finds a new outlet in attempting to govern the body. Tracking temperatures, monitoring diets, and timing intercourse are all traditional tactics for optimizing fertility, but are positioned on film as obsessive and manipulative. Women's over-investment in keeping their bodies in top working order in the name of fertility, from medication to strict regulation of such presumed pleasures as sex and food, adhere to Michel Foucault's notion of power existing at the most intimate level, regulating social and individual behavior and thoughts. Capillary power "touches people's lives more fundamentally through their social practices than through their beliefs," and is "anchored in the multiplicity of ... 'micropractices,' the social practices which compromise everyday life in modern society."[25] Such minute expressions of larger power structures on an everyday, routine level serve to naturalize and further entangle individuals in Foucault's concept of an all-encompassing power/knowledge environment.

As a textual example of women manifesting such micropractices in the name of fertility, *Grace* (2009) introduces monstrous mother Madeline with an opening shot of her and her husband having workmanlike sex to conceive. Later, pregnant after three years of fertility medication and miscarriages, Madeline is chastised by her mother-in-law for maintaining a vegan diet and selecting a midwife over an obstetrician, for in general being too regimented with her pregnancy. Many comedic films make light of such efforts by infertile women to exert control over their bodies, depicting them as neurotic nutcases who require being taught (often by a man) to just relax and be more natural.[26]

The extreme monitoring and futile power plays these women engage in, these films demonstrate, make them manic and in need of regulation within an acceptable, average society. In *Grace*, Madeline refuses that turn to normality. After her husband and still-in-utero baby are killed in an accident, Madeline insists on continuing her gestational regulatory practices and carrying the fetus to term. (Kristine Larsen in this volume details the monstrous ramifications of this decision.) In these films and others, painting such strict self-regulation in a negative light chastises infertile women for calling too much attention to the Foucauldian institutional power/knowledge web that society prefers to remain unseen and unquestioned.

Predominantly, Foucauldian power works its way to the individual level via surveillance—both in the form of physical visibility and, importantly for infertility studies, through scientific, medical means of cataloguing, confession, and examination. Power is productive for Foucault, and indeed the thorough medical study of the female reproductive system has produced positive results, yielding new fertility treatments—and, hence, other means of power over the individual body in particular and social body at large concerned with population and fertility. The close analysis of bodies in infertility's medicalization, inviting scrutiny from doctor's offices to bedrooms, impacts social and personal habits. A socially accepted "normality" of proper bodily functions develops, continuing a historic subjection of women's bodies "to scrutiny, regular surveillance, and dissection at the physical and biochemical level, positioning the female body as a potential site of madness, badness or weakness."[27] In *Grace*, this leads to a dependence on medication, physical monitoring, and emotional reliance upon a midwife to birth the (monstrous) baby. However, Madeline is positioned as particularly deviant and dangerous because she attempts to control such surveillance herself, outside the socially accepted realm of an institutional, male medical practice.

Foucault unites examination and confession in power's control of the individual, just as both physicians and therapists treat infertility. In this dual treatment format, women have physical operations and defects catalogued along with being prompted to "relax" and to stop stress from hindering conception, perhaps to take themselves out of high-pressure (read, masculine) work environments. Elaine Tyler May's "Nonmothers as Bad Mothers: Infertility and the 'Maternal Instinct'" addresses the historical psychoanalytic side of treating infertility and its persistence in contemporary, often-stigmatized views of the condition. She begins with a 1950 quote by Abraham Stone, then medical director of the Margaret Sanger Research Foundation: "Being a woman means acceptance of her primary role, that of conceiving and bearing a child."²⁸ The mid-twentieth century turn to psychoanalysis led to many cases of blaming infertile women for subconsciously denying their innate purpose as a mother. This informed arguments against working women, and the refocus on the family in the 1980s often saw popular culture taking aim at professional and highly educated women, threatening them with horror stories of infertility due to putting childbearing off too long.²⁹ Applying a Foucauldian focus on physical and psychiatric examinations in regard to fertility illuminates how women have become hyper-vigilant of the reproductive deviances in others and themselves, as well as hyper-aware of the abnormalities that would take them into monstrously unwomanly territory.

Abjection and Infertility

A key to monstrosity as employed in this essay is its insidious ability to exist unseen, a silent and hidden threat. Infertility, usually unknown until one attempts to conceive, terrifies in part because it may be lurking within and threatening a woman's identity as such. This quality of infertility as being interior and as upsetting self-definition moves it into Julia Kristeva's notion of the abject, which for many thinkers constitutes the root of horror and monsters. Building on the stigma of infertile women as being obsessed with control, infertility's tendency to overturn life plans and to come as an unforeseen transgression of feminine norms serves to enhance its monstrousness.

Abjection does not "respect borders, positions, rules." It "disturbs identity, system, order."³⁰ Like Carroll's categorization of monsters as defying classification, the abject terrifies because it is in-between delineated groupings, not fully formed in fulfilling any definition. Infertile women fall into abjection because their inability to reproduce keeps them from being female according to the social motherhood mandate. Infertility "disturbs identity," unsettling the placement of infertile women in the social order and undermining assumptions about the relationship between gender identity and reproduction. These uncertainties make the infertile abject, meaning it must be rejected by society.³¹ One means of exclusion is "ritual," in which "societies both renew their initial contact with the abject element and then exclude that element."³²

That horror films are an essential ritual of modern culture grounds Barbara Creed's study of women as abject in her landmark work *The Monstrous Feminine*. While society shuns the abject through ritual demonization, she writes, "abjection is not something of which the subject can ever feel free."³³

Indeed, an infertile woman is never fertile, even if she has children with medical intervention or adoption. She still cannot conceive "naturally." This abjection of infertile women makes them monstrous and unfit to be mothers. Any children they might have, then, are improper and aberrant, carrying monstrosity as an inherited trait.

One means of creating an "unnatural" family for the infertile woman is adoption, and in the horror film this leads to the nurturing of a homicidal, even demonic, child. As women unable to conceive and carry biological children, the adoptive mothers in such films as *The Omen* (1972, 2006), *The Ring* (2002), and *Orphan* (2009) are seemingly punished for ignoring their bodies and turning to artificial means of building a family, raising other people's children as their own. The origins of the otherworldly, murderous child of *The Ring* trace back to her adoption by an infertile couple. "They tried hard for years, but sometimes it's just not meant to be," a therapist who treated the infertile woman explained, recalling the unnatural stigma of infertility. The mother of *Orphan*, Kate, suffers from secondary infertility, the inability to bear children following prior pregnancies. Following a stillbirth, she and her husband adopt a young girl despite suggestions that Kate would prefer a biological child and still mourns her lost baby. Demonstrating the above qualities of abjection detailed by Kristeva and Creed, Kate is treated as suspect and untrustworthy due to that loss, even by her husband. Her adopted daughter quickly disrupts the natural order of the family, from interrupting the parents' sex life and terrorizing the pre-existing children, to finally having Kate committed and murdering her husband.

In both films, the traditional family structure and surrounding community are threatened thanks to a biologically unfit mother. Similar injury comes from the infertile woman in horror who chases motherhood via medical treatment rather than adoption. Here, she transgresses nature's will further, playing God with scientific intervention to counter infertility.

Mad Science and Infertility

First obsessed with herself, then grappling with an abject identity, the monstrous infertile woman becomes an extreme, nearly supernatural threat to humanity itself when she avails herself of experimental science and reproductive technology. "Perhaps because reproduction is the beginning of human life and essential to the continuation of the species, it triggers deep-seated anxieties about power, control, humanity, and the species," writes Kelly Oliver in *Knock Me Up, Knock Me Down*.[34] This fear of tinkering with natural reproduction informs the history of mad scientists in horror and looms larger in the age of ART and genetic research. Creed points out that a woman can be positioned as a mad scientist by her very nature—with her own incubator within, able to grow another being. This can be framed as miraculous and nurturing or, especially in the case of gestation via medical intervention and in-vitro fertilization, ART can be positioned as threateningly all-powerful, correlating infertile women birthing monsters with growing debates over cloning and reproductive technology.[35]

It's Alive unleashed a mutant, murderous baby upon cinemas in 1974. The film faulted a number of potential causes for the creature that ripped the throats of its doctors upon delivery and escaped to terrorize suburban Los Angeles, from pesticides on lawns to parental genetic defects. In the film's opening, older couple John and Lenore Davis prepare for their second child. Upon delivery, however, the newborn mauls every labor and delivery nurse and doctor in the room. While later being questioned by the police, Lenore wails, "I wanted him too much!" and suggests it was "the pills" she took that created her mutant, killer baby. The infant slays others before finally being shot in the sewers of Los Angeles. To close, the police chief receives a call that another killer baby has been born, this time in Seattle—an epidemic of drug-induced monsters is plaguing the nation. While some film scholars have focused on the *It's Alive* baby as the result of legalized abortion or an emotionally distant father, the novelization of the film makes fertility drug usage, and its direct causality for a mutant, killer baby, explicit.[36] The mother popped birth control pills for years, then fertility pills after she could not conceive when she wanted—a "quick fix" to cheat nature. But, the novelization posits, "maybe God was trying to tell us something. About germs and microorganisms and cells. About human cells. You are what you eat."[37]

The *It's Alive* series (*It Lives Again* [1978] and *It's Alive III: Island of the Alive* [1987]) coexisted with and played on a number of growing cultural fears regarding the ramifications of women delaying pregnancy and then necessitating medical assistance in having children. Deformed, even dangerous offspring, the films and book appear to threaten, could strike in real life as the use of ovulation-stimulating drugs like Clomid entered more mainstream obstetrical use in the 1970s and '80s and experiments with in vitro fertilization evolved into routine reproductive treatment. At the same time, suggestions proposed in Shulamith Firestone's landmark 1970 book *The Dialectic of Sex* complicated women's "natural" relationship to childbearing and the alternately liberating and exploitative potential in contraceptive and reproductive medicine, drawing on contemporary polls that revealed a public wariness of scientific intervention in fertility.

The *It's Alive* canon provides not only an exploration of popular skepticism toward science's role in modern mothering, but also a critique of both the choice to delay pregnancy via chemical contraception and the need of some women to turn to drugs when unable to carry children naturally. In *It's Alive*, the mother, fearing what she has brought into the world receives more screen time than her horrific spawn. Lenore wrestles with guilt over her role in what caused her baby's mental and physical deformities and horrific actions, while her husband removes himself from the child, repeatedly saying the baby is not his own, that "it" must be obliterated. "It came from Lenore, for chrissake, and maybe his sperm didn't even have anything to do with it," he thinks.[38]

Returning to Foucault, in his conception of the "socialization of procreative behavior[,] ... the conjugal couple was given both medical and social responsibilities." If not followed, potential results could be "the production of sexual perverts or genetic mutants."[39] So beyond the persistent social stigma of "barrenness," women undergoing fertility treatments must also combat the fear of "mutants" that may result from their unnatural generation. In *It's Alive*, as in so many popular culture texts, these abnormalities are the fault of the mother—infertility is positioned as a woman's problem, with her body having to be "fixed." In horror, too much tampering threatens not just the woman's own body, but also those bodies around her when monstrous, mutant offspring result.

Even more socially taboo than pharmaceutical interference with nature is ART. One figuration of monstrosity, writes Benshoff, comes from "attempt[s] to create life without the aid of procreative sexual union."[40] Recalling the root of monstrosity here as harboring potential to overturn traditional family-based (and patriarchy-based) society as we know it, reproductive technology practices of creating "test-tube babies" and embryos in labs for insertion into human wombs unite horror with science fiction, prompting potential fear for humanity's future. Included in those perceived threats are notably suspicions of technology, the questioned "humanness" of its practices, and worries over absence of men in the process.

Oliver notes that films that include ART as a plot device call attention to the divide between a "real" pregnancy/baby versus a techno-pregnancy/baby. The latter is shown to be suspect and undesirable, inherently unnatural.[41] With conception taking place in a laboratory, wombs are seemingly separated from the body and are therefore horrific, capable of unstoppable generation and incubating unnatural fetuses. The threat of multiples is more likely with

ART, and these broods would result from infertile women who, if nature had its way, would not reproduce at all. These offspring are half human/half science, fulfilling the monstrosity definition of defying categorization and embodying "inhuman possibilities that threaten to overrun humanity with something terrible."[42]

The potential for a brood leads to the positioning of ART as animalistic, echoed in the media coverage of in-vitro patients. Photographs of mothers of extreme multiples—most famously, octuplets in the form of "Octomom" Nadya Suleman—circulate in popular media as people gawk at bellies seemingly swollen to the point of bursting. These women are referenced as having "litters" and positioned as freaks of nature, "conjuring anxieties about the inhuman lurking in new reproductive technologies that move us away from sexual reproduction to embryo or zygote implantation."[43] This reinforces fears of techno-babies as inhuman threats, and positions women who would undergo ART as being even further removed from natural womanhood, and therefore even more monstrous.

Finally, the separation of reproduction from sex animates fears of a paternity being questioned, interrogating the importance of male involvement in reproduction. With ART, both sperm and eggs are handled in laboratories, but the resultant embryo is still implanted into a woman's womb and physically carried to term by her. The father's job is seemingly done at sperm donation. Vivian Sobchack stresses the "paternal figure in decline" as an inspiration for many late-twentieth century horror films in "Bringing It All Back Home."[44] With ART, the paternal figure has gone from decline to invisibility, at least at the point of conception. Creed points out that in horror, "without man, woman can only give birth to a race of mutant murderous offspring ... [as] the child is transformed into a visible image of its mother's desire."[45] If that desire is excessive, the offspring is monstrous. Infertile women are monsters, deviant from the norm and excessive by nature of pursuing ART; therefore, their unnatural children are monsters because of her, but never because of him.

The 2009 film *Splice* combines these fears of technology, inhumanity, and absent fathers into one terrifying child: Dren. Being the result of two scientists (whose names, Clive and Elsa, serve as references to the classic Frankenstein films) tampering with genetics, Dren is part human, but also part fish, bird, and reptile. Elsa supplied her own egg, but no mention is made of Clive's contribution. Elsa is not infertile, but rather chose to grow a custom child in the laboratory (drawing on contemporary cultural fears of ART and genetic testing taken to the extremes of creating "designer babies"). Clive accuses Elsa that she did not want a "normal child" because she was "afraid of losing control." Perhaps channeling Firestone, Elsa also cites not wanting to "bend [her] life to suit some third party who doesn't even exist yet," and she suggests Clive have a biological child once they "crack male pregnancy." As with most attempts at controlling nature in horror films, this one goes horribly wrong, as Dren kills those who threaten her, seduces then slays Clive, and, having morphed into a male, rapes and impregnates Elsa. At the film's end, a heavily pregnant Elsa commits the baby to a pharmaceutical company that hopes to benefit from its chemical compounds, thereby continuing the dangerous cycle of tampering with reproduction and human nature.

Horror films depicting future ramifications of fertility treatments and genetic experiments portray a dire, dangerous world losing touch with humanity.[46] Of particular note is the *Alien* series. These films have already been analyzed at great length regarding their commentary on motherhood; the fourth film, *Alien: Resurrection*, and the tangential *Prometheus* (2012) are of most interest with infertility and ART in mind. In the former, Ripley is figured as both a test-tube baby (created in a "fucking lab" shown to be full of cloning attempts gone wrong) and is also, like many infertile women in horror films, artificially impregnated with something threateningly inhuman. *Prometheus* (described by director Ridley Scott as existing within the same "universe" as *Alien* and its sequels) features an infertile heroine impregnated after her partner ingests an alien substance in the name of science. The experiment cures her infertility, but creates a monstrous fetus that grows to resemble the alien of the first film. Reproduction by infertile women of the future, it seems, is the seed of all humanity's eventual extinction. The series as a whole and these installments in particular draw from and propagate cultural suspicion and fears of science and human interactions, especially in the name of extending "natural" life, as overreaching acts by scientists into generation effect extraterrestrial monstrosities.

Creed describes the Alien queen of *Aliens*, laying row upon row of eggs, as "an unstoppable generatrix; she is totally dedicated to reproduction; and her dedication to reproduction is so fierce that she operates outside of morality and the law, not to mention the realm of the human."[47] These qualities of the Alien queen, a queen of monstrous mothers, echo the qualities of the stereotyped infertile woman as presented in this study: obsessed, baby crazy, with disregard for the health of her body or of the social body at large. Infertility, as depicted on screen, turns a woman into a monster. Medical treatments and ART do not redeem her status as a natural woman, but rather make her veer further into abjection and an even greater risk for humanity by aligning the barren body-made-fertile with such feared, seemingly unstoppable scientific advances as cloning.

By spinning out of control, the infertile female endangers that idealized respite of pro-natalism—the domestic sphere. Sobchack explains: "The horror film deals with moral chaos, the disruption of natural order (assumed to be God's order), and the threat to the harmony of hearth and home."[48] So, too, does the monster cause discord with traditional, hegemonic figurations of presumably God-given gender roles and patriarchal structures. A hidden threat, as figured in this analysis, the monster poses as a presumed fit within ideological norms, but in reality erodes that (heterosexual, reproductive) domestic ideal from within if left unchecked. The monster necessitates stigmatization in the service of driving out the contamination and maintaining a suitable, moral world for our (natural) families.

Sobchack does not address the concept of infertility in her essay on horror, science fiction, and melodrama, but within her definition of the horror film and the villain, women suffering from infertility are undoubtedly a disruption and threat to the nuclear family. They have been made abject on film and, as stereotypes and stigmas carry over from screen to lived reality, in society at large. Additionally, that stigma is passed down to the children of such unnatural conception and family creation, whether in the form of demonic infants or evil adoptees. Fertility medication and reproductive technology tinker with nature's design for mankind as the infertile woman's desperation fused with science is positioned as monstrous—to be feared and shunned for its rejection of nature and for what havoc it might wreak in the creation of aberrant offspring. Especially when infertility-driven measures threaten man's role in reproduction, the traditional home and the stability (and safety) of the family is radically altered. In other words, the immoral, self-obsessed baby-cravings by women who are by nature not meant to be mothers put their children at risk of in turn becoming monstrous and imperiling society itself.

The longstanding tropes analyzed in this essay, of infertile women as being selfish and manipulative, as not wholly female, and as irresponsibly indulgent in altering the natural order, all evidence themselves in contemporary horror films despite increased infertility advocacy and research. Even when films depict those scientific investments, the theories of Foucauldian discourse analysis, abjection, and technological skepticism applied here demonstrate that these works do so with scare tactics that only serve to reinforce the cultural discursive frame of infertile women and their children as unnatural and unwelcome. These stigma persist, betraying the wariness of infertility that is still present in our cultural values and ideals of "true" womanhood, values that serve a pro-natalist society and its members—even those grappling with their own inner demons of infertility.

Notes

1. Harry Benshoff, *Monsters in the Closet: Homosexuality and the Horror Film* (Manchester: Manchester University Press, 1997), 1–2.
2. Robin Wood, *Hollywood from Vietnam to Reagan ... and Beyond* (New York: Columbia University Press, 2013), 66.
3. See Barbara Creed, *The Monstrous Feminine: Film, Feminism, Psychoanalysis* (New York: Routledge, 1993); Carol Clover, *Men, Women, and Chainsaws: Gender in the Modern Horror Film* (New York: Columbia University Press, 1992).
4. While male infertility is statistically as common as female infertility, it is rarely represented on screen. Though this absence is notable, it is not covered by this study.
5. Jane Ussher, *Managing the Monstrous Feminine: Regulating the Reproductive Body* (London: Routledge, 2006), 4–5.
6. Marsh and Romer, *Empty Cradle*.
7. Arthur Greil, *Not Yet Pregnant: Infertile Couples in Contemporary America* (New Brunswick: Rutgers University Press, 1988), 33–34.
8. Greil, *Not Yet*, 34.
9. Assisted reproductive technology (ART) includes fertility treatments "in which both eggs and sperm are handled" (http://cdc.gov/art). This excludes hormone treatment or intrauterine insemination, procedures that are more common and usually employed before ART.
10. Griel, *Not Yet*, 41.
11. Creed; Poole; and David Skal, *The Monster Show: A Cultural History of Horror* (New York: Faber and Faber, 1993).
12. Margaret Marsh and Wanda Romer, *The Empty Cradle: Infertility in America from Colonial Times to the Present* (Baltimore: Johns Hopkins University Press, 1996), 5.
13. Jane Menken, James Trussell, and Ulla Larsen, "Age and Infertility," *Science* 233 (2006).
14. Goffman quoted in Paul Lopes, "Culture and Stigma: Popular Culture and the Case of Comic Books," *Sociological Forum* 21(3): 387–414.
15. Jeffrey Cohen, "Monster Culture," in *Speaking of Monsters: A Teratological Anthology*, eds. Caroline Picart and John Browning (New York: Palgrave Macmillan, 2012), 17.
16. Benshoff, *Closet*, 3.
17. Lee Edelman, *No Future: Queer Theory and the Death Drive* (Durham: Duke University Press, 2004), 2–3.
18. Denise LaVoie, "Woman Held on $500K Bail in Womb-Cut Kidnap Case," Salon.com, September 16, 2009.
19. Cynthia Freeland, *The Naked and the Undead: Evil and the Appeal of Horror* (Boulder: Westview Press, 2002), 2–3.
20. Marsh and Romer, *Empty Cradle*, 5.
21. Noël Carroll, *The Philosophy of Horror: Or, Paradoxes of the Heart* (New York: Routledge, 1990), 32.
22. Poole, *in America*, 172.
23. Elaine Berland and Marilyn Wechter, "Fatal/Fetal Attraction: Psychological Aspects of Imagining Female Identity in Contemporary Film," *Journal of Popular Culture* 26 (3): 1992, 42.
24. Carroll, 31.
25. Nancy Fraser, "Foucault on Modern Power: Empirical Insights and Normative Confusions," *Praxis International* 1(Oct. 1981): 272.

26. See *Baby Mama* (2008), *The Back-Up Plan* (2010), and the television series *Sex and the City* (1998–2004).

27. Ussher, *Managing*, 14.

28. Elaine Tyler May, "Nonmothers as Bad Mothers: Infertility and the 'Maternal Instinct,'" in *"Bad" Mothers: The Politics of Blame in Twentieth-Century America*, eds. Molly Ladd-Taylor and Lauri Umansky (New York: New York University Press, 2008), 521.

29. May, "Nonmothers."

30. Julia Kristeva, *The Power of Horror* (New York: Columbia University Press, 1982), 4.

31. Kristeva, *Power of Horror*, 2.

32. Creed, *Monstrous Feminine*, 8.

33. Creed, *Monstrous Feminine*, 10.

34. Kelly Oliver, *Knock Me Up, Knock Me Down: Images of Pregnancy in Hollywood Films* (New York: Columbia University Press, 2012), 125.

35. Creed, *Monstrous Feminine*, 56.

36. W. Scott Poole, *Monsters in America: Our Historical Obsession with the Hideous and the Haunting* (Waco: Baylor University Press, 2011); Barbara Creed, *The Monstrous Feminine: Film, Feminism, Psychoanalysis* (London: Routledge, 1997).

37. Richard Woodley, *It's Alive* (New York: Ballantine, 1977), 78.

38. Woodley, *It's Alive*, 77.

39. Hubert Dreyfus and Paul Rabinow, *Michel Foucault: Beyond Structuralism and Hermeneutics* (Chicago: University of Chicago Press, 1983), 172.

40. Benshoff, *Closet*, 18.

41. Oliver, *Knock*, 153.

42. Ibid., 186.

43. Ibid., 138.

44. Quoted in Oliver, *Knock*, 160.

45. Creed, *Monstrous Feminine*, 45–46.

46. See *Children of Men* and *The Matrix* for examples of dystopian worlds marked by infertility and artificial reproduction.

47. Quoted in Oliver, *Knock*, 138.

48. Vivian Sobchack, "Bringing It All Back Home," in *Dread of Difference*, ed. Barry Keith Grant (Austin: University of Texas Press, 1996), 144.

When Procreation Becomes Perversion

Zombie Babies

Kristine Larsen

"What's grosser than gross? A garbage can full of dead babies.
What's grosser than that? The one at the bottom is still alive.
What's grosser than that? He has to eat his way to freedom."[1]

One of the reasons why zombies are so fascinating yet simultaneously disturbing is that they defy clear classification. Are they human or not? Are they alive or dead? In this confusion, they epitomize the meaning of "dirt" popularized by anthropologist Mary Douglas as "matter out of place."[2] In order for dirt to be out of place, there first needs to be a culturally defined and accepted natural order for it to be in opposition to. Douglas asserts that human nature "condemns any object or idea likely to confuse or contradict cherished classifications."[3] Mary Bradbury notes that strong reactions to corpses occur precisely because they fall under Douglas's definition of dirt, being "confusing and threatening, human and yet not human."[4] Julia Kristeva takes this analysis further, exploring the important connection between the act of excreting bodily waste and the boundary between life and death. One remains alive—remains on this side of the border with death—by continuing to excrete that which is defiled from one's body. Death corresponds to the loss of extricating the defiled from within us—we have become the defiled.[5] In Kristeva's words, a corpse is "death infecting life."[6] It is for this reason that cultures create elaborate funerary rituals to separate the corpse from society. Interestingly, some of these rituals highlight similarities between birth and death, between "those entering and those exiting our society," for example the traditions of swaddling infants and wrapping corpses in winding sheets.[7]

But a zombie transgresses the boundary between life and death—between the human and the corpse. It eats, but it does not grow. Its heart does not beat, nor do its lungs fill with air, but yet it walks. A zombie is neither alive nor dead—it is, instead, frozen in an interstitial state of being "undead." Barbara Creed argues that it is the transgression of important boundaries such as this that leads to a definition of the monstrous in horror films.[8] Therefore, it is precisely this blurring of the boundary between birth and death that leads to the particular horror with which zombie babies are regarded. In stark contrast to the symbol of the newborn infant as representing life and hope, the rotting corpse reminds us that all will eventually come to dust. Furthermore, the corpse of a child—whether stillborn or having succumbed soon after birth—is a painful sign of life's promise cut short. But more disturbing still is the *undead* corpse of a baby—a zombie baby. The natural human response toward a child in distress is to comfort it, to hold it close and to meet its immediate needs for food, medicine, or shelter. In stark contrast, most humans just as instinctively shun a corpse with repulsion, as it is what Kristeva terms "the most sickening of wastes."[9] As Noël Carroll further describes, "the monstrous in horror stories is not merely a matter of fear ... [but] is compounded by revulsion, nausea, and disgust. The monster is so unwholesome that its very touch causes shudders."[10] As a result, the zombie child is even more of an insult to the natural order than an adult zombie because it creates a dissonance in our supposedly natural (instinctive) reactions to cuddle the child and to cut ourselves off from the corpse. In Carroll's words, zombies and other "undead" creatures "are cognitively threatening. They are threats to "common knowledge" in their unnatural state.[11] Therefore, zombie children, although more rare in film and other media than their adult counterparts, have become a powerful addition to the undead pantheon. *TV Tropes* notes that zombie children are "one of the squickiest things to come out of horror movies," and that in previous decades, while children were "presumably killed off-screen during the Zombie Apocalypse, they weren't turned into the living dead."[12] In contrast, the music video for HEALTH's song "Tears" (written for the video game *Max Payne 3*) openly embraces the horror of zombie children, featuring "the mind-chilling sight of zombie babies playing with eyeballs, bloodied bones, and sucking on pacifiers made from dismembered fingers."[13]

As noted in a comic graphic posted by Andy of Howtobeadad.com, zombies and babies have much in common; for example, zombies' fundamental properties include an "incomplete set of teeth, constant oral excretions, speaks in moans/screams." It is also a "messy eater," has "no sense of right and wrong, [is] bent on destruction, keeps you awake at night in fear, can turn others into zombies."[14] The awkward motor skills of both zombies and babies, and their obvious oral fixations, also make zombies and young children superficially similar. Gillian Brashear exploited these similarities in her 4 minute short *Zombie Baby* (2012), which features toddler Liam Sacrey and his infant brother Nolan. The simple escapades of a toddler in a playground, including affectionately hugging and kissing his brother, take on a nefarious tone when said toddler is dressed in zombie-like garb and make-up, and a horror film-like soundtrack is introduced.[15]

Why are babies as a subclass of humanity so seemingly sacrosanct? Seen through the lens of evolutionary science, they occupy a position of singular importance. The successful production of lively, healthy infants is central to the success of all species on this planet, as fertility and fecundity assure the continuation of the species in future generations.[16] But in the case of *Homo sapiens* in the 21st century, this most natural of biological functions eludes a significant number of couples.[17] Instead, couples increasingly turn to Assisted Reproductive Technologies (ART), including surrogate mothers, egg and embryo donation, and In Vitro Fertilization (IVF), among other techniques, in their quest for a healthy baby, as Brooke Edge discusses in this volume. However, despite the fact that over three million babies have been born using IVF and similar techniques since 1978,[18] many people remain troubled by the ethical and religious issues raised by these technological wonders. Many of these concerns center on the definition of boundaries (such as between life and not-life), and the transgression of those boundaries. Technology has also intruded into other aspects of reproduction—gestation, miscarriage and abortion, birth, and breast-feeding. Therefore, under certain circumstances, reproduction has been considered monstrous, both in life and art.

As Debbora Battaglia argues, popular cinema has a "place of honor in bioethical rhetoric and popular debate about genetically engineered entities" and other technological advances.[19] Zombie reproduction is perhaps the epitome of the unnatural—undead life emerging from the undead—and as such serves as a valuable fictional lens with which to consider all-too-real controversial cases at the intersections between technology, ethics, and human reproduction, including sperm and eggs harvested from dead parents and brain dead pregnant women being kept "alive" by extreme measures just long enough to bring their child to term. This essay argues that procreating zombies and zombie babies horrifically depicted in film and other media construct a mirror whose image forces us to consider these controversial scientific and ethical issues that threaten to transgress a number of biologically and culturally defined boundaries such as those between life and death, natural and unnatural, pure and impure, hope and fear, attachment and repulsion. In short, zombie films can often be seen to frame cutting edge reproductive technologies as being "monstrous" insofar as they play with these transgressions.

Conception

If a zombie apocalypse decimates the human population, reproduction must be considered a top priority—after securing food and shelter—if the human species is to survive. In George A. Romero's *Day of the Dead* (1985), helicopter pilot Johnny notes that the miles and miles of military, governmental, and corporate records stored in their bunker don't mean a thing to the future of humanity. "This is a great 14 mile tombstone," he explains to scientist Sarah. If humanity is to survive, it needs to "make babies and teach them never to dig up these records."[20] But while humans might be able to outthink and out-arm zombies, they cannot hope to out-compete zombies in the reproductive arena since the undead create others of their kind through a simple bite or just as an unavoidable consequence of the death process. Rather than having a 9 month gestation period, zombies animate within a few hours of human death (if not sooner). Because of this rapid reproductive process, medical mathematicians Munz, Hudea, Imad, and Smith found that "only quick, aggressive attacks can stave off the doomsday scenario: the collapse of society as zombies overtake us all."[21]

This reproduction of zombies is not only rapid but also asexual, having more in common with cloning than standard human sexual reproduction. In this way, zombies are more akin to bacteria than humans. Jillian Burcar explains that the zombie "has no gender because it has no biological sex ... [T]hat person ceases to be a person—a person who would deserve gendered pronouns such as he/she, and simply becomes an 'it.'" Furthermore, their non-heteronormative method of reproducing through biting "has its own assortment of symbolism that can be read into, since biting is necessarily a form of penetration."[22] A similar sort of monstrous parody of reproduction is seen in Mary Shelley's classic novel *Frankenstein*.[23] (Sarah Leventer's essay in this volume discusses Shelley's work in more detail.) This lack of ability to reproduce sexually is a clear difference between zombies and humans, at least in the majority of zombie media. But a number of books and films tackle the troubling possibility of zombie babies born from zombie parents. The concept of the undead giving birth to further undead subverts the very essence of human sexual reproduction. This perversion is noted by zombie Andy Warner himself in the novel *Breathers* when he asks, "Is it necrophilia if we're both dead?"[24] When his zombie girlfriend Rita conceives, Andy worries that "finding an ob-gyn who would treat Rita and keep her pregnancy a secret isn't likely.... Zombies procreating would produce a category-five hurricane [in society]."[25] In Peter Jackson's black comedy *Dead Alive* (1992), a dead priest and nurse have animalistic, rutting sex, and she conceives their zombie child, Selwyn, her abdomen hideously swelling in a manner of days.

The ability of zombies to reproduce sexually not only subverts human reproduction but, as previously noted, removes one of the clear boundaries separating humans from zombies. Indeed, in its 1924 decision in Skinner v. Oklahoma, the U.S. Supreme Court associated "the right to procreate with 'human rights' and with 'the right to have offspring,' implying that the right to reproduce is a basic civil right."[26] However, an estimated fifteen percent of married couples now have fertility issues. The decrease in human fertility has been blamed on a variety of issues, from environmental pollution to the increasing propensity of women (and men) to put off childbearing until their 30s, 40s, or even older.[27] Many of these couples turn to medical science to make their dreams of having a genetically-related child possible, through a series of techniques collectively known as ART—Assisted Reproductive Technologies. The juxtaposition of the words "reproduction" and "technologies"—signifying the natural and artificial or unnatural—draws attention to the boundary being transgressed here. It is therefore not surprising that these technologies are considered by some to be inherently unnatural, repulsive, and threatening—in other words, monstrous.

The cases of Selwyn and Andy Warner's post-zombification fatherhood represent a scenario in which zombified (undead but not alive) sperm and egg combine and create a zombified embryo that gestates and results in a "live" birth (more accurately a zombified or undead baby). The closest real-world scenarios are controversial cases involving posthumous reproduction. In these instances, sperm or eggs that have been retrieved and frozen from the parent(s) before their death are used in conception after their death via ART. There are also examples where embryos that were conceived through IVF and frozen are implanted and brought to term after one or both of the biological parents have died. There are a number of ethical and legal issues surrounding these scenarios, and many countries have laws regulating these types of births.[28] There have also been cases where sperm has been harvested post mortem,[29] and in a case in Israel, the parents of a dead 17-year-old girl won the right to have her eggs harvested and frozen for future pregnancies using a surrogate and sperm donor only to have a change of heart later.[30] This ability to produce life from death again transgresses the natural border between humans and corpses, and certainly contains echoes of the Frankenstein trope; the troubling nature of these cases, with all their ethical and legal concerns, parallels the "squickiness" felt at the possibility of zombie conception.

Gestation and Abortion

It is often said that a woman is at her most beautiful while she is with child, having the so-called "pregnant glow." This beauty also reflects the unequaled vibrancy of the process of gestation, the ability to bring forth another life from inside one's own body. But there is another, less flattering, way to view pregnancy, namely as a parasite-host relationship. In this viewpoint, the developing child is seen as an invader, like a tumor growing within the mother's body, feeding on its mother's blood and nutrients. Indeed, figuring out why a pregnant woman's body doesn't just reject and attack the developing child within has been a long-standing area of research in immunology.[31] Despite the fact that many doctors treat pregnant women as a single patient, there are actually two entities involved, with differing and sometimes competing medical conditions and concerns. Examples include preeclampsia and maternal cancers diagnosed during pregnancy, where the mother's health is compromised by the pregnancy. There are also concerns about an expectant mother's emotional and mental health concerning the pregnancy (for example in cases of rape or incest, or in the general case of unintended pregnancies). Here, the embryo or fetus can be considered to be matter out of place, or even "dirt" (as theorized by Mary Douglas). In many of these cases, terminating the pregnancy—abortion—is considered to be the option in the best interest of the woman.

An exploration of all of the medical, ethical, and legal issues surrounding abortion is not relevant to the topic at hand; suffice it to say that in modern culture, abortion is a topic that often leads to heated debates on both sides of the issue, thus making it a topic that filmmakers readily exploit in order to elicit an emotional response from the audience. An example of the emotional intensity of this debate can be found in Romero's original version of *Dawn of the Dead* (1978). Here, the character Fran is completing her first trimester of pregnancy when the zombie outbreak occurs. Her boyfriend (and father of her fetus) Steven explains their situation to Peter and Roger, two former SWAT team members with whom the couple is holed up in a mall, when Fran is struck with a bout of morning sickness. Peter asks Steven, "Do you want to get rid of it? Do you want to abort it? It's not too late and I know how." It is important to note that the fetus is designated "it," possibly a reference to its sex being unknown at this point, but more probably in the sense previously noted—it is not considered a person in this context, but rather an object. Fran overhears this male-only conversation and is upset with the presumption that it is Steven's decision alone to make. "Do you want to abort it?" she accuses. "Do you?" Steven counters, the first time Fran's opinion is sought in a decision that intimately affects her.[32] Romero's inclusion of this discussion in a film released only five years after the historic *Roe v. Wade* decision by the U.S. Supreme Court acknowledges and draws upon the national debate to invoke further feelings of ill-ease and uncertainty in the audience. Over the course of the film the obvious progression of Fran's pregnancy acts as a visual timeline. The film ends before she gives birth, leaving the fate of her unborn child uncertain (as is arguably the fate of any of us in a zombie apocalypse).[33]

Debates about the relative rights of the woman and the fetus often center on the point at which life begins and whether or not the fetus is a person. If it is a person, what is the extent of its "personhood"?[34] What are its inherent rights, and do those rights outweigh the rights of the "fetal container," i.e., the mother?[35] Again, it is not the intent of this essay to explore these controversial issues; rather, it is sufficient to understand that these issues *are* controversial, and therefore provide fodder for filmmakers to draw upon. If the audience has questions or strong opinions about the status of a fetus as human, and if the graphic visuals of aborted fetuses often used by anti-abortion activists are widely considered troubling and gruesome, then it is reasonable to assume that an audience would have a quite visceral reaction to a film centered on not only zombie fetuses, but zombie aborted fetuses. The zombification of aborted fetuses is the central theme of the low budget black comedy *Zombie Babies* (2011). Filmed over two weeks with a budget of only $10,000, the film features not only admittedly inferior gore effects, but in the words of writer, director, and star Eamon Hardimann, "The most awful scene in movie history" in which a man chokes on zombie fetus feces.[36] Indeed, throughout the film, the "filthy" nature of bodily excretions in general (including the aborted fetuses) is highlighted, *à la* Douglas and Kristeva. For example, the coat hanger abortions feature a great deal of exaggerated twisting and pulling motions used to remove large amounts of blood-colored "tissue" from the women.

The basic premise of the movie is that back alley abortionist Burt Fleming attempts to increase his profit margin by having an "Abort-athon" in his rundown hotel. Four young couples accept his offer to get rid of their "zygote problem" and "have the best rest and relaxation for the low, low price of $30" although one couple decides to continue the pregnancy after seeing Burt's facility in person.[37] Burt not only makes his own moonshine in the basement of his hotel but also an age-defying compound that allows him to appear to be no more than about 40 despite his actual age of 117. However, the elixir has "kinks," and when the still explodes, it animates the pile of aborted fetal tissue also kept in the basement. The reanimated fetuses are murderous rather than ravenous, and proceed to murder their own parents (for example, strangling and decapitating one father with an umbilical cord) and then menace the others in the hotel.

The effects used to make those zombie fetuses are rather low-technology puppetry in many cases, but there is sufficient gore and over-the-top offensive dialogue and visuals to draw attention away from this shortcoming. For example, when the zombie fetuses attack, one of the would-be-mothers incredulously remarks, "The whole point is that they kill the babies, right?" Burt turns "heroic" near the end of the film, deciding to stand and fight the zombie fetuses so that the sole remaining couple (the one that did not abort their fetus) can escape. Burt muses "We've made a pretty good living off of kids dying, ain't we.... I ain't no hero. I've won one award in my entire life, and it was for the fastest back alley abortion." After reminiscing over his coat hanger-shaped award, Burt retrieves two gold coat hangers from a suitcase, what his grandfather "used to call the 'final solution.' ... We're gonna kill some fucking babies."[38] The coat hanger motif displayed throughout the film (for example, one zombie fetus still has a piece of coat hanger embedded in it) may seem an obvious one, but curiously many of the current generation do not understand the relationship of coat hangers to abortion's history.[39] In his review of the film, Richard Gary argues that both pro-choice and anti-abortion activists should find offensive fodder for their personal viewpoint in this film, as it is an equal-opportunity offender.[40]

As previously noted, in the original *Dawn of the Dead*, Fran's pregnancy is an important source of tension between the characters, as her boyfriend initially appears to be in charge of making decisions concerning her body. In the 2004 remake, a similar situation occurs in the relationship of a very pregnant woman, Luda, and her boyfriend Andre. When a band of survivors holes up in a shopping mall, Luda is bitten by a zombie, a fact that is only known by her and Andre. When Andre learns that bites always turn the victim into a zombie, he segregates Luda in a baby store in the mall, making excuses for her absence to the other survivors. Yet in reality, he has tied her to a bed as she begins to succumb to the bite, making the decision for both of them to keep her alive at any cost until their child is born. There is no evidence that

Luda is ever told what is happening to her. Luda truly is a "fetal container," having no say over her body or her pregnancy.

Similar cases occur in the real world such as in the case of mothers in vegetative states (irreversible comas) and those who have suffered brain death, mothers whose state of existence threatens the boundary between life and death. In the latter case, the mothers are technically dead, except that their bodies are sustained through artificial means (including ventilators) for the sole purpose of allowing their fetus to develop to the point where it can survive outside of the womb. A recent case in point centered around Texas paramedic Marlise Muñoz, who was kept "alive" for two months by a hospital, against her family's expressed wishes.[41] The alternate terms "postmortem or perimortem pregnancy, cadaveric pregnancy, maternal organism, and posthumous motherhood"[42] used to describe the status of brain-dead pregnant women could just as easily include another: zombie mother. The legal and ethical ramifications of keeping a woman alive without her expressed consent for the purpose of being a womb are myriad, and have been discussed at length in the literature.[43] Such discussions are not merely academic, as several fetuses have been successfully delivered after growing over 100 days in their dead mother's womb.[44]

Night of the Dead: Leben Tod (2006) centers around Dr. Gabriel Schreklich's testing of a serum that reanimates the dead. His protégée is his nephew Peter, who, with his very pregnant wife Anais, live in Schreklich's facility. Anais complains about her "confinement," arguing that the place makes her sick, as do the special vitamins Peter insists she take six times a day. As Gabriel and Peter experiment with the serum, Gabriel explains that he will have better results if he can administer the drug at or before the actual moment of death. If done correctly, the subject enters "a state of *leben tod*, the live-death, almost completely alive—almost."[45] This phrase interestingly parallels descriptions of patients in permanent vegetative states, those in which only the brain stem still functions.[46]

When captive experimental zombies overrun the facility, Peter is bitten and begins to turn, but not before freeing Anais. As he sets her free (with her medical file and a large quantity of the mysterious vitamins in hand), Peter apologizes for the decisions he has made for both of them without consulting her. While the institute burns to the ground, Anais is checked out by a paramedic, who sorrowfully tells her that her baby is most probably dead. She reads her medical records and learns that she herself has been declared brain dead following a stroke. Her body has been stolen from the hospital by her husband after the hospital had wanted to withhold life support and her body had been injected with Gabriel's serum. Gabriel's handwritten notes warn that while she was currently "essentially alive," if she stopped taking the medication six times a day she would return to her "dead state."[47] The film therefore draws upon modern issues of brain dead mothers as "fetal containers," but adds a science fiction twist. One could argue that the horror element is already present to some degree in the real world precedent.

Birth and Breast Feeding

The unnatural transition from life to zombie "undeath" can been likened to a kind of monstrous birth, monstrous in the sense that it transgresses the natural order of birth, life, death, and a birth in that it is a new form of existence. For example, in Robin Becker's 2010 novel *Brains*, lead character Jack Barnes describes his transition from human to zombie as being "whisked into some sort of meat tube, like a large intestine where trapped souls screamed at me from polyp walls and everything was flaming orange and too hot.... And then I was reborn."[48] The comparison between his zombie "birth" and the act of excreting food is a particularly interesting one when considered in light of Kristeva's theoretical framework. Andy Warner, zombie protagonist of *Breathers*, likewise recounts, "When your life is ripped away and you're reborn into an existence of undeath, nothing seems real."[49] Warner later draws connections between his current state and that of an infant: "Born into a world of decay. Relearning how to walk and talk. Suckling from the bosom of hope."[50]

In zombie films, the actual birth of a zombie baby is often depicted as a double monstrosity, as both the process and the progeny (the zombie baby itself) are unnatural. For example, in *Dead Alive* the comic zombie baby Selwyn is first heard moving around Lionel's basement. Lionel tracks the sound to an old radio, and pulls Selwyn out of the device by his feet, a breech birth of sorts. A symbolic monstrous birth takes place in the climax of the film when the overly possessive mother super-zombie threatens Lionel with her pendulous lips, thighs, and breasts (a bloated parody of the famous ancient Venus of Willendorf); her stomach finally opens up and sucks her son inside. Lionel cuts his way out using a medallion given to him by his girlfriend's gypsy grandmother, emerging from this grotesque cesarean birth covered with a mixture of entrails and placenta-like viscera.[51]

Similarly, the greater mass of the fetus pile in *Zombie Babies* amalgamates into a "master baby" that creates a uterus-like cocoon in the basement. Burt fights the master baby with his golden coat hangers, trapping it in its cocoon. He and his assistant Teddy pull the grotesquely bloodied and bloated homicidal monster halfway out of the faux vagina, and it stops moving. Despite the fact that the Master Baby is pulled out head-first (like in the case of a normal birth), it is possible that some connections are meant to be drawn to the controversial D&X (Dilate and Extract) procedure of late-term abortion, more commonly known as "partial-birth abortion." In this procedure, the fetus is drawn out feet-first and the contents of the skull removed so that it can be compacted before its head is delivered, reducing physical damage to the woman.[52]

Other unnatural and repulsive births are found in films with zombie babies. For example, in Snyder's remake of *Dawn of the Dead*, Luda goes into labor at the same time that the zombie infection overtakes her body. While Andre encourages her to breathe as the labor continues, she stops breathing and dies. He kisses her and closes her eyes, but sees her belly move as the unborn fetus struggles to be born. Luda reanimates and attempts to bite Andre, so he muzzles her and turns his attention from his now-dead wife (now a mere fetus container) to his unborn child. Luda delivers the child vaginally, along with an inordinate amount of blood.

Undoubtedly, the most emotionally gut-wrenching birth of a zombie baby is the still-birth of the titular character of *Grace*. Writer and director Paul Solet explains that he based the work on actual medical science concerning a woman's ability to carry a stillborn baby for weeks or more. He calls it "the ultimate kernel of horror on which to grow what became *Grace*."[53] As critic Mark H. Harris observes, the film is "designed to disturb and provoke response" through the main character, a "dead (or undead) baby, whose presence smears a general sense of discomfort across the film, conjuring images of abortion and miscarriage."[54] Grace's apparent stillbirth is made all the more sorrowful by the fact that her parents had so desperately tried to have a child. Madeline had become pregnant twice before while using fertility drugs (a form of ART) but decided to try for a natural conception instead. The tacit accusation here is that the fertility drugs had caused her to miscarry her previous pregnancies.

Madeline is a vegan who insists on a "natural" childbirth, using midwife Patricia (a former girlfriend) and a birthing pool, noting that maternal deaths are more common in hospitals than natural birthing facilities. It is true that modern views of the birthing process itself have changed considerably in the past 100 years. During the past century, the standard of a home birth with a midwife in attendance has given way to the hospital birth where the mother's pain, and in some cases time of delivery, are both manipulated by medication.[55] Finally, the increase in the number of cesarean sections in the Western world takes birth out of the realm of healthy, natural processes and turns it into a surgery—again, reflecting the vision of pregnancy as a disease to be cured by cutting out a tumor. Madeline's viewpoint echoes that of the "natural birth" movement that gained traction in the 1960s, where some women rebelled against the increasingly sterile, impersonal, and alienating hospital birth industry.[56] When her husband and unborn child are killed in a car accident, Madeline decides to carry the pregnancy to term, and still refuses to give birth in a hospital. Instead, she demands that Patricia treat this as a normal birth until the very end, despite the fact that the birthing pool fills with blood.

After the birth, Madeline insists on privacy, cradling the lifeless, gray infant. As Patricia and her assistant Shelly observe from another room, Madeline talks to her dead daughter, begging her to "stay." Shelly notes that Madeline's behavior is "sick" (it is considered unnatural and out of place) and demands that Patricia put an end to it. As Patricia enters the birthing room to remove the stillborn infant, she is amazed to see the baby nursing.[57] For the moment, Grace is normal, motivated by the natural instinct to breastfeed. Madeline's desire to treat her stillborn daughter as a normal infant, if only for a moment, and Shelly's revulsion at her actions, parallel controversies around the Duggar family's funeral for daughter Jubilee Shalom (featuring photographs of the stillborn child)[58] and former presidential candidate Rick Santorum and his wife taking their stillborn son Gabriel home from the hospital in order for their other children to meet him.[59] The controversy derives from the fact that, as previously noted, the culturally dominant point of view is to see the corpse as dirt or waste, something that is inherently repulsive and that one would not wish to intentionally bring into one's home or have children interact with. The Duggars and more directly the Santorums instead actively chose to reject those societal norms and bring their dead children "home," if only briefly. In these cases, the definition of monstrous is clearly in the eye of the beholder.[60] (Renner, in this volume, explores the blind and even obsessive love of mothers in horror films for their monstrous infants.)

The reanimation of another stillborn baby appears in *Night of the Dead: Leben Tod*. Gabriel's zombified daughter Christi survives the fire, and Anais claims to the authorities that she is the girl's mother. The film ends with Anais injecting her abdomen with the serum while Christi looks on. "I don't want the baby to be dead. Not all the way dead," Christi urges. We see the fetus move inside Anais, hear a heartbeat, then after a fade to black we briefly hear and see Anais scream.[61] Luda's baby in Snyder's *Dawn of the Dead* is born alive, or rather undead. When the mall's power goes out, Norma goes to check on the young couple and to bring them some candles. She is shocked to see zombie Luda tied to the bed and growling through her muzzle, while Andre cradles a swaddled zombie infant. "It's a girl," he happily announces. Norma shoots Luda, and in the exchange of gunfire both Norma and Andre are killed. When others run toward the sound of the gunfire, they see the zombie baby still cradled in Andre's arms, and when it utters an unearthly growled cry, nurse Ana shoots it.[62]

Again, it is both the process (zombie giving birth) and the product (zombie baby) that are unnatural, grotesque, and threatening in the case of Luda's child. This dual monstrosity of process and product offers a third possibility in discussions of the ethics of reproductive technologies and bio-engineering. Mary Midgley notes that bioethicists tend to "divide moral objections firmly into two sets, those that point to dangerous consequences and those saying that the act itself is intrinsically wrong."[63] In the case of a newborn zombie baby, there is no such dichotomy. Despite the monstrous (boundary transgressing) nature of both its birth and state of being, Andre clearly sees his zombie child as a child rather than as a zombie. Likewise Lionel attempts to treat zombie baby Selwyn like a normal child in *Dead Alive*, with the exception that the child needs to be sedated with animal tranquilizers and has barbed wire covering his pram to prevent his escape. When the zombies launch an attack on a houseful of partiers at the end of the film, baby Selwyn is able to use his human-like cry to make Paquitta pause for a moment before trying to kill him with a blender. Despite being an obviously comical character, Selwyn nevertheless demonstrates the danger of treating a zombie baby as if it were a normal human infant. Like any zombie, its only desire is to devour human flesh. Grace is no exception. However, as an infant she requires liquid flesh, or blood, which she initially draws from biting her mother's breast. Madeline is increasingly desperate to find out why her daughter won't drink milk like a normal child, but refuses to bring her in for medical tests, lacking trust in the same medical establishment that pronounced her child dead in the womb. This is despite the fact that it becomes increasingly clear that Grace is, if not a classic zombie, indeed a rotting undead creature of some kind (the clues including strange odors emanating from her, flies being attracted to her in droves, unexplained sores, and a low body temperature).

When she accepts that her daughter will only drink blood, Madeline attempts to feed Grace blood from steak packages, but the cold animal blood makes the child physically ill. Dr. Sohn, the personal doctor of Madeline's overbearing mother-in-law, comes to the house and is killed by Madeline when he tries to take Grace away from her. In the original script, Grace eagerly laps up the dead man's fresh blood, but this scene is absent from the film. Perhaps because this was deemed too controversial, in the film Madeline instead takes it upon herself to collect his blood in a baby bottle. Madeline's mother-in-law is also killed when she tries to take Grace, and Madeline, Grace, and Patricia change their appearances and go on the road in a camper. The film ends with Madeline explaining to Patricia that Grace needs more than blood now. "She's teething," as evidenced by the shocking sight of Madeline's partially devoured breast.[64] Therefore, despite the fact that Paul Solet deliberately left Grace's classification ambiguous, she clearly has many of the trademark characteristics of zombies, and should be included as the most human—and hence most terrifying—of the infant undead.[65]

Conclusion

Barbara Almond argues that the "horrifying idea of giving birth to a monster seems to be ubiquitous." Variations on this theme include fears of infertility due to abnormalities with a woman's reproductive system, of the pregnancy sickening or killing women, or women's inability to love the child once it is born.[66] These fears, as well as fears of unwanted pregnancies, stillbirth and an inability to breastfeed, are reflected in the zombie films described in this essay. These films are not specifically about zombie babies, but rather force us to reflect upon how technology has changed the human reproductive process, especially in the 21st century. ART, abortion, brain-dead mothers, and post-mortem conception are at the heart of current debates about definitions of "motherhood, paternity, biological inheritance, the integrity of the family, and the 'naturalness' of birth itself."[67] These debates (especially as they are depicted in film and other media) compel us to reevaluate our personal views of the sanctity of the body, especially the female body, in the face of increasingly intrusive technologies.

As previously discussed, Mary Douglas notes that in order for something to be considered "out of place" there must be a well-defined, agreed upon definition of what that object's rightful place should be. We therefore rely on culturally agreed upon boundaries to define the normal order of things. In the 21st century, these boundaries appear to be shifting as technology progresses. For example, in vitro fertilization was once considered "monstrous" and unnatural; now it is commonplace. In our modern society, we are increasingly forced to ask ourselves where are the acceptable boundaries between life and death, natural and artificial, human and inhuman? As a result, as technology continues to push the envelope of what is possible, there appears to be greater pushback by a significant portion of the population that considers these technologies to be unnatural, repulsive, transgressive, or threatening to the individual and/or society. Does this, in turn, necessarily mandate that we consider all reproductive technologies (as applied from conception through infancy) to be monstrous? If not, where are the boundaries to be drawn, and who should be allowed to define them—scientists, politicians, theologians, ethicists, or the voting public at large? These are uneasy questions with no clear answers. Yet if it disturbs us when zombie babies cry, we would all do well to consider why this is so.

Notes

1. Dead Baby Joke, last modified September 23, 2002, http://www.dead-baby-joke.com/dbj_017.htm.
2. Mary Douglas, *Purity and Danger* (London: Routledge Classics, 2002 [1966]), 44.
3. Douglas, *Purity*, 45.
4. Mary Bradbury, *Representations of Death: A Social Psychological Perspective* (London: Routledge, 1999), 125.
5. Julia Kristeva, *Powers of Horror: An Essay on Abjection*, trans. Leon S. Roudiez (New York: Columbia University Press, 1982), 3.
6. Kristeva, *Powers*, 4.
7. Bradbury, *Representations of Death*, 9.
8. Barbara Creed, *The Monstrous-Feminine: Film, Feminism, Psychoanalysis* (London: Routledge, 1993).
9. Kristeva, *Powers*, 3.
10. Noël Carroll, "The Nature of Horror," *The Journal of Aesthetics and Art Criticism* 46, no. 1 (1987), 53.
11. Carroll, "The Nature of Horror," 56.
12. TV Tropes: Undead Child, TV Tropes Foundation, accessed July 30, 2013, http://tvtropes.org/pmwiki/pmwiki.php/Main/UndeadChild.
13. The Creator's Project, "Zombie Babies Star in the Short Film for HEALTH's 'Tears,'" last modified October 31, 2012, http://thecreatorsproject.vice.com/blog/zombie-babies-star-in-the-short-film-for-healths-tears.
14. Andy, "Zombie vs. Baby," How to Be a Dad Blog, last modified April 19, 2011, http://www.howtobeadad.com/2011/1582/zombie-baby.
15. Gillian Brashear, "Zombie Baby," 2012, http://vimeo.com/52829380.
16. See Lee Edelman's *No Future: Queer Theory and the Death Drive* (Durham: Duke University Press, 2004) for a rebuttal of the politics of "reproductive futurism" in modern society.
17. Rickie Solinger, *Reproductive Politics: What Everyone Needs to Know* (Oxford: Oxford University Press, 2013), 100.
18. Anne Drapkin Lyerly, "Marking the Fine Line: Ethics and the Regulation of Innovative Technologies in Human Reproduction," *Minnesota Journal of Law, Science and Technology* 11, no. 2 (2010): 686.
19. Debbora Battaglia, "Multiplicities: An Anthropologist's Thoughts on Replicants and Clones in Popular Film," *Critical Inquiry* 27 no. 3 (2001): 495.

20. *Day of the Dead*, directed by George A. Romero (1985; Beverly Hills: Anchor Bay Entertainment, 2003), DVD.

21. Philip Munz et al., "When Zombies Attack! Mathematical Modeling of an Outbreak of Zombie Infection," in *Infectious Disease Modeling Research Progress*, eds. J.M. Tchuenche and C. Chiyaka (Hauppauge, NY: Nova Science Publishers, 2009): 133.

22. Jillian Burcar, "Living Appendages of the Machine: Reproducing Sex and Gender in Cyborg and Zombie Narratives, from *Battlestar Galactica* to *The Walking Dead*," in *Creating Humanity, Discovering Monstrosity*, eds. Elizabeth Nelson, Jillian Burcar, and Hannah Priest (Oxford: Inter-Disciplinary Press, 2010), 407.

23. Paul Youngquist, "*Frankenstein*: The Mother, the Daughter, and the Monster," *Philological Quarterly* 70 no. 3 (1991): 339–59.

24. S.G. Browne, *Breathers: A Zombie's Lament* (New York: Broadway Books, 2009), 171.

25. Browne, *Breathers*, 269.

26. Solinger, *Reproductive Politics*, 27.

27. Solinger, *Reproductive Politics*, 100.

28. Daniel Sperling, "Maternal Brain Death," *American Journal of Law and Medicine* 30 (2004): 495–6.

29. Timothy F. Murphy, "Sperm Harvesting and Post Mortem Fatherhood," *Bioethics* 9, no. 4 (1995): 380–98.

30. Adrian Blomfield, "Family Given Permission to Extract Eggs From Ovaries of Dead Daughter in World First," *The Telegraph*, August 8, 2011, http://www.telegraph.co.uk/health/healthnews/8689479/Family-given-permission-to-extract-eggs-from-ovaries-of-dead-daughter-in-world-first.html.

31. P. Nancy, et al., "Chemokine Gene Silencing in Decidual Stromal Cells Limits T Cell Access to the Maternal-Fetal Interface," *Science* 336, no. 6086 (2012): 1317.

32. *Dawn of the Dead*, directed by George A. Romero (1978; Beverly Hills: Anchor Bay Entertainment, 2004), DVD.

33. Space considerations do not allow for an exploration of Lori Grimes's decision to carry her pregnancy to term in *The Walking Dead*, despite the fact that she had had a previous cesarean section and expected to have to have another with this pregnancy. Interested readers are directed to Katherine Don, "Bringing Up Baby: Pregnancy (and Zombies) are Scary on *The Walking Dead*," *Bitchmedia*, last modified November 23, 2011, http://bitchmagazine.org/post/bringing-up-baby-pregnancy-and-zombies-are-scary-on-the-walking-dead.

34. For a detailed discussion of several viewpoints, see Stephen D. Schwarz and Kiki Latimer, *Understanding Abortion* (Lanham, MD: Lexington Books, 2012).

35. Laura M. Purdy, "Are Pregnant Women Fetal Containers?" *Bioethics* 4 no. 4 (1990): 273–91.

36. Eamon Hardimann, "Commentary," *Zombie Babies*, directed by Eamon Hardimann (2011; New York: Independent Entertainment, 2012), DVD.

37. *Zombie Babies*, directed by Eamon Hardimann (2011; New York: Independent Entertainment, 2012), DVD.

38. *Zombie Babies*.

39. Angie Young, "Abortion, Ideology, and the Murder of George Tiller," *Feminist Studies* 35, no. 2 (2009): 419.

40. Richard Gary, "DVD Review: *Zombie Babies*," *Indie Horror Films Blog*, last modified October 22, 2012, http://indiehorrorfilms.blogspot.com/2012/10/dvd-review-zombie-babies.html.

41. For a summary of the case, see Manny Fernandez, "Texas Woman Is Taken Off Life Support After Order," *New York Times*, January 26, 2014.

42. Anita J. Catlin and Deborah Volat, "When the Fetus Is Alive But the Mother Is Not," *Critical Care Nursing Clinics of North America* 21 (2009): 268.

43. For example, Nicola S. Peart, et al., "Maintaining a Pregnancy Following Loss of Capacity," *Medical Law Review* 8 (2000): 275–99.
44. Sperling, "Maternal Brain Death," 453.
45. *Night of the Dead: Leben Tod*, directed by Eric Forsberg (2006; Burbank: The Asylum Home Entertainment, 2006), DVD.
46. Peart, et al., "Maintaining a Pregnancy Following Loss of Capacity," 290–1.
47. *Night of the Dead: Leben Tod*.
48. Robin Becker, *Brains* (New York: Eos, 2010), 36.
49. Browne, *Breathers: A Zombie's Lament*, 98.
50. Browne, *Breathers*, 120.
51. *Dead Alive*, directed by Peter Jackson (1992; Santa Monica: Lionsgate Home Entertainment, 2001), DVD.
52. Solinger, *Reproductive Politics*, 73–4.
53. Paul Solet, "Grace: Conception," *Grace*, directed by Paul Solet (2009; Beverly Hills: Anchor Bay Entertainment, 2009) DVD.
54. Mark H. Harris, "'Grace' Movie Review," *Horror and Suspense Movies*, accessed July 30, 2013, http://horror.about.com/od/theatricalhorrorreviews/fr/gracereview.htm.
55. Katherine Beckett, "Choosing Cesarean: Feminism and the Politics of Childbirth in the United States," *Feminist Theory* 6, no. 3 (2005): 251.
56. Beckett, "Choosing Cesarean," 253.
57. *Grace*.
58. Eryn Sun, "Duggars' Memorial Service for Stillborn Baby Celebrates Short Life," *Christian Post*, last updated December 15, 2011, http://www.christianpost.com/news/duggars-memorial-service-for-stillborn-baby-celebrates-short-life-64953/.
59. David Sessions, "Rick Santorum's Dead-Baby Ritual," *The Daily Beast*, last updated January 3, 2012, http://www.thedailybeast.com/articles/2012/01/03/rick-santorum-s-dead-baby-ritual0.html.
60. The status of anencephalic infants (infants born with only a brainstem) is also a related case, but lies beyond the scope of this essay. For information on ethical considerations concerning this medical condition, see Ferhaan Ahmad, "Anencephalic Infants as Organ Donors: Beware the Slippery Slope," *Canadian Medical Association Journal* 146, no. 2 (1992): 236–44.
61. *Night of the Dead: Leben Tod*.
62. *Dawn of the Dead*, directed by Zack Snyder (2004; Universal City: Universal Studios, 2004), DVD.
63. Mary Midgley, "Biotechnology and Monstrosity: Why We Should Pay Attention to the 'Yuk Factor,'" *Hastings Center Report* 30, no. 5 (2000): 7.
64. *Grace*.
65. Solet, "Grace: Conception."
66. Barbara Almond, *The Monster Within: The Hidden Side of Motherhood* (Berkeley: University of California Press, 2010); 53.
67. Cris Shore, "Virgin Birth and Sterile Debates: Anthropology and the New Reproductive Technologies," *Current Anthropology* 33, no. 3 (1992): 295.

PART II

Frankenstein's Kindergarten

"My hideous cinematic progeny"

Rosemary's Baby, Eraserhead *and* Frankenstein

SARAH LEVENTER

According to legend, before shooting *The Shining*, Stanley Kubrick screened two films for his production crew: Roman Polanski's *Rosemary's Baby* and David Lynch's *Eraserhead*. This Kubrick legend has proven difficult to verify, an apparent product of vaguely similar plots and cinephiles' wishful thinking. However, the legend's endurance suggests a strongly felt kinship between these films. Understanding that kinship may involve looking to one of the few sources Kubrick did admit to consulting, Mary Shelley's *Frankenstein: The Modern Prometheus*. *Rosemary's Baby* and *Eraserhead* in fact reanimate *Frankenstein* on multiple levels, making the films two important points on the monstrous child continuum detailed in the introduction to this volume.[1] Both films follow *Frankenstein*'s central narrative—a protagonist "artificially" creates life with horrific consequences—but more importantly, the films use "monstrous-childness" to elaborate on *Frankenstein*'s central projects—undermining the rational order personified by male-centered, Enlightenment logic and revealing the irrational world beneath.[2]

In the 1831 introduction to *Frankenstein*, Mary Shelley famously used "my hideous progeny" to refer both to her novel and the offspring (Frankenstein's Monster) birthed within it. This term suggests the way Shelley envisioned the affinity between her project and Victor Frankenstein's as well as her connection to the Monster. As with Victor Frankenstein, the Monster is Shelley's "progeny" and her doppelganger. Like her protagonist, Shelley conceived and inflicted a terrifying product on the wider world. Like the Monster, Shelley's involuntary alterity fated her to be an unwitting messenger of terrible knowledge; the Monster and Shelley's novel show the monstrous implications of the creative drive so important in the Romantic era.[3] As is oft remarked upon, Shelley was a divided authorial entity, both the Monster and its creator, the victim and perpetrator of a cruel reproduction. Her novel, her hideous progeny, is a warped product of those divisions (victim/creator, monstrous/civilized, rational/irrational, deformed/normative).[4]

Shelley's novel provides the model for many of the texts discussed in this volume, as well as the teratological theory applied to them: nearly every character is some combination of doppelganger/monstrous child. Frankenstein's Monster is the enduring symbol of these myriad doublings and divisions, following exactly the pattern of monstrous-childness detailed in the introduction to this collection. He begins the novel as emblem of Victor Frankenstein's (and the larger Industrial Revolution's) boundless faith in science and reason but transforms into a repository for sexual, familial, and ideological nightmares. The same can be said for the Monster's updated iterations—the children in *Rosemary's Baby* and *Eraserhead*.

In *Frankenstein*, *Rosemary's Baby* and *Eraserhead*, the child is an icon: it briefly embodies the protagonist's best hopes, only to descend in esteem to the level of the monstrous, the darker half of the "divided self" trope so prominent in Dark Romantic/Gothic tales. In Polanski and Lynch's films, this monstrous child also carries additional historical/theoretical import. By *Rosemary's Baby*'s release in 1968, the nation had lost thousands of soldiers in the Vietnam War as well as leaders whose deaths were previously unthinkable: Martin Luther King, Jr., John F. Kennedy, and Malcolm X, among others. However, America's realization of its role as an exporter of violence began to crystallize with the military failure of the Tet Offensive, also in 1968. The nation's division revealed itself in the clash at the Democratic National Convention in 1968 and continued to deepen through key events of the 1970s: the escalation of the Vietnam War, Watergate, the continuing increase in political activism and the violence of Kent State and Altamont, all of which occurred before *Eraserhead*'s release in 1977. Rosemary and Henry (the respective protagonists of *Rosemary's Baby* and *Eraserhead*), too, cause catastrophic events, and are victims of the same: their children embody the historical and psychological divisions of their makers.

In both films, the children's appearance triggers psychological crises that show the devastating effect of such identity-shattering historical incidents. Their births initiate a return to the Romantic (a return to the inexplicable, subjective experience beyond reason) by a cinema and nation that considered themselves resolutely modern. The erupting conflict between a Romantic and an Enlightenment worldview—one governed by reason, empiricism, and the endless perfectibility of the human mind—is also what structures *Frankenstein*. Victor Frankenstein, an Enlightened subject driven by the hermeneutic impulse to know and to master the inner workings of the world, begins his quest by declaring, "Life and death appeared to me ideal bounds, which I should first break through, and pour a torrent of light onto our dark world. A new species would bless me as its creator and source; many happy and excellent natures would owe their being to me."[5] As he pursues his monster across mountains and seas, he learns that the mind is not perfect, but limited and earthbound, and the "true" natural world cannot be conquered or even fully understood by humans. His deformed monster is an uncanny reminder of nature's inexplicability as well as the compromised nature of the doctor's project to know and control that world.

As filmmakers and theorists from George Méliès to Linda Williams have explored, the hermeneutic impulse is also a key drive of the cinematic apparatus. The desire to know is expressed in narrative film's drive to penetrate the visual world, its use of the camera to "get at" the logic underpinning that world. The hermeneutic drive assumes that the world proceeds according to logic, and further, that the human mind cannot only understand that logic but replicate it in its own acts of cinematic creation. Polanski and Lynch intervene in this impulse in the same way Mary Shelley's novel did. In *Rosemary's Baby* and *Eraserhead*, the initially well-ordered, rational world is transformed when the irrational ruptures through in the form of a tiny, malformed body in a crib. These only partially glimpsed bodies typify Gilles Deleuze's concept of the monstrous, as noted in the introduction to this volume, defined as the "pure unformed," brutally remonstrating against our presumption to know.[6] By the end of these films, the entire cinematic apparatus, built on visuality and resolution, is undone.

Rosemary's Baby follows young newlyweds, Guy (John Cassavetes) and his pregnant wife, Rosemary Woodhouse (Mia Farrow), on what seems an exceedingly normative journey: finding and settling into an apartment. However, at the end of Rosemary's strange, illness-filled pregnancy, she gives birth to what may be Satan's child. The child's ontology provokes further anxiety for Rosemary and audience alike because it remains offscreen and forever unknowable. The child's absence troubles the hermeneutic impulse and its ancillary practice, psychoanalysis, at a time when knowing and finding oneself became particularly urgent, and particularly difficult.[7] Psychoanalysis is structured on the principle that to understand herself, a subject must investigate the neuroses formed in her childhood. As stated in the introduction to this volume, psychoanalysis uses the child to explain adult impulses, but seeing and understanding the child is paradoxically impossible for the adult subject. As Virginia L. Blum observes, "Psychoanalysis [...] is the preeminent twentieth-century discourse about childhood, a discourse that [...] refuses to examine the inevitable aporias occurring when adult subjects treat as ultimately knowable a position they have both internalized and forsaken."[8] By not picturing the child, *Rosemary's Baby* casts the child's position in an appropriately unknowable way—this partially constitutes its enduring terror for adult audiences.

Rosemary's Baby's resolutely anti-visual ending sets our unconscious free: what *is* that child, and what has its existence unleashed? What does it suggest about the world we thought we knew? How much else don't we know? *Rosemary's Baby* uses its child's non-appearance to provoke profound fear. However, as close analysis of two key scenes of *Eraserhead*—a dream sequence in which protagonist Henry's head falls off and is replaced by the rising, phallic head of his infant, and an earlier moment when the infant eviscerates—reveals, seeing the monster-child does nothing to diminish the feeling of unspeakable dread in the worlds of Polanski and Lynch.[9]

The opening of *Rosemary's Baby* sets up Manhattan's familiar, Enlightened topography, but it also subtly telegraphs the impending irrational breakdown of that world. A lilting score and pink, swirling title script play over a bird's-eye shot of New York City. Eventually, the audience is introduced to Rosemary and Guy viewing an apartment in the Bramford Building, which overlooks Central Park. As production designer Dick Sylbert notes, "[Polanski] said 'I thought this was a soap opera,' and that was the best clue he had, and we used it. *Rosemary's Baby* opens like a Doris Day picture, and that's the whole point."[10] The first few moments of *Rosemary's Baby* create the impression that the film is a reliable construction of reality, one that will progress in a logical way to a conclusion that offers resolution.

However, just before the audience meets the couple, the image of Central Park, (that apparently civilized space) is made strange by its juxtaposition against a precariously high-angle shot of the Bramford, which appears to be lifted, and perfectly preserved, from a nineteenth-century Gothic novel. From this point, the film metaphorically zooms further and further into the Woodhouses' lives until Rosemary descends completely into madness, and the opening shot of the film is shown in reverse as a zoom-out. All the qualities of the first shot are inverted, and the subversive invocation of Central Park is revealed.

Urban parks, like the "checkerboard-patterned" fields that replaced much of the English wilderness, are emblems of rational thought: they transform untamed nature, once the vaguely terrifying site of the sublime, supernatural forces that accounted for the mysteries of human experience, into orderly, subdivided spaces.[11] The creation of these spaces is part of the Enlightenment practice of dismantling the superstitious medieval worldview and replacing it with one based on empirical logic and scientific reasoning. By forcing a prolonged confrontation with the irrational and occult, and by visually inverting the image of Central Park, however, Polanski also inverts the Enlightenment worldview, reasserting the power of the supernatural, and making the notion that the inexplicable world can be civilized seem counterfeit and absurd. Upon reflection, the viewer is confronted with the realization that the soap opera aesthetic is a dark satire, and the artificially boundaried Central Park is the first indication of the ugliness of Rosemary's world. In fact, these hints very possibly go unnoticed during initial viewing of the film, which is perhaps the most frightening realization of all.

By the film's end, the odd angle of the bird's-eye shot of the Bramford seems obviously malevolent, as do the medieval architecture, dissonant chords and lilting score, which now sounds like a carnivalesque, deranged lullaby. The film's slightly amplified color scheme, especially concentrated on whites and yellows, and exaggerated furniture scale also express something malevolently too-perfect. All of these visual details speak to the concept of excess and decadence, two defining aesthetic qualities of the Dark Romantic/Gothic genre; they confirm Diane Waldeman's assertion of the film's structural similarities to texts like *Frankenstein*: "the structure has all the earmarks of the Gothic mode (the naïve woman, the opaque husband, the awesome mansion, supernatural events)."[12] However, similarities between *Frankenstein* and *Rosemary's Baby* run much deeper, to the shared style and biographical details of their authors.

Connecting Polanski to his literary predecessor begins with perhaps the most obviously Dark Romantic quality of his films: his propensity for animating the objective world with the interior life of his protagonist.[13] This is particularly true in what is often referred to as his apartment trilogy: *Repulsion, Rosemary's Baby*, and *The Tenant*. The *Rosemary's Baby* poster, for instance, superimposes a baby buggy over Rosemary's profile, making it appear her child (and the film) emerged directly from her mind.[14] In *Repulsion*, Polanski immerses the viewer in his protagonist Carole's (Catherine Deneuve) perspective and offers no "break" as she slowly goes insane. The world Carole experiences becomes more and more surreal, but the line between her perspective and her environment remains unclear—her projections become the audience's reality.

Unfortunately, for all the self-reflective energy expended to resolve Carole's situation, Polanski's main character and the viewer are rewarded with what film scholar John Orr calls a "final incomprehension," the knowledge that the world is somehow less understandable than when the viewer started her mental heavy-lifting.[15] In many of his films, the protagonist's journey is an exercise in psychic entropy, making Polanski a continuation of the Dark Romantic tradition of portraying the awakening of perception as a traumatic, solitary event. In the films of Polanski and his literary antecedents, the hermeneutic impulse to know, control, and resolve results in the failure of reason and discovery of the true world just beneath civilized society—a world in which suffering and dilemma are endemic, but simultaneously incomprehensible in terms of rational thought and language. This fall into solipsistic, abyssal experience—embodied by Rosemary's stunned state at the end of *Rosemary's Baby* or Victor Frankenstein's guilt-ridden wandering in Mary Shelley's *Frankenstein*—is the central similarity that unites Polanski with Shelley.

When examining Romantic works, critics run the risk of over-relying on biographical details and conflating author and protagonist. However, as literary scholar George Levine notes, because *Frankenstein* is a self-admitted product of authorial preoccupations, considering Shelley's worldview is crucial. This is particularly true when comparing her to Polanski, as a similarly random tragicness pervades their work, and parallels their life experience.[16] What Elzbieta Ostrowska says of Polanski, who was a perpetual culprit and victim of tragic circumstances, could easily be extended to Shelley: "In his work ... motherhood never takes the form of a nostalgic space of safety, but rather indicates all the horrors of human life that begins at the moment of conception."[17,18]

Shelley's father, William Godwin, was a political radical who inspired many of the Romantic writers (including Shelley's husband, Percy), as did her mother, Mary Wollstonecraft. Unfortunately, Wollstonecraft died ten days after Shelley's birth. From the very beginning of her life, then, the understanding that birth could be terrible, that Shelley herself could be marked with guilt for her mother's death in addition to being a victim of loss, was profound. The difficulties continued throughout the Gothic author's life, which is significant as it demonstrates that for Shelley, who began writing *Frankenstein* in 1816 and published it in 1818, death, ugliness and birth were always intertwined.[19] As Anne Mellor notes, likely as at least a partial reaction to the random suffering and disproportionate burden of responsibilities in Shelley's personal experiences, with each rewrite *Frankenstein* became more Hobbesian and less suffused with the primacy of free will so central to her father's views:

> In 1818 ... Victor Frankenstein possessed free will or the capacity for meaningful moral choice—he could have abandoned his quest for the "principle of life," he could have cared for his creature ... but in the revised text [published in 1831] ... [h]e is the pawn of forces beyond his knowledge or control. Again and again Mary Shelley reassigns human actions to chance or fate.[20]

In her later work, "years after writing *Frankenstein* Mary would have Katherine Gordon, a character modeled after herself in her novel *Perkin Warbeck,* admit 'I am doomed to a divided existence, and I submit.'"[21] *Perkin Warbeck* has very little to do with birth or creation, which suggests that although *Frankenstein* may speak to female fears of motherhood, the condition of motherhood Shelley's work examines is more precisely a metaphor for the modern malady of divided existence. As Levine observes, *Frankenstein* implies that the "civilized man or woman contains within the self a monstrous, destructive and self-destructive energy."[22] As suggested in the beginning of this essay, Frankenstein's "hideous progeny" is a projection of this monstrous-childness energy, as is Rosemary's: all are oddly familiar, radically defamilarized Other halves.[23]

Essentially, Mary Shelley relocates the classic drama between God/Satan, once conceived as external forces fighting over one's soul, into one body composed of a public, proper self and a private, darker side.[24] Frankenstein and Rosemary's respective shadow selves, their children, are frightening and attractive to modern consciousness because they force a confrontation with that uncanny side of ourselves buried by years of purportedly polite, civilized society. The children overturn the Enlightenment precedent that such a society has summarily conquered and dismantled such taboo drives of the human experience. As Levine notes, the confrontation with these beings "promises to reveal to us our deepest and most powerful desires and enact them."[25] The horror of *Frankenstein* is the horror of *Rosemary's Baby*: the purportedly civilized subject becoming acquainted with her "authentic self," an especially potent drive in post–Freudian America, and being frightened by what she finds.

Polanski spins the contrast between uncanny human drives and civilized society, using it as a source of the film's horror and humor. As Maximilian Le Cain notes of the Woodhouses' apartment: "To the last, it is a conspicuously bright, clean space, the blandly cheerful vision of a glossy magazine distressingly unmarked by the obscene happenings it is witness to."[26] Rosemary's husband, Guy Woodhouse, desperately clings to what Le Cain refers to as the "constrictive façade of normality," as seen when, after making his ugly trade with Satan (his wife's body for his success), he brings Rosemary yellow daisies and announces that he bought a shirt he saw in the *New Yorker*. Later in this scene, when Rosemary claims their neighbor Roman Castevet is actually Satan-worshipper Steven Marcato, Guy nervously retorts "It's 1966!" as if the fact that they live in a modern world, with reason and *New Yorker* styled lives, precludes the existence of ineffable evil. The Scrabble pieces Rosemary uses to figure out that "Roman Castevet" is an anagram for "Steven Marcato" serve not only to lampoon bourgeois atmosphere, but also point to another subtle theme of the film, the function of language.

While arranging the Scrabble pieces, Rosemary's short haircut and oversized dress make her resemble a child learning her letters for the first time, a quality that is heightened by Mia Farrow's natural aloofness. In short, this scene suggests "the baby" is not the only alterior child in the film. By arranging the Scrabble letters, then reading a book once owned by a benevolent (and prematurely taken) mentor, Rosemary learns the language of the alien world order (in this case, the supernatural, inexplicable world) in a progression similar to Frankenstein's Monster. Rosemary is prevented from learning more about the Castevets' coven when Guy throws away her book. Ironically though, even if she had finished the book, none of the explanations it provided could have prepared her for the awful sight of her child and her final confrontation with the Other world.[27]

The inadequacy of language to a person in Rosemary's predicament reflects the fractured nature of Shelley and Polanski's work and anticipates the Deleuzian "crisis of the action image" that structures many New Hollywood films. According to film historian Christian Keathley, in times of extreme trauma (as portrayed in post World War II Italian cinema, for instance), the Hollywood rhetoric of active human agency—that one can always *do* or *say* something—proves utterly inadequate and untrue to the experience of that trauma. Keathley traces the narrative of films that showcase Deleuze's "crisis of the action image," easily fitting for *Rosemary's Baby* ending, this way:

> The [protagonist's] sense of control is progressively revealed as illusory ... these films often leave their protagonists not dead, but rather wounded and helpless, disconnected from their surroundings, often muttering to themselves in a catatonic traumatised state ... each film concludes with its protagonist literally trapped in a reaction shot.[28]

When Rosemary obsessively repeats, "This isn't happening," and rocks her child's crib, she carries the trauma Keathley notes, and also becomes complicit in her husband's odious project. Victor Frankenstein's act of creation occurs much earlier in *Frankenstein*, but the confrontation facing him throughout of his novel—to kill or embrace his hideous progeny—is the same as Rosemary's. Having created the being that will destroy her world, Rosemary resigns herself to her fate and soothes her child, but her destruction is no less total than Frankenstein's. As does Shelley's novel, Polanski's ending deemphasizes agency and choice, reassigning human actions to chance or fate.[29] In fact, Polanski's tale has an aspect that makes it even more Romantic than its source material; as feminist critic Lucy Fisher notes, "It seems significant that, as Rosemary rocks the cradle, we never fully glimpse her infamous baby, who remains forever offscreen."[30]

Central to the Enlightenment worldview is the mimetic impulse to portray events realistically and to objectify the occult by giving it a recognizable face, thereby making its dimensions finite and controllable. As mentioned earlier, the same impulse guides much of mainstream American cinema. The hermeneutic drive manifests most obviously in the cinematic obsession with demystifying the body. As Jeffrey Jerome Cohen elaborates, the hermeneutic impulse to know and thereby to demystify also fuels our cultural obsession with monstrousness: "a fixation that is born of the twin desire to name that which is difficult to apprehend and to domesticate (and therefore disempower) that which threatens."[31] The cultural solution to sating cinematically both anxious fixations has been to make the onscreen body hyper-available to the eye. Even films that initially refuse to picture their monsters (*Cat People, Jaws,* etc.) eventually do so, with a double-barreled payoff of revelation and palliative resolution of the anxiety of the un-pictured (and uncontrolled).[32]

When Polanski refuses to picture the monstrous-child body, he reverses the generic terms of the horror movie by unleashing the ambient social anxiety that generates monsters rather than foreclosing it in the revelation of "the evil being." Put in another way, he amplifies the disease of civilized social anxiety rather than offering resolution of its symptoms. What ultimately makes *Rosemary's Baby* so terrifying—its refusal in the non-appearance of Satan and his offspring to declare evil conquerable—is also what makes it an anti-cinematic product of counter–Enlightenment values. *Rosemary's Baby* is Mary Shelley's nightmare realized, dramatized in brilliantly paradoxical detail.

While it would be specious to assume that *Rosemary's Baby* was the sole film responsible for reigniting interest in Romantic storytelling conventions, it did anticipate the 1970s' predilection with the idea that the world is ultimately unknowable, even in circumstances that initially appear comprehensible (*Chinatown, The Conversation, The Parallax View*, etc.). The film also seemed to spark an increase in monstrous-birth films, beginning with the conspicuously titled *It's Alive!* (1974) and its sequel *It Lives Again* (1978), and extending through the decade with films like *Embryo* (1976), *Demon Seed* (1977), *Alien* (1979), *The Brood* (1979), and most Romantically baroque of all, David Lynch's *Eraserhead* (1977).

Although almost a decade separates Lynch's first feature from Polanski's film, the two men actually make surprisingly good bedfellows. Both directors share an interest in Polish cinema and the absurdist work of Jan Svankmajer.[33] More importantly for the purposes of this analysis, both of their monstrous birth narratives also lack a defining quality of 1960s and 70s art—distanciation. As weird as the images in *Eraserhead* can be, as Todd McGowan argues, Lynch is a director of proximity, "whereas Godard ... works to alienate spectators and force them to recognize their distance from the images on the screen, Lynch tries to close this distance to an even greater extent than typical Hollywood films."[34] The viewer may be repulsed by *Eraserhead*; yet it is almost impossible to be detached from the film when watching it. Like Polanski, Lynch offers no respite from the film's weird mindscape. *Eraserhead*'s impossibly subjective nature recalls *Frankenstein* in the same way *Rosemary's Baby* does.[35]

Also like *Rosemary's Baby*, *Eraserhead* invokes the power of the irrational to dwarf that power of science and logic, and in fact deepens the dramatization of the world beyond rational comprehension. *Eraserhead* is set entirely within the inexplicable realm that *Rosemary's Baby* only glimpses at with its paradoxically unseen child. This is a realm in which reality markers like cause-and-effect logic have no place (i.e., when Henry's girlfriend Mary X has an unprovoked seizure, her mother combs her hair; the cutting of a chicken provokes a seizure in Mrs. X, etc.). In setting, tone, and order of events—which all change capriciously—the film amplifies the omnipresent feeling in *Rosemary's Baby* that the world is about to shift beneath one's feet, that some cataclysmic event or entity threatens to overwhelm characters and audience alike. The feeling of apprehension created by both viewing experiences frequently registers often as frustration in reviews of *Eraserhead*:

> Here either everything is real, or nothing is. We can discern no degrees of reality because there is no baseline to which we can point as *rational*. There can be no distinction between what really happens and what someone thinks is happening because here thought is instantaneously manifest as event.... In fact, it seems that very little actually does happen in the film, although something momentous is always *about* to happen.[36]

This critic describes viewing *Eraserhead* as a subjective experience without rational comprehensibility, one in which the imminence of something momentous and potentially apocalyptic generates an unformed terror. In other words, the critic describes *Eraserhead* as an extended confrontation with monstrous childness, as defined earlier in this essay. *Eraserhead* challenges the viewer to appreciate a narrative that withholds knowledge; the film's denial of predictability takes the terror of the unformed to new heights, with important cinematic and historical implications.

Eraserhead's resistance to the rules of implicit causality shatters Hollywood tradition and reflects the trauma of the times even more than other films that may initially seem more "of the era."[37] As Keathley notes:

> Certain of the century's key events ... the Kennedy assassination, the Vietnam experience ... mark the limits and beyond of the realist discourse that relies on continuity, cause-and-effect, and agency.... Instead, [Hayden] White argues, such traumatic historical events demand a modernist style of representation, for the formal strategies of fragmentation, discontinuity, chance, and incoherence that are common to modernism are also the characteristics that mark one's experience of a traumatic event. The filmmakers of the post-traumatic cycle seem to have intuited this necessity ... employing modernist formal devices to show that realist practice is strained to the breaking point.[38]

Lynch's film is an exercise in straining realist practices to their breaking point, and its setting and protagonist bear an uncanny similarity to the traumatized subjectivity Keathley describes. As McGowan notes, "Visually, the burnt-out industrial setting connotes an enjoyment located elsewhere—in the years past, before the steel barrels, pipes and chains."[39] To be sure, Henry's perpetual blank stare taken together with the idea of "enjoyment elsewhere" seem to indicate that the bleak, diseased landscape robbed him of something essential: human warmth.

As critics have noted, Henry recalls poker-faced silent film stars like Buster Keaton, but he also closely resembles another classic personality: Frankenstein's Monster. As in *Rosemary's Baby*, the "baby" in *Eraserhead* is not the only "child." Like Frankenstein's Monster, Henry is technically human, but he appears to have been birthed fully formed from the landscape itself. He is defined throughout by his out-of-placeness, which often registers as mechanical; he moves awkwardly, seldom speaks with any affect (if he speaks at all), and, as McGowan notes, "does not dress like someone who fits comfortably within the world he occupies," throughout walking with deliberation in pants two inches too short.[40] Like the Monster, Henry wanders through a world that he was born in but that he nonetheless seems at a loss to comprehend.

The other characters who populate this world seem less alienated than Henry, though they share his odd, mechanical qualities. All body animations in the inexplicable world of the film are a weird facsimile of organic movement. Humans break down like robots freezing mid-operation, as Mary's father, Bill X (Allen Joseph), does at the dinner table; or short-circuit, as Mary and her mother Mrs. X (Jeanne Bates), do during their seizures. The product of the one organic sexual act spoken of is a robotic simulation of an infant. Even sexuality in this realm seems illegitimate or perverted, though, of course, none of this is explained within the film. Lynch is confronting the inexplicable world through repeated machine failures, as Chris Rodley infers in *Lynch on Lynch*.[41]

Lynch reorders the animate/inanimate schema, and the birth process, by showing aliveness and deadness in unexpected places. Even the elevator in Henry's building awakens with a primitive consciousness of sorts, as Schneider argues, "intentionally and perhaps spitefully 'teasing' Henry."[42] As Schneider describes this scene:

> What follows after the [elevator] doors open is an extremely disconcerting period of waiting (approximately 13 seconds) for them to close again, and then an equally disconcerting rise up to Henry's floor. It is not so much that anything happens during this sequence—though the lights in the elevator flicker, and briefly go out a couple of times—but our sense of foreboding is primed nevertheless.[43]

An example of the unformed anxiety previously described, this sequence is also a literal example of electricity breathing "life" into an ordinarily "dead" object, though it is not the only time electricity plays a role in the film. The "machine failures" of humans in *Eraserhead* seem more specifically to be electrical failures. Characters jolt in unnatural, unexpected ways, creating confusion over their ontological status. Is Grandmother X, for instance, alive, dead, asleep, conscious? *Eraserhead*'s purposeful confusion and electrical reanimation of dead objects connect the film to its origins in *Frankenstein*.

As Shelley famously said in the introduction to her text, discussions of galvanism prompted her to hypothesize: "Perhaps a corpse would be reanimated ... perhaps the component parts of a creature might be manufactured, brought together, and endued with a vital warmth."[44] Describing her subsequent dream in which *Frankenstein* allegedly came to her, Shelley further says:

> I saw—with shut eyes, but acute mental vision—I saw the pale student of unhallowed arts kneeling beside the thing he had put together. I saw the hideous phantasm of a man stretched out, and then, on the working of some powerful engine, show signs of life, and stir with an uneasy, half-vital motion.[45]

What Shelley goes on to say of how she imagined Dr. Frankenstein's reaction to his creation is similar to Henry's probable desire as he stands over his dubiously created baby: "He would rush away from his odious handiwork, horror-stricken. He would hope that, left to itself, the slight spark of life which he communicated would fade; that this thing, which had received such imperfect animation, would subside into dead matter.... He sleeps; but he is awakened; he opens his eyes; beholds the horrid thing ... at his bedside."[46] Unlike Victor, Henry does not fully comprehend the "thing" he created and does not demonstrate the same desire to kill his offspring, who also stirs with an uneasy, half-vital motion, until late in the film.

After seeing the Beautiful Girl Across the Hall (Judith Roberts) with another man, Henry turns to look at his baby, who appears to laugh spitefully at him. Just after this encounter, Henry angrily removes the baby's bandages. Yet even he does not anticipate the truly gruesome outcome of his actions: the baby immediately eviscerates. As Schneider notes, "By fashioning Henry's baby skinless, boneless and poised to spill its guts out, Lynch forces Daddy and audience alike to contemplate a living, breathing (temporarily, at least) transgression of the deeply-entrenched cultural opposition, inside vs. outside."[47] In this moment Lynch again disrupts cause-effect logic and the dead/alive schema with one important difference: there is someone to blame for this adverse event (Henry), though the effect is grossly disproportionate to the cause.[48]

The heavy price Henry pays for his one spontaneous act, his existence in a world that perpetually mystifies him, and his responsibility for a being that he does not understand call to mind Dr. Frankenstein and the Dark Romantic hero more generally, as described by G.R. Thompson:

> In Romantic Gothic literature man is confronted with an ambiguous world structure rather than the clearcut world of the Middle Ages. Instead, he faces a world that he has no hope of comprehending and in which he cannot make the proper moral choices, even though he is yet held responsible by some occult power for such choices.[49]

Like the Gothic subject described above, Frankenstein, and Rosemary, Henry transubstantiates from an initially unwitting, alterior victim into a fatefully complicit actor in an odious creative/destructive project. The ramifications of Henry's act and his disproportionate punishment escalate to the end of the film, when the world explodes. Just before this apocalyptic moment though, when Henry fantasizes about his beloved Lady in the Radiator, his head suddenly pops off and is replaced by the slowly rising, phallic head of his infant. If there is doubt as to whose perspective *Eraserhead* is told from, this image seems proof that the terror expressed at this moment is Henry's. Freudian readings aside, "the horror of this sequence is the horror of attack from within, whether psychically, socially ... or at a more primitive bodily level."[50] In this final moment, as in *Rosemary's Baby* and *Frankenstein*, the monstrous child, in all of its terror—its inexplicability, ineffability, and uncontrollability—overtakes the rational world of its maker. These nearly unprecedented reversals epitomize the generative power of the unformed that Deleuze found so compelling, and suggest that the appeal of *Eraserhead, Rosemary's Baby* and *Frankenstein* is precisely the same as the horror they enact: that of the monstrously divided self.

Notes

1. According to biographer John Baxter, Kubrick asked Diane Johnson, *The Shining's* co-screenwriter and professor of the Gothic, what she thought of one text: *Frankenstein*. John Baxter, *Stanley Kubrick: A Biography* (New York: Carroll & Graf, 1997), 307.

2. As is argued in the introduction to this collection, childness-engaged beings like Frankenstein's Monster, Rosemary's baby, and protagonist Henry's child in *Eraserhead* evoke "an elusive quiddity ... something extra-discursive, extra-linguistic, and even ineffable." In other words, these monstrous children confront us with how much we do not know and cannot control. This is an especially terrifying prospect within fictional words defined by logic and empiricism: the Enlightened sphere of Dr. Frankenstein, and the insistently civilized, post-industrial universes of *Rosemary's Baby* and *Eraserhead*.

3. Shelley's perspective on the limited, earthbound nature of the human constitution made her anomalous among her Romantic counterparts, who generally saw human capability as limitless.

4. These divisions are myriad, but include Victor's culpability/victimhood in the deaths of those closest to him, his civilized/despicable nature, his sexuality, and his belief system structured on logic but challenged by the illogical being he creates. For a full discussion of these divisions, and a deeper investigation of the plot mechanisms of *Frankenstein*, see Mary Lowe-Evans, ed., *Critical Essays on Mary Wollstonecraft Shelley* (New York: G.K. Hall, 1998).

5. Mary Shelley, *Frankenstein: The Modern Prometheus* (New York: Bedford/St. Martin's, 2000), 49.

6. Gilles Deleuze, *The Logic of Sense* (New York: Columbia University Press, 1990), 107.

7. The concurrent rise of New Age spiritualties and evangelical religion in the 1970s can easily be understood as an assimilative response to the dissociative events of the 1960s.

8. Virginia L. Blum, *Hide and Seek: The Child Between Psychoanalysis and Fiction* (Urbana: University of Illinois Press, 1995), 25.

9. The child in *Eraserhead* is so unrecognizable that debate still rages over what kind of animal (or composite of animals) was used to create it.

10. "Retrospective Interviews," *Rosemary's Baby*, dir. Roman Polanski, 1968. prod. Robert Evans; (Hollywood: Paramount, 2008) DVD.

11. For an extensive discussion of the impact of this "checkerboard subdivision," and Industrialization on the Romantic movement, see M.H. Abrams "The Romantic Period," *Norton Anthology of English Literature: 3rd Edition*, ed. M.H. Abrams (New York: W.W. Norton, 1976), 1285–1286.

12. Diane Waldeman as qtd. in Lucy Fischer, "Birth Traumas: Parturition and Horror in *Rosemary's Baby*," in *The Dread of Difference*, ed. Barry Keith Grant (Austin: University of Texas Press, 1996), 417.

13. For a subsection of Romantic writers, termed the Negative or Dark Romantics, the experience of the sublime, solipsistic focus on the self, and the pressure on their creative imaginative abilities, resulted in psychic crises instead of conventional Romantic ecstasy and

awe. What D. G. James says of all Romantic writers may be an overstatement for writers like Wordsworth, but more appropriately describes the Dark Romantics including Thomas De Quincey, Mary Shelley, Percy Shelley, and Lord Byron: "The Romantics achieve their heights by placing impossible demands for certitude on creative imagination—and finding the results unsatisfactory or ultimately insubstantial, they collapse back in despair." James as qtd. in Robert D. Hume, "Exuberant Gloom, Existential Agony and Heroic Despair: Three Varieties of Negative Romanticism," in *Gothic Imagination*, ed. G.R. Thompson (Tacoma: Washington State University Press, 1974), 110.

14. The question of whether the events of the film actually happen, or only happen in Rosemary's mind, is left open-ended. In either case, the audience cannot escape Rosemary's perspective on those events, which implies that she creates the meaning of these events for the audience by virtue of the claustrophobic subjectivity the audience is forced to share with her.

15. John Orr, "Polanski: The Art of Perceiving," in *The Cinema of Roman Polanski: Dark Spaces of the World*, eds. John Orr and Elzbieta Ostrowska (London: Wallflower Press, 2006), 12.

16. For evidence of the semi-autobiographical nature of *Frankenstein*, see Shelley's 1831 introduction to her novel, as well as George Levine, "The Ambiguous Heritage of *Frankenstein*," in *Critical Essays on Mary Wollstonecraft Shelley*, ed. Mary Lowe-Evans (New York: G.K. Hall, 1998), 25–39.

17. Elzbeita Ostrowska, "*Knife in the Water*: Polanski's Nomadic Discourse Begins," *The Cinema of Roman Polanski: Dark Spaces of the World*, eds. John Orr and Elzbieta Ostrowska (London: Wallflower Press, 2006), 75.

18. Polanski's mother died in the gas chambers, and he narrowly survived the Holocaust himself. He lived through the murder of his pregnant wife, Sharon Tate, in 1969, and in a cruel irony, was publicly considered a suspect for the crime due to the dark nature of *Rosemary's Baby*. Polanski's criminal history is well documented, but worth mentioning because it confirms the (albeit qualified) culprit/victim position he shares with Shelley. He was charged with, and pled guilty to, unlawful sex with a minor, which has infamously kept him out of the United States since 1977.

19. Shelley delivered her first live child (who died a month later) in 1815, and over the next three years survived two more pregnancies and two more deaths. During the same time span, she also lived through the suicides of her half-sister, Fanny Imlay, and a pregnant Harriet Shelley (her husband's first wife).

20. Anne Mellor as qtd. in David J. Skal, *Screams of Reason: Mad Science and Modern Culture* (New York: W.W. Norton, 1998), 54.

21. Mary Lowe-Evans, "Introduction," *Critical Essays on Mary Wollstonecraft Shelley*, ed. Mary Lowe-Evans (New York: G.K. Hall, 1998), 2.

22. Levine, 34.

23. Gothic tales like *Frankenstein* most often take place in aristocratic society and infamously employ multiple sets of doppelgangers or divided characters (i.e., Dr. Jekyll/Mr. Hyde) to suggest the dark underbellies of such societies. *Rosemary's Baby* features its own host of doubles, including former Bramford residents, the Trench sisters. These proper Victorian ladies cannibalized their neighbors. Like Central Park, these briefly depicted characters are meaningful as they suggest a common theme of *Frankenstein* and *Rosemary's Baby*—the idea that monsters are not aberrant elements who enter society from without, but rather that they are birthed from within.

24. As George Levine notes, "Morality, as it were, was replaced by schizophrenia," 34.

25. Levine, 34.

26. Maximilian le Cain, "Into the Mouth of Madness: in *The Tenant*," *The Cinema of Roman Polanski: Dark Spaces of the World*, eds. John Orr and Elzbieta Ostrowska (London: Wallflower Press, 2006), 122.

27. Throughout the film, in fact, there are a number of tongue-in-cheek plays on the limited power of language: the incomplete note that Rosemary finds the first time she views the Bramford apartment which reads "I can no longer associate ..." the realtor's prescient observation that "we'll never know" why the previous tenant covered up her linen closet; Dr. Saperstein's warnings to Rosemary not to read; and Rosemary's near-mute state at the end of the film.

28. Christian Keathley, "Trapped in the Affection Image: Hollywood's Post-Traumatic Cycle: 1967–1976," in *The Last Great American Picture Show: New Hollywood Cinema in the 1970s*, eds. Thomas Elsaesser, Alexander Horwath and Noel King (Amsterdam: Amsterdam University Press, 2004), 297.

29. Mellor, as qtd. in Skal, 54.

30. Fischer, 413.

31. Jeffrey Jerome Cohen, Preface to *Monster Theory: Reading Culture*, ed. Jeffrey Jerome Cohen (Minneapolis: Minnesota University Press, 1996), vii.

32. See Dennis Giles, "Conditions of Pleasure in Horror Cinema," *Planks of Reason: Essays on the Horror Film*, ed. Barry Keith Grant (Metuchen, NJ: Scarecrow Press, 1984), 38–53.

33. Lynch and Polanski have been reticent to discuss similarities between their films, but film scholars have certainly drawn parallels: none more evocative than Erica Sheen and Annette Davison's description of the child at the center of *Eraserhead*: "Although ... nowhere in the published interviews does Lynch make actual reference to *Repulsion* (Roman Polanski 1965), J. Hoberman and Jonathan Rosenbaum must be onto something when they describe the baby as 'an illegitimate monster—a mewling, eye-rolling first cousin to the skinned-rabbit centerpiece of Roman Polanski's [film]." Erica Sheen and Annette Davison, "Introduction," *The Cinema of David Lynch: American Dreams, Nightmare Visions*, eds. Erica Sheen and Annette Davison (London: Wallflower Press, 2004), 1–4.

34. Todd McGowan, *The Impossible David Lynch* (New York: Columbia University Press, 2007), 12.

35. It is difficult to imagine anyone other than Lynch directing the film, and just as difficult to escape the protagonist's perception as it is in *Repulsion*.

36. K.G. Godwin, "*Eraserhead*: The Story Behind the Strangest Film Ever Made, and Cinematic Genius Who Directed It," *Cinefantastique* 14.5 (September 1984): 48.

37. *Eraserhead* actually debuted in 1977, after the bulk of New Hollywood films were produced.

38. Keathley, 302.

39. McGowan, 35–36.

40. McGowan, 35.

41. Chris Rodley, *Lynch on Lynch* (London: Faber and Faber, 2005), 73.

42. Steven J. Schneider, "The Essential Evil in/of *Eraserhead* (or, Lynch to the Contrary)," in *The Cinema of David Lynch: American Dreams, Nightmare Visions*, eds. Erica Sheen and Annette Davison (London: Wallflower Press, 2004), 9.

43. Schneider, 9.

44. Shelley, 23.

45. Shelley, 24.

46. Shelley, 24.

47. Schneider, 13.

48. The other parallel to be drawn between *Eraserhead* and its predecessors is the heavy price Dr. Frankenstein and Henry pay for their one spontaneous act (creating The Monster and removing his baby's bandages, respectively), a narrative rendering of the concept of entropy. According to the theory of entropy, the energetic benefit of creation within a closed system is never equal to the amount of energy expended. For his one act of creation, Frankenstein loses his younger brother, family friend Justine, wife/cousin Elizabeth, best friend Henry,

and father. In *Eraserhead*, not only does Henry's monstrous baby decompose before his eyes, but the planet also explodes, seemingly as a direct result of his actions.
 49. G.R. Thompson, "Introduction: Romanticism and the Gothic Tradition," *Gothic Imagination: Essays on Dark Romanticism*, ed. G.R. Thompson (Tacoma: Washington State University Press, 1974), 6.
 50. Schneider, 15–16.

Doesn't everyone want their parents dead?

Monstrous Children in the Films of Ridley Scott

Colin Yeo

Published anonymously in 1818, Mary Shelley's novel *Frankenstein; or, the Modern Prometheus* is a landmark text that addresses the possibility of creating artificial life and the repercussions of these actions. Since its publication in the nineteenth century, Shelley's text has continued to garner critical attention. Studies have often read the character of the Monster as the "son" of Victor Frankenstein. This "father-son" relationship between Frankenstein and his Monster, along with the subject of creating artificial life, are themes that also persist in Ridley Scott's science fiction film oeuvre. From *Alien* (1979) to *Blade Runner* (1983) and *Prometheus* (2012), Scott's films feature patriarchal characters who are analogues of Victor Frankenstein: masculine, technologically savvy individuals, who, like Frankenstein, are responsible for the creation of artificial offspring. Like Shelley's Monster, the artificial children represented in these films have one thing in common. These children cause their creators' deaths. In destroying their fathers, these children can be aligned with an evil moral positioning, allowing for a reading of these children as "monstrous." In this essay, I propose a different reading of these children's patricidal traits. While the act of destroying their creators might be construed as heinous, from the point of view of the audience, these monstrous children can be read as morally ambivalent. In destroying their fathers, they end the oppressive patriarchal order depicted in these films, an order that is synonymous with technological power. Unlike the tragic Victor Frankenstein, the creators of these monstrous children are cast as tyrannical characters possessed by hubris. By destroying their creators, these children serve as a rectifying force, counterbalancing their creators' hubris. These monstrous children can be read as "monstrous" as they destroy their paternal figures, but their actions resist classification as evil by virtue of the fact that they act as a retributive force. These children are cast as neither evil nor good, but rather as occupying a liminal space between these two moral positions.

Defining the Child and the Monstrous

Before engaging in my analysis of these three film texts, I want to first outline the parameters of what the concepts of "child" and "monster" entail in the context of this essay. As outlined in the introduction to this volume, the concept of "childness" has many definitions and interpretations. The character of Shelley's Monster offers a template for my reading of the child in light of "childness." The characters Roy Batty, the Xenomorph and David from these films can be regarded as children in the same way that the Monster is regarded as a child of Victor Frankenstein. Harold Bloom remarks, for example, that the Monster's exclusion from the world of man gives it the characteristic of an "abandoned child."[1] Similarly, Elisabeth Bronfen remarks that Victor Frankenstein's downfall stems from the fact that he fails to accept the Monster as his child.[2] The relationship that exists between Frankenstein and his creation can be extrapolated in an analysis of the representation of the child in *Alien*, *Blade Runner* and *Prometheus*. These children are artificial creations that are *produced* by their fathers. Like the Monster, David and Batty are artificial human beings, androids, who, unlike Frankenstein, are acknowledged by their respective creators as sons. The android David is said to be the "closest thing to a son" that his creator Peter Weyland has, and similarly, Batty's creator Tyrell calls him a "prodigal son." As the creators of the Xenomorph's eggs, the masculine looking Engineers seen in *Prometheus* can be equated as the Xenomorphs's father figure(s). The eggs are the artificial products of the Engineers' experiments in creating life, much like Weyland and Tyrell's attempts to create artificial human beings. These children are *created*, rather than *birthed*. In this respect, my essay displays a departure from the paradigms established in the two essays in this volume by Brooke Edge and Kristine Larsen. While their essays utilize primarily maternal figures as a starting point for their inquiries, mine addresses the role of the paternal in the creation of artificial life in the creation of children in these films.

The definition of "monstrous" for these children can be broken into two separate categories. The first is that of unnaturalness. A common defining trait of the monstrous is the alignment of monstrosity with the unnatural. In the simplest sense, as artificial creations, these children can be classified as "unnatural" and hence as monsters. The "natural," in this regard, can be read in two ways. The first is in terms of the "natural" *process of childbirth*, a process that is subverted in the creation of these children. The Xenomorph from *Alien* is birthed from a host regardless of its host's gender. The androids in *Prometheus* and *Blade Runner* are artificial creations that are likened to items in a production line by their creators. The second way in which the concept of "natural" can be read is the utilization of the human condition as a baseline for what is "natural." In other words, these children are unnatural because they are *not human*. Recognizing the Xenomorph's abilities, the character Ash lauds the Xenomorph as epitomizing perfection. For Ash, the Xenomorph's only flaw is that it has a hostile streak. The Xenomorph is a primal force that has no knowledge or awareness of the concepts of good or evil, and as the Android Ash states, it is an organism that is unclouded by "delusions of morality." The Xenomorph is possessed of pure instinct, rendering a moralizing conscience as void.[3] This is what defines the Xenomorph as unnatural and thus monstrous. The absence of a capacity for reason and morality are characteristics that define what it means to be human and, lacking these, allows it to be read as monstrous. The character David from *Prometheus* is regarded as not human by his creator, and his unnaturalness is acknowledged by Weyland:

> His name is David, and he is the closest thing to a son I will ever have. Unfortunately, he is, he is not human. He will never grow old, and he will never die. And yet he is unable to appreciate these remarkable gifts, for that will require the one thing that David will never have—a soul.

Weyland regards David's creation as unnatural since to him, David is bereft of a soul. To be human, for Weyland, is to age and to die. Therefore, because David cannot age and die, he is classified as unnatural and non-human by his creator. Tyrell's androids from *Blade Runner*, however, are built with a life span. Their unnaturalness stems from the fact that they possess physical attributes that surpass ordinary humans. For example, Roy Batty is seen to have a resistance to extreme cold, and has the strength to punch through a brick wall. To recap, the "children" featured in these three films are thus not children in the strictest sense, but share a symbolic son to father relationship with their creators. These children are created in ways that are independent of natural birth processes. They are monstrous because they are unnatural creations.

These children resemble human beings but have traits that designate them as different from humans.

Despite resembling ordinary humans, the characters of the Xenomorph, Roy Batty and David have attributes that surpass the ordinary. The second definition of "monstrous" has to do with behavior. In addition to their unnaturalness, these children can be regarded as monstrous because of their patricidal inclinations. Like Frankenstein's monster, the Oedipal impulses displayed by these children allow them to be coded as monstrous. In her essay "The Queer Ethics of Monstrosity," Patricia MacCormack suggests that "[t]hus monstrosity, in its final definition as the simple turbulence that collides or harmonizes with the fluidity of our own selves, is nothing more than a wondrous possible in all things that requires not the monster as entity, but *monstrous encounter*"[4] (italics added for emphasis).

MacCormack raises the idea of an encounter, or an occurrence that contributes towards the definition of the monstrous. The "occurrence" in these texts, I suggest, is the act of patricide. The first of these children, the Xenomorph, is birthed by bursting out of its host's chest, a process that destroys its host. Similarly, the androids in *Blade Runner* and *Prometheus* destroy their fathers in an act of violence. Like the Xenomorph, *Blade Runner*'s Roy Batty kills his father in a show of physical violence. Batty confronts his creator Eldon Tyrell and asks that Tyrell extend his lifespan. After realizing that Tyrell cannot help him, he gouges Tyrell's eyes out in a symbolic, Oedipal gesture. Batty's act is horrifying. A shot of Tyrell screaming in pain is visible, with blood streaming down Tyrell's face. This graphic display of violence characterizes Batty as a monster, one who brings death, specifically to the one who created him. While Batty's killing of Tyrell is undertaken in a direct manner, the android David from *Prometheus* is responsible for the death of his creator in an indirect manner. David is initially characterized as completely subservient to his creator Weyland, but an exchange between David and the character Shaw reveals a darker side to his character:

> SHAW: What happens when Weyland isn't around to program you anymore?
> DAVID: I suppose I'd be free.
> SHAW: You want that?
> DAVID: Want. Not a concept I'm familiar with. That being said, doesn't everybody want their parents dead?

This conversation between Shaw and David hints at a darker side to the android's personality. His casual, matter-of-fact tone betrays his patricidal impulse. This exchange is carried out behind Weyland's back with an element of subtlety as wanting Weyland dead would not be something David would openly admit in front of his father. David, in addition to the Xenomorph and Roy Batty, is therefore another one of the "children" depicted in Scott's films who causes the death of his father. This patricidal impulse, I propose, allows these characters to be classified as monstrous. By destroying their parents, these children violate a fundamental moral positioning, allowing them to be read as monstrous. By destroying their creators, and in several instances other individuals as well, these children become monsters, patricidal creations who, in the words of the character David, "want their parents dead." The phrase "want" designates a sense of culpability, and as the characters David and Batty are directly responsible for the deaths of their creators, the notion of intent makes their actions morally objectionable, and therefore evil. Batty, for example, has been outlined by critics as resembling Satan, a reading that underscores Batty's revolt against his maker and the morally objectionable act of patricide. For Desser, Batty's designation as an analogue with Satan has precedents in Shelley's *Frankenstein*, and earlier in Milton's *Paradise Lost*.[5] Patricidal intent is also a characteristic of *Prometheus*'s David, and his actions in bringing about the death of his creator are suggestive of a characteristic of ambiguous morality. From the point of view of the audience, these characters are read as the "villains" of each text, monstrous children who cause their creators' deaths. But as the characterization of David hints at, the relationship between creator and child is not a straightforward one. While these children might be denigrated for their patricidal streaks, their fathers are not portrayed as one-dimensional victims. This is because these father figures are often associated with oppression and tyranny. Patricide, in these cases, can be seen as a necessary evil that serves to disrupt the overbearing nature of masculine oriented power in these texts.

The Father's Hubris and Masculine Oriented Technology

The father figures featured in these films are cast as hubristic individuals who wield a considerable amount of power. The characters Tyrell and Peter Weyland are aligned with the divine, evoking their hubristic strive for power. Power, in their case, is associated with patriarchy. Their destruction at the hands of their children allows for another reading of these monstrous children, a departure from the negative reading I have posited earlier. Because of the fact that their fathers are portrayed as hubristic, these children's revolt against the patriarchal forces that created them allows them to be read as a retributive force. In a world that is dominated by patriarchy, these children balance out their fathers' hubris by destroying them. In doing this, these children occupy a liminal space between good and evil. They are "evil" in that they destroy their fathers, but are also "good" in that they counteract their fathers' acts of hubris.

While the paternal characters featured in these films are synonymous with the act of creation, they do not conform to the one dimensional, stereotypical filmic convention of the "mad scientist" a la Colin Clive's Henry Frankenstein. Instead, these characters' mastery of technology is regarded as being analogous with the divine. Rather than the biological conception of the child via the mother, or Eve figure, the father figure in these texts attempts to invoke the generative power associated with gods. The Engineers, the creators of the Xenomorphs, are equated with the divine. A series of cave paintings on Earth discovered by the protagonists of *Prometheus* indicates that the Engineers are believed to have visited primitive civilizations in Earth's past, and were worshipped as gods. The Engineers' human counterparts are the characters Peter Weyland and Eldon Tyrell, characters who are also aligned with the divine. Weyland's success in creating artificial life that is "indistinguishable" from ordinary humans leads him to develop a god complex, equating himself with the mythological Titan Prometheus. The viral campaign of *Prometheus* features a faux TED talk by the character of Weyland, who delivers the following address as part of his TED speech: "At this moment in our civilization, we can create cybernetic individuals who, in just a few short years, will be completely indistinguishable from us. Which leads to an obvious conclusion: We are the gods now."[6] Despite using the plural form in his address, the characterization of Weyland indicates that the equation of technology with godhood is an analogy that Weyland applies to himself. His self-assigned association with godhood underscores his arrogance. His haughty declarations and their hubristic implications exemplify the transgressive nature of his technological dominance. Like the Engineers and Peter Weyland, *Blade Runner*'s Tyrell is portrayed as a godlike figure. When we first meet Tyrell in his office, his deification is symbolized by the bright color scheme used in this sequence. Batty's remark about the "god of biomechanics" letting Tyrell into heaven is another marker of how Tyrell's power is associated with the divine. As a wielder of divine power, Tyrell acknowledges Batty by calling him the "prodigal son."[7] These father figures' ability to create artificial life thus aligns their power with the divine. In associating these father figures with divinity, Scott sets them up as patriarchs who display a streak of hubris. The consequence of this extension of power into the realm of the divine is the breaking of an unspoken taboo. These actions thus warrant a retributive force that acts against their transgressions, a force that results in their demise.

As another form of hubris, the technologically determined patriarchal order in Scott's science fiction narratives asserts its control over a natural process that cannot be accorded to the male gender. In these texts, the process of creating artificial life displaces the role of the mother. Ian Barnes addresses the appropriation and subversion of the feminine in the role of reproduction in his article on cinematic iterations of the Frankenstein story. Barnes outlines that this uprooting of the female in the act of reproduction is rooted in Victor Frankenstein's "psychosexual" ambition:

> A related feminist variant of this reading of the Frankenstein narrative interprets Victor's monstrous creation as a metaphor for his (and modern science's) unacknowledged psychosexual ambition to establish a masculinist domination over nature through technology which displaces both females from reproduction and subjectivity and femininity from nature through the reconstruction of nature in mechanistic and objectivist terms.[8]

Like Victor Frankenstein, the scientists Eldon Tyrel and Peter Weyland and the alien Engineers symbolize the persistence of this masculinist domination over natural reproductive processes. In their hubris, in their attempts to attain godhood, these fathers commit the ultimate transgression. This is an attempt to subvert death itself. As Gena Corea addresses in her essay on cloning, patriarchy's control over life and death can be realized via reproductive technologies:

> The cycle of birth, growth, and death in nature, a cycle venerated in the Goddess religion and epitomized by a woman bearing a child is one against which patriarchal man has long railed. He does not want to die.... His desire to control birth through the reproductive technologies, then, is also a desire to control death.[9]

These texts question patriarchy and foreground the implications of the control of life and death by a male dominated order. If there is an underlying message that is consistent in these three films, it is the severe ramifications of this element of masculine control over a process that is naturally allocated to the female gender. On the part of these father figures, this critical oversight results in a false sense of security that is a consequence of the compelling ramifications of bypassing the role of the feminine in the act of reproduction.

In her introduction to *The Mother Machine*, Corea proposes that "Reproductive technology is a product of the male reality. The values expressed in the technology—objectification, domination—are typical of the male culture. The technology is male-generated and buttresses male power over women."[10] While the masculine is privileged with power in these films, a dual dialectic of masculine power arises. While technologically determined patriarchal power is a display of mastery over the creation of artificial life, it is paradoxically undermined by an inability to reign in these monstrous children and maintain some semblance of control over them. The technological displacement of the maternal in Scott's films ultimately has the unintended consequence of self-destruction, as these fathers are destroyed by their own creations. Technology has had a tradition of being associated with the male gender. The pervasiveness of male centric power, as depicted in these films, can be described as hegemonic. Connell and Messerschmidt's essay on "hegemonic masculinities" addresses the complex nature of masculine power, such as the challenges associated with male power and the relationship dynamics of male power with female agency. In the section "The Dynamics of Masculinities," they propose that hegemonic masculinities involve division and emotional conflict due to their association with gendered power.[11] The child's relationship with the father, they propose, is a "likely focus of tension" that arises from the inscription of hegemonic masculine power. This conflict between father and son is what arises in these films. Here, the monstrous child's patricidal streak is framed as a reactionary force to the oppressive nature of patriarchal regimes. In her study on cyberbodies in films, Claudia Springer proposes: "In a world without human bodies, the films tell us, technological things will be gendered and there will still be patriarchal hierarchy. What this reconfiguration of masculinity indicates is that patriarchy is more willing to dispense with human life than with male superiority."[12]

Patriarchal order, especially in the films *Alien* and *Prometheus*, epitomizes the gendered nature of technology. This manifests as a willingness to exert power without regard to the costs or repercussions. Peter Weyland's corporation is responsible for the destruction of Ripley's crew, all for the sake of acquiring the Xenomorph. The human crew of the Nostromo is regarded as "expendable" to the corporation, exemplifying the willingness of patriarchal forces to sacrifice even human lives in the name of science and technological advancement.

Conclusion

From the landmark *Alien* in 1979, to *Blade Runner* in 1982, and *Prometheus* in 2012, themes of technology, patriarchy, and the monstrous child are powerfully grappled with. Vacillating between hero and villain, perfection and destruction, the monstrous children in the science fiction films of Ridley Scott defy attempts at categorization. In *Alien* and *Prometheus*, however, we witness the emergence of a counterpoint to the overbearing patriarchal order represented by the Weyland Corporation. This is the representation of female agency in the characters Ripley (*Alien*) and Shaw (*Prometheus*). Ripley and Shaw outlive their crews, and symbolize tenacity and rationalism in a world that is governed by hubristic patriarchs. They are characters who literally have the last word in these texts. Their electronic journal logs are recited as voice-overs at the close of *Alien* and *Prometheus*. Both characters are made to suffer the consequences of patriarchy's hubris, but eventually overcome the destruction wrought by the monstrous children present in these texts. The survival of these characters underscores the role of the feminine. Ironically, Ripley and Shaw are mothers themselves, and they are the ones who survive. In the sequel to *Alien*, we discover that Ripley is a mother. *Prometheus's* Shaw is impregnated with a foreign fetus, but successfully extracts it in a caesarean section. These films thus place an onus on feminine oriented reproduction rather than artificial reproductive methods. If there is an underlying moral message that is consistent in these three films, it is the severe ramifications of this element of control over a process that is allocated to the female gender. Man's technological prowess is always aligned with the masculine, and in particular, male oriented power that oppresses female agency. The creation of monstrous children thus results from the hubristic actions of male power. By destroying their fathers, these monstrous offspring balance out their fathers' attempts at attaining godhood, highlighting the flaws of masculine technological determinism. In both *Alien* and *Prometheus*, these female characters are presented as cautious, placed in direct opposition with the recklessness of male characters. The survival of feminine characters suggests that patriarchy lacks certain traits such as rationality and humility, traits that are essential to the survival of man. If these films envision patriarchy as oppressive and tyrannical, the persistence of patriarchal forces they represent is counterbalanced by their female characters, characters who display the requisite characteristics and traits needed to survive in a technologically advanced world.

In these films, the heedlessness of Shelley's Frankenstein resurfaces time and time again, and the patricidal behavior of the monstrous children in these films serves as a warning. This warning is that the potentialities and repercussions of being able to create artificial life should not be taken lightly. Such an act carries with it the notion of transgression, and these fathers' deaths at the hands of their children can be read as the consequence of their fathers' hubris. In Ridley Scott's science fiction universe, the Xenomorph, the David android and Roy Batty are products of a technologically advanced patriarchal order. These texts can be read as Frankensteinian analogs, texts that eschew the perceived arrogance that goes hand in hand with technological prowess. Technological determinism in these films carries with it the notion of transgression, and these fathers' deaths at the hands of their children can be read as the consequence of their hubris. As such, the act of patricide in these texts is one that is morally ambivalent. These fathers' hubris results in their deaths at the hands of their offspring. The act of murder, in these cases, can be read as a reaction to the overreaching aspirations of patriarchal power. The children via their acts are monstrous in that they destroy their fathers, but in this, they bring an end to the dominance of oppressive patriarchy in these texts. These children can be regarded as neither good nor evil, but straddling both moral positions, indicative of what this volume terms "monstrous childness." The character who exemplifies this ambiguity is the Xenomorph. But for the Xenomorph child, the Alien differs from Batty and David in that it is a creature that is devoid of intent. The character Ash describes the creature as one that is "unclouded" by conscience or morality. The primal Xenomorph is incapable of grasping the concept of morality, and unlike Batty and David, acts on pure instinct. Its destruction of its hosts is an imperative, as the body of the Xenomorph's father is presented as literal confining structures. The Xenomorph can therefore be regarded as a morally ambiguous creature, one that acts in consistency with Karen Renner's concept of the "Feral Child." Renner proposes that the feral child's defining feature is that the child's "appetites and beliefs" supersede notions of morality and empathy, and the actions of the Xenomorph are in concordance with this.[13] The Xenomorph is possessed of pure instinct, rendering a moralizing conscience void.[14] After developing her concept of the feral and the possessed child, Renner subsequently questions the social factors behind the creation of these children. She proposes that these children can be read as products of a "faulty family or society," bringing into question the greater picture of whether or not these children be considered evil when placed against the forces that are responsible for their creation.[15] Ultimately, these children are the products of the indiscriminate wielding of technological prowess. Creation, Scott's films remind us, can be self destructive if it is not tempered with an element of restraint.

Notes

1. Martin Tropp "The Monster," in *Mary Shelley's Frankenstein*, edited by Harold Bloom (New York: Chelsea House, 2007), 24.
2. Elisabeth Bronfen, "Rewriting the Family: Mary Shelley's Frankenstein," in *Frankenstein, Creation and Monstrosity*, ed. Steven Bann (London: Reaktion Books, 1994), 33.
3. Sydney Palmer, "Virginity in Alien: The Essence of Ripley's Survival," in *The Culture and Philosophy of Ridley Scott*, eds. Adam Barkman, Ashley Barkman, Nancy Kang (Lanham, MD: Lexington Books, 2013), 270.

4. Patricia MacCormack, "The Queer Ethics of Monstrosity," in *Speaking of Monsters: A Teratological Anthology*, eds. Caroline Joan S. Picart and John Edgar Browning (London: Palgrave Macmillian, 2012), 264.

5. David Desser, "The New Eve: The Influence of Paradise Lost and Frankenstein on Blade Runner," in *Retrofitting Blade Runner: Issues in Ridley Scott's Blade Runner and Philip K. Dick's Do Androids Dream of Electric Sheep?*, ed. Judith Kerman, (Wisconsin: University of Wisconsin Press, 1997).

6. http://www.weylandindustries.com/tedtalk.

7. Sharon Gravett, "The sacred and the profane: Examining the religious subtext of Ridley Scott's Blade Runner," in *Literature/Film Quarterly*, vol. 26, no. 1 (1998).

8. Ian Barns, "Monstrous nature or technology?: Cinematic Resolutions of the 'Frankenstein Problem,'" *Science As Culture* vol. 9, no. 1 (1990): 16.

9. Gena Corea, *The Mother Machine* (New York: Perennial Library, 1985), 262–263.

10. Corea, 4.

11. R.W. Cornell and James C. Messerschmidt, "Hegemonic Masculinity: Rethinking the Concept," *Gender Society* 19 (2005): 852.

12. Claudia Springer, "The Pleasure Of the Interface," in *Cybersexualities: A Reader On Feminist Theory, Cyborgs and Cyberspace*, ed. J. Wolmark (Edinburgh: Edinburgh University Press, 1999), 48–49.

13. Karen J. Renner, "Evil Children in Film and Literature II: Notes Towards a Taxonomy," *Lit: Literature Interpretation Theory* 22, no. 3, (2011): 183.

14. Sydney Palmer, "Virginity in Alien: The Essence of Ripley's Survival," in *The Culture and Philosophy of Ridley Scott*, ed. Adam Barkman, Ashley Barkman, Nancy Kang, (Maryland: Lexington Books, 2013), 270.

15. Renner, 188.

Of Radioactive Sprites and Diminutive Tyrants

Hammer's Monstrous Children

REBECCA A. BROWN

Hammer films typically conjure a myriad of gruesome, lascivious images, such as Peter Cushing's dynamic body wrestling a moldering creature, and Christopher Lee's demonic eyes mesmerizing an ample-bosomed maiden. While these horror films helped redefine the genre in the 1950s and 1960s, alongside Herschell Gordon Lewis's and Roger Corman's works, the studio also produced several less renowned fantasy, sci-fi, suspense, and historical films.[1] David Pirie (1973, 2008) and Peter Hutchings (1996) have perceptively written about Hammer horror, while Bruce Hallenbeck (2011) and David Huckvale (2014) have recently begun mapping the company's uncharted cinematic terrain.[2] However, these critical contributions do not extensively focus on the "monstrous" children and teenagers that haunt the studio's oeuvre. From the animalistic youth in *The Curse of the Werewolf* (1961) to the mentally imbalanced teen in *Nightmare* (1964) Hammer's youngsters, almost always relegated to supporting roles, reconceptualize monstrosity in multifarious ways.

This essay responds to these genre-based and thematic oversights by examining child monstrosity in Joseph Losey's sci-fi film *The Damned* (1963) and Seth Holt's psycho-thriller *The Nanny* (1965). The former movie initially focuses on a group of violent Weymouth Teddy Boys who assault American tourist Simon Wells (Macdonald Carey). After Simon absconds to Portland Bill with Joan (Shirley Anne Field), sister of Teddy Boy King (Oliver Reed), the film's narrative shifts to dramatize a group of radioactive preteens' attempts to transform the couple into an adopted family and to escape Bernard (Alexander Knox), their surrogate father. In contrast, *The Nanny* focuses on ten-year-old Joey (William Dix), who helps dismantle his family by trying to defeat the titular caregiver (Bette Davis), a woman who embodies patriarchal and matriarchal authority. Both films, despite significant narrative differences, create dominant figures that possess excessive power and use it to contain or to destroy monstrous children.[3]

My definition of monstrosity underscores both the corporal and the behavioral, drawing upon Jeffrey Jerome Cohen's and Stephani Etheridge Woodson's work. Cohen posits monsters' bodies as "metaphoric crossroads, as an embodiment of a certain cultural moment" that "quite literally incorporates fear, desire, anxiety, and fantasy (ataractic or incendiary), giving them life and an uncanny independence."[4] As he elaborates, monsters "are disturbing hybrids whose externally incoherent bodies resist attempts to include them in any systematic structuration."[5] Losey's children and Holt's tyrant possess bodies that are "metaphoric crossroads" because they represent a range of postwar socio-historical anxieties. Yet their forms are not "externally incoherent" like humans with animalistic "attribute[s]" displayed in Renaissance fairgrounds[6] or the putrefying living dead that inhabit horror films. Instead, the children's physical normativity and incomplete or excess knowledge enables them to unleash unwittingly lethal behavior (*The Damned*) and to perform non-lethal, transgressive behaviors (*The Nanny*). Consequently, the youngsters reinforce Woodson's remarks that, "If a child is unable or unwilling to conform to expected socialization parameters, that child is labeled deviant or poorly socialized. An 'uncontained' child then becomes a 'dangerous' child."[7] Importantly, being and behaving monstrously has an underlying productivity in these films that enables the children—none of whom are truly evil—to challenge the inimical adults who threaten the heteronormative family, thereby aligning them with monstrous-childness as defined in the introduction of this volume.[8]

Since this essay is concerned with youngsters' (dis)empowerment within family structures, I initially use the term "children" to refer to post-infant preteens who are dependent upon adults for financial, moral, mental, and physical well-being. This description serves as an apropos point of departure for considering socio-historical and cinematic contexts that frame the films.[9] Janet Fink states, "In 1945, the rebuilding of British family life was considered central to the broader social and economic reconstruction of the country."[10] Responding to "the separation of married partners, the [wartime] evacuation of children" and other factors, "There was ... a widespread belief that to ensure society's well-being in the postwar years, the family's moral, emotional, and material stability had to be restored."[11] *The Damned* and *The Nanny* expose the romanticization of these ideologies by portraying physically and behaviorally monstrous children who are largely created by their own malevolent caretakers and parents. In both films, the signifiers "child" and "monster" become so malleable that they catalyze the collapse or reconstruction of the heteronormative family.[12] Thus, Losey's and Holt's movies reveal that outside of the horror genre, Hammer's monstrous children exemplify a range of psychological and socio-cultural issues. Simultaneously, they provide a Janus-faced meditation on child monstrosity by continuing the work of *The Bad Seed* (1956), *Village of the Damned* (1960), and *The Innocents* (1961) and anticipating *The Others* (2001), *Joshua* (2007), and *Orphan* (2009).

Radioactive Sprites

The Damned engages in timely British psychological, political, and moral discourses centered upon children.[13] Fink explains, "Legislation in the early postwar years ... sought ... to address concerns about children's wartime experiences and to improve the care and protection provided to children by the state."[14] She maintains that one of the 1948 Children Act's "priorities had been to rescue children from neglect and violence and to provide appropriate care for those children removed from their family homes."[15] Roy Kozlovsky also affirms that this legislation "endowed children with subjective rights, such as the right to happiness and a loving, supportive family environment."[16] In *The Damned* Bernard, a civil servant in charge of the Edgecliff facility, serves as the nine children's "surrogate father" and educator.[17] He explains to his former lover Freya (Viveca Lindfors) towards the film's conclusion that the children "were born as they are. Their mothers were exposed to an unknown kind and level of radiation by an accident."[18] In continuity with 1960s horror film conventions and cultural anxieties, the maternal womb is configured as a deadly, infected site that damages rather than nurtures offspring and implicitly damns the absent women as well.[19] Since the missing mothers are unable to care for their children and the youngsters' bodies are diseased, Bernard's parental duties additionally include containing the preteens in an underground bunker.

The youngsters' social invisibility reinforces Bernard's gendered socio-political power.[20] Peter Hutchings posits that "Authority is inalienably patriarchal in Hammer horror of this period [1956–1964]."[21] He additionally underscores patriarchal power's "associat[ion] with celibacy" and that it is "always the property of the professional, the man ... who knows exactly what he is doing and why."²² *The Damned* is not a horror film, but it nonetheless coheres with these conventions and repurposes them. The civil servant, who remains romantically detached from Freya through the film's duration, harnesses the role of a revisionist "regenerative colonial patriarch" in Portland Bill, benevolently victimizing his radioactively rather than racially othered children in a modernized, subterranean compound rather than a distant land.²³ Unlike the paternal characters in Hammer's *The Mummy* (1959) and *The Hound of the Baskervilles* (1959) who seek to empower decaying family lineages, Bernard's containment of the brood solely aims to revitalize an emasculated Cold War Britain.²⁴

Bernard's nationalist anxieties reveal that in the post-war era, "the child could serve a number of cultural functions at once."²⁵ He tells Freya, "To survive the destruction that is inevitably coming, we need a new kind of man. An accident gave us these nine precious children, the only human beings who have a chance to live in the conditions which must inevitably exist when the time comes."²⁶ Adrian Bingham's discussion of the British popular press's portrayal of atomic weapons illuminates the issues the patriarch alludes to. He explains, "In the period from the successful atomic test in Oct 1952 to the national humiliation in the Suez crisis at the end of 1956, the popular press portrayed Britain as a resurgent great power confidently bestriding the international stage."²⁷ However, "Such euphoria did not long survive the Suez fiasco. By the late 1950s and into the 1960s, pride in Britain's nuclear capability was increasingly tempered by the growing recognition of how dependent Britain was upon the United States for the production and maintenance of its deterrent."²⁸ For Bernard, the children are not miniature weapons or sickly dependents, but rather metonyms for British atomic and imperial power in the world's imminent apocalypse. As he intimates, they can restore Britain to its position as the global power par excellence, its status in the late–Victorian era when one-third of the map was "in pink." Thus, the patriarch reveals that if the postwar child had a multiplicity of cultural uses, here, the child can "heal" a once great nation.²⁹

The patriarch, though, must deprive the youngsters of social knowledge and knowledge of their contagion to ensure their malleability. These occlusions, in turn, emphasize other facets of the preteens' monstrosity. In his exploration of Renaissance monsters and monstrosity, Mark Thornton Burnett discusses "incompletion" and "excess" by examining human bodies that are non-normative due to their extraordinary size, diminutive size, and/or anatomical aberrations.³⁰ In a Cold War context, horror films such as *Them!* (1954), *Godzilla* (1954), and *It Came from Beneath the Sea* (1955) expose the ways that nuclear power and the men who create it produce enormously threatening animalistic bodies. Cinematically, radioactivity is metonymically associated with monstrosity because of its horrifically, large-scale destructive capabilities while culturally, the British popular press also propagated these associations. For instance, the *Mirror* "portrayed" the H-bomb "as having almost demonic capabilities" and even titled a photograph of a "'monstrous mushroom cloud'" "'The monster.'"[31] However, *The Damned* inverts these conventions, enabling them to play out microcosmically. The youngsters' lack of social knowledge can be construed as a form of internal incompletion that affects their mental/social growth; their excessive radiation, which can only be interpreted by placing a Geiger Counter near their skin, sickens their own bodies and the bodies of others. As a result of their complex attributes, Bernard's protection/victimization does not fully ensure his wards' malleability or their containment. Instead, he produces a group of dangerously innocent preteens—rather than hulking beasts—who corrupt several adults.

The youngsters unwittingly seduce Simon and Joan, since their physical normativity and innocent behavior coheres to a conventional definition of "child" rather than "monster."[32] Lack of human contact makes them cloyingly affectionate with the couple in the cavern, while the fanciful origins stories they share imply "childishly" over-active imaginations. Even when the adults apprehend the group's irrationally cold skin, they still remain blinded to the disease and death the youngsters represent. Judith/Jack Halberstam in exploring Victorian and filmic monstrosity writes, "[s]kin ... becomes a kind of metonym for the human; and its color, its pallor, its shape mean everything within a semiotic of monstrosity.... Skin houses the body and it is figured in Gothic as the ultimate boundary, the material that divides the inside from the outside.... Slowly but surely the outside becomes the inside and the hide no longer conceals or contains, it offers itself up as text, as body, as monster."[33] Radiation absorbed in the womb, the ultimate interior space, shifts from inside the mothers' bodies to inside and outside of the children's bodies, rendering their skin a site of ontological perplexity. Later in the film, King touches the children's cold skin and declares that they are "dead" and "zombies"; at the movie's conclusion, he calls Henry "poison."[34] The Teddy Boy's words affirm that the children's "'un-natural'" coldness makes them "physically threatening" (like a zombie or poison) and "cognitively threatening" (like a zombie or dead body).[35] But Simon and Joan do not possess the same non-normative features that enable King to recognize the children's monstrosity. Because the youngsters' skin bears no visual disfigurement and their behavior seems so "childlike," the couple willingly become saviors, fulfilling the children's own expressly and pictorially articulated dreams of having parents.[36]

The proliferation of meanings the film's adults generate for and graft onto the children's bodies contribute to the youngsters' own behavioral changes. When the patriarch confronts the children through a television monitor, explaining, "I know that you have some big people in your hideout.... If you do not help me, I will be forced to take your hideout away from you," Victoria responds, "We want to keep them here, sir."[37] The girl's rejoinder, shot in a close-up to reveal her youthful, freckled face, is uttered with no ill-intent; nonetheless, her statement is inimical because she echoes the civil servant's treatment of his wards. Given her vital role as the group's leader who "mimics" Bernard's words and often serves as a miniature parent,[38] here she demonstrates her doubly "uncanny independence": Victoria defies her father's authority, and she challenges social taboos by verbally transforming the adults from sentient beings into possessions that the children can control and unwittingly destroy. The aptly named preteen illustrates that "[p]arental identification may be the means by which we gleefully produce the healthy, balanced child ... but it also signals the degree to which we cannot control exactly what the child will identify with or incorporate."[39]

Victoria's metamorphosis into a defiant offspring catalyzes the other youngsters' transformations, thereby further affirming that "identifications" between the child (group) and adult (Bernard) "rarely inscribe themselves on tabulae rasae."[40] Bernard tries to reinstate his paternal role by declaring, "I love you, children, and I'm trying to protect you," but the children renounce his words by chanting, "You don't!"[41] For the first time in the underground bunker, the children become verbally then physically rebellious: they run around the classroom, covering up the video cameras so that the patriarch and his men cannot see the destruction they cause. Although the preteens initially function as a group when they rescue Simon and Joan, they also behave as individuals throughout the adults' sojourn in the cavern. But in this scene, their monstrosity is exposed through "massification,"[42] as well as behavioral metamorphosis and spatial transgression. Nonetheless, the children's actions only result in temporary liberation, due to Simon, Joan, and King's aid. Their swift re-entrapment by Bernard's subordinates demonstrates the triumph of patriarchal authority and the death of the youngsters' collective dreams to belong to a heteronormative family.

Bernard's chilling speech to Freya following his children's immurement not only exposes the socio-historical issues discussed earlier in this paper, but also links the youngsters' monstrosity to a *barren* futurity. The etymology of the word monster has often been evoked to portend future events. As Burnett explains, "In 1572, Lewes Lavater argued that 'monsters' manifested '*shewing[s] or warnyng[s] [of] some thyng to happen afterward,*' confirming for 'monsters' a prodigious power."[43] He additionally contends, "In its apocalyptic positioning of the 'monster' alongside bloody rains, comets, earthquakes, eclipses and tempests, for instance, Revelation could be used to lend authority to contemporary attempts to link the 'monstrous' body with the end of the world."[44] The religious overtones associated with monsters, warnings, apocalypse, are displaced in a Cold War world with the inevitability of horrifying nuclear destruction, since, as conventional wisdom holds, the scientist and the politician trump a Judeo-Christian God. When Bernard finally exposes his devastating future plans for the youngsters, he yokes the idea that the "potential—the future—is made corporeal in the body of a child" to the monsters he has helped create.[45] Since the onus of siring the British/human race rests upon radioactive children, the patriarch ultimately forecasts a desolate prospect: either "humans" will die because the diseased children cannot reproduce, or they become monstrous (radioactively diseased). In either scenario, the heteronormative family will be terminated because it is queered in its strictest definition (non-reproductive) or queered in its other definitions (sexually othered, different, etc.).[46] Although the notion of queered family structures has enormously positive political, sexual, and gendered potential, particularly in an apocalyptic future, it does not cohere with the patriarch's own heteronormative perspective.

Ultimately then, the film's final images expose the culmination of Bernard's patriarchal power by emphasizing that his omnipotent control is as destructive as the children's radioactive bodies. King, Simon, Joan, and Freya, all directly or indirectly involved with the children's escape, are killed, die, or depart.[47] To further emphasize these terrifying outcomes, the camera swerves across the water to a long shot of the Weymouth hotels and beach. Overlaying this serene image is the sound of a male child screaming, "Someone help us!"[48] The camera's cut from the cave to the distant Weymouth mainland, full of seaside resorts, distorts the Romantic theory that "If the quintessential child is both source and goal of humanity, this essentialized being can play that role only when set apart from humanity."[49] Before the film's end, Simon and Joan's reiteration of the word *children* fixed the group in a "timeless" state of "isolation,"[50] Bernard's appropriation of the term linked them to empowerment and futurity, and King's resistance to calling them children affirmed that they represented contagion and microcosmic destruction. But at the film's conclusion, the children are deprived of the agency both "children" and "monsters" might possess. There are neither children nor monsters in the cave; there are—and perhaps only ever were—ghosts. If "the monster is always coming back, always at the verge of irruption," the only character who embodies this statement is Bernard himself.⁵¹

Diminutive Tyrant

While *The Damned* concludes with the radioactive children's harrowing, ghostly cries, *The Nanny* more explicitly engages in discourses of spectrality and haunting, particularly through the film's visual and thematic evocation of Jack Clayton's horror-suspense film, *The Innocents* (1961). Joey, *The Nanny*'s ten-year old protagonist, resembles Clayton's Miles (Martin Stephens) in his subtly incestuous desires for an adult woman and his traumatic knowledge that negates his innocence.⁵² Whereas Miles's sexual and social knowledge is supernaturally inflected due to his possession by Peter Quint, Joey too is possessed although metaphorically rather than paranormally. His knowledge derives from his precocious powers of observation since he believes he saw Nanny drown his sister Susy in the bathtub. Unlike Miles, who verbally flaunts patriarchal power, Joey's family silences his accusations and emasculates him through a two-year imprisonment at a psychiatric institution. As in *The Damned*, the non-normative child who represents an excessive social threat must be contained.

Similar to *The Innocents*, *The Nanny* begins with preparations for the male child's homecoming, but in Holt's film, returning home is a disquieting event that underscores the house's and family's dis-ease. Kim Newman explains in his discussion of Hammer's psycho-thrillers that these films "tend to revolve around the theme of trouble within the family, often harking back to *The Old Dark House* (1932) by using decaying mansion settings ... to represent a decadent, inbred milieu that harbours scheming, calculating evil ... and psychotic, random violence.... The world of these films is essentially that of Agatha Christie, preserving the values and cruelties of the classic country house whodunnit while the rest of Britain is getting on with the 1960s."⁵³ Newman acknowledges a Gothic trope that resonates with the films he discusses—the house as a symbol of the "family" and the nation.⁵⁴ *The Nanny*, filmed in black and white, channels Bly's darkness and shadows within a contemporary setting and has a "whodunnit" mystery at its core. Nonetheless, the movie does not resemble the Agatha Christie "classic country house." In *The Nanny*, the potently symbolic late-eighteenth- and nineteenth-century gothicized overtones of female entrapment, male tyranny, and subversive otherness (with the child and domestic playing the role of "other") are recast within the domestic space, microcosmically reverberating in the landscape of early 1960s England. The film, in sum, is concerned with national dis-ease but utilizes the house, with its "sick" family and multiplicity of disquieting performances, to exemplify these tribulations.[55]

The movie's opening domestic scene reinforces these socio-cultural resonances by staging the first of several domestic dramas. Joey's youthful mother Virginia sits on the bed in her son's room hysterically refusing to accompany her husband Bill (James Villiers) to pick up Joey. Bill coldly tells her, "It's high time you started behaving like an adult. You're a mother," thereby insisting that she subsume her identity within a cluster of traits associated with normative upper-middle class motherhood.[56] Although Bernard in *The Damned* is a patriarchal absent presence, towards the film's conclusion, his imposing body, domineeringly positioned on a cliff high above all the protagonists, asserts his embodied authority over everyone's life. Bill, though, becomes a tyrannical yet spectral patriarch throughout the film, leaving for Beirut the day after Joey's arrival, haunting the movie through Virginia and Nanny's empty threats to the child that his father will punish him when he returns. Furthermore, his wife fails to exemplify the vitality of idealized postwar motherhood and more generally demonstrates the permeation of female domestic, social, and political oppression within the 1960s.[57] The biological family was the postwar Labour Party's ideal vessel for maintaining children's emotional and physical health.[58] Nonetheless, *The Nanny*'s opening scene instantly posits an upper-middle-class family in a state of psychic, social, and gendered disintegration, held together and simultaneously torn asunder by the hired help.[59]

Nanny, rather than Virginia, initially embodies the idealized image of motherhood since she cooks, cleans, and mediates between husband and wife; nevertheless, she is a monstrous being. The matriarch is monstrous because she possesses and wields excessive power: she possesses the patriarchal authority Bill grants her and the matriarchal authority that she amassed by rearing Virginia and her sister Pen (Jill Bennett) in a household that has implicitly been deferred to her rule, because she has symbolically displaced the mother after her death. The nature of her vocation inscribes her with additional layers of dominance. Sally Mitchell maintains, "The full-fledged nanny [of Victorian and Edwardian culture] was a professional who had full charge of the children and their upbringing. Mothers recognized their own amateur status and deferred to Nanny's training and experience."[60] Virginia follows her predecessors by consistently relying on Nanny for Joey's care and her own care. The matriarch notably differs from that exemplar of the 1960s filmic imagination—Mary Poppins—a benevolent, if not occasionally controlling spinster who bettered the life of her employers and wards.[61] Instead, she is Virginia's evil doppelganger who may also be considered monstrous because of her microcosmic acts of destruction since she ostensibly kills her own child and Virginia's.

Although no one explicitly refers to Nanny as a "monster," the three adults Joey torments refer to him as one, testifying to the child's own destructive proclivities.[62] Joey's monstrosity largely relies on his physical normativity. He is a small, skinny ten-year old boy with blonde-brown hair; his persistently pouty lower lip characterizes him as a child in need of maternal affection. Huckvale remarks, "William Dix is excellent at pouting and staring in an ambivalent manner, so we are always unsure if he is telling the truth or not."[63] The boy's skin thus reveals even less within conventional discourses of monstrosity than the children in *The Damned*, suggesting instead an association with the postmodern Gothic. Halberstam contends,

> The postmodern monster is no longer the hideous other storming the gates of the human citadel, [sic] he has already disrupted the careful geography of human self and demon other and he makes the peripheral and the marginal part of the center. Monsters within postmodernism are already inside—the house, the body, the head, the skin, the nation—and they work their way out. Accordingly, it is the human, the facade of the normal, that tends to become the place of terror within postmodern Gothic.[64]

Although *The Nanny* may not, at first glance, seem like a postmodern narrative, due to the film's reverberations with so many other genre films and Joey's own behavioral resonances with other evil children in horror films—such as Rhoda Penmark in *The Bad Seed*—the movie and the child can be considered pastiches. Both Joey and Rhoda are "already inside" the house, the head, and, implicitly, the nation. Similar to Rhoda, a physically perfect façade becomes an essential weapon in his arsenal against adults for transforming monstrosity into a performance.

Joey's performative agency begins early in the film and is tantamount to his defense against Nanny and his accumulation of patriarch power. Woodson, in discussing the interconnections between children's (dis)empowerment and performance, writes, "childhood exists as a type of performance space—a cultural geography—in which identities are performed on, in, and through child bodies."[65] When Bill arrives at the psychiatric institute to take Joey home, the child enacts the performance of suicide using a rope. The inimical prank, which occurs in another room, is intended to thrill the boy and scare the female adult (nurse), shifting the power dynamic between the two. Joey's performance also exposes a relevant connection to Renaissance actors' monstrosity, particularly since, as Huckvale notes, "*The Nanny* has certain things in common with Shakespeare's play. Joey is an infant Hamlet, devoted to but alienated from his mother. Nanny resembles King Claudius (who killed Hamlet's father)."[66] Burnett explains, "the [Renaissance] actor presented a tricky ontological problem. Less of a prodigy portending the end of the world, the actor was a 'monster' in a double sense—'monstrous' in constantly changing his attire and 'monstrous' in the commercial profit that he reaped from making a spectacle of his own body."[67] Joey, who not only changes attire throughout the film but also has an arsenal of props at his disposal, does not make a commercial profit from his performances. Instead, his profit is epistemological, psychological, and (in this opening scene) sadistic. The power he establishes in this scene is extended to several others in the movie, such as when the youngster dictates the room he wishes to inhabit at home and insists that Nanny give him his privacy in the bathroom. In each of these instances, Joey's attempts to maintain his independence from the domestic and amass his power are perceived as a kind of abnormality by his parents, rather than an asset.[68]

Joey, however, does not just perform monstrosity; he, like Hamlet, is also possessed, which makes his monstrosity all the more multifaceted. Dr. Beamaster (the boy's psychiatrist) articulates the child's non-normativity in horror film coded language: "Our job is to search out their little devils and exorcise them. I'm afraid we failed Joey, failed him miserably."[69] The failure to exorcise the child's demons emphasizes his metaphoric possession, but the psychiatrist, like all the film's other adults, misreads the youngster, grafting a narrative of guilt and mental illness on him. Karen J. Renner maintains that in some child possession narratives, "a child is not literally taken over by a spirit but naively falls under its influence, never suspecting that it has insidious intentions."[70] In contrast, Joey is possessed by an entity (Nanny) and a memory (seeing Nanny drown Susy), succumbing to the influence of one (entity) and haunted by the other (memory), because of his visual prowess and failure to escape adult scrutiny. Renner explains the significance of these works by writing, "The possessed child narrative ... performs important ideological work that has less to do with the child—who in many ways remains an innocent figure taken advantage of by a more powerful spirit—and more to do with his or her parents."[71] Joey, as the film eventually reveals, is innocent of his sister's murder; instead, Nanny, who embodies and threatens both patriarchal and matriarchal power, insidiously overwhelms the boy and his family. Nevertheless, he continually amplifies his theatrical performances in an attempt to upstage his nemesis.

Joey demonstrates an even fuller range of his physical and behavioral monstrosity through his interactions with the fourteen-year-old daughter (Pamela Franklin) of the doctor who lives above him.[72] On his second day at home, the child relays one of Nanny's attempts to murder him in a fearful manner to his aunt, but in the teenager's room, he lays on her bed, clad only in a towel, nonchalantly claiming, "She tried to kill me."[73] Burnett elaborates on the monstrous nature of the Renaissance actor by stating, "To label the player a 'monster' was ... to alert audiences to the shape-shifting strategies whereby he muddled God-given identifications, unmaking himself, turning 'monstrous' and becoming, in the process, worryingly unclassifiable."[74] While the socio-historical context is significantly different, this scene and the subsequent one where the preteen offers to play doctor, demonstrate how the child's performances are reliant upon vocal inflections, mood transformations, and even costume changes, magnifying his unclassifiability and his empowerment. Since "childhood exists as a space in which culture, identity, and significance are repeatedly and overtly stamped onto children in order to recover them from, or to reiterate, their otherness," Joey's performances, following on from his attempted murder, continually exemplify his efforts to maintain agency over his otherness.[75] Flaunting his youthful manliness through his flippancy, half naked body, and performance of an adult male role (doctor), he counteracts his embodied otherness—specifically his physical and vocal vulnerability/helplessness—that Nanny has invested in.

Unfortunately, the child's accumulation of patriarchal power, gained through his father's absence, tormenting his mother, and altering the teenager's perspective about Nanny, is deflated at the film's climax. To eliminate the child's threat to her rule, the domestic attempts to kill Joey by drowning his body in the bathtub. However, after a brief flashback to Susy's bathtub demise, she pulls the boy from the water, resurrecting him through her frantic, yet affectionate gestures and words. Renner claims that child possession narratives, "often culminate in an exorcism which may or may not succeed."[76] *The Nanny* merges exorcism with baptism, freeing and cleansing both Nanny and Joey from the haunted past and offering an alternative to the end of *The Innocents* where the governess implicitly kills her male ward. Nanny's final performance with a live child creates a restorative rather than disruptive effect on the Fane household: the child no longer needs to perform monstrosity and Nanny, the more insidious, psychopathic character, will finally be contained.

The film's concluding scene, an affectionate reunion between mother and son in the hospital, undermines viewers' expectations by affirming that neither possession nor monstrosity vanishes with Nanny's removal. Renner writes, "Possession narratives act as cautionary tales that warn us, in symbolic terms, that children are vulnerable to dangerous influences when traditional family structures are damaged and parents are negligent in their duties. In some cases, if parent figures reassume their proper roles, the child can be saved; other times, it is simply too late."[77] Joey, clearly vulnerable to Nanny's perilous presence, reinforces Bill and Virginia's negligence and dependence upon the domestic. The absent father never reassumes his role, and the mother only assumes hers after Nanny's psychic destruction. Joey is ironically saved because Nanny disavows her triadic power and finally plays the role of the nurturing domestic. As Virginia holds her child, he promises, "I'll look after you now. I promise," enumerating the myriad domestic duties he will engage in.[78] Joey, in sum, promises to symbolically displace his father and as a result, he finally accumulates the independence he has sought for the film's duration. But even as he affirms that his exorcism/baptism has dispelled one aspect of his possession (the memory of a traumatizing event), it has also resurrected another aspect of it. Nanny, like the children at the end of *The Damned*, is no longer an entity; she is a ghost. Yet she maintains the agency they lack since Joey domesticates himself after Nanny's model, offering his mother several new performances, foreshadowing that the monster will likely return.[79]

Conclusion: Growing Up Monstrous

The Damned and *The Nanny* reinforce an implication in Steven Bruhm's investigation of Gothic children in postwar American fiction and film—that monstrosity is not only the manifestation of parental fears in transforming socio-cultural milieus but also functions as a coping strategy for children (fictional and otherwise) growing up in the postwar era.[80] This, in turn, establishes additional connections to "monstrous childness," as the term "childness" can be yoked to adults, particularly in redefining adult-child relations that create "monsters" to begin with. Joey and the radioactive brood, victimized by adults who wield social, psychological, and gendered power, unwittingly contaminate and wittingly perform as monsters, respectively, in an effort to not only make their voices and desires heard, but to exert the agency they are continually deprived of. Although *The Damned*'s children are ultimately disempowered despite their efforts, Joey's mom's affirmation of his innocence, her affectionate bonding with the boy, and his relative freedom to harness patriarchal and matriarchal roles grants him the agency he seeks throughout the film. While Joey's success might be attributed to little more than a last minute change on Holt's part to appease audiences, it also reaffirms the triumph of patriarchy in 1960s Britain amidst the more visible rise of second wave feminism and the reinforcement of heteronormative ideologies, however symbolically displaced the father-figure is.[81] That the radioactive brood is forever severed from society alarmingly resonates with filmic and fictional trends of the era (and now) that the child or children who kill, whether wittingly or unwittingly, are deprived of the right to live.

Acknowledgments

Eternal thanks to Paul Anthony Johnson, Michael Falcone, and Yesenia Camacho for their feedback and support while writing this essay.

Notes

1. David Simmons notes, "Though the last few years have witnessed a growing amount of critical discussion concerning the horror output of the Hammer film studio, there has been comparatively little analysis of the important part that science fiction and the scientific has played in its output." David Simmons, "Hammer Horror and Science Fiction," in *British Science Fiction Film and Television: Critical Essays*, eds. Tobias Hochscherf and James Leggott (Jefferson, NC: McFarland, 2011), 50.

2. David Pirie, *A New Heritage of Horror: The English Gothic Cinema* (London: I.B. Tauris, 2008). Peter Hutchings, *Hammer and Beyond: The British Horror Film* (Manchester: Manchester University Press, 1993). Bruce G. Hallenbeck, *British Cult Cinema: Hammer Fantasy & Sci-Fi*, ed. Denis Meikle (Bristol: Hemlock Books, 2011). David Huckvale, *Hammer Films' Psychological Thrillers: 1950–1972* (Jefferson, NC: McFarland, 2014).

3. For *The Damned's* production history see Hallenbeck, *British Cult Cinema*, 114–120. For *The Nanny's* production history see Marcus Hearn and Alan Barnes, *The Hammer Story: The Authorised History of Hammer Films* (London: Titan, 2007), 92–93. *These Are the Damned* (1965) is the film's American title, but I refer to the movie by its British title, *The Damned* (1963), throughout this essay.

4. Jeffrey Jerome Cohen, "Monster Culture (Seven Theses)," in *Monster Theory: Reading Culture*, ed. Jeffrey Jerome Cohen (Minneapolis: University of Minnesota Press, 1996), 4.

5. Cohen, "Monster Culture," 6.

6. Mark Thornton Burnett, *Constructing "Monsters" in Shakespearean Drama and Early Modern Culture* (Basingstoke: Palgrave Macmillan, 2002), 16.

7. Woodson, who primarily investigates "evil" children in film, theater, and popular culture, draws these conclusions from Shirley Steinberg and Joe Kincheloe's discussion of "the corporate construction of childhood." Stephani Etheridge Woodson, "Mapping the Cultural Geography of Childhood or, Performing Monstrous Children," *Journal of American Culture* 22.4 (Winter 1999): 34, accessed May 24, 2013, doi: 10.1111/j.1542-734X.1999.2204_31.x.

8. Monstrous and evil are frequently not but not always synonymous. See Joe L. Kincheloe, "The New Childhood: *Home Alone* as a Way of Life," in *The Children's Culture Reader*, ed. Henry Jenkins (New York: New York University Press, 1998), 164–165.

9. My use of the term British often refers to English. However, there is also blurring amongst sources I use between these words, especially concerning the "British horror film" and the "postwar British family." Also, for clarification Bernard in *The Damned* is Scottish, so "British" rather than English seems especially apropos for this film.

10. Janet Fink, "Natural Mothers, Putative Fathers, and Innocent Children: The Definition and Regulation of Parental Relationships Outside Marriage, In England, 1945–1959," *Journal of Family History* 25.2 (Apr. 2000): 178, accessed May 5 2013, doi: 10.1177/036319 900002500203.

11. Fink, "Natural Mothers," 178, 179. Sue Bruely and Fink maintain that the heteronor-

mative family remained the ideal in the 1950s and the first part of the 1960s. Sue Bruley, *Women in Britain Since 1900* (Basingstoke: Macmillan, 1999), 130–131.

12. Hutchings, in discussing 1970s horror, explains, "Horror films have often explored familial tensions.... [But] British horror, usually set in the past, away from everyday reality dealt more with the psychological effects of the family structure." Hutchings, *Hammer and Beyond*, 166–167. His insights have resonance within the 1960s horror film as well.

13. Hutchings and Pirie provide a cinematic context for Losey's film by comparing it to *Village of the Damned* (1960) and *Children of the Damned* (1964). Hutchings, *Hammer and Beyond*, 93. Pirie, *A New Heritage*, 155.

14. Fink, "Natural Mothers," 180.

15. Fink, "Natural Mothers," 186.

16. Roy Kozlovsky, "Adventure Playgrounds and Postwar Reconstruction," in *Designing Modern Childhoods: History, Space, and the Material Culture of Children*, eds. Marta Gutman and Ning de Coninck-Smith (New Brunswick: Rutgers University Press, 2008), 176.

17. Tony Shaw too refers to Bernard as a "surrogate father." Tony Shaw, *British Cinema and the Cold War: The State, Propaganda and Consensus* (London: I.B. Tauris, 2006), 183.

18. *These Are the Damned*, directed by Joseph Losey (1961; Culver City: Columbia Pictures, 2010), DVD.

19. David J. Skal, *The Monster Show: A Cultural History of Horror* (New York: Penguin, 1993), 290, 292, 294.

20. This point is fairly paradoxical because the children all possess the names of England's former monarchs.

21. Hutchings, *Hammer and Beyond*, 67.

22. Hutchings, *Hammer and Beyond*, 67, 66.

23. See Anne P. McClintock, *Imperial Leather: Race, Gender and Sexuality in the Colonial Contest* (New York: Routledge, 1995), 239–250. Of the setting, Losey remarks, "this part of the country is Thomas Hardy and John Cowper Powys territory..." referring to Weymouth and Portland Bill. Michel Ciment, *Conversations with Losey* (London: Methuen, 1985), 198.

24. Hutchings explains that Hammer's horror films from this period engage in a number of socio-cultural anxieties, including the loss of Empire. He states, "On one level, *The Mummy* does seem to operate as an interrogation of aspects of imperialism which conflates this with a representation of troubled masculinity" (71). He also sees postwar gender conflicts within *The Hound of the Baskervilles* (81).

25. Steven Bruhm, "Nightmare on Sesame Street: or, The Self-Possessed Child," *Gothic Studies* 8.2 (2006): 100, accessed April 15, 2013.

26. *The Damned*.

27. Adrian Bingham, "'The Monster'? The British Popular Press and Nuclear Culture, 1945-early 1960s," *The British Journal for the History of Science*, 45.4 (Dec. 2012): 622, accessed April 28, 2013, doi: 10.1017/S0007087412001082.

28. Bingham, "'The Monster,'" 622.

29. Bruhm, "Nightmare," 100.

30. Burnett, *Constructing "Monsters,"* 11, 20.

31. Bingham, "'The Monster,'" 617.

32. Gardner states, "with their stilted RADA delivery and stiff, prep-school elocution the children are more like over-rehearsed amateur thespians than typically rambunctious pupils, a frightening contrast to the violent but nonetheless very human and instinctive Teds." This statement oversimplifies the children's behavior as well as their significance in the film. Colin Gardner, "From Mimicry to Mockery: Cold War Hybridity in Evan Jones's *The Damned*, *Modesty Blaise* and *Funeral in Berlin*," *Media History* 12.2 (2006): 182, accessed June 25, 2013, doi: 10.1080/13688800600807999.

33. Halberstam, Judith /Jack, *Skin Shows: Gothic Horror and the Technology of Monsters* (Durham: Duke University Press, 1995), 6–7.

34. *The Damned.*

35. Noël Carroll, *The Philosophy of Horror or Paradoxes of the Heart* (New York, Routledge, 1990), 34. Carroll draws upon Mary Douglas's famous study *Purity and Danger* (1966, 2002) to formulate his conclusions. Since Burnett also uses Douglas's study, there's some resonance between Carroll's discussion of horror fiction and filmic monsters and Burnett's exploration of Renaissance monstrosity.

36. Gardner writes, "The children are convinced that these adult 'strangers' are their long-lost parents—up to now they have made do with simulacrum families in the form of cut-out magazine photos of mismatched couples—and react with delight and amazement at the human warmth of their bodies" (108–109). Colin Gardner, *Joseph Losey* (Manchester: Manchester University Press, 2004).

37. *The Damned.*

38. In his discussion of *The Damned*, Gardner explores "mimicry" and colonial power ("From Mimicry to Mockery," 183–84). He sees this as "a strategy of *inclusion*" in relation to the children in Losey's film; in other words, "an acceptance of the 'good' Other in the form of the interpellated children of *The Damned...*" (184).

39. Bruhm, "Nightmare," 105.

40. Bruhm, "Nightmare," 105.

41. *The Damned.*

42. Carroll, *The Philosophy of Horror*, 50. Carroll indicates, "As with the case of magnification, with massification it is not the case that any kind of entity can be grouped into horrific hordes. It must be the sort of thing we are already prone to find repellent..." (50). Since Bernard's minions are terrified of the children due to their deadly radioactivity, the youngsters qualify as "repellent" beings to this particular group of people.

43. Burnett, *Constructing "Monsters,"* 29.

44. Burnett, *Constructing "Monsters,"* 30.

45. Woodson, "Mapping," 39.

46. For the various definitions of "queer" I'm drawing upon, see Andrew Smith and William Hughes, *Queering the Gothic* (Manchester: Manchester University Press, 2009), 1–10.

47. Hallenbeck refers to Freya as "the film's moral conscience" (115).

48. *The Damned.*

49. Judith Plotz, *Romanticism and the Vocation of Childhood* (Basingstoke: Palgrave, 2001), 30.

50. While the time periods, socio-cultural contexts, and geography differ, Simon and Joan's reading of the children resonates with Judith Plotz's insightful explanation of De Quincey's portrayal of the solitary, rural Romantic child: "Because such isolation sequesters the child from time and change, the Romantic child can become an emblem of fixity rather than of growth and development. In its rural isolation childhood is timeless and stable" (24).

51. Cohen, *Monster Theory*, 20.

52. Joey harbors these desires for his mother, Virginia (Wendy Craig), while Miles harbors them for his governess Miss Giddens (Deborah Kerr). Joey is the same age as Henry James's Miles in *The Turn of the Screw* (1897) and implicitly Clayton's tyrant, placing the three children on the brink of puberty. See also Fredrik Tydal's essay in this collection.

53. Newman, "Psycho-Thriller," 76. Kim Newman claims, "the psycho-thriller (as opposed to the psychological thriller, which is something else again) deals with the horror of madness." Kim Newman, "Psycho-thriller, qu'est-ce que c'est?" in *British Horror Cinema*, eds. Steve Chibnall and Julian Petley (London: Routledge, 2002), 71. Intriguingly, Huckvale uses "psychological thriller" rather than "psycho-thriller" throughout his study.

54. Newman, "Psycho-Thriller," 76, 80.

55. Newman indicates that *The Nanny* is "the most rooted in reality of all Hammer psycho movies" (77), and while he briefly mentions the eighteenth-century Gothic male tyrant/killer that the psycho-thrillers revise (79), he does not examine Holt's film in this context.

56. *The Nanny*, directed by Seth Holt (1965; Beverly Hills: Twentieth-Century–Fox, 2008), DVD.

57. See Andrew August, "Gender and 1960s Youth Culture: The Rolling Stones and the New Woman," *Contemporary British History* 23.1 (March 2009): 80–83, accessed May 17, 2013, doi: 10.1080/13619460801990104

58. Fink, "Natural Mothers," 179.

59. For a discussion of "mutuality" in postwar marriage see Marcus Collins, *Modern Love: Personal Relationships in Twentieth-Century Britain* (Newark: University of Delaware Press, 2003), 168–173.

60. Bill and Virginia have an upper-middle-class household due to his vocation and their home. Mitchell writes, "The idealized nanny was largely a figure of late–Victorian and Edwardian upper-class households." Sally Mitchell, *Daily Life in Victorian England* (Westport, CT: Greenwood Press, 2009), 150. http://www.worldcat.org/title/daily-life-in-victorian-england/oclc/34117508/viewport.

61. Huckvale also states that *The Nanny* "*is* a dark shadow of *Mary Poppins*, the Walt Disney film adaptation which had appeared only in the previous year (1964)." Huckvale, *Hammer Films*', Kindle Locations 3039–3040. Mary Poppins, as portrayed in P.L Travers's books, was far less benevolent than her filmic counterpart. In the words of several former children's literature students, "she's mean."

62. *The Nanny*.

63. Huckvale, *Hammer Films*, Kindle Locations 3027–3028.

64. Halberstam, *Skin Shows*, 162.

65. Woodson, "Mapping," 31.

66. Huckvale, *Hammer Films*, Kindle locations 2965–2966.

67. Burnett, *Constructing "Monsters,"* 10.

68. This insistence on independence is motivated by metaphoric possession—his fear that Nanny will kill him. His parents' fear of his "uncanny independence" thus marks another significant aspect of his behavioral monstrosity. Also, for Hammer horror father-son tensions see Hutchings (70–6).

69. *The Nanny*.

70. Karen J. Renner, Introduction, in *The 'Evil Child' in Literature, Film and Popular Culture* (London: Routledge, 2013), 7.

71. Renner, *The 'Evil Child*,*'* 7.

72. The connection between *The Innocents* and *The Nanny* is further reinforced by the presence of Pamela Franklin, who plays Flora in the former film.

73. *The Nanny*.

74. Burnett, *Constructing 'Monsters*,*'* 9.

75. Woodson, "Mapping," 32.

76. Renner, *The "Evil Child*,*"* 7.

77. Renner, *The "Evil Child*,*"* 8.

78. *The Nanny*.

79. Cohen, *Monster Theory*, 20.

80. Bruhm, "Nightmare," 100–103.

81. Hearn and Barnes contend, "Some time after shooting was complete, Twentieth-Century–Fox insisted that a happier, less ambivalent, [sic] ending be tacked on to the end of the picture. [Jimmy] Sangster reluctantly wrote a brief scene where Joey visits his recovering mother in the hospital, and the actors concerned were recalled" (93).

Part III

The Adoption Papers (Adaptations)

What About Grendel's Son?

Shades of Monstrosity in Beowulf and Grendel

Danny Gorny

They fuck you up, your mum and dad.
They may not mean to, but they do.
They fill you with the faults they had
And add some extra, just for you.
—Philip Larkin, "This Be the Verse"

Beowulf is a poem notoriously difficult to adapt to film. Although it is replete with heroic set-pieces and fights with monsters, the poem relies too heavily on its allusive digressions to figures such as Scyld, Sigemund, Heremod, and Modþryð to form a fully-contained narrative arc suitable for such a visual medium. The poem's third episode, which occurs fifty years after the protagonist's first two battles and in another country entirely, creates additional narrative complications difficult to resolve without straining an audience's credulity or patience. *Beowulf* is often adapted to new media, but never, it seems, satisfactorily.

Adaptations of *Beowulf* have always needed a degree of mediation so great that they are worth considering not only as adaptations, but also as readings. As Linda Hutcheon argues in *A Theory of Adaptation*, the point of adapting a text into a new medium is "repetition, but repetition without replication."[1] Hutcheon suggests that we do adaptations a critical disservice when we instinctually respond to them primarily on account of their fidelity to their sources:

> All ... adapters relate stories in their different ways. They use the same tools that storytellers have always used: they actualize or concretize ideas; they make simpli-

fying selections, but also amplify and extrapolate; they make analogies; they critique or show their respect, and so on.[2]

Adapting *Beowulf* has always led to interpretations that have needed to be judged on their own merits. Marijane Osborn argues that "translations and paraphrases of the poem have served as acts of literary criticism, continually reinterpreting *Beowulf* in the currently or locally accepted idiom."[3] Various adaptations have turned *Beowulf* into a fairy tale, set it in its "native" Scandinavia, or transposed it to a more modern context. Illustrations from a 1965 Spanish translation depict the hero in fifteenth-century armor as he fights what Osborne describes as a "mildly cubist brachiosaurus."[4] The 1975–76 DC comic book series portrays Beowulf as a Conanesque figure, perpetually saving busty ladies from slimy monsters.[5]

Two somewhat recent films have been the most successful of the lot: *Beowulf and Grendel* (2005) directed by Sturla Gunnarson, and *Beowulf* (2007) directed by Robert Zemeckis.[6] Both take a similar tack in "resolving," as William F. Hodapp puts it, the question of Grendel's father. Drawing attention to Hrothgar's remark that the people who named Grendel "no hie fæder cunnon" [know of no father],[7] Hodapp suggests that filmmakers' concern for the identity of Grendel's father constitutes an attempt to provide modern audiences with an explanation for his attacks on Heorot.[8] Likewise, both films add a sexual component, also absent from the poem. As E.L. Risden suggests, "sex reconfigures *Beowulf* entirely: we get not the epic with its ideals of heroism, loyalty, and personal accomplishment balanced with martial service and self-sacrifice, but exoticisization and titillation that reshape the story as fable about the problems of male sex-drive."[9] What both films do most effectively is challenge the poetic account by claiming that its story is somehow incomplete, and that additional content must be added to remedy this fault. And yet even as they do so, the success of both adaptations relies on their ability to reformulate the moral and interpretive questions asked by the poem and impose them upon their audience.

As Laurence N. de Looze observes, when we read *Beowulf* "the voice of the implied author is authoritative at all times. It gives no sign of being unreliable."[10] And yet adapters of *Beowulf* persist in their perception that certain omissions in the narrative require filling; these omissions are usually sexual, but they can also be factual. De Looze draws our attention to Beowulf's attempt to find historical examples on which to model his own paradoxical situation when forced to face the dragon, suggesting that he invents history in his analogy to the old man watching his son swing on the gallows, as signaled by the simile "swa bið" [it is like].[11] The poem provides us with a similar sense of uncertainty in the verbal challenge Unferth offers to Beowulf upon his arrival, when he questions Beowulf's bravery in his swimming contest with Breca.[12] Here, although Beowulf acquits himself well in his retelling of the story, the reader may still question whose account is truest. *Beowulf* explores the relationship between tale-telling and reality, developing a kind of epistemological ambiguity applicable to men and monsters alike.

Adaptations of the poem such as Zemeckis's and Gunnarson's invoke its ambiguity when they offer answers to some of the questions that arise from Grendel's unknown parentage and the near-complete absence of women with whom the hero can interact. Paradoxically, these putative answers provoke new questions. Because the narrative must be fleshed out with new characters and new relationships, new points of ambiguity tend to arise in the resolution of old ones. By focusing so intensely on questions of parentage and sexuality, as both films do, adaptations of *Beowulf* become reconfigured as tales of domestic violence. Both films integrate Grendel into a family by accounting for his parentage while portraying Beowulf more as a sexual interloper than as a redemptive hero. In Zemeckis's film, the dual revelations of parentage— first when Grendel is revealed to be Hrothgar's son, and then when the dragon is revealed to be Beowulf's—serve not only to reconfigure the poem to focus on Grendel's mother (Angelina Jolie) and the violent consequences of her monstrous sexuality, but also to suggest that these monsters (and perhaps, by extension, *all* monsters) owe their existence equally to the deviant sexuality of powerful men. While Gunnarson's treatment adds a sexual component to the narrative and even gives Grendel his own son, the film itself is not about sex and parenting so much as it is about the ambiguousness of childhood. *Beowulf and Grendel* retains the moral ambiguity of its source by depicting children as liminal figures.

Among the changes Gunnarson's *Beowulf and Grendel* makes to the poem is the removal of most of its Christian allusions and the expansion of the culture at Heorot as a dynamic society. Gunnarson also creates a history for Grendel by opening the film with an episode entitled "Prologue: A Hate is Born," in which Hrothgar (Stellan Skarsgard) spares Grendel's (Ingvar E. Sigurdsson) life after killing his father. The most jarring change is the addition of another major character: Selma (Sarah Polley), whose character fits with none of the major female roles that have traditionally been identified within the poem. Selma, being a "witch," does not fall into the three roles (hostess, peaceweaver, and ritual mourner) the poem tends to reserve for women.[13] As Shari Horner observes, women tend to be carefully circumscribed in *Beowulf*, and their voices tend to be silenced.[14] Selma resists this tendency. Aside from being a love interest to both hero and monster, as demonstrated in the juxtaposed sex scenes, Selma provides the audience with running commentary on Beowulf's adventures. Moreover, Selma offers a perspective on the events at Heorot that competes successfully with the aggrandizing commentary of Thorkel (Ronan Vibert), the warrior-*scop* who composes the "original" poem while accompanying the hero on his quest.[15] Most remarkably, *Beowulf and Grendel* uses Selma as a medium by which Grendel is rendered comprehensible, and consequently less monstrous, more familiar, more human.

In his provocative article "Monster Culture (Seven Theses)," Jeffrey Jerome Cohen suggests that the figure of the monster is "pure culture": the displaced embodiment of cultural anxiety.[16] For Cohen, Grendel is liminal: he patrols the limits of cultural identity and unsettles our construction of the human by embodying the self-estrangement intrinsic to the foundation of social and cultural boundaries.[17] In this sense, Grendel's monstrosity has more to do with his symbolic potential than with any of his intrinsic or essential qualities. Caroline Joan Picart and John Edgar Browning nuance the meanings of monstrosity in their introduction to *Speaking of Monsters*, in which they link the Latin *monster* with the Greek *teras* to call the study of monsters "teratology."[18] Picart and Browning's initial concern with etymology is suggestive, for while we might read a *monster* as, to borrow Cohen's phrase, pure culture, we do so because the name we have to describe such creatures is derived from the verb *monstrare*, "to show." *Teras*, however, includes concepts of freakishness, especially with respect to birth defects, and thus teratology might well be said to be the study of both physical abnormality and monstrosity together.[19] Put more succinctly, a monster *must* signify, but sometimes a freak just *is*.

With this distinction, we are left to question whether monstrosity is a cultural or a physical category. Childhood complicates the question further. When we consider an adult to be monstrous, we do so as a consequence of his or her words or actions, implying that such a "monster" has chosen to become monstrous. In such a case, a root cause of insanity or deformity returns us to the realm of the *teras*, the freak. Because children are not adults, our categories of monstrosity—normal, monster, freak—are insufficient to describe the experience of childhood so long as we imagine that there exists a fundamental difference between childhood and adulthood. Although Philippe Ariès has hypothesized in his provocative study *Centuries of Childhood* that childhood was not understood to be a concept radically distinct from adulthood until the onset of modernity, Nicholas Orme has recently demonstrated that children, even medieval children, have *always* been symbols of our aspirations: even in the Middle Ages childhood was considered a phase of social development distinct from the rest of life, and consequently parents' relationships with their offspring were genuinely caring rather than apathetic.[20] Childhood is not an end-state of being, but a waypoint on the road to adulthood; by its very nature, the existence of a child invites us to imagine its future, in the sense that a child can always be taught, redeemed, reformed or civilized. To categorize a child as monstrous is to entrap it in an inescapable present by denying its potential to develop. Thus, while a regular monster is, as Cohen suggests, difference embodied, a monstrous *child* is as likely to be the embodiment of sameness made alien. And while a regular monster patrols the borders of civilization, a monstrous child occupies its threshold as a symbol of uncertainty.

In *Beowulf and Grendel*, Selma asks us to reject the easy interpretation of Grendel as monstrous. As J.R.R. Tolkien has famously argued, the monsters of *Beowulf* are "essential ... to the underlying ideas of the poem," and as we shall see, one of the ways the monsters can be seen as central is the persistence with which the poet's language undermines the distinction between the monster and the hero.[21] Selma's role in the story is to ask all who approach her to reconsider their own relationships with monstrosity. She does this largely by questioning motivations and remembering history, and in doing so, she renders the nature of monstrosity compelling by making it a matter of interpretation. As Selma draws our attention to the film's points of ambiguity, and as the development of the plot gives the audience increasingly good reasons to agree with her, we become increasingly suspicious of interpreting Beowulf as heroic. Although it at times falls flat, *Beowulf and Grendel* successfully adapts the poem to the screen by limiting its account to the poem's two contiguous narrative episodes featuring the fights with Grendel and his mother (Elva Ósk Ólafsdóttir). Gunnarson replaces the forward-looking episode with the dragon when he adds a third "monster": the silent red-headed child of Selma and Grendel (Benedikt Clausen) who by his very existence threatens to continue the feud after Beowulf departs. Because we see Grendel's son only as a child, his character works as a nexus for the ambiguities (heroism/monstrosity, action/reaction, childhood/adulthood) Selma asks us to ponder.

Beowulf and Grendel follows its source's lead in challenging us with a series of interpretive difficulties, especially when questions of childhood and children become complicated by the discourse of monstrosity. Beginning with an image of Grendel as a child, continuing with images of Grendel acting childishly, and ending with an image of Grendel's child, *Beowulf and Grendel* imbues the concept of childhood with all the ambiguous liminality we tend to reserve for monsters. As Browning's essay in this volume suggests, a common character type in contemporary horror cinema is that of the Adult Child, a kind of antagonist who terrifies us by means of its deranged pursuit of vigilante revenge with a childlike demeanor. Gunnarson's Grendel is one such figure, in that he is neither fully childlike, nor fully an adult. Selma, too, is a transgressive figure: one who facilitates Gunnarson's depiction of Beowulf (Gerard Butler) and Grendel along a continuum of monstrosity. And we have difficulty reading Grendel as human until he becomes situated within the new familial context heralded by the introduction of his son. We cannot call Grendel's son a terror, whether holy or unholy, as his speechlessness makes him a cypher. Gunnarson takes full advantage of Grendel's son to demystify the hero, to humanize the monster, and to problematize the resolution of Beowulf's mission to save the Danes from Grendel.

Gunnarson does much to preserve the poem's points of interpretive tension.[22] Even though it sometimes employs Christian imagery, *Beowulf* is not a wholly Christian poem. Moral examples rooted in pagan concepts such as *wyrd* (destiny or providence) compete with the Christian narrator's occasional reflections on the doomed nature of the pagan characters, as when he remarks of the first men Grendel kills that their fate is unknown because "ne wiston hie drighten God" [they did not know the lord God].[23] As Paul Taylor and Ruth Waterhouse have suggested, Grendel gains much of his terrifying power from his location at the intersection of Christian and Pagan mythologies.[24] On the one hand, Grendel is defined over and again in Old Testament language. He is "Caines cynne. þone cwealm gewræc"[the kin of Cain, that wreaks death], "feond mancynnes" [enemy of mankind], he "Godes yrre bær" [bore God's anger], is "Godes andsacan" [God's adversary], a "cwealmcuman" [murderous visitor], who was "fag wið God" [in a state of feud against God].[25] Grendel's mother is defeated only through the power of the sword found in her lair, which has inscribed upon it in runes the story of Noah's flood:

> On ðæm wæs or writen
> Fyrngewinnes; syðþan flod ofsloh
> gifen geotende giganta cyn,
> frecne geferdon; þæt wæs fremde þeod
> ecan dryhtne; him þæs ende lean
> þurgh wætteres wylm waldend sealde.[26]

On it was the origin of ancient strife written, ever since the Flood slew, with pouring sea, the race of giants; the terrible suffering of that alien people, the Eternal Lord banished them to their final reward through surging waters.

The lines that tell the story of the Flood define Grendel and his kin as alien people that bear the curse of an angry Hebraic deity. The problem is that Beowulf and the Danes are pagans. Consequently, critics such as Mary Parker suggest that "it is because the Danes are heathen, king and people, that Grendel is permitted to afflict them."[27] Moreover, though the poem is clearly influenced by the Scriptures, this influence is limited to the Old Testament; there is little sense of the kind of eternal salvation heralded by Christ. Parker suggests the poem stresses implicitly that the redemptive value of heroic sacrifice for pagans is merely temporary by pointing out that neither Beowulf's killing of Grendel nor his slaying of the dragon "redeems society or offers salvation or eternal life," and reminds us that in the end "Heorot will perish by fire and Beowulf's people will be attacked."[28] In this way, *Beowulf* occupies the liminal space between Christianity and paganism, rendering them competitive but not mutually exclusive.

As the runes on the sword Beowulf recovers from the mere suggest, the Danes are threatened by monsters derived from Biblical history. Although these monsters can be killed by the poem's pagan hero, the tentative Christianization offered by the poet does little by way of promising a permanent salvation. Gunnarson disposes of most of the poem's Christian references, but he retains this tension by showing the Danes and the Geats alike to be pagan cultures only freshly introduced to Christianity, and thus still in the process of integrating its tenets into their own belief systems. The characters in *Beowulf and Grendel* gain little benefit from being introduced to Christianity. What the new religion adds most immediately to the film is a way to understand the importance of mercy, especially towards children, in hopes of preventing an eternal feud. It is fitting that such scenes bookend the film.

Beowulf and Grendel preserves the poem's categorical ambiguity in its depiction of both heroism and monstrosity. Katherine O'Brien O'Keefe has argued persuasively that the language used to describe Beowulf and Grendel is initially disparate, converges as they approach each other, and then diverges again when distance is put between them:

> Preconceptions in the glossing, translating, and editing of the text have substantially affected our picture of Grendel. The word *aglæca* is an instance of an unfortunate glossing which seriously affects the interpretation of the text. The word is used twenty times in *Beowulf,* chiefly ... for Grendel and the dragon. Yet *aglæca* is also used for Beowulf and Sigemund. [The most common solution] is to gloss *aglæca* as "wretch, monster, demon, fiend" when it refers to Grendel and the dragon and as "warrior, hero" when it refers to Beowulf and Sigemund. Building such a distinction into the glossing of the word completely ignores the possibility that the poet has deliberately chosen to use the same word to describe two sets of characters.[29]

O'Keefe thus demonstrates that we can read Beowulf to be as monstrous as Grendel is human, and, more significantly, that the poet shows that their identities are marked by patterns of convergence and divergence. Consequently, we can see that both characters are situated within the same continuum of identity, and that neither is purely monstrous nor purely human. Andy Orchard, in *Pride and Prodigies*, concurs, suggesting that "of all the monsters [in *Beowulf*], it is Grendel who is most consistently depicted in human terms, particularly in the constant evocation of exile imagery to describe his plight."[30] Both characters exist within a continuum of monstrosity. In *Beowulf and Grendel* this continuum finds expression in the juxtaposed Beowulf/Selma and Grendel/Selma sex scenes. How can we distinguish between the hero and the monster if both seem to be equally heroic and equally monstrous?

Beowulf and Grendel can be differentiated by their powers of speech. Much of what we know of Beowulf's heroism is told to us by the hero himself. By contrast, Grendel is a character who is spoken of, but never one who speaks, and his silence makes it easy for his enemies to define him. As Gabe Foreman suggests:

> In *Beowulf*-criticism, there has been little attention given to Grendel's lack of speech, but at the same time, considerable effort has been expended to show that the monster possesses human characteristics. The more human Grendel is, the more inexplicable becomes the fact that he does not speak. For this reason, Grendel's monstrosity may be seen as deriving from his silence.[31]

The Grendel of the poem is silent and obscure, but the Grendel of Gunnarson's film is not. Here, he has a voice: we hear him refer to his father as "papi" in the prologue, and once again when he comes to Heorot to take revenge against Hondscioh (Tony Curran) for defiling the shrine in his cave. These are the only two times Grendel's speech can be understood without Selma's translation, and both moments are significant because they cast Grendel as reactionary. Just as Grendel's feud with the Danes begins when Hrothgar kills his father, his feud with the Geats begins with Hondscioh's action in the cave. Grendel is at his most immediately comprehensible when he reminds us that he was once a child.[32] If Grendel's silence renders him monstrous, his voice renders him human.

Grendel's monstrosity derives from his silence, ancestry and form, while Beowulf's heroism derives from his voice, parentage, and strength. Yet Gunnarson's presentation of Grendel's ability to communicate undermines these differences and thus the nature of monstrosity within his film. The *Beowulf*-poet has Grendel and Beowulf meet in a linguistic atmosphere in which the distinctions between man and monster have been deliberately obscured— where "the mark of the assailant is measured as much in terror and anger as in corporeal harm."[33] In the poem, Beowulf and Grendel are aligned linguistically within a continuum of monstrosity. Gunnarson adapts this continuum to accommodate the audience's emotional response to the plot. John Niles suggests the poet treats Beowulf as a reactionary figure, whose presence is necessitated by the arrival of the monsters he is to fight:

> Rather than see Grendel as an anti-hero, one can regard Beowulf as a kind of "anti-monster" ... it is the monsters who call Beowulf into being, not the reverse. *He responds to them*, and if there had been no Grendel there would never have needed to be a Beowulf.[34]

By Niles's assessment, Grendel is something of a force of nature, a creature whose challenge to Heorot comes because the Danes have imposed their civilization upon the wilderness. Grendel's actions require someone like Beowulf to respond to them, but the poet does not suggest the Danes were responsible for making the monster monstrous: being *caines cynne* suffices to explain Grendel's distaste for civilization. As opposed to the poem, the assignation of agency is central to the question of responsibility in *Beowulf and Grendel*.[35] Here, Grendel is no longer a descendant of Cain, but rather a marginalized figure who clearly responds to his childhood trauma by revisiting Hrothgar's earlier violence towards his father upon the Danes he leads.

Although he still terrorizes Heorot, Gunnarson's Grendel is not the same Grendel who, in the poem, strikes out against the abrasive hall-building Danes who encroach on his territory. Nor is he the Grendel who, according to O'Keefe "negates Heorot's function as the locus of civilized life."[36] Gunnarson's Grendel does not defend his territory; he punishes his father's killers. Niles suggests the poetic Grendel and Beowulf play similar roles to different effects:

> Grendel represents the pure perversion of the will. He is the grinder, the destroyer, the devourer ... he lives beyond the pale of society and that we are always nonetheless reminded of him ... Beowulf too is a destroyer, but he destroys to preserve what is bright and beautiful: the peaceful community of human beings living together without treachery or fear.[37]

In the poem, Grendel's exile is a consequence of his ancestry. He is a freak because he is a descendant of Cain, whose whole bloodline is marked for eternity "þæs þe he Abel slog" [because he slew Abel].[38] Grendel can be wholly monstrous if, and only if, we accept that Heorot is in fact a peaceful community living together without treachery or fear. Gunnarson does not only reject this proposition in its prologue, he reverses it by showing Grendel's family to be the community without treachery or fear, whose way of life is violently interrupted by the hall-building Danes.

The poetic Beowulf's history is also fraught with murder. Foreman reminds us that it is Hrothgar, and not the narrator, who reveals Beowulf's tainted lineage by reminding him that "gesloh þin fæder fæðe mæste; / wearþ he Heaþolafe to handbonan / mid Wilfingum" [by fighting, your father brought about the greatest feud. He became the hand-slayer of Heatholafe among the Wilfings].[39] The poet regularly draws attention to this history by referring to Beowulf as "bearn Ecgþeowes" [Ecgtheow's son], and yet Gunnarson does not treat Beowulf's lineage as a significant part of his character.[40] With Selma, Gunnarson replaces the poem's reminders of Beowulf's parentage with reminders of Grendel's. In doing so, he renders the hero's history opaque while rendering the monster's history sympathetic. By drawing attention to Grendel's childhood in this way, Gunnarson invites us to read the parallels in Grendel's son's relationships with his own family. Grendel is the only character Gunnarson portrays as having once had an idyllic life, but the recollection of this lost innocence is what drives him to attack the Danes. Grendel's son does not have such memories, and yet Selma and Beowulf both recognize that the child might also become a "destroyer" in response to his own childhood trauma.

Both *Beowulf* and *Beowulf and Grendel* are at their most ambiguous when they demand a moral response from their audiences. We are never sure whether we ought to judge the characters as pagans or as Christians. Nor are we completely sure of the extent of Beowulf's monstrous strength, the moral rectitude of the Danes, the relationship between their society and their outcasts, or how many generations of men and monsters will suffer from a history of violent feuds. For Gunnarson, these uncertainties invite meditation on the relationship between the truth and its telling. *Beowulf and Grendel* begins with a narration that evokes the opening of the poem, framing the old text as one of many possible interpretations:

> Hwæt! Great are the tales of the Spear-Danes
> How they broke and bloodied their foes
> How they tamed the Northern seas.
> Some tales sail, others sink
> Below the waves, but no less true...

The film thus invites a direct comparison against the poem, which it presents as an aggrandized rendition of the plot composed throughout the film by Thorkel, a warrior-*scop* in Beowulf's company. Although Beowulf and his company come to Heorot to rid Hrothgar of the "troll" who torments him and kills his men, Grendel shies away from battle against those who have done him no wrong.[41] For most of the film, Beowulf's role is reduced to that of an investigating detective. As a *scop*, it is Thorkel's role to employ his power of speech to render his lord heroic.

The viewer's first introduction to Grendel is as a playful child forced to witness his father's murder and who only escapes death himself on account of Hrothgar's mercy. Formally, Gunnarson gives us a clear sense of Grendel's identity from the film's very first scene, in which the poem's *sceadugenga* [shadow-walker] is introduced to us in full daylight.[42] The high angle of the shot of Hrothgar as he decides to spare Grendel evokes a sense of pity. Gunnarson then shows Grendel reclaiming his father's body from the bottom of a cliff, and placing its head on a pedestal in his lair. Later, the high angle shots, as Grendel is shown stalking about the bluffs around Heorot alone, imbue him with a sense of loneliness rather than dread, and the tracking shots of Grendel running across the landscape give his movement a sense of purpose. Gunnarson's Grendel does not *scryð* [stride] as he travels across the landscape, but bounces and rolls with childish glee.[43] Throughout the film, we watch Grendel take pleasure in his own power. When Grendel attacks the guards at Heorot, he kills them with a mischievous grin on his face, and there is a certain boyish charm in Grendel's decision to annoy the Geats on their first night in Heorot by urinating on the threshold. In a later scene, we watch as he plays a game of bowls with some rocks and the skulls of some of the Danes he has defeated. These moments suggest Grendel is impulsive, an assessment made explicit in the flashback where he has sex with Selma, and yet he does not seem to have a sense of fear, nor does he know his own limits. Although Grendel clearly has sufficient fortitude to survive on his own, his easy confidence suggests he is permanently childlike, a creature of impulse rather than one of thought.

When Grendel appears alongside normal people, he is shot in such a way as to visually establish his physical superiority. In the rare scenes where he interacts with others as equals, he is shot from a wide angle so that both parties are on the same plane. Whenever Grendel approaches the hall, he is shot at a tight angle in order that the focus is kept on the monster rather than his prey. And when he interacts with Beowulf, Grendel is shot from a low angle, which makes him tower above the hero and implies his superiority. Likewise, because Beowulf is shot from a high angle in these scenes, his minimized stature becomes an indication that he is a reactive hero. The wide angle shots by the hall tend to show men in a similar state of aloneness, but the fog limits the scenery, portraying them objectively. Furthermore, there is very little movement of the camera in these shots, implying that the Danes are static, while shots of Grendel alone involve movement and cuts that provide the viewer with a sense of motion and activity. Gunnarson uses close-ups of Grendel when he is near the hall to focus the action on the terrorist rather than the terrorized. It is not until the morning after any given attack that we are shown the effects of Grendel's violence, which often seems justified when the victims are removed from the frame. Although Beowulf works to defend Danish society, it is evident that he is cast as being secondary to the monster he has come to challenge. Gunnarson thus guides us in our viewing by making us *look up* to Grendel just as we *look down* on Beowulf.

As Beowulf learns more about Grendel's history and attitudes in his conversations with Hrothgar and with Selma, he comes to the realization that Grendel is an aggrieved party who pursues his feud with directed bloodshed rather than with random violence. Beowulf is faced with a moral dilemma as he learns that he has unwillingly become an agent whose duty requires him to pursue an unjust feud. Night after night Beowulf awaits Grendel in Heorot, but Grendel refuses to fight him. After learning that Selma can translate for Grendel, Beowulf asks her why he will not fight him. Selma's laconic response is "Why should he? You've done nothing to him." This conversation forces Beowulf to aggressively seek battle with the "troll" who seems to be interested in pursuing his feud only against Danish warriors, refusing to harm women, children, or old men, including Hrothgar.

As Beowulf gains insight into Grendel's motivation, he comes to regret the apparent inevitability of bloodshed. Shortly after he and his troops find Grendel's cave and Hondscioh defiles the severed head of Grendel's father—the relic that is the focus of a small shrine in Grendel's cave—Beowulf again implores Selma to find him a way out of violence when he tells her that "he needs to know; I know he was wronged. But if he doesn't leave here I can't stop [his death]." That night, Grendel attacks the Geats in Heorot in order to take revenge on Hondscioh. Beowulf is forced to defend his company, and Grendel escapes with a mortal wound.

The following night, Grendel's mother comes to take revenge for her son. However, her very presence complicates Grendel even further. In the poem, Grendel is a character often described as one who approaches humanity with an air of ire or malice.[44] Yet as we have seen, Gunnarson does not portray him so. These emotions are reserved for his mother, a screeching, gigantic hag, complete with leathery skin and pointed teeth. Grendel's mother is depicted almost exactly as the poem portrays her: a force of nature entirely without the power of speech, uncontainable, and comprehensible largely in terms of her biological function.[45] Although any viewer familiar with the poem is bound to expect her arrival, we have been made to think about Grendel and his relationship with his father (and so little about even the presence of his mother) for so long that her appearance comes as something of a surprise.

In showing us his father, mother, lover, and son, Gunnarson turns Grendel into a freak with a family: a participant in a social structure whose successive generations are as decreasingly monstrous in appearance as they are increasingly capable of communication. Grendel and his father clearly share a bond, but the only time we see Grendel with his mother is as a corpse. The question of Grendel's relationship with his mother is as open as the question of the relationship between his parents. Grendel's mother's cave contains a hoard of treasure, so why does Grendel live alone in the cliffs? It is unlikely that this question can be explained through Grendel's inability to swim because he might well have inherited his mother's ability to breathe underwater. Considering the apparently estranged relationship between Grendel and his mother, why does she take revenge on the Danes rather than on Selma, who lived under his protection and bore him a son? And why does Grendel's son live with his grandmother instead of with either of his own parents? Does Grendel even *have* a relationship with his son? Considering his veneration of his father's relics it would be uncharacteristic of him not to. Why did Selma not tell Beowulf about Grendel's mother? And can we really treat Grendel as a human if his mother is so monstrous (or so freakish)? Grendel's father and Grendel's childhood produce a series of deeply problematic questions about the relationship between monstrosity and family.

It seems as though Gunnarson wants us to imagine Grendel as neither a monster nor a freak, but as a human. The morning after Beowulf's combat with him, one of the Geats suggests that Grendel may be in the process of re-growing his arm, since trolls are known to regenerate limbs, just like some kinds of worms are known to do. Beowulf expresses doubt at this postulation when he responds by saying, "This thing's no more a worm than you or I." Here, after Grendel has been defeated, Bewoulf realizes they are alike. Shortly afterwards, he learns that Selma mourns him. Selma tells Beowulf how Grendel slept with her right before she makes a pass at Beowulf. In Selma's bed, hero and monster are indistinguishable. After killing Grendel's mother, Beowulf visits Selma one last time. Knowing that Beowulf has been told of Hrothgar's mercy towards Grendel in the past, Selma chastises him for his ignorant treatment of Grendel's child in the sea-cave when she says, "Hrothgar taught you nothing." Beowulf chooses to spare Grendel's child, but we are not sure why. Perhaps he did not want the fight, or perhaps he saw something of himself in the small boy wielding a very large sword, or perhaps he saw Selma in his red hair. Selma's remarks emphasize that the child might pose a threat, Beowulf builds a cairn to Grendel on the seashore before he sails away. The film ends much as it began, with a monster and his parent standing side-by-side on the landscape.

Gunnarson's adaptation of both Beowulf and Grendel reverses their portrayal in the poem. However, there is something intrinsically human about all the poem's monsters. Andy Orchard has shown that despite their clear antagonism towards the world of men, *Beowulf*'s monsters are more than merely "the pure perversion of the will," they are also motivated by comprehensible (if remote) conditions and emotions: Grendel is an exile, his mother is driven by vengeance, and the dragon is chasing a thief.[46] This anthropomorphism allows the poet to ascribe human reactions to the monsters. Moreover, Orchard explains that Beowulf himself has monstrous attributes: he "fights monsters because only then is he well-matched. When he does face human champions, like the Frankish Dæghrefn, his methods are distinctly inhuman, one might almost say monstrous."[47] Grendel's mother and the dragon are reactionary, and merely act in retaliation to wrongs done to them, but Grendel himself is the least reactionary of the monsters, and moreover the one most consistently depicted in human terms, such as when the poet describes him as one who "earmsceapen/ on weres wæstmum wræclastas træd" [wretchedly trod on the paths of exile in the form of a man].[48] In attributing moral superiority to Grendel rather than to Beowulf, Gunnarson transforms the monster into an object of sympathy.

My point is that despite its additions and deviations, *Beowulf and Grendel* is an effective reading of the poem. As with other adaptations of literary works, the change in medium requires a change in plot. Gunnarson employs the suggestive liminality of children to keep intact the moral ambiguity of his source. This ambiguity is partly soteriological, as we can see in the poet's evocation of Christian mythology in order to cover up for pagan beliefs and practices. It is also epistemological, as we can see in the poet's description of man as monstrous and of monster as man. In *Beowulf*, Grendel is introduced as an unambiguously monstrous creature: *caines cynne*. *Beowulf and Grendel* concludes with Thorkel imposing this appellation in retrospect. As the Geats sail away from Daneland, Thorkel composes the following lines:

> Born of scum and swampy things,
> Lurking in his mother's moss;
> The mark of Cain came to his brow,
> Of evil and a sea-hag born.
> Grendel: grinder of lost men's bones,
> Felt hate towards the happy Danes.

Listening to the tale, one of the Geats asks Breca (Rory McCann) about the relationship between Cain and Grendel, to which Breca responds, "I think Thorkel's saying that Grendel's like Cain: a killer." The first Geat dismisses Breca's interpretation, stating simply, "We all are."

The exchange above suggests that if *Beowulf* is about the monsters,

Beowulf and Grendel is about monstrosity. Nowhere is this more evident than in the film's treatment of children. Grendel's monstrosity is to some extent intrinsic, in the sense that his freakishness disturbs us, but he acts the part of the monster as a result of his childhood trauma. The potential monstrosity of Grendel's son becomes uncertain when Beowulf builds the cairn to honor his fallen enemy. Children are pliable creatures, whose future outcomes are unpredictable. In this sense, children possess a latent potential that manifests itself largely as they develop into adults. Gunnarson develops Grendel's character by situating him within a network of (fraught) familial relationships His son therefore becomes the character who may finally escape the cycle of exile and bloodshed that dominates the film. As Beowulf and his company sail away from Daneland, the boy's fate is left as an open question. By his parentage, Grendel's son is half-monster and half-human. In his challenge to Beowulf in his grandmother's lair, we see that he is also brave enough to become a hero. The child's brief interaction with Beowulf may well have put the feud to rest. We will never know whether prejudice, bad luck, or fate will influence Grendel's son to become a monster like his father, or whether he will defend the weak against the depredations of the strong as Grendel did for his mother. Grendel's son's silence prevents him from expressing his intentions, but the audience has learned that like Grendel, past wrongs can be laid to rest. At the close of the film, we see a mother and child standing on the coast looking out to the sea, the Danes freed to think beyond the imminent collapse of their civilization, and the Geats sailing eagerly home. Gunnarson invites the audience to join these characters in imagining the future, and we do so because we concede to Grendel's son the choice to pursue his monstrous potential.

Notes

1. Linda Hutcheon, *A Theory of Adaptation* (London: Routledge, 2006), 7.
2. Hutcheon, 3.
3. Marijane Osborn, "Translations, Versions, Illustrations," in *A Beowulf Handbook*, eds. Robert E. Bjork and John D. Niles (Lincoln: University of Nebraska Press, 1977), 343.
4. Hutcheon, 355.
5. Michael Usulan, *Beowulf: Dragon Slayer* (New York: DC Comics, 1975–76).
6. *Beowulf*. Dir. Robert Zemeckis (Paramount, 2007); *Beowulf and Grendel*. Dir. Sturla Gunnarson (Equinoxe, 2005).
7. All references to line numbers and all citations refer to Fulk, Bjork, and Niles, *Klaeber's Beowulf, Fourth Edition* (Toronto: University of Toronto Press, 2008), line 1355. Translations are my own unless otherwise noted.
8. William F Hodapp, "'No hie fæder cunnon': But Twenty-First Century Filmmakers Do," *Essays in Medieval Studies* 26 (2010): 101.
9. E.L. Risden, "The Cinematic Sexualizing of Beowulf," *Essays in Medieval Studies* 26 (2010): 109.

10. Laurence N. De Looze, "Frame Narrative and Fictionalization: Beowulf as Narrator," in *Interpretations of Beowulf: A Critical Anthology*, ed. R.D. Fulk. (Bloomington: Indiana University Press, 1991), 242.

11. De Looze, 248. Cf. *Beowulf*, 2444–59.

12. *Beowulf*, 499–528.

13. Alexandra Hennesey Olsen, "Gender Roles," in *A Beowulf Handbook*, eds. Robert E. Bjork and John D. Niles (Lincoln: University of Nebraska Press, 1977), 314.

14. Shari Horner, "Voices from the Margins: Woman and Textual Enclosure in Beowulf," in *The Postmodern Beowulf: A Critical Casebook*, eds. Eileen A. Joy, Mary K. Ramsay, and Bruce D. Gilchrist (Morgantown: West Virginia University Press, 2006), 468.

15. Cf. Risden, 112.

16. Jeffrey Jerome Cohen, "Monster Culture (Seven Theses)," in *Monster Theory: Reading Culture*, ed. Jeffrey Jerome Cohen (Minneapolis: University of Minnesota Press, 1996); 3–25.

17. Cohen, *Of Giants* (Minneapolis: University of Minnesota Press, 1999): 1–28.

18. Caroline Joan S. Picart and John Edgar Browning, eds., *Speaking of Monsters: A Teratological Anthology* (New York: Palgrave Macmillan, 2012), 1.

19. I draw my definition here from the *Oxford English Dictionary*, def. 2: "A person, animal or plant with an unusual physical abnormality."

20. Philippe Ariès, *Centuries of Childhood: A Social History of Family Life* (New York: Vintage, 1962); Nicholas Orme, *Medieval Children* (New Haven: Yale University Press, 2001). Sadly, Orme's contribution to this debate is not as well-known as Ariès's. Orme draws his evidence from primers, journals, coroners' records, and clothing (especially shoes).

21. J.R.R. Tolkien, "Beowulf: The Monsters and the Critics," *Proceedings of the British Academy* (1936): 245–95. (Reprinted in Fulk, ed., *Interpretations of Beowulf*, 14–44, 24.)

22 Kuo-Jung Chen, "The Untold Stories of Beowulf: Cinematic Renditions and Textual Interpretations," *Tamking Review* 41.1 (2010): 124–25.

23. *Beowulf*, 181b. *Wyrd* is a very strong theme within the poem, and is referred to in lines 455, 477, 572, 734, 1056, 1205, 1233, 2420, 2526, 2574, 2814, and 3030. See Bertha S. Phillpotts, "Wyrd and Providence in Anglo-Saxon Thought," *Essays and Studies* 13 (1928): 7–27 (Reprinted in Fulk, ed., *Interpretations of Beowulf*, 1–13, for a reading of *wyrd* as representative of pagan attitudes.)

24. Paul Taylor, "Heorot, Earth, and Asgard: Christian Poetry and Pagan Myth," *Tennessee Studies in Literature* 11 (1966), 128, and Ruth Waterhouse, "*Beowulf* as Palimpsest," in *Monster Theory*, ed. Jeffrey Jerome Cohen (Minnesota: University of Minneapolis Press, 1996), 26.

25. *Beowulf*, 107, 164b, 711b, 786b, 792a, 811b.

26. *Beowulf*, 1688b-93.

27. Mary A. Parker, *Beowulf and Christianity* (New York: Peter Lang, 1987), 94.

28. Parker, 87.

29. Katherine O'Brien O'Keeffe, "Beowulf, Lines 702b-836: Transformations and. the Limits of the Human," *Texas Studies in Language and Literature* 23 (1981): 484–85.

30. Andy Orchard, *Pride and Prodigies: Studies in the Monsters of the* Beowulf-*Manuscript* (Toronto: University of Toronto Press, 1995), 30.

31. Gabe Christian Foreman, "The Shape of the Unspoken," *Egotistics* 1.1 (2000), http://www.bama.ua.edu/~ego/vol11/11foreman.htm.

32. By contrast, Zemeckis's Grendel is definitively childlike: impulsive, whiny, and utterly beholden to his mother. This depiction is fitting for a film so deeply concerned with questions of parentage. Gunnarson is more interested in interrogating the consequences of mercy. The possible monstrosity of Grendel's child is, of course, an open question, and one that the child's voice is never used to resolve. It is attractive to imagine this unresolved question stands as such in part because the child is not demonstrably a killer.

33. Orchard, 37.

34. John D. Niles, *Beowulf: The Poem and Its Tradition* (Cambridge: Harvard University Press, 1983), 21–22.

35. Responsibility is central also to Zemeckis's adaptation, where the rulers of Heorot find themselves unable to resist the sexual allure of Grendel's mother, and equally unable to acknowledge the destructive return of their own monstrous progeny.

36. O'Keefe, 491.

37. Niles, 20–21.

38. *Beowulf*, 108b.

39. Foreman. Cf. *Beowulf*, 459–61a.

40. *Beowulf*, 529b.

41. Gunnarson's reimagining of Grendel as a "troll" is not unprecedented. As Liuzza notes in his translation, one possible interpretation of Beowulf's description of Grendel as possessing some kind of glove or pouch hanging from his belt ("Glog hangode," line 2085) is that he is casting Grendel as a troll (116n2). Cf. Seth Lerer, "Grendel's Glove," *ELH* 61.4 (1994), 721–51.

42. *Beowulf*, 703a.

43. *Beowulf*, 703a.

44. Orchard, 36.

45. Cf. Horner 482–84.

46. Orchard, 29–30.

47. Orchard, 32–33.

48. *Beowulf*, 1351b-52a.

Bringing Out Henry James's Little Monsters

Two Film Approaches to The Turn of the Screw

FREDRIK TYDAL

The most recent Penguin UK edition of Henry James's 1898 novella *The Turn of the Screw* uses as its cover art John Singer Sargent's *Edouard and Marie-Louise Pailleron* (1881). The painting features two children, looking at the artist in a way that may be described as detached and intense at the same time—creating a vaguely disturbing impression. In this context, then, the children in the painting are made to serve as visual representations of Flora and Miles, the two siblings of James's story, whom the reader may experience as similarly unsettling.

As a paratextual element that shapes reader reception, the cover illustration not only suggests that Flora and Miles are central characters in the story, but in using Singer Sargent's distinctly eerie painting, it also links the two children to the sense of gothic dread that fairly emanates from the work. Today, when children and horror are routinely connected in popular culture, the choice of cover art seems virtually a given, capturing as it does what the contemporary moment would find gripping about the story. At the same time, however, it is easy to forget that the two children in *The Turn of the Screw* have not always been granted such prominence. In fact, their presence and role in the story have long been overshadowed not only by the more overt horror represented by the two ghosts, but also by the main character of the novella: the narrating governess figure, whose reliability critics have debated endlessly.

In the following, I want to explore how the ability of James's children to shock and terrify has largely been brought out by cinematic engagements with the story. Specifically, I will look at two film approaches to the novella, both produced in England and separated only by a decade: Jack Clayton's 1961 adaptation *The Innocents* (starring Deborah Kerr) and Michael Winner's 1971 prequel *The Nightcomers* (starring Marlon Brando), which takes place before the events of James's original story. Together, as I will show, these two films could not only be seen as instrumental in bringing about the shift in critical and popular focus towards the children of the novella, but may in this sense also have a part in consolidating the figure of the monstrous child that would go on to become so prevalent in 1970s cinema.

The Location of Monstrosity

The Turn of the Screw is a horror story without a clearly identifiable monster; what frightens, rather, is the monstrous. Put differently, for while there is no abominable creature roaming the halls of the grand old estate in which James's story is set, the horror and dread which we would normally associate with such a thing is unmistakably present, suffusing almost every page of the narrative. This is even reflected at the level of lexical choice, for while the adjective "monstrous" is used six times in the story, its root noun "monster" never appears in the text once. This curious presence-absence would seem to align James with a conception of monstrosity as culturally produced rather than inherent and corporeal. As Jeffrey Jerome Cohen has pointed out, the word monster is derived from the Latin *monstrum*: that which shows or reveals, even warns. In this light, monsters—and by extension the monstrous—could be said to function as the screen on which the fears and anxieties of a certain time and place may be projected. Monsters are thus culturally and historically contingent, and from this follows that they are also elusive; Cohen muses that the monster always escapes. "We see the damage that the monster wreaks," he writes, "but the monster itself turns immaterial and vanishes."[1] In *The Turn of the Screw*, then, the monster is so elusive that it never appears in unequivocal form; what we get, rather, is a profound sense of the monstrous. This displacement of monstrosity is crucial to the story's enduring power, providing the basis for its defining mode of ambiguity. In effect, it sends the reader searching, in what might well be characterized as a monster mystery—or even a monster *hunt*. Something frightens us in the story, but what exactly?

At the time of its original publication and throughout the first decades of criticism, the monstrous in *The Turn of the Screw* was predominantly associated with the two ghosts of the story: Peter Quint and Miss Jessel, the former staff members. This is of course unsurprising, given that the idea of the undead have served as a repository for popular and folkloric horror down the centuries. More substantially, however, it is worth pointing out that the cultural understanding of ghosts bears a certain relation to the etymological roots of the monstrous: throughout history, ghosts have of course been viewed as harbingers, as that which shows and indeed warns. And in their obscure sexual relations, which is what seems to doom them, Quint and Miss Jessel also give us the dangerous connection between *eros* and *thanatos*, which had at the time recently frightened late–Victorian audiences in Bram Stoker's *Dracula* (1896). On the whole, then, it is almost as if contemporary readers were predisposed to receive their chills from the accursed revenant lovers.

In the 1930s, however, the monstrous began to be located elsewhere, as the great literary critic Edmund Wilson brought to widespread attention the idea that what is really frightening about the story is in fact the governess. Basically, Wilson argued that that *The Turn of the Screw* is psychological rather than supernatural in nature: the ghosts do not exist, but are rather figments of the governess' imagination. Wilson's argument is Freudian in nature: "the story is a neurotic case of sex repression," he writes, suggesting that the young woman's obsession with the two ghostly lovers stems from her own sexual self-denial.[2] Put simply, it is all in her head: "there is never any reason for supposing that anybody but the governess sees the ghosts," he asserts, after marshaling a series of symbols and imagery as evidence.[3] As Wilson confidently concludes: "When one has once got hold of the clue to this meaning of *The Turn of the Screw*, one wonders how one could ever have missed it."[4] By his own admission, Wilson was not the first to make this claim; however, due to his position as one of the leading literary critics of his generation, the article had an impact that exceeded anything that had gone before it. In time, there were attempts to refute the thesis, and soon, battle lines were drawn: either the governess was accepted as a perfectly reliable narrator committed to the well-being of her charges or, conversely, viewed as an unstable neurotic who in fact constitutes the real threat to the children. As a result, two distinct camps appeared: the *apparitionist* and the *non-apparitionist*, as they have come to be known in James scholarship; the former, as should be clear, hold that the ghosts do exist, while the latter contend that they are merely products of the governess's imagination.

As I have already indicated, the debate sparked by Wilson's essay was implicitly also a debate about the location of monstrosity. For while the apparitionists saw the ghosts as for all intents and purposes being real, constituting monstrous forces from which the children must be saved, many of the non-apparitionist critics came to view the governess as the actual monster of the story, in the sense of causing the children direct harm and actually bringing about Miles's death.[5]

Compelling as the debate was, it also had a limiting effect. On both sides of the divide, critics were fairly obsessed with the governess, trying either to indict or defend her, with the result that other elements of the story were often left unconsidered. In Wilson's own words, "the story is primarily intended as a characterization of the governess," and in his reading, the children become little more than the victims of her neurosis.[6] To the extent that their behavior is odd or abnormal, Wilson suggests it is because they, along with Mrs. Grose, are actually afraid of the governess. As he writes: "The housekeeper insists that she does not see [the ghosts]; it is apparently the governess who frightens her. The children too become hysterical, but this is evidently the governess' doing."[7]

In its emphasis on the governess's psychological state, then, Wilson's essay and the long-standing debate it generated effectively drew attention away from the children of the story. The two films in my study, I propose, could both be seen as redressing this imbalance, by giving the children a focus they had largely not been afforded before. But it is not merely a question of expanding their roles; rather, and more substantially, both *The Innocents* and *The Nightcomers* may also be seen as engaging with the critical history of the novella. As I have already shown, the central question posed by *The Turn of the Screw* concerns the nature of what frightens the reader, and as I have also outlined, early critics identified the ghosts with the monstrous, while Wilson and his followers came to view the governess as that which truly terrifies in the story. Placed in this context, then, the two films continue this trajectory, by offering a new interpretation of the nature of the monstrous in the story: the children.

While the identification of the children with the monstrous might be seen as speculative or played out for shock value, the idea does have a certain support in James's original story. *The Turn of the Screw* begins with an intricate and sometimes neglected prologue, in which a group of friends sit around a fire sharing ghost stories. After one particularly spine-tingling tale, involving a young boy awakened by an apparition, the friends agree that ghost stories where children play a prominent part are the most chilling; the presence of little ones in the face of the spectral, as it is put, provides "another turn of the screw." Much to the delight of everyone present, one of the men in the party announces that he also knows a story falling under this category. What is more, not only is the story allegedly true, but it also has the added attraction of involving *two* children—giving "two turns" to that same screw. The story the man proceeds to tell then becomes the story we are reading, as the governess proceeds to take up her position at Bly House.

While the prologue does not necessarily attribute monstrous agency to the children, it does suggest that their role in the story is central to the reader's experience of horror. As I will show, both films not only pick up on this idea, but also take it further. In this sense, I view the films as not only adaptations, but also as forms of interpretation, and—by extension—interventions into a critical debate.

The Ambiguity of Innocence

When Jack Clayton set to adapt *The Turn of the Screw* for the cinema, he was very much aware of the critical debate surrounding the work.[8] Thus, it comes as no surprise that the film pays tribute to both the apparitionist and non-apparitionist perspectives. In doing so, it also encourages viewers to locate the monstrous with either the ghosts or the governess: on the one hand, we see the intimidating figures of Quint and Jessel on the screen before us, but on the other, we also observe the governess acting in ways that seem both unstable and menacing. However, as I have already indicated, the film does not merely reflect then-current scholarship (by allowing for these two interpretations); rather, it contributes to the critical debate as well by inviting the audience to also locate the monstrous with the children.

Clayton's first interpretative act is using *The Innocents* as the title of his adaptation. In making that choice, he achieves two things. First, of course, he foregrounds the role of the children. But second and more importantly, he also invites the viewers to reflect on the children's innocence and to compare their behavior in the film against the epithet conferred on them by the paratextual title. As we shall see, this produces a certain juxtapositional irony, when the children start acting in ways that are far from innocent. For in examining the differences between novella and film, it becomes clear that most of the new additions concern the children—and, specifically, the question of their innocence.

One of the most significant yet least acknowledged differences between *The Innocents* and James's original story pertains to the relationship between narrative chronology and dramatic effect. In *The Turn of the Screw*, the governess begins to observe that the children are acting strangely only after she has witnessed the ghosts, suggesting that her view of Flora and Miles is influenced by what she has or thinks she has seen. But in Clayton's film, the children's possible malevolence is introduced as a thematic issue before the appearance of the ghosts and thus before any doubts about the governess's sanity have been raised.

The first example of this shift in narrative chronology is found already on the evening of the governess's arrival to Bly. While saying her prayers before going to bed, Flora makes a slip: "If I should wake before I ..." she starts to recite, before correcting herself and putting it in the right order ("If I should die before I wake, I pray the Lord my soul to take"). But what Flora was about to say—"If I should wake before I die"—is not actually nonsensical; rather, it suggests the wakeful dead. This suspicion is confirmed by the exchange that follows between Flora and the governess—or Miss Giddens, as she is named in the film.

> FLORA: Miss Giddens, where would the Lord take my soul to?
> MISS GIDDENS: To heaven.
> FLORA: Are you certain?
> MISS GIDDENS: Yes, of course, because you are a very, very good girl.
> FLORA: But I might not be. And if I weren't, wouldn't the Lord just leave me here to walk around? Isn't that what happens to some people?

Later, in the night, Flora rises from her bed and, in a by-now classic horror trope, proceeds to watch the governess as she sleeps. From her tossing and turning as well as her sighing and whimpering, it is clear that the governess is not experiencing peaceful dreams—a fact which, sinisterly, makes Flora smile. Then, the girl moves to the window, and from there apparently watches for something or someone in the garden, while humming the vaguely eerie song "O Willow Waley," as if a mystical summons.

At this point in the film, the viewer has little reason to believe that anything is afoul at Bly, since no ghosts have yet appeared. So, while Flora's behavior would from a broader critical perspective seem to endorse the apparitionist view, she simply appears as creepy in the context of the unfolding narrative. In other words, we are introduced to the idea of the potentially monstrous children *before* the idea of the potentially insane governess. In the following scene, taking place the next day, the letter announcing Miles's expulsion from school arrives, in which the boy is described as being "an injury to the others." Coupled with Flora's behavior during the night, the viewer is led to assume that there is something wrong with these children—again, before any doubts have even been raised about the reliability of the governess.

Now, from a non-apparitionist perspective, it might be argued that this is just a ruse on the part of Clayton—that he is deliberately using the children as a red herring, so as to keep us from immediately seeing the real monster of the story: i.e., the mad governess. However, the persistence with which the film focuses on the children suggests something else. Consider, for example, another scene not present in the novella: when Miles surprises the governess in the attic during a game of hide-and-seek. While the governess is kneeling on the floor, examining a photograph, Miles suddenly jumps at her from behind, throwing his arms around her neck. The following exchange occurs:

> MILES: Now you're my prisoner!
> MISS GIDDENS: Oh, Miles, let me go …
> MILES: Why?!
> MISS GIDDENS: You're hurting me.
> MILES: Am I?
> MISS GIDDENS: Yes, Miles, please let me go.
> MILES: Why?!
> MISS GIDDENS: I told you: you're hurting me. Now, Miles, I mean it!
> MILES: Do you?

At this point, Flora enters the attic, and Miles loosens his grip. Granted, the scene is open for interpretation: on the one hand, it is late in the evening and they have been playing, so Miles may simply be laden with excess energy. But on the other hand, there is also something stubborn and almost programmatic about Miles's behavior, which suggests possession. This impression is reinforced by a later scene, in which the children dress up and put on a small performance for the governess and Mrs. Grose. As part of this, Miles recites a poem he has composed:

> What shall I sing to my lord from my window?
> What shall I sing, for my lord will not stay?
> What shall I sing, for my lord will not listen?
> Where shall I go, for my lord is away?
> Whom shall I love when the moon is arisen?
> Gone is my lord, and the grave is his prison.
> What shall I say when my lord comes a-calling?
> What shall I say when he knocks on my door?
> What shall I say when his feet enter softly,
> Leaving the marks of his grave on my floor?
> Enter my lord, come from your prison.
> Come from your grave, for the moon is arisen.

The poem is so explicit as almost not to require any commentary. In essence, it puts words to the governess's deepest fears, namely that Miles remains Peter Quint's disciple even after the latter's death. After the recital, the boy gives the governess a long, unsettling stare. In the novella, the governess feels as if she is "fighting with a demon for a human soul"; in the film, then, Miles seems to be confirming this impression through his recital.[9]

From these examples, we can see the film is more interested in exploring the apparitionist issue through the behavior of the children rather than through the psychological state of the governess. Put simply, the question asked by the film is not so much whether the governess is mad or not, but rather if the children are, in fact, little monsters—and not only in the colloquial sense of the term. This idea is brought to the fore by the governess's ironic reference to the children as innocents, in a key scene with Mrs. Grose. Having given her a sense of what life was like at Bly before the governess's time, Mrs. Grose goes on to assure her that the children cannot possibly have been corrupted by Quint and Miss Jessel. "Master Miles is a good boy," Mrs. Grose almost pleads with her, "there's nothing wicked in him." To this, the governess retorts: "Unless he's deceiving us; unless they're both deceiving us," after which she stops for a second, to then carefully articulate: "The innocents..."

The delivery of the line is striking: it is as if the governess realizes the irony of what she is saying at the moment she speaks it. Standing out due to its invocation of the film's title, the comment goes to the very heart of the difference between the novella and Clayton's adaptation, namely how it shifts the weight of titillating ambiguity from the insanity of the governess to the monstrosity of the children. In doing so, *The Innocents* also opens up a site of potential horror that was indeed present in the original tale, but which had been obscured by the polarization of the critical debate: the secret world of childhood.

In his preface to *Émile, or Treatise on Education* (1762), Jean-Jacques Rousseau reflected on how childhood is something fundamentally mysterious and inaccessible to the adult world: "We know nothing of childhood," he writes, "and with our mistaken notions the further we advance the further we go astray."[10] *The Innocents* could be seen to dramatize this idea through scenes that have no equivalent in the novella, but which nonetheless carry its spirit. In a conversation with the children, the governess comments on how large the house is. This prompts Miles to inquire about her own family home: "Your house, where you used to live, was that a big house too?" When she answers that it was actually very small, Miles follows up with another query: "Too small for you to have secrets?" At this moment, without the governess noticing, the two children give each other a knowing look. Without grasping the subtext, which the viewer is made to discern, the governess notes: "Secrets require a privacy that our little house did not provide." In other words and by implication, the spacious estate of Bly allows the children to maintain their world of secrets to which the adults are not privy. Later in the film, the governess will show her horror at this notion: "They are both playing, or are being made to play, some monstrous game," she comments to Mrs. Grose. "I can't pretend to understand what its purpose is; I only know that it is happening—something secretive and whispery ... and indecent." Having grown up in a small house, the governess cannot imagine such privacy as the children enjoy, and is therefore frightened of what it may at once contain and conceal. From a non-apparitionist perspective, of course, it could be said that the governess is simply projecting her own anxieties about "indecency" onto that fearful space of privacy. But what if her fears are right? We have, after all, seen the children behaving in ways that are more than a little disturbing to the viewer.

Later, while walking to church with Mrs. Grose, the governess expands on her fears: "they are not living with us," she comments, "we have no part in their real life." But where are the children living, if not with her and Mrs. Grose? As the governess goes on to imply, they are living in the spirit world: "Look at them," she says, and points to Flora and Miles who are walking ahead of them. "What do you think they are saying? They're talking about *them* [Quint and Miss Jessel], talking horrors." Yet what frightens her could just as well be that mysterious world of childhood, which she, like Rousseau, knows very little of. In fact, regardless of whether we subscribe to the apparitionist or non-apparitionist perspective, the idea speaks to that added element of horror that *The Innocents* extracts from James's novella: the horror of not knowing whether that secret world of childhood could serve as a breeding ground for the monstrous.

This epistemological anxiety, inherent in James's text and brought to the fore by Clayton's adaptation, may be further understood with reference to Eve Kosofsky Sedgwick, who has taken note of the "definitional binarisms" that shape and structure Western thinking.[11] Enumerating a series of such opposites (including secrecy/disclosure, private/public, innocence/initiation, health/illness, cognition/paranoia), she argues that the understanding of these categories as mutually exclusive has left a space of ambiguity in between them. This space, she suggests, has the potential to "represent[ ] the hidden, perhaps dangerous truths about a culture to itself."[12]

It is this space, then, that James mines, and which Clayton continues to work with in his film. For in both the novella and its adaptation, the appearance and behavior of Flora and Miles oscillate between child-like/childish and adult-like, between angelic and monstrous, between innocent and corrupted. In this light, the critical polarization surrounding the original novella may be seen as symptomatic of an inability to confront these in-between spaces in the story. For as the critics deadlocked around the issue of the governess's sanity, the binary thinking which underpinned the debate must also have carried over to the view of the work as a whole. In fact, there is something conspicuous about the staunchly diametrical nature of the debate: the governess is either sane or mad, and cannot be anything in between. Of course, Edmund Wilson recognized ambiguity as the guiding principle of the novella, but even so, he still seemed unwilling to engage with these indeterminate spaces, being so intent on proving the governess's insanity—even revising his essay over the years as he found new evidence to prove his point. Wilson, we may say, was more interested in resolving the ambiguity of the text, rather than exploring its strange spaces. So too were the critics who followed him. As Edward J. Parkinson has shown in his exhaustive study of the novella's critical history, it was not until the 1950s that anything resembling a synthesis between the apparitionist and non-apparitionist perspectives began to emerge—so entrenched, in other words, were the definitional binarisms in the critical mindset.[13] What hidden, perhaps dangerous truths were lurking in these spaces, that made the critics hesitant to approach them?

Ten years later, another director would return to the strange spaces of James's novella. But unlike *The Innocents*, which explored these spaces with both care and refinement, the resulting film would dive headfirst into them—to brutal, but also enlightening, effect.

From Innocence to Savagery

Michael Winner's *The Nightcomers* (1971) is one of those films that may strike the viewer as more interesting than necessarily enjoyable: an artifact of its time, whose main draw—aside from seeing Marlon Brando in his pre-*Godfather* career slump—rests on the sheer audacity of tampering with the fundaments of James's classic work. As a prequel, taking place before the events of the original story, the film explores the relationship between Peter Quint and Miss Jessel while they were still among the living, as well as what influence they exerted on Flora and Miles during their tenure at Bly. While the original novella and *The Innocents* describe the relationship between the valet and his lover in imprecise and euphemistic terms, *The Nightcomers* shows it to be of a sado-masochistic nature—explicitly so. This is not to imply, however, that the film is a sexploitation affair; rather, it is somewhat more complex than what it initially seems since it actually engages with both James's novella and

The Innocents in intriguing ways. So, in what follows, I will have the chance to put up a small defense for what is an often slighted film, by examining it in the context of the fictional world it seeks to extend.

As the film opens, Flora and Miles are playing an outdoors game of hide-and-seek with Quint. Although he is the one being pursued, Quint is able to outsmart the children at every turn, as he moves between hiding locations. We first see him up in the tower, and later, he successfully hides in a treetop, watching the children as they pass by underneath. In a way, the opening serves as an important piece of character continuity, reminding us of the control that Quint was said to have exerted over the children while he was alive. By implication, the character continuity also extends to Flora and Miles: while wandering around the premises looking for Quint, they appear as vulnerable—or at least at the mercy of the valet's cunning and control.

Yet the beauty is that the opening is also a kind of setup. For while the hide-and-seek sequence accurately represents the power relationship between Quint and the children suggested in the source text and *The Innocents*, the film as a whole could be said reverse this relationship. In the novella, Quint is variously described as a "creature," a "hound," and a "wretch"—on top of which "depraved" almost seems like a compliment. *The Innocents* gives much the same impression: Mrs. Grose speaks of there being "vicious things" in Quint's life, and we are made to understand that she was afraid of him. Since the premise of *The Nightcomers* is to show James's ghosts in the flesh, those familiar with the original story would rightly expect to witness a real villain, if not a monster. This, however, is not the case; for instead, *The Nightcomers* portrays Quint as a soft-spoken eccentric with a philosophical bent. Moreover, there is also a child-like quality to him, which allows him to forge a close relationship to Flora and Miles: in addition to playing hide-and-seek, he is shown entertaining the children with stories and helping them to fly a kite. If we view *The Nightcomers* in the context of the fictional world into which it inserts itself, then Quint simply appears to be misunderstood, as his supposed depravity only seems based on his unconventional yet by all accounts consensual relationship with Miss Jessel. In fact, the only time we see Quint's sadist tendencies expressed outside his affair with Miss Jessel is when he subjects a toad to a bizarre form of torture in front of the children. But this could just as well be viewed as child-like—like pulling off the legs of a spider. Contrary to expectation, then, the horror of *The Nightcomers* does not reside with Quint; rather, as the narrative unfolds, it comes to be placed with the children. This idea is built up slowly, so that the viewer is almost ambushed by its realization at the end. At its core, the reversal of expectations hinges on a subtle but crucial difference from both James's story and Clayton's adaptation.

In *The Turn of the Screw*, Quint and Miss Jessel are described as being careless and irresponsible in their relations. "Quint was much too free," Mrs. Grose comments at one point; later, she adds that he and Miss Jessel "were both infamous."[14] In *The Innocents*, this is expanded on, as the governess pressures Mrs. Grose into revealing more about the affair:

> MRS. GROSE: Miss, there's things I've seen ... I'm ashamed to say.
> MISS GIDDENS: Go on!
> MRS. GROSE: Rooms... used by daylight as though they were dark woods.
> MISS GIDDENS: They didn't care that you saw them?
> MRS. GROSE: [shakes her head]
> MISS GIDDENS: And the children?
> MRS. GROSE: I can't say miss; I don't know what the children saw.

While the novella is perhaps too vague on the issue, *The Innocents* quite clearly suggests that there was something exhibitionist about the couple. But in *The Nightcomers*, it is Miles who actively seeks out Quint and Miss Jessel as they are engaged in their nocturnal activities. At first, he is simply curious, asking Quint: "What do you do to Miss Jessel when you love her, and what does she do to you?" To this, Quint responds in a deliberately vague manner, as any responsible adult would: "We just trick around.... That's all." Apparently not satisfied with this answer, Miles later sneaks out in the middle of the night to see for himself. Peering in through Miss Jessel's window, a captivated Miles observes the two adults "tricking around" until the early morning, and later, he lets a curious Flora know all about what he saw.

Now, there is of course nothing strange in being curious about the adult world, as Miles is shown to be. However, what this change from the source text does is alter the chain of causality implicit both in James's original story and Clayton's adaptation, namely that Quint and Jessel willfully corrupted the children through their careless behavior. But in *The Nightcomers*, the situation is the exact opposite since the two adults are actually very secretive about their relations. In fact, Miss Jessel does not even allow Quint to address her by first name in public. The effect of this modification is that it makes Quint less monstrous than he is made out to be in the novella and Clayton's adaptation ("creature," "hound," "wretch"), and by implication, it forces the viewer to locate the monstrous elsewhere. This is a horror film, after all, with the expected ambiance and stylizations of the genre (eerie score, quick jump cuts, sudden close-ups, disturbing imagery). So, where is the actual horror, if not with Quint? This is where *The Nightcomers* is actually faithful to James's original story—in that it carries over that lurking sense of dread, rendered all the more powerful by the obscurity of its source.

While practicing archery, Quint tells Miles of a Chinese saying: "If you think about the target hard enough, you can hit it—blindfold." Having a try at this technique, Miles takes aim with his eyes closed and to his own surprise hits the bull's eye. Later, while alone, Miles sees Mrs. Grose at a distance, and with Quint's advice in mind, takes aim at her. In a gruesome sequence of shots, we then see the arrow hitting the old woman in the throat, as blood starts coming out of her mouth. While she writhes in pain on the ground, Miles gives a radiant smile. A second later, however, we understand that this sequence was just Miles visualizing the target in his mind, since in the next shot, we see the boy taking aim for real. This time, however, the arrow narrowly misses Mrs. Grose: "Miles, that could have been dangerous," she scolds him. Nevertheless, the disturbing nature of the scene remains, as Miles clearly had the intention to hit her. At the same time, though, the violence remains within the realm of fantasy, and so ultimately, the scene produces a similar ambiguity to the one found in *The Innocents*. Taken together, the scene places the viewers on the threshold: the children may or may not be dangerous, but no conclusion can be drawn for certain at this point. Now, while Clayton strongly suggested the children's malevolence, he never actually crossed this threshold, preferring to honor the ambiguity of the original story. *The Nightcomers*, on the other hand, will eventually leap above and beyond that threshold, since following the bow and arrow scene, a series of events is set in motion that ultimately leads to a brutal crescendo, shedding all ambiguity.

After Mrs. Grose has finally had enough of Quint's eccentricities, she forbids him from entering the house, thus putting a stop to his nightly visits to Miss Jessel. Learning about this, the children endeavor to help the two lovers resume their relationship—by trapping Mrs. Grose up in their tree-house, allowing Quint and Miss Jessel to meet for a midnight tryst. This time, both Flora and Miles observe the two with interest as they take up their forbidden affair again. However, things seem to escalate beyond whatever unwritten parameters the couple have set up for their relationship, as Quint, after a perceived slight, starts to slap Miss Jessel in the face, as well as take a stranglehold on her. The next day, the children copy what they saw during the night, with Miles putting a stranglehold on Flora in the same way as Quint did to Miss Jessel. Aghast at this, Mrs. Grose puts two and two together and figures out that the children have been influenced by the adults, and announces her intention to do something about it. Realizing that she has but little choice, Miss Jessel at this point decides to leave her position. But Flora and Miles do not want her to go away: this would imply breaking up her relationship with Quint, a relationship from which the children seem to derive some obscure vicarious pleasure. So, in the night, Miles chops a hole in the floor of Miss Jessel's boat, after which the children lure her out on the lake with the false promise that Quint is there to meet her on the other side. In the middle of the lake, the boat starts taking in water, and a panicked Miss Jessel falls over and eventually drowns. On the shore, we see Flora watching the whole drama unfold, without lifting a finger. The next day, Quint also falls victim to the children. In a fairly grotesque scene, Miles first hits Quint with an arrow in the back. Then, he walks up to his victim, and at close range fires another arrow right into his head. Afterwards, the boy casually pulls out the arrow and pushes the lifeless body of Quint into the lake.

On the original film posters for *The Nightcomers*, the tagline read: "Two adults, two children—one unspeakable crime." It is fair to assume that few people going into the movie theaters would have guessed that the crime would be committed by the children against the adults, especially not those familiar with James's story. But there is in fact a logic in the film, albeit a twisted one. Throughout the film, Quint has been philosophizing about death in front of the children, a subject in which they seem inordinately interested.

> MILES: You remember when you told me about the dead and where they go, Quint?
> QUINT: Yes.
> MILES: Tell me again.
> QUINT: Well, the dead go nowhere, because they've got nowhere to go, you see; there's no heaven or hell or that nonsense ... and later on, well, we all join them.

But in the film, there is nothing all that sinister about Quint's reflections on death. Rather, he apparently makes these comments to help the children cope with the loss of their parents, who have passed away from an accident in India. Earlier in the film, when the bodies are to be brought home for the burial, Quint consoles the children by saying that they are coming back to "stay with us forever." In this way, the film suggests, Flora and Miles are made to believe that killing Quint and Miss Jessel will actually make them stay, stopping their impending separation. More broadly, and less straight-forwardly, there is also an obscure way in which Quint's pontifications about love influence the killings. "If you really love someone, sometimes you really want to kill them," he comments at one point. It is the conflation of these two ideas that seem to inform the logic of the children's actions: "We don't want you to go, we want you to stay with us," Flora calls to the drowning Miss Jessel. "You see, you must stay: we love you."

But something disturbing remains, left unaccounted for by this twisted logic: namely the sheer brutality of the action. Earlier in the film, Miss Jessel has mentioned to Flora that she cannot swim and has also shown that she is in fact terrified of water. Thus, there is something particularly cruel about the method of murder, in letting Miss Jessel die in sheer terror. In addition, the children are also shown burning dolls resembling Quint and Miss Jessel in a ritualistic fashion. More generally, the fact remains that both children are strangely drawn to Quint and Miss Jessel's relationship and also seem fascinated if not obsessed with its violent nature.

What *The Nightcomers* does, I believe, is take us back to the fin-de-siècle context of James's original novella, where the Victorian idealization of the child was being increasingly challenged by emerging ideas in evolutionary anthropology about childhood as the savage state in human development. In *Figurations: Child, Bodies, Worlds* (2002), Claudia Castañeda highlights a brief, almost anecdotal article by Charles Darwin, in which he comes to observe parallels between his son Doddy and a savage, following a visit to the zoo.[15] This notion, as Castañeda goes on to expound, is emblematic of the tendency from the mid–1800s onwards to view childhood as the primitive state in human evolution. By implication, this in turn meant that people who were perceived as primitives were also viewed as children; think of, for example, William H. Taft's reference to Philippine colonial subjects as "our little brown brothers." So, the child-savage analogy served a twofold and mutually reinforcing purpose: chiefly, of course, to legitimize colonization, but also to help manage a rising young population—and, in particular, to combat youth delinquency. In the same way that colonial subjects had to be civilized to rid them of brute behavior, so too the tendencies towards simple-minded mischief and even terror had to be curbed in children. Scientifically, the idea found support in Ernst Haeckel's theory of recapitulation, which stated that, in the course of evolution, "the individual organism goes through the same stages as does the species."[16] By the end of the century, the child-savage analogy had turned into a popular commonplace. For example, it was invoked by William Dean Howells, that other great American novelist of James's generation, who in 1890 wrote:

> The Young People may have heard it said that a savage is a grown-up child, but it seems to me even more true that a child is a savage. Like the savage, he dwells on an earth round which the whole solar system revolves, and he is himself the centre of all life on the earth. It has no meaning but as it relates to him; it is for his pleasure, his use; it is for his pain and his abuse.[17]

Howells' topic is childhood memories, and so the tone is predominantly jocular and nostalgic. But the mention of pain and abuse here could be seen to stick out and disrupt the mood, suggesting that what had become a popular commonplace still contained something disturbing underneath.

Credit must thus be given where credit is due: rather than bastardizing the original novella, *The Nightcomers* seems to accurately dramatize a particular anxiety about childhood that was very much present in Henry James's own time. In fact, there is a disturbing element in the film that suggests a clear familiarity with the child-savage analogy. For in their assault on the adults, the children make use of practices that would in the colonial era have been associated with primitive cultures: Miles uses a bow and arrow to kill Quint and, together, the children ceremonially set fire to dolls representing their victims. In this sense, it may be said that *The Nightcomers* illustrates the threat posed by the child-savage analogy, or the dangerous truth it contained, to again invoke Eve Kosofsky Sedgwick. For while the surface function of the analogy was to imply an evolutionary parity between children and native peoples, it must also have reflected a deeper fear of the era, namely that both of these subordinated categories could very well rise up against their masters—be they colonial or parental.

But even as *The Nightcomers* bludgeons the carefully wrought ambiguity of *The Innocents* by making the children vicious killers, it also takes us back to the comment by Rousseau, namely that childhood is something inherently mysterious and inscrutable to analysis. In this regard, it might be said that Flora and Miles are able to commit their terrible acts because they are, so to speak, under the cover of childhood. They do get away with it, after all: in the closing sequence of the film, the children are introduced to their new governess, presumably the one of the original novella, suggesting that things go on as normal. But as Miles suddenly pulls a frog out of his hand as a prank, the viewer is made to remember that this show of normality—this performance of childhood innocence—is but a thin veneer. And as the lifeless bodies of Quint and Miss Jessel are then intercut with the scene, we realize it is impossible to ever again read *The Turn of the Screw* without seriously considering the role of the children.

Coda

In the prologue to *The Turn of the Screw*, the friends sitting around the fire are in agreement that the most terrifying horror stories involve children. If we view *The Innocents* and *The Nightcomers* as evidence of this proposition, then it would seem that children bring this added element of terror not because of their innocence (as the frame story suggests), but rather because of their potential monstrosity. While the "legions of cinematic monstrous children" currently advancing through popular culture might have rendered this a commonplace notion,[18] it is still worth taking a step back to consider its implications. Of course, Henry James was not the first to write a horror story about children—but, he was the first to write one which self-reflexively commented on its own internal dynamics. What *The Innocents* and *The Nightcomers* did was to amplify these dynamics, by considerably expanding the roles of the children—each film, as I have shown, giving another turn of the screw.

In this light, it is appealing to imagine the combined engagement with James's story constituted by these two films as a previously neglected impetus for the ubiquity of the monster child in 1970s cinema. All those movie-goers who were disturbed and terrified by Regan and Damien in *The Exorcist* and *Omen* would probably have been in agreement with James's fire-side listeners: it is the presence of children which adds that extra chill to the spine in such narratives. In this way, even though neither *The Innocents* nor *The Nightcomers* include elements of James's prologue, they could still be said to incorporate its *spirit*. And it was this very same spirit that would dominate the horror genre for years to come, as it produced more and more monstrous children, tightening that screw a little harder each time.

Notes

1. Jeffrey Jerome Cohen, "Monster Culture (Seven Theses)," in *Monster Theory: Reading Culture* (Minneapolis: University of Minnesota Press, 1996), 4.
2. Edmund Wilson, "The Ambiguity of Henry James," in *The Triple Thinkers: Twelve Essays on Literary Subjects* (New York: Oxford UP, 1948), 88.
3. Wilson, 90.
4. Ibid., 94.
5. For an example of the former viewpoint, see Robert Heilman, "*The Turn of the Screw* as Poem" in *A Casebook on Henry James's* The Turn of the Screw, ed. Gerald Willen (New York: Crowell, 1960), 175. In this essay, originally published in 1948, Heilman writes that "the ghosts are evil, evil which comes subtly, conquering before it is wholly seen; the governess, Cassandra-like in the intuitions which are inaccessible to others, is the guardian whose function it is to detect and attempt to ward off evil." For an example of the latter perspective, see Osborn Andreas, *Henry James and the Expanding Horizon: A Study of the Meaning and Basic Themes of James's Fiction.* (Seattle: University of Washington Press, 1948), 46. In Andreas's view, the governess subjects the children "to all the vagaries of her progressively more and more deranged mind, until through sheer terror Flora goes into a delirium with brain fever, and Miles, harder pressed than Flora, is literally scared to death."
6. Wilson, 94.
7. Ibid., 90.
8. Neil Sinyard, *Jack Clayton* (Manchester, UK: Manchester University Press, 2000), 93. As Sinyard notes, a typed-up copy of Edmund Wilson's essay can be found among the director's personal papers, included with the first master script of the film. See also Christopher

Frayling, "Filmed Introduction," *The Innocents*, directed by Jack Clayton (London: BFI, 2010), DVD. As Frayling comments, even though Clayton was very taken with Wilson's argument, the director wanted to preserve the ambiguity of "whether this is the story of a [sexually] frustrated governess or whether it's a real ghost story"—that is, he wanted to present both sides of the critical debate.

9. James, "The Turn of the Screw," 257.

10. Jean-Jacques Rousseau, *Émile, or Treatise on Education*, trans. Barbara Foxley (London: Everyman, 1995), 1–2.

11. Eve Kosofsky Sedgwick, *Epistemology of the Closet* (Berkeley: University of California Press, 1990), 11.

12. Kosofsky Sedgwick, 56–57.

13. Edward J. Parkinson, "*The Turn of the Screw*: A History of Its Critical Interpretations, 1898–1979." PhD diss., Saint Louis University, 1991.

14. James, "The Turn of the Screw," 177, 184.

15. Claudia Castañeda, *Figurations: Child, Bodies, Worlds* (Durham: Duke University Press, 2002), 12.

16. Hugh Cunningham, *The Children of the Poor in England: Representations of Childhood Since the Seventeenth Century* (London: Blackwell, 1991), 123.

17. Williams Dean Howells, *A Boy's Town: Described for "Harper's Young People"* (New York: Harper, 1890), 6.

18. Markus P.J. Bohlmann, and Sean Moreland, "Introduction: Holy Terrors and Other Musings on Monstrous-Childness," 11.

The Monstrous Child

Replacement and Repetition in The Shining

Dustin Freeley

While "family" may not be the first word that comes to mind when discussing typical themes in Stanley Kubrick films, according to Michel Ciment's biography of Kubrick and retrospective of his films, it persists as "the continuation of war in society by other means."[1] If the family is a locus of conflict, then it stands to reason that the child or children within that family are equally sites of tension and conflict. In Kubrick's films, there is recurring, underlying animosity in the relationships between parents and their progeny. Lolita, for example, sleeps with her stepfather, Humbert Humbert, and drives him to murder. In *Barry Lyndon*, "Bullingdon symbolically castrates his [stepfather] by having him physically mutilated."[2] In *A Clockwork Orange*, the ultraviolent Alex is incarcerated, prompting his parents to replace him with the bucolic Joe. In *2001: A Space Odyssey*, the in-utero-child image at the end is more a foreboding anticipation of the intellect that incepts Hal than it is one of hope. The climax of *Full Metal Jacket* leaves the remaining brotherhood of marines staring at the bleeding, gasping figure of a barely-teenage sniper. In *Eyes Wide Shut,* the unnamed, under-aged daughter of a costume shop owner cavorts in her underwear with older businessmen.

All told, these offspring defy the binary depiction of children as either evil or innocent. Instead, Kubrick fashions them in such a way that they are unable to be defined specifically. The young characters paradoxically exist to "subvert cultural notions of the child as needing to be protected" and are "something that must be protected against: they are frighteningly 'other.'"[3] In typical depictions, children are others to adults, who have long since moved from the conception of innocence into experience. At the same time, however, Kubrick's children defile this blank slate. Fashioned as adults, they are fully capable of, and willing to indulge in, violence, sexuality, and death. The effect here is two-fold: it both shatters the illusion of innocence and threatens the socially constructed hierarchy within the adult/child dynamic—a movement akin to the concept of "monstrous childness" taken up by this volume. In no other Kubrick film is this dichotomy surrounding the figure of the child clearer than in *The Shining*.

Because Danny is set opposite his axe-wielding father, Jack, he is often seen as the film's victim. However, Danny is more than what a helpless child would suggest. Rather, Danny embodies the subliminal definition of socially constructed patriarchy. This is not anomalous to Kubrick's exploration of family. Studies done in the late seventies and early eighties on the social perception of childless parents versus parents with children suggest that Danny, as a physical body, represents financial, familial, and (ironically) mental stability,[4] as well as a "lower risk of marital disruption."[5] Therefore, society's gaze on Danny translates the Torrances from middle of the road transients into a successful middle class couple. At the same time, however, Danny masks the deficiencies found within their family unit from society at large: Jack's alcoholism, his and Wendy's apparently sexless marriage, and Jack's unhappiness with his career and social standing. This view of the parent-child dynamic positions Danny as a symbol of Jack's success as American man. However, within this discourse of biopolitics, Danny contains a dimension of monstrosity that, according to Andrew Hock-Soon Ng, is "the product of cultural, social and historical anxieties."[6] Thus, while Danny represents the success of American patriarchy, he simultaneously illuminates Jack's rising anxieties over his role as patriarch and his station in society's hierarchy. In other words, the mask that Danny provides is as fragile and as temporal as his youth. When he becomes uncontrollable, and his actions become unknown, Jack is relegated to Danny's mercy, as opposed to the inverse commonly associated with the father-son dynamic.

In Jack and Danny's dynamic, Danny is a body produced to cloak the Torrances in the façade of stability, but is also, in truth, a burden *because* of his production. Danny bestows a sort of *promissory* identity on Jack, but he is also a threat to Jack's ideal existence because Danny is a triptych representation of what his father should be, isn't, and reluctantly must be: a financially stable, responsible American father. As such, Danny's presence threatens Jack's social standing with a constant reminder about the impending, unpredictable future and Jack's inevitable irrelevance. And as this carrier, Danny moves from the image of *child* to something murkier found in the definition of *childness* that positions the child as both the familiar and the unfamiliar. Danny's existence pushes these anxieties to the forefront, representing both an extension of Jack that throughout *The Shining*, provides an identity located in posterity for the Torrances, but Danny's monstrosity threatens Jack's position as patriarch, suffocates his creativity, and becomes a symbol of perpetuated violence.

In T.S. Eliot's "The Waste Land," the question "What you get married for if you didn't want children?"[7] is ironically posed to show the devaluation of marriage to an artery for procreation. A similar sentiment exists in Lee Edelman's reference to "reproductive futurism," which results from what he calls the "social consensus," or the belief that the "Child remains the perpetual horizon of every acknowledged politics, the fantasmatic beneficiary of every political intervention"[8] and "the pervasive invocation of the Child as the emblem of futurity's unquestioned value."[9] Edelman's lament over this focus on posterity pertains to culture's shifting perception from *value of the present individual* to the *value of the future child* and its inchoate symbol of futurity. Such a shift compels a wealth of anxiety, first when the individual is conditioned to believe that perpetuation is the primary goal, and then when the individual understands his or her devaluation inversely to the child's increasing value.

In *The Shining*, these anxieties exist between Jack and Danny, with much of the anxiety borne through socially constructed pressures to procreate. As Lee Edelman asserts, if there are no children, "then the blame must fall on the fatal lure of sterile narcissistic enjoyments understood as inherently destructive of meaning."[10] Thus, the blame for such destruction would fall heavily on the shoulders of adults who choose to be childless. This fear of race suicide or the coercion to have children is not something exclusive to *The Shining*. Studies conducted between 1975 and 1985 suggest similar rhetoric that reveals "Nonparents are generally aware of unfavorable reactions to their family size preference" and "feel pressure to conform to the 'socially acceptable' norm of two to three children."[11] Danny's mere presence therefore is a constant reminder to Jack of what he is pressured to be and what he would rather not be: a father.

Throughout Kubrick's film, Jack rejects this role of father. Early on, we learn that he injured Danny after having drank too much, and his relationship with Wendy appears perfunctory when he refers to her as "the sperm bank upstairs." There is also some question as to Jack's sexual orientation. As Patrick Webster asserts, "Jack's lack of heterosexual interest in his wife might potentially point toward a homoerotic discourse."[12] Evidence for this discourse is suggested as Jack reads a *Playgirl* magazine,[13] when Wendy discovers the two fellating men in the same hallway as the Torrance's living quarters,[14] or in Jack's placement opposite Stuart Ullman—All Man. While it's not abundantly clear that Torrance is a homosexual or that Kubrick is offering a direct commentary on homosexuality, Jack's interest in the homoerotic derives from his narrow focus on his own future. Heterosexual parents are familiar with what Edelman refers to as "the pervasive invocation of the Child as the emblem of futurity's unquestioned value."[15] However, Jack, in his move to Colorado, follows the opposite ethos inasmuch as he moves his family to find peace and quiet for himself and work on his writing. Edelman also notes that "the queer comes to figure the bar to every realization of futurity, the resistance, the internal to the social, to every social structure or form."[16] This would seem to be more appealing to Jack inasmuch as his every motive and action would center on himself, as opposed to Danny. Thus, Jack's flirtation with the homosexual confirms his reluctance to see Danny replace him as well as emphasizes Danny's affront to the constructed order of father and son. Jack's emphasis on his own futurity can also be seen when he refers to Wendy as the "sperm bank upstairs." Here, much in the way that Wendy is stripped of her role as *wife*, she is re-categorized as a repository, wherein the sperm is unutilized. Ergo, there is no pregnancy, which assures Jack's perpetuation, not his replacement.

The antagonistic homosocial relationship between Danny and Jack is further on display as Danny disrupts Jack's attempts to be a writer. As Randy Rasmussen notes, Jack, who is "formerly a school teacher," now a "writer," "distances himself from and belittles his teaching job by relegating it to the status of financial prop for his chosen career."[17] If Rasmussen is correct and we continue with the theory that Jack has reluctantly entered into both marriage and fatherhood, then we can view Jack as a struggling artist caught in the gears of the capitalistic machine. Presumably, Jack's entry into the machine is the result of needing to provide for his family, and more specifically Danny. Ironically, Jack abandons his job as a teacher to take on another job that submerges him deeper into the capitalist machine, as his position requires the employee to follow a set of rote instructions each day to ensure that the building continues to function properly.

Ideally, Jack's position as caretaker is supposed to provide the peace and quiet in which he can write. However, in Jack's inability to compose, Danny becomes an additional site of tension for Jack. If it is true that the presence of a child is a presumed reflection on the father's ability to gather "the financial resources necessary for having several children,"[18] then Danny's presence for Jack is a glaring contradiction to how Jack intends to be viewed. The Torrances are not financially well off; Jack is (mostly) unemployed, and we find that their move out west is futile, as is Jack's attempt to write. When he does write, it's a tome comprised of the line "All work and no play make

Jack a dull boy." Between the repeated lines, we read that Jack is stuck, unable to break free of monotony and mechanization, or burgeon as a writer. In tandem, his role as the Overlook's caretaker (no matter how inadequate he is) likens him to the father in Lacan's symbolic order. In both circumstances, Jack's purpose is to maintain the status quo and insure the perpetuation of external objects: the hotel and his son. All told, both caretaking positions symbolize Jack's mechanization, as well as provide a bit of mordant irony inasmuch as Danny is all that he can, reluctantly, produce. While Danny represents "a preservation against [the] extinction"[19] of the Torrance name, he also gums up the symbolic order of father-son. He is simultaneously "an assurance of immortality" via posterity to "the ghastly harbinger of death"[20] that elucidates what Jack is: a failed teacher, father, husband, caretaker, and—because of Danny—murderous ax-man. In effect, Danny's youth is ripe with promise, reminding Jack of his failures and his mortality.

It's with this understanding that Danny embodies the uncanny for Jack. Danny "arouses dread and creeping horror"[21] because he can be thought of as what is "*not* known and familiar."[22] As a whole, Danny is *un*familiar. He *is* Jack's son, but his specific intentions and future actions are "not known." As Kathryn Bond Stockton notes about the dichotomous nature of children, "we are threatened by the specter of their longings that are maddeningly, palpably opaque; their leisure-time activities that don't often include us; and their robust consumer wishes that lessen our control."[23] When Danny plays, he plays alone. He follows the specter of murdered sisters, and he wanders into nefarious rooms, including 237, where he is (perhaps) attacked by a ghostly woman. Ultimately, Wendy blames Jack for Danny's bruised neck, despite evidence that he had been sleeping while Danny played. In this particular instance, Danny's actions are unknown, but the bruises inflicted because of his actions ultimately indict Jack as an abusive father—or, at the very least, a failure as Danny's caretaker. Furthermore, Danny embodies an additional facet of Freud's look at the uncanny: the double. While father and son are not physically identical, Danny "possesses knowledge, feeling and experience in common with the other."[24] These inexplicable commonalities between Jack and Danny prohibit Jack from controlling his own agency. In a sense, Danny's ability to see into the future and the past removes much of Jack's agency in that it's already been foretold and anticipated—even if it fails to be prevented. For example, Danny's frightening experience with the ghostly woman foreshadows Jack's equally horrific experience with the woman. From the beginning of the film, Danny is hesitant about the move out west, and Jack's death at the end of the film results from Danny leading him—and ultimately trapping him—in the hedgerow labyrinth.

Most importantly in these symbols of failure and mortality is the transfer of language from Jack to Danny. Throughout, Jack's "novel" is replete with typos ("Jaca," "bog," "noplay," etc.)[25]; the formatting moves from clean and firm against the margin to wonkily set and hastily done. The sloppiness reflects both his inadequacies as a writer and father-figure, as well as the transition of value between him and Danny. Building from Freud, Lacan believes that the child exists in an imaginary world until language makes the child a symbol of agency.[26] In the same way that the double is a symbol of immortality until it gains agency through language, Lacan believes that "it is the world of words that creates the world of things."[27] It stands to reason that Danny's agency is solidified as he writes and speaks. Thus, the inverse must also be true: Jack loses agency as his ability to speak and to write disappears. This is most apparent as Jack enters the height of his rage and Danny writes "redrum" on Wendy's bedroom door. Whereas Jack's redundant opus is devoid of meaning, Danny's single word is clear, to the point, and reflects actions that have occurred, and are occurring, within the hotel. In effect, Danny is the more successful of the two writers. After "redrum" is scrawled on the door, Danny begins screaming "redrum" in his own voice as opposed to the scratchy voice of Tony. Therefore, Danny develops his own voice and adopts the language that is conversely abandoning Jack. Three brief scenes occur consecutively here: Danny speaks and is established as a person separate from Tony; Wendy wakes to see the reflected "redrum" in the mirror; Jack begins chopping at the bedroom door with an axe. The significance here is that, upon Danny becoming his own person, Jack must eliminate him as the actual—as opposed to imaginary—successor. Essentially, Danny—the writer, the speaker—becomes "the monster [that] is no longer spectral but a (corpo)realized entity betokening our worst fears and anxieties."[28] Danny persists as the abstract threat stemming from Jack's cultural and social anxieties, embodied as what Deleuze refers to as "the pure unformed."[29] Danny's ability to speak shatters Jack's understanding of Danny as subservient *child* and repositions Danny as an authority with his own agency.

If it is true that "once the monster is articulated—that is, once it is embodied in words—it can no longer be unsaid,"[30] then we can accept the complete emergence of Danny as a symbol of anxiety after Jack establishes himself as linguistically bankrupt insomuch as Jack's most cogent lines are plagiarized from other sources.[31] He chops through the bedroom door, sardonically announcing, "Honey, I'm home," a line taken from any number of fifties-centric sitcoms. He follows this with "Come out, come out wherever you are," a reference to the child's game hide and seek (or a Frank Sinatra song if you fancy Torrance a musical gent). He then imitates the Big Bad Wolf from the "Three Little Pigs," announcing his intent to "huff and [...] puff." And in what might be the most famous line of the film, Torrance announces, "Here's Johnny!" While this progression is iconic, from here out, Jack is theriomorphized, offering only various guttural versions of "Danny!" that are more akin to a grunting boar, snarling bear, or baying wolf. Taking a Lacanian approach to Jack's final words, we can see that "Danny!" – as opposed to "Daddy!" – becomes the dominant figure as he is beckoned into a bodily existence that surpasses Jack's. With one word, he exposes Jack's well-rounded set of failures and most importantly emphasizes an outgrowth from his father figure.

While *The Shining*'s third act drives home Danny's ascension to a patriarch of the Torrance family, there are moments from the beginning of the film that highlight the antagonized homosocial relationship between Danny and Jack as well as further link Danny to a symbol of culturally- and socially-constructed anxieties. Kathy Merlock Jackson takes note of the conflict between parents and children in films of the 1970s when she writes that this filmic image reflects "the combined responsibilities of work and family in a world that was becoming increasingly more fragmented and demanding."[32] As *The Shining* was filmed through the final year of 1979 and released in 1980, it is fair to suggest that the anxiety over this inability to balance works and family is showcased between Jack and Danny. Similarly, in his look at the horror-film series *The Omen* (1976), Andrew Scahill contends that "parental-replacement anxiety figures strongly in child horror—priming youth to command the future but fearful of what the future will contain."[33] Whereas *The Omen* offers a more obviously wicked child, a similar tendency to supersede the father and a similar anxiety present in the father exists in an intellectual battle between Danny and Jack as they travel to Colorado. As Danny and Jack—in an act of doubling—both stare out through the windshield, Danny complains of hunger to which Jack responds, "You should have eaten your breakfast." Here, Wendy immediately chimes, "We'll get you something as soon as we get to the hotel." In our first viewing of Jack and Danny in the same frame, Jack's patriarchal ruling is dismissed in favor of Danny's needs, and no less importantly, Wendy's decision.

Within the same exchange, Danny becomes Jack's intellectual equal when Wendy inquires about the Donner party. Jack relays the infamous party's fate, but as he gets to the part about eating each other to survive, Danny announces that he knows all about cannibalism because, as Jack snarkily mimics, "he saw it on the television." In this brief exchange, Jack and Danny are intellectually equalized in this father-son dynamic, which makes Jack—as the father figure—useless inasmuch as the information he provides is unneeded. While it's logical that Jack has more experience than Danny, the child here once again represents both the uncanny and a disruption of the symbolic order. He and Jack—at least in part—share similar knowledge, yet Jack is unaware that Danny has gained such knowledge until Danny tells *him*. Furthermore, Danny usurps Jack's attempted explanation of cannibalism and becomes the dominant lecturer within the car.

The exchange in the car further represents Danny's ability to tailor Jack's life around his own. Prior to their move, Jack injures Danny, who had "scattered some of his school papers all over the room." The injury compels Jack to "never touch another drop of alcohol." Even though Danny is the object of Jack's anger, his injury should be seen as an additional point to understanding Danny's monstrousness, or a manifestation of Jack's anxieties. Borrowing from Lacan and Freud, Andrew Hock-Soon Ng asserts that "trauma is the disappearance of the Symbolic and the resurfacing of its excess, the Real."[34] Looking at Jack's violence, we see that it stems from Danny's agency and his unwanted, unprovoked scattering of important papers. If we take Hock-Soon Ng's subsequent assertion that "the monster rejects its place in the Symbolic"[35] then we see that, prior to the film's beginning and our introduction to him, Danny disrupts the symbolic order of father and son; he disrupts Jack's role as teacher, thus positioning himself as the aggressive agent that "insist[s] on being realized."[36] In turn, Jack's resulting sobriety makes him a grounded adult subservient to the child. Danny's presence is a constant reminder that relegates Jack to the position of punished progeny spending "five miserable months on the wagon and all of the irreparable harm it's caused." In *The Shining*, we should not view Jack's time on the wagon as redemptive. Rather, we should see it as the result of containment, one that forces Jack to focus once again on Danny's futurity rather than on his own.

For the viewer, the image of a frozen Jack Torrance in *The Shining*'s penultimate scene typically signals the cessation of a threat. However, Danny's survival offers another dimension of monstrosity, one in which he becomes the agent in the construction of future cultural and historical anxieties. As Geoffrey Cocks asserts, "*The Shining* is a rueful contemplation of how history shows that human beings learn nothing, or at least not enough to overcome the malevolent forces that surround and inhabit them."[37] If Cocks is correct, then we can interpret the last scene of *The Shining*, in which the audience is left looking at a black and white photo of Jack Torrance attending a gala in 1921, as a symbol of repetition that mixes the past, the present and the future. Despite Jack's inability to remember that he has "always been the caretaker,"

Kubrick uses the final image to suggest that history is a circuit of repetition. Furthermore, if we consider Kubrick's notion that "a work of art is a dialogue between past and future from which the present ... has been extended,"[38] then Danny is the "extended" and yet integral part of this dialogue.

Danny as a perpetuation of Jack is apparent in Deleuze's theory of repetition, in which he notes, "Repetition is truly that which disguises itself in constituting itself, that which constitutes itself by disguising itself."[39] Therefore, we shouldn't view Danny as an exact replica of Jack, but rather as an extension disguised, groomed, and shaped by external forces, which, in *The Shining*, take the form of advertisement-laden clothing and television. The first time we meet Danny in the kitchen he wears a white, long-sleeved shirt with blue sleeves, embossed with Bugs Bunny on the front, single red bands of white stars around each bicep, and the number 42 on his right arm. Like Stuart Ullman, Danny is a U.S. flag personified, and, as such, is a symbol of a culture indoctrinated with blind patriotism. Linking the number 42 to January 1942, the month in which "the Nazis organized the Final Solution" and planned the extermination of the Jews, Geoffrey Cocks recounts the repeated use of "42" within *The Shining*: "Television news reports $42 million spending bill, and Wendy watches the American home-front war movie *Summer of '42* (1971) [...] It is also the product of the three digits in 237, the number of the double-doored room of mystery and murder that embodies the dark past of the Overlook."[40] Also of note, there are 42 cars in the Overlook's parking lot as we see it from above, and there are 6 pallets of 7Up in the hallway leading from the kitchen area.[41] Finally, the number 42 adorns the shirt that Danny wears before and after he has a vision of the elevator gushing blood for the first time. Cocks's assertion about this number's significance as a symbol of Nazi aggression in combination with Deleuze's theory about repetition associates Danny with this aggression that is being subliminally disseminated through innocuous-seeming attire.

Most interesting in this dissemination is how "aggression" becomes disguised in its repetition. While Danny is ostensibly the victim in *The Shining*, we've seen how his very presence is an aggressive act upon Jack. Thus, through Danny and his clothing, Kubrick seems to offer a commentary on a fetishized aggression that appears more peaceful and justified when placed in contrast to other horrors. Simply put, Danny is innocent because he is not obviously connoted with violence, such as the historical Holocaust, Jack's axe-wielding, or blood gushing from the elevator. However, Danny's aggression is merely sublimated because we are trained to see children as "embodiments of innocence,"[42] clothing as innocent attire, and television as harmless entertainment.

As Chuck Jackson notes, we are often unable to confront a character whose "face of evil carries with it an uncanny reminder of the face of innocence."[43] However, in *The Shining*, Kubrick flips the script and portrays Danny as the face of innocence and obscures the evil, tempting us to see the child as a vehicle for sanctioned aggression. Perhaps Danny, in the future, will be able to put these images behind him and revolt against their indoctrinations, but this goes against a common theme in Kubrick's films, that "revolt ends in failure. Each of his films tells a story of fragmentation and disintegration."[44] That said, the child in a Kubrick film is far from off limits, particularly one with the "shine."

In Kubrick's film, each "shine" offers a moment from the past. Instead of making Danny clairvoyant, Kubrick allows the child to see horrific snippets, with each snippet provided by Danny's imaginary friend Tony. In this dynamic, Tony acts as the provider of memory. On the theory of memory, Deleuze asserts, "Memory is the fundamental synthesis of time, which constitutes the being of the past (that which causes the present to pass)."[45] Simply put, memory defines what we experience as the past. Transitively, it also constitutes what we remember from the past, and how we synthesize this into our present, and by extension, our future. Similarly, the "shine" is both a reflection of moments that have been forgotten from the past and moments that will occur in the future. Even though Danny appears cursed with the ability to shine in that he is tasked with seeing everything forgotten by the other characters around him, his ability to "shine" is more interesting in what he *fails to do* after he shines: he tells no one, which signals a perpetuation of the violence that he witnesses. By default, he perpetuates the historical anxiety that terrifies his father, Jack. More importantly, he continues to be the child that embodies the frighteningly "other." If Geoffrey Cocks is correct when he asserts, "*The Shining* is a rueful contemplation of how history shows that human beings learn nothing," then Danny's ability to shine and failure to warn anyone are poignant examples of this. Certainly, we could chalk this up to a child being scared of scary things, but his alter ego, Tony—a representation of historical memory that informs Danny of past horrors—commands Danny "never to tell."

Tony is not the only force keeping Danny silent. Dick Halloran, who can also "shine," tells Danny they're "just like pictures in a book; it isn't real."[46] Ironically, Halloran, an ancestral victim of similar tragedies, also suffers from this culturally constructed amnesia. Perhaps this is why Kubrick offers a different fate for Halloran than the heroic one depicted in King's novel. There, Halloran rescues Wendy and Danny, but in Kubrick's film, Jack murders Halloran. In one sense, this could be Kubrick separating himself from King. More importantly, Halloran's demise is Kubrick reasserting that history repeats. Halloran knows the horrors that have happened, are happening, and will happen at the Overlook but is unable to prevent them. Of equal importance is Halloran's linking these visions to a book, which is perhaps a way of suggesting that recorded history is adjusted to suit those writing it. This too damns Danny's future as heroic child and keeps him categorized as the representation of historical anxieties. Danny's sloppily scrawled "redrum" officially undoes Jack, but it also signifies that Danny fails to fully understand the written word either. While Wendy comprehends the gravity of what she sees in the mirror—only when it's blatantly spelled out for her—Danny does not. Thus, in his inability to understand the implications of the history being written, Danny is further linked to a destiny of repetition, insomuch as he is unable to understand the subliminal aggression that he portends.

A final, foreboding prophecy concerning Danny's monstrous intentions and history's tendency to repeat itself can be found in the opening and closing music of the film. Whereas the ominous "Dies Irae" opens *The Shining*, Al Bowlly's "Midnight, the Stars, and You" plays over the end credits and reminds us that "I'll be remembering you, whatever I do." Perhaps this is Kubrick's way of leaving us on a high note. Perhaps it's his way of telling us that things will be okay. But this song, juxtaposed with a photo of Jack Torrance from a ball on July 4, 1921 is an eerie reminder of what we forget. Optimistically, we could say that Danny will write his own future. We can hope that he and Wendy had a long talk on their way down the Sidewinder, and that he will avoid indoctrination, but throughout *The Shining*, we've also borne witness to the difficulties of change. All in all, *The Shining* is not a movie *for children* any more than it is a movie *about children*. However, it is a film that concerns how we linguistically define *the child* and *childhood*. Kubrick's interpretation of King's novel is one that focuses on the social and cultural anxieties kindled by family and exacerbated by the constructs of patriarchy and duty. Most importantly, *The Shining* removes the culturally constructed barriers placed between parents and children, shining a light on the anticipated parent-progeny hierarchy that can so easily fall to pieces.

Notes

1. Michel Ciment, *Kubrick* (New York: Holt, Rinehart and Winston, 1983), 122.
2. Ciment, 120.
3. Sage Leslie-McCarthy, "'I See Dead People': Ghost-Seeing Children as Mediums and Mediators of Communication in Contemporary Horror Cinema," *Lost and Othered Children in Contemporary Cinema* (Lanham, MD: Lexington Books, 2012), 1.

4. Marcia G. Ory, "The Decision to Parent or Not: Normative and Structural Components," *Journal of Marriage and the Family* 40 (1978): 535.

5. Howard Wineberg. "Delayed Childbearing, Childlessness and Marital Disruption," *Journal of Comparative Family Studies* 21:1 (1990): 100.

6. Andrew Hock-Soon Ng, *Dimensions of Monstrosity in Contemporary Narratives: Theory, Psychoanalysis, Postmodernism* (New York: Palgrave Macmillan, 2004), 5.

7. T.S. Eliot, "The Waste Land," *Collected Poems 1906–1962* (New York: Harcourt Brace, 1963), 162.

8. Edelman, *No Future*, 3.

9. Edelman, *No Future*, 4.

10. Edelman, *No Future*, 13.

11. Ory, 535.

12. Patrick Webster, *Love and Death in Kubrick: A Critical Study of the Films from Lolita through Eyes Wide Shut* (Jefferson, NC: McFarland), 99.

13. Stanley Kubrick, *The Shining*, directed by Stanley Kubrick (1980; Hollywood: Warner Bros, 1999.) DVD, approximately 20:22.

14. *The Shining*, approximately 2:09:48.

15. Edelman, *No Future*, 4.

16. Edelman, *No Future*, 25.

17. Randy Rasmussen, *Stanley Kubrick: Seven Films Analyzed* (Jefferson, NC: McFarland, 2001), 238.

18. Denise F. Polit. "Stereotypes Relating to Family-Size Status," *Journal of Marriage and the Family* 40 (1978): 108.

19. Sigmund Freud, "The Uncanny," *Literary Theory: An Anthology* (Malden, MA: Blackwell, 1998), 162.

20. Ibid.

21. Ibid., 156.

22. Ibid., 154.

23. Kathryn Bond Stockon, *The Queer Child, Or Growing Sideways in the Twentieth Century* (Durham: Duke University Press, 2009), 126.

24. Freud, "The Uncanny," 162.

25. Kubrick, *The Shining*, approximately 1:42:35.

26. Jacques Lacan, "The Symbolic Order," 185.

27. Lacan, "The Symbolic Order," 185.

28. Hock-Soon Ng, *Monstrosity*, 17.

29. Gilles Deleuze, *The Logic of Sense* (New York: Columbia University Press, 1990), 107.

30. Hock-Soon Ng, *Monstrosity*, 3.

31. Kubrick, *The Shining*, all lines begin at approximately 2:01:02

32. Jackson, *Images of Children*, 137.

33. Andrew Scahill, "'It's All for You Damien!' Oedipal Horror and Racial Privilege in *The Omen* Series," in *Lost and Othered Children in Contemporary Cinema*, eds. by Debbie Olson and Andrew Scahill (Lanham, MD: Lexington Books, 2012), 97.

34. Hock-Soon Ng, *Dimensions of Monstrosity*, 8.

35. Ibid.

36. Lacan, *The Seminar*, 326.

37. Geoffrey Cocks, "Death by Typewriter: Stanley Kubrick, the Holocaust, and The Shining," in *Depth of Field: Stanley Kubrick, film, and the Uses of History*, eds. by Geoffrey Cocks, James Diedrick, and Glenn Perusek (Madison: University of Wisconsin Press, 2006), 200.

38. Ciment, *Kubrick*, 66.

39. Giles Deleuze, *Difference and Repetition* (London: Athlone Press, 1994), 17.

40. Cocks, "Typewriter," 205.

41. Kubrick, *The Shining*, approximately 29:09.

42. Jackson, *Images of Children*, 27.
43. Chuck Jackson, "Little, Violent, White: *The Bad Seed* and the Matter of Children." *Journal of Popular Television and Film*. (2000): 66.
44. Ciment, *Kubrick*, 96.
45. Deleuze, *Difference*, 80.
46. Kubrick, *The Shining*, 32:00.

PART IV

TROUBLED TEENS AND IN-BETWEENS

Demon Drugs or Demon Children

Take Your Pick

SHARON PACKER

In 1973, *The Exorcist* convinced viewers that demons caused Regan's bad behavior—but her doctors conducted an exhaustive evaluation before reaching that conclusion. When Dr. Klein (Barton Heyman) suggests that Regan (Linda Blair) may be depressed, her actress-mother looks askance. The doctor elaborates, reminding Ms. McNeil (Ellen Burstyn) about her recent separation from Regan's father and hinting that this event might affect Regan.

When the mother seems reluctant to accept that line of reasoning, he takes a different tactic and heads toward biological territory. Dr. Klein then diagnoses "brain dysfunction," which was shorthand for "minimal brain dysfunction." In those years, children who showed outward signs of this disorder were labeled as "hyperkinetic" or "hyperactive" by their schools.

MBD caused controversy in the 1960s and 1970s, not just because the medical data was called into question, but because schoolteachers assumed unofficial (and unlicensed) diagnostic authority and identified children that "needed" prescriptions. Debates about this disorder raged before, during and after *The Exorcist* went into production.[1] As Sean Moreland tells us in *A History of Evil in Popular Culture*,[2] the demand for exorcisms increased after the film's debut. There is no evidence that demonic diagnoses proliferated in the scientific literature, although additional articles on stimulant-treatment of MBD appeared.

Academic articles about stimulant use in MBD surfaced in pediatrics journals as early as 1937,[3] five years after Smith, Klein and French synthesized the first stimulant, Benzedrine, in 1932. Methylphenidate arrived several years later, in 1944. It was marketed as Ritalin in 1950, by Ciba Pharmaceuticals.[4] The research seemed promising, on the surface. It was not long before detractors—and public protestors—arrived on the scene, disparaging these treatments.

The Exorcist's Dr. Klein seems confident in his assessment of Regan. Wearing shirtsleeves, without a suit jacket, and leaning back, while extending his elbows outwards, he clasps his arms behind his head (to expose his armpits in an awkward and off-putting pose). The doctor attempts to explain how stimulants work, while admitting how little of their operations are understood.

Again, the mother is skeptical. She says that she expected a tranquilizer. She asks if Regan needs psychiatric consultation. Dr. Klein assures her that there is no such need. He is convinced that a few weeks of Ritalin will suffice. (His conclusion proves premature, given that he does not foresee the need for psychiatric and parapsychiatric consultation in the near future.)

Dr. Klein's glibness demeans the credibility of the medical profession, and casts doubt on its ability to diagnose MBD accurately. The film echoes the ethos of the time—and of our time, as well.[5]

As it turns out, Ritalin worsens Regan's condition, so she gets a workup for a seizure disorder. That makes sense, since she lost bladder control during one of her "episodes" (as happens with seizures). She seems oblivious of everything that occurred (as also happens during epileptic states). In other words, she has "amnesia" about her behavior during her altered state. She has rhythmic body movements, and her eyes roll back in her head, like an epileptic. Her guttural syllables are similar to sounds emitted as a seizure starts, when the glottis closes. Equally importantly, she shows "religious preoccupations" (with crucifixes) and experiences dreamy (oneroid) states, which have been reported in persons with temporal lobe seizures.

Had that movie been made in 2013, instead of in 1973, a sleep specialist might have suggested REM behavioral disorder—but sleep medicine is a relatively new invention and was not recognized as a subspecialty in the 1970s. It would be unfortunate if Regan received a diagnosis of REM behavioral disorder, considering that it often presages Parkinson's disease or Lewy Body dementia, both of which carry ominous prognoses, even worse than possession.

Better yet, a sleep specialist might have suspected narcolepsy, because frightening visions commonly accompany narcolepsy. A few probing questions about spontaneous daytime sleepiness or feeling "weak at the knees" and losing postural control would have made this prospect seem less likely. Still, Regan's experiences were scary, for both her and for the audience. She sees demons, among other things. Those of us who screamed at the sight of the possessed Regan were not alone; many critics and watch lists consider *The Exorcist* to be one of the most frightening films ever made.

Director William Friedkin fretted about adding too much medical detail—yet he delighted in tapping into a contemporary medical controversy: MBD. Medical, pediatric, psychiatric and psychological journals carried news of MBD, as did education publications. At the same time, many community newspapers, national magazines and some politicos railed against the diagnosis and treatment of MBD. Well-respected journals such as *JAMA* (*Journal of the American Medical Association*) published studies of this perplexing syndrome.[6]

Writing in *JAMA*, Dr. Sulzbacher frets about diagnostic labels, perhaps even more than film director William Friedkin worried about over-inclusion of medical minutiae in his movie. In his December 1, 1975, article, Sulzbacher affirms, "It is an unfortunate truism that most of the diagnostic procedures used with children who have learning disabilities and hyperactivity are not helpful in deciding on treatment. Although at least 92 diagnostic terms have been used to describe behavior and learning disorders in children with average intelligence, the terms "learning disability," "minimal brain dysfunction" (MBD), and "hyperactivity" seem to have gained widespread acceptance.

We have been forewarned. If Dr. Sulzbacher identified "at least 92 diagnostic terms" in 1975, it should not be so surprising that the MBD of the mid–1970s morphed into 21st century ADD and ADHD. Dr. Sulzbacher and others might have been surprised to learn that these labels are applied to toddlers so much more frequently in 2014. A heading for the *New York Times* on May 16, 2014, reported "Thousands of Toddlers Are Medicated for A.D.H.D., Report Finds, Raising Worries." Specifically, 10,000 American toddlers currently have prescriptions for stimulants. Those children are not old enough to come to the attention of schoolteachers, who stepped in as first-line diagnosticians some forty or fifty years ago.

The numbers of prescriptions written for ADD/ADHD have risen dramatically in recent years. Currently, 9.5 percent of school-age U.S. children and teens (6–17 years old) carry ADHD diagnoses.[7] The *New England Journal of Medicine*, perhaps the premiere general medical journal published in the U.S., suggests that DTC (direct-to-consumer) advertising, as well as Big Pharma funding to physicians, and possible parental demands for success, have driven the explosion of such diagnoses. After examining the statistics, *NEJM* suggests that ADHD is overdiagnosed in the United States (but perhaps underdiagnosed in African and Mideastern countries). *NEJM* advises caution before prescribing to preschoolers, and recommends behavioral techniques and parental training before reflexively resorting to Ritalin or related medications.

Not surprisingly, none of the current medical journals attributes behavioral dyscontrol to demons, although ethnographic studies acknowledge some patients' belief in demonic possession, and bestselling author M. Scott Peck, MD, professes success in exorcising demons.[8]

Considering that *The Exorcist* remains one of the top-grossing films of all times, with so many Academy Award nominations, it surprises me that so few realize that this stimulant controversy is on "rewind." Today, however, the "demon" appears to inhabit the drugs, or the drug companies and their DTC advertising, and perhaps the doctors who overprescribe these medications to toddlers or to those who have no clinical need for them.

Notes

1. H.B. Levy, "Minimal Brain Dysfunction/Specific Learning Disability: A Clinical Approach for the Primary Physician," *Southern Medical Journal* 69: 5 (1976): 642–53.

2. Sean Moreland, "Occupied America(ns): Contemporary Trends in American Possession-Horror Films," *A History of Evil in Popular Culture: What Hannibal Lecter, Stephen King and Vampires Reveal About America*: Vol. I, eds. Sharon Packer and Jody Pennington (Santa Barbara, CA: ABC-CLIO, 2014), 211–222.

3. C. Bradley, "The Behavior of Children Receiving Benzedrine," *American Journal of Psychology* 94:3 (1937): 577–588.

4. C. Bradley, "Benzedrine and Dexedrine in the Treatment of Children's Behavior Disorders," *Pediatrics* 5 (1950): 24–37.

5. Sharon Packer, *Cinema's Sinister Psychiatrists* (Jefferson, NC: McFarland, 2012), 15, 63, 81–3, 89, 102. 6. S.I. Sulzbacher, "The Learning-Disabled or Hyperactive Child: Diagnosis and Treatment," *JAMA* 234 :9 (1975): 938–941. doi:10.1001/jama.1975.03260220042017.

7. C.A. Boyle, S. Boulet, L.A. Schieve, et al., "Trends in the Prevalence of Developmental Disabilities in U.S. Children, 1997–2008," *Pediatrics* 127 (2011): 1034–1042.

8. M. Scott Peck, *Glimpses of the Devil: A Psychiatrist's Personal Accounts of Possession, Exorcism, and Redemption* (New York: Free Press, 2005).

Disability and Slasher Cinema's Unsung "Children"

JOHN EDGAR BROWNING

"I think we shoot a lot of stuff, and then 20 years later we find out what it really meant."—Tobe Hooper, *The American Nightmare* (2000)[1]

The horror film industry has been rife since its very inception with images of disability in the guise of the physically and psychologically monstrous. A notable early example lay with the Pre-Code "talkie" *Freaks* (1932), whose director, Tod Browning, inaugurated the horror genre[2] just a year earlier with *Dracula* (1931). The focus of my critical gaze, however, when turned towards the intersections of disability and horror, is routinely directed away from the horror genre proper. Within the genre itself, structurally, "Any kind of alterity," to solicit one of Jeffrey Jerome Cohen's postulates, "can be inscribed across (constructed through) the monstrous body," even though, as Cohen adds, "for the most part difference tends to be cultural, political, racial, economic, sexual."[3] Herein I reconsider this axis through engaging critically with a familiar subgenre of horror, though one I often avoid in a classroom setting because it bifurcates the standard horror and teratological conventions of which Cohen speaks: the Slasher film.

Unfortunately, getting at a consensual definition[4] of Slasher cinema often proves harder even than defining its parent genre. Traditionally, though not always in practice, the central monster of a typical horror film occupies, at least in Western cinema, simultaneously the space of both social deviant (i.e., the "sinner") *and* the physical or mental anomaly in the narrative (Count Dracula, for example, is not only physically aberrant but morally transgressive as well). Slasher cinema, on the other hand, according to the classification I adopt, features a monster who, generally speaking, commits few or no other sinful or unlawful acts beyond trying to police (murder) the film's otherwise "normal" scharacters who've now absorbed the role previously occupied by the monster of social transgressor. Put in another way, the Slasher film's *socially transgressive* protagonists, with whom adolescent viewers ideally are meant to identify, are killed off one by one for their "sins" by the film's *physically anomalous* Slasher. Indeed, it is this very feature that, by my account, categorically distinguishes Slasher cinema within the horror genre.

Curiously, featured in the role of the physically or mentally anomalous Slasher in these films is a predominance of disabled killers. Sharon L. Snyder and David T. Mitchell, though they don't specify the Slasher subgenre, draw this connection in their study *Cultural Locations of Disability* (University of Chicago Press, 2006), stating, "In horror films the terror of an expected meeting with the villain (often disabled), and anxiety over potential or actual violence, produces an accord of sensations between characters and members of a viewing audience."[5] To exacerbate this anxiety, it is telling that many of these disabled killers adopt the practice of wearing a mask, or feature faces that are effectively rendered mask-like from genetic malformation or through some disfiguring accident. Yet there is also, within the subgenre, one other highly visible, albeit frequently undertreated motif: the disabled, child-minded (i.e., mentally underdeveloped) killer, whom I shall call simply an "Adult Child." This breed of antagonist generally starts off his narrative as a child, only to maintain afterwards, as an adult, a child-like emotional and behavioral demeanor, inciting terror while pursuing what can only be described as some sort of deranged moral *vigilantism*. *Halloween*'s Michael Myers and *Friday the 13th*'s Jason Voorhees, for example, as well as a whole slew of other, less prominent Slasher villains, as I'll elaborate later, share between them an early, originary traumatic moment, conflict, or history that has previously left them physically and/or psychologically disabled; fundamentally, it is this key moment or incident which narratologically echoes into the villain's adulthood with his repeated policing of socially transgressive behaviors that visually or conceptually footnote his own traumatic past. However, the nebulous meanings affixed to Slasher cinema and the multiple, often competing discourses surrounding it have invariably fueled my reluctance to develop more fully and commit singularly to one analysis of the role the "Adult Child" plays in the subgenre. Necessarily, then, the line of inquiry I engage here reflects that sense of on-going negotiation and takes as its primary aim the incitation of serious and sustained thought and discussion.

Of course, the only thing harder than defining Slasher cinema is agreeing upon which film(s) started it all. Michael Powell's *Peeping Tom* (1960) and Alfred Hitchcock's *Psycho* (1960), two films often attributed to the subgenre's teratogenesis, are not what I would term Slasher films proper. Nevertheless, they supply the subgenre with several crucial conventions. Mark (Carl Boehm) the sympathetic, scopophiliac killer who wields a spike-bearing camera in *Peeping Tom*, "has survived in adulthood the spectatorial cruelties of his childhood," writes Carol J. Clover,

> by splitting and reenacting them—on one hand through the assumption of his father's role, using the camera to "kill and fuck" (as Stein puts it) and on the other through the obsessive re-viewing of his own boyhood experience of having been on the *receiving* end of his father's cinematic "killing and fucking."[6]

Clover describes *Peeping Tom* as a narrative "shaped around the experience of fear and pain,"[7] but this quality foregrounds the portrayal of Adult Child killers in Slasher films in general. Indeed, in *Peeping Tom*, Mark doesn't merely "reenact" his childhood experiences; he literally channels his childhood persona through his crippling shyness and social ineptitude, and in the security blanket–like protective function of his camera. Similarly, as Mark is to his father in *Peeping Tom*, the character of Norman Bates (Anthony Perkins) is to his mother in *Psycho*. Norman, the son of a sexually repressive, over-bearing woman, can hardly suppress his boyish giddiness at meeting Marion Crane (Janet Leigh) upon her arrival at the Bates Motel. This, as well as the repeated references to Norman as "boy" by his angry, suspicious "mother" off-camera moments after we're introduced to him, help to set him up early on as an Adult Child figure. However, what we don't yet know at this point in the film is that he's also a killer. In the iconic "shower scene," Norman murders Marion, whose character in the first 30 minutes of the film had been sexually unscrupulous with her lover ("post-coital lunchtime lovers" is the phrasing David Greven aptly uses in *Psycho Sexual: Male Desire in Hitchcock, De Palma, Scorsese, and Friedkin* [2013][8]) before committing grand larceny. Similarly, *Peeping Tom*'s Mark dispatches a prostitute, a pornographer, and an upstart movie extra unopposed to breaking rules and undermining professional conduct. It's also telling of their demeanor that both Mark and Norman innocently serve milk to their respective female interests upon meeting them. Yet, for all their adolescence and naiveté, Mark and Norman are still at least capable of some measure of reason and speech, and their lives are marked by some intermediary "sin"; Mark is a sexual deviant, and Norman a cross-dresser. The Adult Child killers that emerge from the rise to prominence of Slasher cinema some two decades later are terrifyingly more infantile and disturbingly more innocent, and for this reason, resolutely more dangerous.

The conventions established in 1960—targeted "punishment"-killings and the marked adolescence of the killer—culminate in the subgenre's reputedly first installment with the independent picture *Halloween* (1978), written (with Debra Hill) and directed by John Carpenter. *Halloween* is generally billed as the *locus classicus* of Slasher cinema, and in it Carpenter supplies the Slasher industry with its most recognizable archetype to date in the masked character of Michael Myers. Notably, the "poster child" for the subgenre's inaugural film is also characteristically an Adult Child, one who is so cold, so singular in his objective, that viewers can scarcely help admiring the purity of his malevolence. Michael Myers's doctor, Sam Loomis (Donald Pleasence), tells in *Halloween II* (1981) of the terror awaiting the mid-western community of Haddonfield, Illinois: "He was my patient for 15 years. He became an obsession with me until I realized that there was nothing within him, neither conscience nor reason, that was even remotely *human*." Yet, "If *Peeping Tom* clearly established the camera as the machine between us and it," Clover writes, "*Halloween* seeks to efface the intervention of the photographer, to try for the direct connection: we are invited to look not through a murderous camera, but with our own murderous eyes, listening to the beat of our heart and the breathing of our lungs."⁹

The film begins fifteen years in the past on Halloween night when Michael, a six-year-old boy, returns home from trick-or-treating to discover the late-night escapades between his sister and her date. We know by the end of Michael's (nearly seamless) 4-minute long Steadicam POV shot that his

Figure 1. Will Sandin plays the young Michael Myers in *Halloween* (U.S., 1978).

sister has just had sex, even though we don't actually see it happen; every pre- and post-coital cue is present. For this reason, Michael dons a mask then plunges, with repeated action and force, a long kitchen knife into her naked body. She falls limp to the floor, and Michael leaves in the same methodical manner in which he came. He descends the stairs and is exiting the house when his parents arrive home, confronting him on the lawn. Michael's father calls to him, tearing the mask from his face. The shot reverses, and we see the boy who has just murdered his sister, his hand still wielding the bloodied knife (see Figure 1).

Ironically, it is only by accident that Carpenter and Hill produce the conventions that become unique to Slasher cinema. The producers wanted Carpenter to make a picture about babysitters being pursued by a killer, and the question arose: What do babysitters do? Better still, what do teenagers do when adults aren't around? Perhaps they fornicate with their boyfriends, consume alcohol or smoke a little grass, or commit some other moral transgression. As chance would have it, the killings occurred *after* these activities. So, naturally the conclusion is drawn that the antagonist in Slasher films is a sort of moral avenger, and these transgressions are somehow tied to the very grievance that helped to define the killer. Perhaps it was too much for Michael to bear that his sister, who was supposed to be watching him, engaged in premarital sex. After the murder, Michael's body matures into a young adult, but his mind effectively remains that of his six-year-old self. In *Halloween II*, Dr. Loomis underscores Michael's disability in a short monologue: "He waited with extraordinary patience. There was a force inside him biding its time. The staff [at the mental hospital] grew accustomed to his immobility and silence. In many ways he was the ideal patient. He didn't talk, he didn't cry, he didn't even move. He just waited." After Michael's return to Haddonfield, it is the behavior—and defining moment—of his childhood that he re-enacts in his pursuit of Laurie Strode (Jamie Lee Curtis) and her friends. This formula, successful as it was in *Halloween*, was tested again two years later and met with even greater success.

The *Friday the 13th* (1980–) franchise develops further the notion of Slasher cinema's disabled Adult Child killer. In the first installment, we learn by the end of the film that the one killing Camp Crystal Lake's counselors is Mrs. Voorhees (Betsy Palmer), a disgruntled mother whose facially deformed, mentally disabled son, Jason (Ari Lehman),[10] had been left unattended two decades earlier at the same camp and drowned while the counselors charged with watching him were off having sex.

In the final chase scene, Mrs. Voorhees begins talking to herself using her son's voice and even imbues her final, murderous actions with a child-like peculiarity. This scene is mirrored in part in the important final scene of *Part II* (1981), in which Jason, now a murderous, hooded young man, confronts the character of Ginny (Amy Steel). Ginny, who's studying child psychology, dons the sweater of Jason's mother (which Jason has been keeping all these years, along with her severed head) and bids him to listen to her, as a mother would a young child. Pacified, Jason complies with Ginny's ("Mrs. Vorhees's") commands, and with this haunting scene our picture of his psychopathology is completed: Jason, like Michael, is a murderous child. At the time, this trend proved to be as popular with Jason's character as it had been with Michael's, but the honor wasn't theirs alone.

The short period following *Halloween*'s release is beset with a myriad of other pictures that utilize an Adult Child antagonist, not least among them, *Don't Go in the House* (1979) and *Don't Answer the Phone!* (1980). In the former, Donald "Donny" Kohler (Dan Grimaldi), a disturbed young man whose religiously devout mother used to purify him with fire by holding his extremities over a gas stove ("burn the evil out of him," she called it), returns home one night to discover his mother has passed away. At first saddened, he quickly realizes his new found freedom and begins jumping on the furniture and playing his disco music loudly; he also develops an affinity for fire and, donning an aluminized fire proximity suit (complete with hood and mask), uses it, with a child-like enthusiasm, to purify women he invites back to his home who remind him of his mother, whose corpse still sits peacefully upstairs. In *Don't Answer the Phone!* (1980), strangler Kirk Smith (Nicholas Worth), who suffered physical and emotional abuse from his parents, is "a Vietnam vet who pissed the bed until he was 18.... Prone to laughing hysterically like some forgotten cartoon character and suddenly sobbing uncontrollably, he veers from brutish to child-like."[11] Following *Friday the 13th*'s release, more titles emerge, among others *The Funhouse* (1981), which features a severely facially deformed adolescent villain (credited as "The Monster" [Wayne Doba]) whom Steven West and Paul J. Brown dub simply, in *Slash Hits: Teens in Trouble* (2007), "a drooling, squawking retard."[12] Another popular favorite of the period is *Hell Night* (1981), whose Adult Child killer, writes one *New York Times* reviewer, "is 'a gork.'"[13] The reviewer continues, "It is unclear what this means, although it is axiomatic in the new horror films [i.e., Slashers] that the handicapped, whether Mongoloid, deformed or gork, are wicked."[14] And following in a long line of '80s Adult Child Slasher films of the camping/wilderness variety (see, for example, the *Sleepaway Camp* [1983–] franchise) is the gritty *Just Before Dawn* (1981). A film trailer warns, "How could they know the heat of their

Figure 2. John Hunsaker plays both of the "Mountain Twins" in *Just Before Dawn* (U.S., 1981).

bodies was the magnet that would draw the terror to them," the "terror," in this case, being a pair of over-sized, machete-wielding, mentally handicapped, playful "Mountain Twins" (see Figure 2).

Finally, in 1982's *Humongous*, a band of adolescent friends is shipwrecked on a wooded lake island after their yacht explodes. The island's former inhabitant, Ida Parson (Shay Garner), was raped on the island many years earlier and afterwards resigned herself there, in seclusion, for the remainder of her life. With the help of her diary, which the marooned adolescents locate in her dilapidated estate, we soon learn of the sad but ghastly truth of what awaits them. In it, Ida tells of her tragic past, of her disdain for men, and of her large, immensely strong son afflicted by acromegaly. Her decision to remain on the isolated island, we learn, was an attempt to protect him from the "evils" of the outside world. Following his mother's death, the son resorts to killing the island's animals for food, which, but for the newly arrived adolescents, have all but run out (see Figure 3).

These films continue to see production well into the late–1980s, and traces of them linger even today. Observe, for example, *Mask Maker* (2010) whose deformed Adult Child killer, Leonard (played by Jonathan Breck, and referred to during the film as "a retard"), witnessed, as a young boy, his mother's persecution as a witch, and finally her murder. Our fascination with these films, as with any horror film, seems intimately tied up with the experience of

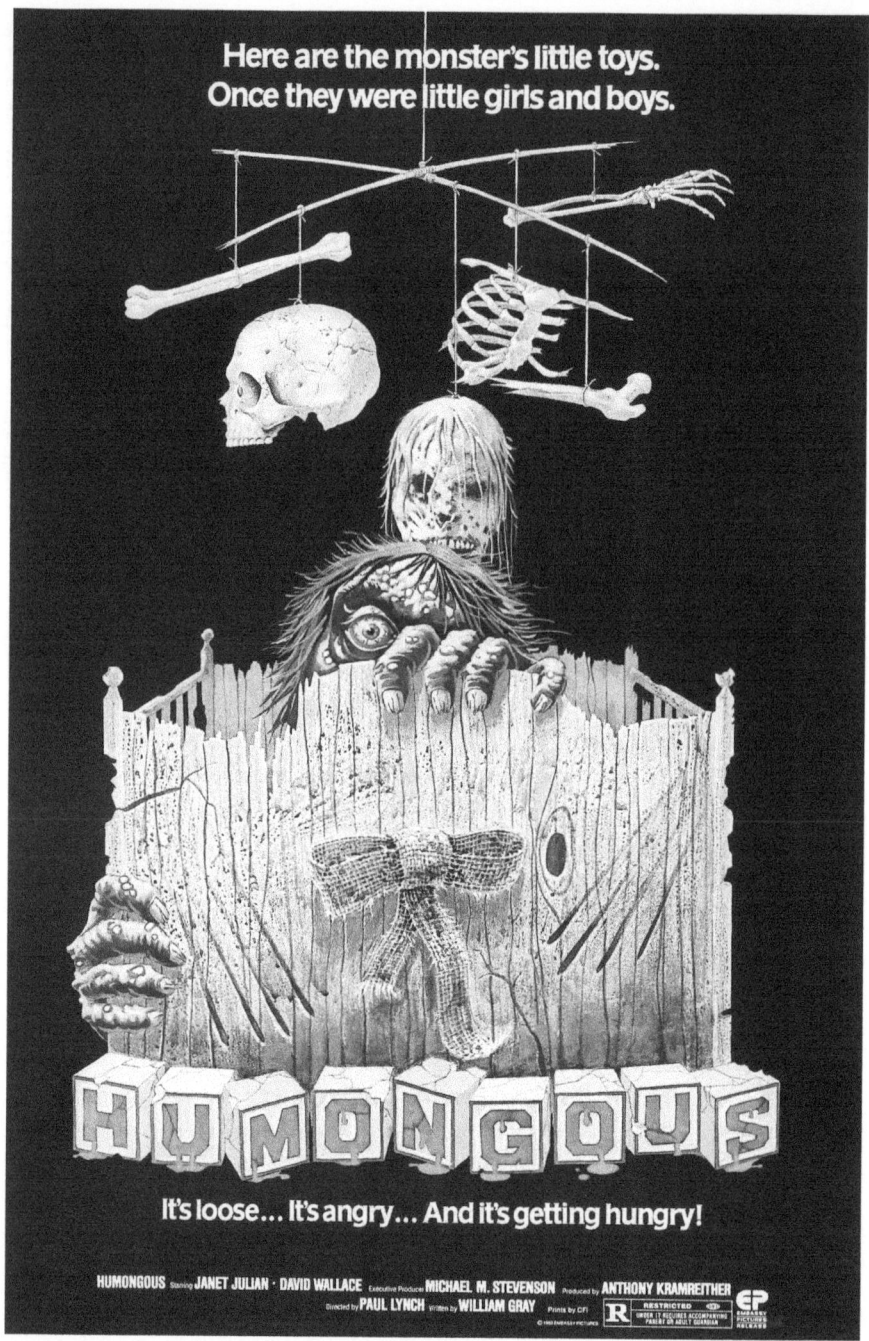

Figure 3. Poster art for *Humongous* (Canada, 1982).

extreme or excessive emotions. For Snyder and Mitchell, however, the corollary is much clearer. To them, it is *"disabled bodies,"* more than any other in the cinema, that *"have been constructed cinematically and socially to function as delivery vehicles in the transfer of extreme sensation to audiences."*[15] Thus, "an anatomy of disabled bodies," posit Snyder and Mitchell, "can deepen our comprehension of the system and structure"[16] of what Linda Williams calls "body genres,"[17] wherein (as with the horror genre) bodily displays of terror on the screen evoke in audiences a similar reaction as well.

Indeed, Adult Child killers do frighten us. Yet, strangely, like no other monsters in the annals of cinematic history, they are also capable of moving us, a bodily reaction associated more with melodrama (another of Williams's "body genres") than with horror. Clover reminds us that while the killer's-eye-view "is probably the most widely imitated—and widely parodied—cliché of modern horror," "this first-person, assaultive gaze" is a gendered one, "figured explicitly or inexplicitly in phallic terms…. Slasher films draw the equation repeatedly and unequivocally: when men cannot perform sexually, they stare and kill instead."[18] However, Clover's assessment fails to account adequately for Slasher narratives that, again, use some early, originary traumatic moment, conflict, or history to breed Adult Child antagonists (who are also all virgins, presumably). Any thematic inquiry into horror cinema that intends to use the genre's history to trace the general development of evil *vis-à-vis* monstrosity is effectively disrupted by the Slasher film. Slasher cinema, as I've defined it, makes visible a vital dichotomy between the frequently homogenized notions of moral transgression and physical monstrosity. Adding to this, among the films I have cited, is what this anthology's editors have termed "monstrous childness"—the killer's innocence, as it were, which unsettles even a category as porous as monstrosity. The masked figure in these Slasher films is at heart a faceless terror, conceptually a killer uncorrupted whose mask doubles as a blank screen onto which we ably project any fear that suits us. Yet his pathology is ostensibly that of a *socially*—even, by crude extension, *legally*—innocent child, a quality which effectively separates him from the vast majority of other teratological figures.

To stake Count Dracula or gun down Rosemary Woodhouse's (Mia Farrow) neighbors in *Rosemary's Baby* (1968), to slay the shark in *Jaws* (1977) or total out the car in *Christine* (1983), feels understandably like one's "moral duty," and the feeling afterwards is pleasantly buoyed by a sense of justification. Yet to kill an Adult Child Slasher, in any one of the examples I've cited, seems unsettlingly akin to euthanasia: a form of mercy killing seemingly designed to "put down" some black, heavy thing upon the human psyche. The question arises, then, as to whether we fear more the Adult Child killer in these films or the very people with whom, ideally, we're meant to identify, the young protagonists. Can it be simply that their transgressions—often the same variety which helped to birth their disabled stalker—lie too heavy on our collective conscience? In "Avenging the Body: Disability in the Horror Film," Travis Sutton's treatment of a particular disabled stalker that bears upon our discussion, one whom he calls the "Obsessive Avenger," Sutton points out that "Revenge is a theme in all kinds of genres and is particularly useful in the horror film to justify monstrous behavior."[19] Yet, when the act of revenge "is tied to a disability, as it is with the Obsessive Avenger, then such stories draw upon able-bodied assumptions that people in the disabled community are usually bitter and angry about their disabilities."[20] The assumption that members of the disabled community lament their disabilities and covet the able-bodied "reveals more about the cultural hierarchy of dis/abilities and the insecurity of dominant positions," argues Sutton, "than the wide spectrum of experiences and perspectives of those people who have a disability.[21] Snyder and Mitchell offer a different view to Sutton's position, instead proclaiming that "order and mastery," which we associate with the able-bodied, are central to the "fantasy of bodily control among audience members," and it is *this* which "becomes the target of body genres as a fiction deeply seated in the desire for an impossible dominion over our own capacities."[22]

Curiously, the figure of the Adult Child Slasher fits comfortably in neither camp but seems, rather, to vacillate across vengeance *and* order. For his part, he murders in vigilante-style (*à la* the *Death Wish* [1974–1994] franchise) the culprits of sinful ways, ways which haunt his own traumatic past, yet in the process his actions restore order to a present afflicted by transgressions tied almost exclusively to the body. In the end, it's his "childness" which effectively exonerates him of his deeds; unaccountable in his destruction, like some macabre divinity, he punishes us—protagonist and viewer alike—for our sins, and the sense of relief that follows assures returning sales.

Notes

1. Dir. Adam Simon, *The American Nightmare* (Minerva Pictures, 2000).
2. As David J. Skal explains, before *Dracula*, "horror movies of the genuinely fantastic, supernatural variety had not been invented yet, at least not in America, where conventions dictated that supernatural occurrences always be 'explained away.'" See David J. Skal, *Hollywood Gothic: The Tangled Web of Dracula from Novel to Stage to Screen*, (rev. ed.) (New York: Faber and Faber, 2004 [1990]), 165.
3. Jeffrey Jerome Cohen, "Monster Culture (Seven Theses)," in *Speaking of Monsters: A Teratological Anthology*, eds. Caroline Joan S. Picart and John Edgar Browning (New York: Palgrave Macmillan, 2012), 17.

4. Worthy examples include, among others, Carol J. Clover's exhaustive treatise on Slasher cinema in *Men, Women, and Chain Saws: Gender in the Modern Horror Film* (Princeton: Princeton University Press, 1992), as well as recent general studies of horror like Rick Worland's *The Horror Film: An Introduction* (Malden, MA: Blackwell, 2007) and Brigid Cherry's *Horror (Routledge Film Guidebooks)* (New York: Routledge, 2009), in which the Slasher film is treated succinctly yet effectively.

5. Sharon L. Snyder and David T. Mitchell, *Cultural Locations of Disability* (Chicago: University of Chicago Press, 2006), 159.

6. Carol J. Clover, *Men, Women, and Chain Saws: Gender in the Modern Horror Film* (Princeton: Princeton University Press, 1992), 174.

7. Clover, *Men, Women, and Chain Saws*, 174.

8. David Greven, *Psycho-Sexual: Male Desire in Hitchcock, De Palma, Scorsese, and Friedkin* (Austin: University of Texas Press, 2013), 89.

9. Greven, *Psycho-Sexual*, 185–86.

10. According to an interview with Betsy Palmer, Tom Savini, the film's lead makeup artist, termed his creation "a mongoloid." See Dir. Jeff Mcqueen, *Going to Pieces: The Rise and Fall of the Slasher Film* (Starz Entertainment, 2006).

11. Steven West and Paul J. Brown, *Slash Hits: Bloody Beginnings*, vol. 1 (Northamptonshire: Midnight Media, 2006), 39–40.

12. Steven West and Paul J. Brown, *Slash Hits: Teens in Trouble*, vol. 2 (Northamptonshire: Midnight Media, 2007), 21.

13. John Corry, "'Hell Night,' Initiation Rite," review of *Hell Night* (1981), *The New York Times*, Sept. 6, 1981.

14. Corry, "'Hell Night,' Initiation Rite."

15. Snyder and Mitchell, *Cultural Locations of Disability*, 162.

16. Ibid.

17. Linda Williams, "Film Bodies: Gender, Genre, and Excess," in *Film Theory and Criticism*, eds. Leo Braudy and Marshall Cohen (Oxford: Oxford University Press, 1999), 701–15.

18. Clover, *Men, Women, and Chain Saws*, 186.

19. Travis Sutton, "Avenging the Body: Disability in the Horror Film," in *A Companion to the Horror Film*, ed. Harry M. Benshoff (Malden, MA: John Wiley, 2014), 79.

20. Sutton, "Avenging the Body," 79.

21. Sutton, "Avenging the Body," 79.

22. Snyder and Mitchell, *Cultural Locations of Disability*, 163.

Monstrous Mammies in Lee Daniels's *Precious*

Debbie Olson

In 1810, ship surgeon Alexander Dunlop returned to England from South Africa bearing numerous curiosities from the Dark Continent. One of these specimens was a San woman named Saartjie Baartman, who would later be known throughout Europe as the "Hottentot Venus." Dunlop sold Baartman to Hendrick Cezar, a showman in London, who promptly set Baartman up as a cultural "oddity" because of her unusually large buttocks (steatopygia) and her "primitive" genitalia—an elongated labia.[1]

The practice of putting dark-skinned people on display for white visual consumption has a long history in the West.[2] During the years of heightened colonialism (17th to the mid 19th centuries), such ethnographic displays of people from colonies inhabited by non-whites were common throughout Europe and America. This spectaclization of difference based on romantic and pastoral notions of "the primitive" quickly became the European narrative frame through which any discourse related to colonial peoples was presented. Saartjie Baartman's humiliating display functioned in a unique way to establish and reinforce cultural notions of the superior beauty (milk-white skin; straight, flowing hair; small nose and lips; "delicate" facial features) and femininity (weakness, modestly, self-control, compassion, sensitivity, tolerance, fragility, submissiveness, graceful movements) of white women, and helped establish perceptions of black women as the "monstrous" opposite to the white female model. In the introduction to this volume, Moreland and Bohlmann define the term monstrous, through Deleuze, as something unknowable, that "escapes human comprehension." This definition accurately describes the persistent pattern of Western beliefs about non-white peoples. In the context of race, John Block Friedman explains that the "monstrous races were always far away, in India, Ethiopia," places that "evoked mystery."[3] Ethnographic displays, like that of Saartjie Baartman, reinforced the monstrousness of these ethnically "unknowable" dark peoples encountered in colonized territories. For my purposes, monstrousness refers to difference, unknowingness, and incomprehensibility of the raced body, particularly the obese raced body.

Saartjie Baartman's experience, and particularly her *visual* depictions, her "on-display-ness," underscores the way the black body has been systematically linked to notions of abnormality, i.e., monstrous, in relation to the white body. George Yancy, in his compelling book *Black Bodies, White Gazes,* describes the way the black body is ritually defined in relation to whiteness:

> From the perspective of whiteness, the black body *is* criminality itself. It *is* the monstrous; it is that which is to be feared and yet desired, sought out in forbidden white sexual adventures and fantasies; it is constructed as a source of white despair and anguish, an anomaly of nature, the essence of vulgarity and immorality.[4]

As Yancy points out, the demonization of the black body shows that, for whites, "black *existence* constitutes a threat."[5] Yancy argues the black body is a discursive entity, bound to the interstices of "social semiotics" where the black body is "less of a thing or being, than a shifting or changing historical meaning that is subject to cultural configuration and reconfiguration."[6] And although cultural configurations are constantly in flux, the way the black body is discursively juxtaposed against the white body—"Momma, See the Negro! I'm frightened!"[7]—continues the Western myth of white superiority.

The white myth of superiority remains a constant within the semiotic field of culturally raced identities.[8] By exaggerating and then denigrating physical differences, whites are able to construct an ordered universe that privileges whiteness (especially European whiteness) over any other ethnicity.[9] This belief extends to black genders also, as they are defined by their otherness to white genders. W.E.B. du Bois introduced the notion of "double consciousness" in which blacks know themselves through a "two-ness," a doubling of their identity that frames their (personal) identity through the "revelation" or (social) lens of the "other [white] world."[10] This identity doubling also extends to gender, resulting in specific racial stereotypes about the inherent nature of black *genders*. Gender distinctions within stereotypes about blackness work to reify and naturalize both stereotypes. According to popular media images, to be black *and* female is to exist in a space of negation of all that whites consider feminine, while to be black *and* male is to be identified as inherently criminal and beastly.[11]

In *Toons, Coons, Mulattoes, Mammies, and Bucks,* Donald Bogle outlines the many different stereotypes about African Americans that have been replicated throughout American popular culture. As Bogle explains, these stereotypes functioned not just to entertain whites, but to reinforce and "[stress] Negro inferiority. Fun was poked at the American Negro by presenting him as either a nitwit or a childlike lackey."[12] Interestingly, the "childlike" qualities that were attributed to African Americans were not the endearing qualities—innocence, purity, and perpetual wonder—normally associated with children. Instead, African American stereotypes characterize innocence as ignorance, purity was either non-existent or presented as a type of savagery, and notions of childlike wonder were instead presented as perpetual—and inherent—dumbness, signifying both silence (a voice) and a lack of intelligence.

While black children populate many Hollywood films, they are rarely the star or protagonist. When they do assume the atypical protagonist role, these children are often portrayed as the Other, as an outsider, and in the context of Western notions of childhood, as existing in a space that is neither innocent nor pure, are often presented as "victims in the making,"[13] or infantilized for the paternalistic white gaze. These children are positioned within a discursive framework that renders their images as modern reworkings of colonial-era stereotypes. In this essay, I will examine the black female child through the framework of childhood studies, critical race and film theories in order to interrogate the space black children occupy within popular conceptions, and expectations, of what the West believes children and childhood should be.

Precious-ness

Adam Phillips, in *The Beast in the Nursery*, observes that "in the old, modern fable of civilization and its discontents, either the child or the culture is demonized."[14] Such is the case in Lee Daniels's 2009 film *Precious*, based on the novel *Push* by Sapphire, which showcases many of society's ills—welfare, poverty, isolation, drugs, and abuse. On the film's surface, Precious, beautifully played by Gabourey Sidibe, is constructed as an object of pity and sympathy; we cringe when she is verbally abused by her mother, yet the film's subtext sends a very different message. It presents the dark cultural spaces where Precious resides, along with her children born of incest, amidst all that white society rejects. Though decades away from the distasteful ethnographic zoos and the carnival displays of nineteenth and early twentieth century freak shows of Saartjie Baartman's time, *Precious* nevertheless replicates what Rosemarie Garland Thompson calls the "discourse of the anomalous body" through the film's exaggerated visual presentation of difference.[15] What is most disturbing about the aesthetic geography of *Precious* is its validation—indeed, its naturalization—of the monstrousness of the black female: mother and child—Precious's abusive mother, Precious and her daughter (by her own father) whom she calls "Mongo," slang for Mongoloid (the child has Down Syndrome), a trilogy of black females that suggests a generational aberration. The film, while not a traditional horror film in the sense of having supernatural or slasher elements, presents instead the "horror" of race, of the black underclass that threatens to spill out into the mainstream, into White middle-class America; a horror that is reinforced throughout the film by the portrayal of the monstrous feminine, or, in the case of Precious Jones, the monstrous mammy.

Rooted in Western (white) notions of the inherent innocence of children, black children and black childhood are often ostracized from the landscape of the cultural normative ideal of childhood. *Precious* forces to the surface the notion of the "monstrous feminine"[16] which is realized in the "monstrous black child" through what David Hevey terms "enfreakment," a cultural process by which bodily differences are skillfully embellished and foregrounded while at the same time they are degraded and marginalized—i.e., freaked.[17] Though this process elicits only a conditional sympathy for Precious—a sympathy that oscillates between compassion and repulsion—it essentially reinforces comforting white racist beliefs about the Otherness of African Americans and the monstrousness—not innocence—of black children.

Mammies, Pickaninnies and Orphans

Stereotypes of black females as oversexed, asexual, or animalistic not only apply to adult females but also to black female children. And while the most historically common stereotype of the black child is the pickaninny character—an unkempt, ragamuffin black child normally with bulging eyes and a cacophony of ponytails that stick up all around the child's head—many of the general stereotypes about black adults are also recreated in portrayals of black children.

In *Imagining the Black Female Body: Reconciling Image in Print and Visual Culture,* Carol E. Henderson argues that black women are placed "outside the 'acceptable' conceptualizations of womanhood that have historically made black women the monstrous Other, and white women the emblems of virtue and beauty."[18] Black women have been historically portrayed as either the oversexed Jezebel character—in such films as *Birth of a Nation* (1916), Pam Greer's (in)famous *Foxy Brown* (1974) and Halle Berry's role in *Monster's Ball* (2001), (Angela Bassett was first offered the role, but refused specifically because it was a stereotypical Jezebel role) or the passive and nonsexual mammy character—such as in *Birth of a Nation, Gone with the Wind* (1939), *Pinky* (1949), Whoopie Goldberg's role in *Corina, Corina* (1999), and more recently, perhaps arguably, Tyler Perry's Medea character. These two characters are a variation of the "Madonna/Whore" construct in which many women, of all races, are depicted in popular culture as either angelic with limited sexual needs, subservient, and in need of protection, or independent, sexually deviant and deserving of punishment. Henderson states that when the black female was depicted visually it was either as a "sexualized mythology or a neutered anomaly, defined by her sexuality, or her lack of it."[19] A woman who enjoys sex, who is active in pursuing sex, is viewed culturally as less feminine than a woman who is subservient to men and sexually non-aggressive. As victims of white oppression and slavery, black women have historically had to fight the racism battle on two fronts: their humanity and their femininity.

Similar to the historical white strategy of emasculating black men, and thereby subjugating the black male, white slave-masters had to de-feminize the black female to excuse their systematic rape of her, and to raise the status of white womanhood. If black women were not "real" women, then they cannot be raped. As Henderson suggests there is an "inextricable link between idea and subject formation and the historic conditions that shape our perspectives of flesh and bone."[20] Such discursive conditions during slavery gave life to beliefs (which still persist today) that black women were somehow not real women. As David Pilgrim writes:

> The mammy caricature was deliberately constructed to suggest ugliness. Mammy was portrayed as dark-skinned, often pitch black, in a society that regarded black skin as ugly, tainted. She was obese, sometimes morbidly overweight. Moreover, she was often portrayed as old, or at least middle-aged. The attempt was to desexualize mammy. The implicit assumption was this: No reasonable white man would choose a fat, elderly black woman instead of the idealized white woman. The black mammy was portrayed as lacking all sexual and sensual qualities. The de-eroticism of mammy meant that the white wife—and by extension, the white family, was safe.[21]

As Norma Manatu argues, from the first encounter with white people, black African women were not viewed as women, but as less-than white women because of their "perceived absence of femininity,"[22] a myth that has been, and still is, perpetuated through visual images of the black mammy figure in American popular culture.

The polar opposite of the mammy figure, however, is the Jezebel character, who, as a stereotype rooted in old European notions of the "lusty Moor,"[23] depicts black career women or autonomous black women (deemed "aggressive") as oversexed. Manatu suggests that "no matter how virtuous the black woman, no matter how feminine, she is more likely than not to be viewed as hypersexed because black women's virtue has had no place in the 'feminine' mythos of U.S. culture."[24] Whites have historically put forth the notion that blacks were "intellectually inferior, culturally stunted, morally underdeveloped, and [express] animal-like sexually."[25] Black women are regularly portrayed in cinema as animalistic, overly-sexual, and aggressive. As Sander Gilman argues, the "Hottentot remained representative of the essence of the black, especially the black female."[26] Described in the "Jim Crow Museum,"

> The Jezebel images which defame African women may be viewed in two broad categories: *pathetic others* and *exotic others*. Pathetic others include those depictions of African women as physically unattractive, unintelligent, and uncivilized. These images suggest that African women in particular and black women in general possess aberrant physical, social, and cultural traits. The African woman's features are distorted—her lips are exaggerated, her breasts sag, she is often inebriated. The pathetic other, like the Mammy caricature before her, is drawn to refute the claim that white men find black women sexually appealing. Yet, this depiction of the African woman has an obvious sexual component: she is often placed in a sexual setting, naked or near naked, inebriated or holding a drink, her eyes suggesting a sexual longing. She is a sexual being, but not one that white men would consider.[27]

Today the Jezebel stereotype is regularly splashed across television-particularly music videos, cinema, and the internet. The image of the Jezebel provides a "framing of the black female experience" for the white audience, who are gratified at "witnessing" what they have long believed about the hypersexed black woman.[28]

Both of these two stereotypes are classic cinematic iconography for black women. But both stereotypes are also part of the way young black girls are presented in cinema. Today, it is common for black teen girls to be portrayed as Jezebels:

> Jezebel images also [reveal] that black female children are sexually objectified. Black girls, with the faces of pre-teenagers, are drawn with adult sized buttocks, which are exposed. They are naked, scantily clad, or hiding seductively behind towels, blankets, trees, or other objects ... [which] suggests that black females are sexually active and sexually irresponsible even as small children.[29]

Though slavery is 150 years past, these are not new stereotypes or characterizations; rather, they are very old beliefs repackaged and re-presented within new frameworks. Today, black girls are routinely depicted in reality television shows and music videos as hypersexual and aggressive. Such images, in contrast to white child images, which often emphasize innocence and purity, instead suggest "the overt sexuality of the black child," and especially poor black girls.[30]

Black children have historically been portrayed as savage in relation to white children and Western notions of childhood, a juxtaposition that helps "constitute a larger cultural politics of innocence" from which the black child is ritually excluded.[31] Early depictions of black children were of a harmless, though ignorant savagery (uncivilized, uncultured, animalistic), such as the portrayal of Sunshine Sammy, Farina, Stymie, and Buckwheat of the *Little Rascals/Our Gang* series.[32] This type of savagery was presented within the context of culturally dominant beliefs about inherent black stupidity, and amid prevalent fears of black (mostly male) aggression, particularly sexual aggression. Hill-Collins states that poor and working class black children are often portrayed in the media as "aggressive, undisciplined, unruly, and unsuitable playmates for white children of any social class."[33] Such widespread portrayal of black children as renegade and undisciplined has evolved to more positive portrayals in a few Hollywood films, for instance the recent *After Earth* (M. Night Shyamalan, 2013) co-starring Jaden Smith, son of Will Smith (also co-starring) and Jada Pinkett-Smith. But Jayden Smith is quite the exception to the rule.

Monstrous Mammy—*Precious Jones*

Precious: Based on the Novel "Push" by Sapphire, directed by Lee Daniels, and produced by Oprah Winfrey and Tyler Perry, was released in 2009 to wide critical acclaim. It is the story of a morbidly obese black teen girl who suffers horrendous abuse at the hands of both her mother and her father. She is raped by her father (and has two children by him), beaten by her mother (who hates Precious for "stealing my man") and is bullied at school by the other teens. The film was praised by some reviewers as a "must see," a rare cinematic experience that "exhibit[s] the courage and perseverance that gives us all hope."[34] Teresa Wiltz, of *The Root*, claims *Precious* is a film that will make the viewer "feel with her, *through* her,"[35] while David Hennessee argues that *Precious* is "singular, moving, and disturbing," with a narrative that suggests we "feel good about a character's struggles because they are ultimately overcome."[36] Yet not all the critical response to *Precious* has been so uplifting. Ed Gonzales, of *Slant* magazine (slantmagazine.com), describes the film as an "impeccably acted piece of trash—an exploitation film that shamelessly strokes its audience's sense of righteous indignation" and a film "For The Stuff White

People Like" genre. Gonzalez opines that the film "simplifies" Precious's longing for escape and for a loving, secure family.[37] Armond White, writing for *NYPress*, characterizes the film as "ghetto tragedy," a "post hip-hop freak show" in which the film's star, Gabourey Sidibe, is "so obese her face seems bloated into a permanent pout." White states that "not since *Birth of a Nation* has a mainstream movie demeaned the idea of black American life as much as *Precious*."[38]

In their disparaging descriptions of Precious (Sidibe), many of the critics used language that enfreaked her, discursively positioning her body as monstrous other. The monstrous body deviates from what is considered normal and acceptable, those things beyond just difference, but are perceived as horrible, disgusting, aberrant, repulsive, and bestial. The film also locates this monstrousness in the urban environment that is often used to portray black life in America, where the "inner-city dweller is irredeemably lost in the dystopic urban core" from which there is little hope of escape.[39] As Rosemarie Garland Thomson describes, the monstrous child (as Other) "emerges from culture-bound expectations" that reside in the interstitial space between "wonder and error."[40] Garland Thomson's description is particularly astute because Precious's existence resides in the liminal space of adulthood while looking back at, and desiring, a lost [white] childhood, indeed a position of "error." As Karen Renner explains "converting the improperly sexual girl into a monster allows her to be excluded from the domain of proper [i.e., white] childhood."[41] And while the film *Precious* does not exclusively monsterize Precious (it also monsterizes her mother and Precious's child, Mongo, albeit differently), it does highlight Precious's monstrousness above all and the monstrousness—the inherent Otherness—of the black child.

The film opens with Clarice Precious Jones dressed in a beautiful ballroom-style gown, happy and smiling. She is morbidly obese, yet this opening scene does not foreground her bodily difference, rather it is her happy demeanor that captures the scene. She is approached by a tall, slim, regal-looking older black woman, wearing an orange princess gown, with an African style headress. The smiling woman anoints Precious with a red-orange, flame-colored, scarf by laying it on Precious's shoulder, a symbolic passing of a "torch." They look into each other's eyes with a sense of understanding. The opening of the film, then, visually connects Precious to a fairy-godmother character that alludes to traditional African philosophical beliefs in the deep spiritual connectedness between the living and the ancestors. Such an allusion at the opening of the film also suggests that the monstrousness of the modern black female is an extension of old colonial beliefs about African women: aberrant, uncivilized, unfeminine, Other. This important filmic nod to African women, African spirituality, and colonialist attitudes will ultimately be reinforced as the film progresses. That the film opens with this scene is significant, as I will show, because so many of the scenes in *Precious* suggest notions of a generational monstrousness rooted in those historic first encounters between whites and the "monstrous" black/brown races.

The first few scenes in *Precious* present a young teen girl in school who daydreams about being on the cover of a magazine, about her white teacher being in love with her, about finding a light-skinned boyfriend, and that she will someday live in the suburbs—all things that any typical American teenage girl dreams about.

The classroom, however, is exactly what white America imagines an inter-city classroom to look like (and what Hollywood typically portrays): white male teacher in front of a wild and out-of-control room full of disrespectful children of color. The landscape of this classroom is oft repeated in such films as *Blackboard Jungle* (Richard Brooks, 1955), *Dangerous Minds* (John N. Smith, 1995) and *Freedom Writers* (Richard LaGravenese) that reinforce viewer familiarity with "those" kinds of classrooms and "those" kinds of kids; this familiar, stereotypical classroom lends an air of authenticity, of truthfulness to an inner city "condition" that belies the film's overt scriptedness. The black boys are particularly unruly and their behavior is foregrounded significantly—the way they tease Precious is by making animal noises (barking), a long-held stereotype of the "animalistic" nature of black children, especially males. The barking noises also begin a trope that lasts throughout the film of equating Precious with a dog.

Throughout the film, Precious is cast as unfeminine: she is morbidly obese and is displayed as vulgar, both of which are considered types of cultural deviancy and socially unfeminine. At home, Precious is a servant to her mother—a mammy in all senses of the word. In the classroom, she forcefully hits a boy upside his head because he would not be quiet while the teacher was speaking. Black women are often portrayed as violent and lacking self-control and this scene naturalizes such stereotypes. Her voice over discusses how she has "Mr. Wicher's back," also a part of the mammy character—protection of the white master (in this case, the teacher). Precious's aggressive slap is also repeated in the Each One, Teach One classroom, where one of the girls calls her fat, and she quietly walks by, then quickly turns around and slaps the girl's head. Yet, oddly, in a later scene when a group of boys verbally assault Precious as she walks home. She does not lash out at them physically as she did to the students in both classrooms, but is pounced on from behind and knocked face-first to the ground, a violent act that sends her into one of her out-of-body escape fantasies.

Precious's vulnerability in this scene works in tandem with the ensuing fantasy, in which she is dancing provocatively with a light skinned man, to assert that in the "real" world, obese black girls do not get light-skinned boys. As she imagines the young light-skinned man nibbling lovingly on her ear, she reluctantly fades back to reality to discover, as she lays face down in the street, it is a dog licking her ear, a gesture in which resides Precious's desire *for* loving kisses, and her marginalization as undeserving of them from a man. She is physically depicted on the ground at the level of the dog, and therefore more deserving of kisses from an animal.

The notion of physical violence committed by the monstrous black child is complicated where Precious is concerned. On the one hand, in the classroom she demonstrates aggression and even violence, but outside the classroom, and most particularly at home, she is passive and vulnerable and is physically and emotionally abused. This oscillation between aggression and vulnerability is a part of the film's practice of enfreaking Precious. Her large frame and her occasional acts of lashing out physically seem to suggest an adult power and an underlying ruthlessness, an uncontrollability, perceptions rooted in a culture that equates power with size (short men are seen as less powerful than tall men, for instance) and blackness with aggression. In the mythos of female obesity, the belief that a large woman is physically strong is common and as a result the viewer is not really surprised when Precious strikes her adversaries; yet the film interrogates this notion of a mannish strength when we witness Precious's large body vulnerable when her mother, Mary, beats her. Precious's position as mammy is also interrogated in the scene when her father rapes her. Instead of a victim, she becomes the Jezebel, as Mary blames Precious—"you fuckin' ho, stole my man!"—for "stealing" her man. This "doubling" of Precious's character is in play throughout the film as she oscillates between pretty/ugly, love/hate, skinny/fat, ignorance/knowledge, abuser/abused.

In *Suffering Childhood in Early America*, Anna Mae Duane examines the "complex relationship between vulnerability and violence that [Little Eva from Harriet Beecher Stowe's *Uncle Tom's Cabin* (1852)] helped articulate in early America." The little white child Eva, in contrast to the wild, uncivilized black girl-slave Topsy, became a defining icon for childhood itself—the site of "vulnerability, suffering, and victimhood"[42] that is still in use today. Conversely from the novel, the slave child Topsy became the blueprint for the Pickaninny character. Though Precious is no pickaninny character, she does represent a "traumatized slave child"[43] in the sense that, as Riché Richardson argues, she is "essentially her mother's servant," a child-mammy who has been "dehumanized and devalued ... treated like an animal"[44] by her peers and in her own home by the one person who should be protecting her. Precious's vulnerability in some cases, such as when her mother abuses her and when her father rapes her, elicits sympathy and yet her aggressiveness at times cancels out that sympathy, reminding the viewer that *black* children are abject: "while the film draws the audience by soliciting a particular type of affective response, it simultaneously performs a critique of the structures of looking that inform the spectacle of sexual violence."[45] The film forces the traditionally non-sexualized obese mammy into a sexualized position, discombobulating long held beliefs about the sexuality of black women and children, obese females, and the mammy character.

In some ways, Precious's size itself becomes the catalyst for the continual oscillation between sympathy for her and the belief in her own complicity. In the field of Attribution Studies, Robert T. Muller, et al., explain that for people who believe the world in general is ordered, just and fair, the "victim-blame" phenomenon results when people try to justify good things happening to people who they feel do not deserve it, and conversely, when bad things happen to good people (like themselves). Muller argues that "individuals respond to such inequities by altering their perception of the victim, [particularly] the victim's behavior, so that the victim is devalued and blamed for [their own] misfortune."[46] The intersection of sympathy and blame contribute to Precious's monstrousness—her abject sexuality as a child victim of rape, and of her obesity—the abject body, reinforced in the scene where she steals and eats an entire bucket of chicken. The film implies that Precious was in some way complicit in both of these conditions—her rape and her obesity. As Michelle Jarman notes, "Sidibe's nonnormative body is often situated as the primary problem of the film ... critical fixation on her weight trumps the abuse, literacy, and economic issues faced by the protagonist."[47] Yet Precious's size perhaps functions as a discursive framework for her lost childhood. Her most poignant scenes reveal both a black girl and fat girl who, much like Toni Morrison's Pecola Breedlove, believes she is ugly and desires to be thin, white and loved.

It would be hard to deny the resemblance of Clarice Precious Jones to Toni Morrison's Pecola Breedlove in *The Bluest Eye:* "Long hours she sat looking in the mirror, trying to discover the secret of the ugliness, the ugliness that made her ignored or despised at school, by teachers and classmates alike."[48] There are quite a few parallels between the two girls: both were raped by their fathers and became pregnant, both were abused by their mothers (though Pecola was not sexually abused by her mother), both girls escaped abuse through dissociative means, both girls see themselves as ugly, and both hate and blame their blackness as the cause of their condition. Pecola's meditations on her physical appearance mirror Precious's self-contemplation in the bedroom scene, one of the few scenes in the film that reminds us that Precious is still a child. The scene opens with Precious in the shower, getting ready for her day at Each One, Teach One, then cuts to her mother masturbating in bed. The juxtaposition of both scenes suggests Precious's desire to wash the stain of incest away (a common trope in rape narratives), and a "point of transfer of power"[49] in which Precious's bathing signifies renewal of both her desire to learn (taking pains with her appearance for the alternative school) and rejection of her mother's sexual abuse. The camera next does a slow pan of Precious's bedroom: posters of skinny, beautiful pop singers and light-skinned hunks line her wall. She appears in frame and steps to the mirror. Instead of her own reflection she sees a thin, blonde girl looking back at her, a "visualization and reinvention" while simultaneously rejecting her own identity and body.[50] Precious here "imagines conforming to the hegemonic discourse of beauty she's absorbed from white society" as the way to love and security.[51] As Mask describes her, "Precious's learned self-devaluation [is] the convergence of abuse, internalized racism (or more specifically, colorism), and weight discrimination."[52] Much like Pecola Breedlove imagined that having blue eyes would help her escape abuse and despair, Precious believes that being socially acceptable and deserving of a better life requires being thin and having lighter skin. Unlike Pecola, however, Precious's journey is not into insanity, but rather, away from. She is not a silent victim and at first takes tentative but stubborn steps towards her own salvation, such as attending Each One, Teach One. As those few steps garner significant progress (like reading and having friends for the first time), she finds the strength to reject abuse, leave her mother's home, and strike out on her own with little Abdul.

The film presents the subtle confirmation of the belief in the dysfunction of the black family as intergenerational, beginning with the very first scene where the older woman passes the orange scarf to Precious. In the scene of the welfare worker's visit, *Precious* visually suggests deep familial corruption by showcasing four generations of black female monstrous others: the ineffective grandmother, Toosie (perhaps a victim of abuse herself), Mary (Precious's mother), Precious, and her daughter Mongo (see Figure 4).

In this scene, the outward façade of a functioning family unit is presented to the welfare worker (and us) by Mary, who puts on a wig, lipstick, and holds a squirming Mongo in a falsely loving embrace. Mary's voice is soft and humble as she works to convince the welfare worker that she has been looking for

Figure 4. Precious, Mary, and Mongo—three generations of "monstrous" black women.

work and caring for Mongo. As soon as the welfare worker leaves, Mary pushes Mongo off her lap, calls her a "goddamn animal" and proceeds to berate Precious's "stupidity" for somehow being the "cause" of the welfare worker's scrutiny. Precious here is positioned squarely as a child, yet only as a means to her mother's welfare check, and only in front of the worker. The moment the welfare worker leaves, Mary begins to treat Precious as a servant, a mammy, while the silent grandmother looks on. The intergenerational nature of both physical and sexual abuse is suggested by the grandmother's extreme passivity, and her obvious fear of her daughter, Mary. In Mary's aggression toward, and verbal abuse of, little Mongo, one may infer (particularly in light of a later scene where Mary intentionally drops newborn baby Abdul to the floor) that until the child was placed with the grandmother, she may have also been the victim of Mary's wrath.

All the people in the film who are positive influences, who are kind and help Precious, are light-skinned: Ms. Weis (the welfare worker), Ms. Rain (her teacher) and her lesbian partner, and Nurse John. The only meaningful support that is offered Precious comes from these light-skinned folks, reifying whiteness as the savoir, as the answer to Precious's (and by inference "The Hood's") problems. Such a message elides the very real socio-economic and political processes and matrices that often converge in urban poor areas to create real obstacles for those who wish to improve their lives. The film's rhetorical strategy renders "happiness, safety, and security [as] particularly synonymous with a white suburban configuration of the American Dream,"[53] leaving no other avenue open for success. Even Precious's own grandmother, who is dark-skinned like Precious, does not, will not, or cannot help. Toosie's lack of involvement in preventing her granddaughter's abuse at the hands of her own daughter Mary suggests again the intergenerational impotence and dysfunction of the black family.

The scene of the welfare worker's visit does more than just suggest the family's dysfunction; it echoes the most disturbing and racist opinions of the notoriously paternalistic 1965 Moynihan Report, which concluded that the "Negro family" is disintegrating because of the predominance of single mothers (i.e., Jezebel behavior), their dependence (generationally) on public assistance, residing in urban ghettos, and a lack of "strong father figure[s]" who have the freedom to "strut" like all "male animals."[54] The stereotypes about crumbling African American families inherent in the Moynihan Report unfortunately remain today and have been the source of both public policy shifts (i.e., welfare reform under the Clinton administration—a media inspired, moral panic response to the demonized, and mythical, black "Welfare Queen") and persistent processes of institutional racism in such areas as medical care and schools.

One of the recurring allusions in *Precious* is to the (colonial) notion of the animalistic black female. Throughout the film, at key moments, dogs appear as visual metaphors that suggest the animalistic nature of Precious and her family. The little white and brown Jack Russell Terrier first appears when the boys knock Precious to the ground. As I stated earlier, in her fantasy she is being kissed by her light skinned prince, but she wakes to find the dog licking her face as she is face down on the street and on the same level as the dog. A short time later, we see Precious steal then devour an entire bucket of chicken, a scene in which the character performs the most racist of stereotypes about black people and fried chicken. When Precious is in the hospital, her grandmother berates Precious that "not even a dog would drop a baby then leave, not even a dog." Most significantly, however, is the scene when a bloody and disheveled Precious, cradling the newborn Abdul, escaping from her mother's vicious assault, hears music and stops in front of a church. As she listens to the church choir, she slides into one of her dissociative excursions and imagines herself singing with them. Next to her fantasy self is her light-skinned boyfriend holding the little Jack Russell terrier. That the dog becomes an ambient character in her dreams is indicative of her struggle to redefine her identity, to escape the framework of "ghetto tragedy," to escape the echo of the barking and grunting noises the boys in her public school class made towards her, and to resist the label of animal that has defined her life until Ms. Rain and the Each One, Teach One school.⁵⁵ But in this choir scene, the dog is contained by the fantasy boyfriend instead of sharing the street space with Precious, a suggestion that resonates with her new liminality and her reclamation of identity.

And while the fantasy choir scene shows a smiling and singing Precious, admired with the loving gaze of the light-skinned boyfriend (and the dog), the street scene instead positions a giant billboard above Precious that reminds the viewer of her and her children's (and her family's) monstrousness. The billboard sign recommends people "spay and neuter" their pets (producing "Happy, Healthy Pets") and is juxtaposed with an abused Precious, protectively cradling her child (of incest). The billboard message, which hovers over Precious, is the literal discursive framing of Precious as abject: the moment when her body, her sexuality, and her progeny are fully monstrous—wholly Other, and that monstrosity threatens to spill over into the suburbs she dreams of inhabiting—that dream is the film's "horror." Blackness, therefore, must be "neutered." The triangulation of the billboard, Precious and Abdul, and the church presents the viewer with a "trinity of judgment"; an intersection in which the church (moral authority) and the sign (as the establishment) both play to historical theories of Eugenics, to Margaret Sanger's 1929 *The Negro Project*, in which she recruited NAACP founder W.E.B. Du Bois to support her push for widespread birth control for African American women so they would stop "breeding." Du Bois, an unlikely supporter, had stated at the time that: "The mass of ignorant Negroes still breed carelessly and disastrously, so that the increase among Negroes, even more than the increase among whites, is from that portion of the population least intelligent and fit, and least able to rear their children properly," a sentiment Sanger repeated often in her quest to eradicate the Negro. Sanger pushed for government-sponsored clinics that gave out free birth control to poor black women.⁵⁶ Du Bois's statement "least intelligent and [least] fit" reaches out from history to marginalize Precious Jones, who is portrayed as both. The message to "spay and neuter" black women and girls, to keep the horrors of aberrant black sexuality and its monstrous un-femininity out of middle-class, white America is fully realized in this image.

Conclusion

Despite the film's clear message of uplift through education and self-love, the subtext of *Precious* resides with old notions of whiteness, slimness, and middle-class suburbs as the only paths to happiness. Though Precious finds freedom from her mother's tyranny and discovers what it's like to be loved, she holds on to the model of whiteness, and white childhood, as her ideal goal. The film does a respectable job of leaving Precious in the interstitial space between child and adult, but it is the juxtaposition of adult knowledge (particularly sexual) with the childlike fantasies (being a star, a princess, being desired by a "white" knight in shining armor, or in this case, a light-skinned young man) that highlight Precious's exclusion from notions of childhood itself. For Precious, who wants to *be* a child in the idealized sense, her fantasies of having a loving mother, adoration by fans, and the love of a light-skinned man frame her forced position of adulthood, her desire for knowledge, and her vow to be the loving mother to Abdul and Mongo that she never had. But as Duane, rightly, suggests, "[t]he continued equivalence of childhood, and particularly black childhood, with a state of perpetual victimhood needs to be rethought."[57] Unfortunately, *Precious* does little to rethink the black child's position within social matrices and instead, rather *supports* notions of black children as victims. And while we feel sorry for Precious and her predicament, at some level that sympathy is replaced with the belief in the righteousness of whiteness, as throughout the film achieving whiteness was the *real* goal for Precious all along.

At the end, Precious and her dysfunctional family have been "displaced onto the invented domain of the [urban] primitive,"[58] a primitiveness that instills fear in white middle-class sensibilities. And while the film voyeuristically caresses, yet enfreaks, Sidibe's obesity, it does so in such a way that highlights the "malice underlying the infantilization of blackness,"[59] its Otherness/monstrousness. And rather than leave the viewer with hope for a brighter future for Precious and her children, the white viewer is left shivering at the unspoken threat that Precious and her family just might make it; just might move to the suburbs and take up residence.

Notes

1. Bernth Lindfors, "Ethnological Show Business: Footlighting the Dark Continent," in *Freakery: Cultural Spectacles of the Extraordinary Body*, ed. Rosemarie Garland Thompson (New York: New York University Press, 1996), 208–9. See also *Exhibiting Cultures: The Poetics and Politics of Museum Display*, eds. by Ivan Karp and Steven D. Lavine (Washington, D.C.: Smithsonian Institution Press, 1991); Sadiah Qureshi "Displaying Sara Baartman, The Hottentot Venus," *History of Science* 42.136 (2004): 233–257.

2. According to Lindfors, "live Eskimos [were] exhibited in Bristol as early as 1501, of Brazilian Indians building their own village in Rouen in the 1550s, of 'Virginians' on the Thames in 1603, and of numerous other native human specimens from the New World,

Africa, Asia, Australia, and the Pacific Islands being conveyed to European cities and towns as biological curiosities" (207).

3. John Block Friedman, *Monstrous Races in the Medieval Art and Thought* (Syracuse: Syracuse University Press, 2000), 1.

4. George Yancy, *Black Bodies, White Gazes* (Lanham, MD: Rowman & Littlefield, 2008), xvi.

5. Yancy, xx.

6. Yancy, xxii.

7. Franz Fanon, "The Fact of Blackness." full text online at http://www19.homepage.villanova.edu/silvia.nagyzekmi/postcol/Fanon%20The%20Fact%20of%20Blackness.pdf. 8. Yancy, 3. 9. Mary Douglas, *Purity and Danger* (New York: Routledge, 2002/1966), 5.

10. W.E.B. Du Bois, "Strivings of the Negro People," *Atlantic Monthly*, August 1897. http://www.americasinging.com/wordpress2/wp-content/uploads/2009/11/WEB-DuBois.pdf

11. For more discussion of black masculinities, see Ronald L. Jackson, III, *Scripting the Black Masculine Body: Identity, Discourse, and Racial Politics in Popular Media*, (New York: State University of New York Press, 2006) and Kathryn Bond Stockton, *Beautiful Bottom Beautiful Shame: Where "Black" Meets "Queer"* (Durham: Duke University Press, 2007).

12. Donald Bogle, *Toms, Coons, Mulattoes, Mammies, and Bucks* (New York: Viking Press, 1973), 4.

13. Duane, 127.

14. Adam Phillips, *Beast in the Nursery* (New York: Pantheon, 1998), 14.

15. Rosemarie Garland Thomson, ed., *Freakery: Cultural Spectacles of the Extraordinary Body* (New York: New York University Press, 1996), 2.

16. Creed, 67.

17. David Hevey, *The Creatures That Time Forgot: Photography and Disability Imagery* (New York: Routledge, 1992), 53.

18. Carol E. Henderson, ed., *Imagining the Black Female Body: Reconciling Image in Print and Visual Culture* (New York: Palgrave Macmillan, 2010), 3.

19. Henderson, 29.

20. Henderson, 5.

21. David Pilgrim, "The Mammy Caricature," Jim Crow Museum, http://www.ferris.edu/jimcrow/mammies/, 26 May 2013.

22. Norma Manatu, *African American Women and Sexuality in the Cinema* (Jefferson, NC: McFarland, 2003), 18.

23. Pilgrim, "Jezebel," http://www.ferris.edu/jimcrow/jezebel.htm.

24. Manatu, 19.

25. Pilgrim, "Jezebel," http://www.ferris.edu/jimcrow/jezebel.htm.

26. Sander L. Gilman, "Black Bodies, White Bodies: Toward an Iconography of Female Sexuality in Late Nineteenth-Century Art, Medicine, and Literature," *Critical Inquiry* 12 (1985): 204–242, 206.

27. Jim Crow Museum, http://www.ferris.edu/jimcrow/jezebel.htm.

28. Maria del Guadelupe Davidson, "'You … You Remind Me of….': A Black Feminist's Rejection of the White Imagination," in *Imagining the Black Female Body*, ed. Carol E. Henderson (New York: Palgrave Macmillan, 2010), 191–205, 199.

29. Pilgrim, "Jezebel," http://www.ferris.edu/jimcrow/jezebel.htm.

30. Gilman, 212.

31. Yancy, 171.

32. See Christopher P. Lehman, *The Colored Cartoon: Black Representation in American Animated Short Films, 1907–1954* (Amherst: University of Massachusetts Press, 2007), Richard Neupert "Trouble in Watermelon Land: George Pal and the Little Jasper Cartoons," *Film Quarterly* 55.1 (2001): 14–26; and Kelvin Santiago-Valles, "'Still Longing for de Old

Plantation': The Visual Parodies and Racial National Imaginary of U.S. Overseas Expansionism, 1898–1903," *American Studies International* 37.3 (1999): 18–43.
  33. Patricia Hill-Collins, *Black Sexual Politics: African Americans, Gender, and the New Racism* (New York: Routledge, 2005), 138.
  34. Monica Sweeney, "A Precious and Painful Life," *The Lancet* 375 (2010): 189–190. Web.
  35. Teresa Wiltz, "Oprah Is Wrong About *Precious*," *The Root*, November 6, 2009. Web.
  36. David Hennessee, "Some Thoughts on *Precious: Based on the Novel Push by Sapphire*," *Moebius* 8.1 (2010): 155–160. Web.
  37. Ed Gonzalez, "*Precious: Based on the Novel Push by Sapphire*," *Slant Magazine*, October 9, 2009. Web.
  38. Armond White, "Pride and Precious," *NYPress.com*, 4 November 2009. Web.
  39. Cameron McCarthy, Alida Rodrquez, Shuaib Meecham, et al., "Race, Suburban Resentment, and the Representation of the Inner City in Contemporary Film and Television," in *Off White: Readings on Power, Privilege, and Resistance*, eds. Michelle Fine, et al. (New York: Routledge, 2004), 163–174, 163.
  40. Thomson, 3.
  41. Karen Renner, "Monstrous Schoolgirls: Casual Sex in the Twenty-First-Century Horror Film," *Red Feather Journal* 3.2 (2012): 34–50, 1.
  42. Anna Mae Duane, *Suffering Childhood in Early America* (Athens: University of Georgia Press, 2010), 3.
  43. Duane, 146.
  44. Riché Richardson, "Push, Precious, and New Narratives of Slavery in Harlem," *Black Camera* 4.1 (2012): 161–180, 165.
  45. Régine Michelle Jean-Charles, "'I think I was raped': Black Feminist Readings of Affect and Incest in *Precious*," *Black Camera* 4.1 (2012): 139–160, 153–4.
  46. Robert T. Muller, Robert A. Caldwell, and John E. Hunter, "Child Provocativeness and Gender as Factors Contributing to the Blaming of Victims of Physical Child Abuse," *Child Abuse and Neglect* 17 (1993): 249–260, 249.
  47. Michelle Jarman, "Cultural Consumption and Rejection of Precious Jones: Pushing Disability into the Discusson of Sapphire's *Push* and Lee Daniel's *Precious*," *Feminist Formations* 24.2 (2012): 163–185, 168.
  48. Toni Morrison, *The Bluest Eye* (New York: Alfred A. Knopf, 1993), 45.
  49. Jean-Charles, 154.
  50. Richardson, 171.
  51. Mia Mask, "The Precarious Politics of *Precious*: A Close Reading of a Cinematic Text," *Black Camera: An International Film Journal* 4.1 (2012): 96–116, 99.
  52. Mask, 99.
  53. Mask, 99.
  54. Moynihan Report, "The Negro Family: The Case for National Action," 5–12, http://www.stanford.edu/~mrosenfe/Moynihan%27s%20The%20Negro%20Family.pdf.
  55. White.
  56. Harriet A. Washington, *Medical Apartheid: The Dark History of Medical Experimentation on Black Americans from Colonial Times to the Present* (New York: Anchor Books, 2006), 195–198.
  57. Duane, 159.
  58. Anne McClintock, *Imperial Leather: Race, Gender, and Sexuality in the Colonial Contest* (New York: Routledge, 1995), 214–215.
  59. Duane, 159.

Violent Nymphs

Vampire and Vigilante Children in Contemporary Cinema

Lisa Cunningham

The problem with much common discourse about "childhood" or "the child" is that the collapsing of multiplicitous and complex identities into those singular, unifying categories is a serious oversimplification. Idealized versions of children are culturally produced and repeated in media and in cultural storytelling, often in ways that completely disregard any individual or noncompliant desire children themselves might have. These reductive narratives of childhood and its possible expressions often limit the child to a realm of acceptable performance that focuses on the child's desirability and innocence; this focus, for little girls in particular, both requires and is couched in dialogue about their culturally-presumed nonviolence (both the lack of a predilection for violence and the lack of a capability to enact it). James Kincaid's *Erotic Innocence*, a study on the cultural construction of universalizing narratives of the desirable child, notes that such narrowness of identity definition is dangerous:

> by formulating the image of the alluring child as bleached, bourgeois, and androgynous, these stories mystify material reality and render nearly invisible—certainly irrelevant—questions we might raise about race, class, and even gender. Such categories are scrubbed away in the idealized child, laved and snuggled into Grade-A homogeneity.[1]

Collapsing children into a single sanitized category thus leads to widespread rhetorical practices of norming, of excluding any non-hegemonic narratives of childness, a term introduced in the introduction of this volume. If these narratives of "normal" or "acceptable" childhood are all that is provided, they will not only shape our discourse surrounding childhood; they will then, naturally, govern our reactions and expectations when faced with real, embodied, problematic children. Thus, oppositional narratives of girlhood are both positive for the discursive space of girlhood as a whole and necessary to keep systems that devalue the girl subject from being wholly reductive of girlness. The violent little girl—specifically here, the vampire or vigilante little girl—is a confrontational reminder to the audience that it is impossible to reduce girlness to its social components; she asks that the audience "[relocate] the talk [...] tease the storytelling into a new territory, find new possibilities."[2] Violent girls in cinema, particularly in these films of "impossible" and impossibly violent girlhood, have uniquely overt ways of exposing the social narratives of what "little girls" must be and the dangers of subscribing to that minimizing narrative.

As Rose points out, the social interest in maintaining a simplified, stable image of the child is one of maintaining the signifying status quo: "Children may, on occasions, be disturbed, but they do not disturb us as long as that sequence (and that development) can be ensured. Children are no threat to our identity because they are, so to speak, 'on their way' [...] Their difference stands purely as the sign of just how far we have progressed."[3] So long as "childhood" and its boundaries are considered sacrosanct, the adult can tell himself that he has left "all of that"—any sexual ambiguity or uncertainty—behind, as the now-adult has progressed past the stage in which those concerns are presumably resolved. As Rose explores, however, "childhood is something in which we continue to be implicated and which is never simply left behind. Childhood persists."[4] "Childhood," as a finite biological or developmental stage, has been redefined repeatedly in terms of medical and historical discourse, but it is the less tangible "childhood" of psychoanalytic and cultural discourse—the "childness," as articulated in the introduction to this volume—which itself is a powerful destabilizing force. It is perhaps not childhood that persists, but childness. The biological stage can be left behind, but the decentering effects of childness are always already occurring in the self.

Terminologically, the discussion surrounding children and childhood is complex, riddled with vocabulary that is only subtly, connotatively distinguished. "Childhood," for example, generally refers to the biological/developmental period before puberty—the age during which one is externally identified as a "child." Freudian thought traditionally sees childhood as a stage, developmentally separate from adulthood, during which certain behaviors/mannerisms manifest, are worked through, and are discarded from the self before the adult self is realized. Such separation of childhood from adulthood, however, is as problematic as any binary relationship; implying that the two have no intrinsic connection or are somehow inherently different leads inevitably to the social assignation of certain qualities, traits, and value to each category. The biological separation of these two stages by the apparent marker of puberty (as though one's body does not continue to change over time) makes it easier to separate specifically "adult" from "child" developmentally, by an apparently impermeable boundary, and to invest childhood (as a unified, iconic category) with these hegemonic significations.[5]

This investment is seen most apparently in language used to describe children and those traits and objects that are considered part of the realm of the child. "Childlike" is an adjective used to describe qualities that are expected and accepted in children, traits that are considered generally innocent or otherwise "harmless"; for example, enthusiasm or exuberance.[6] The intentional and semantic simile of child-"like" denotes the positive, comparative relationship that its use signifies between the quality being commented upon and "childhood." "Childish," conversely, refers to those actions or behaviors that are undesirable, that are invested with negative value. Many of these traits are those that are actively abjected by adults, who are enabled by the false division of childhood from adulthood to see themselves as beyond or developmentally past "childish" behaviors, which are conscripted entirely to the distanced realm of the "child."[7] Both "childlike" and "childish" can refer to traits exhibited by both adults and children—the main differentiating factor in their use is the tonal conveyance of approval or disapproval of the action or behavior, respectively.

"Childlike" is a useful term to reference the performance of behaviors or mannerisms that are expected from and/or accepted in children. So long as certain significant behaviors can be maintained as "childlike," they become qualities that are abjected by the adult, conscripted to childhood.[8] As Kincaid points out, the qualities that adults attempt to foist onto children are, for the most part, those defined by negation: "the child was the one who *did not have*. Its liberty was a negative attribute, however much prized, as was its innocence and purity."[9] Childness, then, allows for the reappropriation of those qualities into a structure that reminds adults that abjection, the very act of defining oneself by "radically exclud[ing]"[10] or denying certain characteristics, is an unproductive and ultimately irresponsible method of identification and identity formation.[11]

Certain cultural values (or concerns) can, of course, be more easily projected or inscribed onto a conceptual category of identity than on an actual subjective individual. Childhood, and what is considered "childlike" in particular, seems vulnerable to this kind of targeted rereading, and the construction of the modern girl is more demanding of that emptiness than of the modern boy. Kincaid identifies a few specific qualities that social constructions of "childhood" and of "desirable femininity" often share: "among other things, sweet, innocent, vacant, smooth-skinned, spontaneous, and mischievous."[12] These qualities, many of them popular in advertisements for young girls' dolls, all share a blankness, a vacancy that indicates the stillness and emptiness these kind of valuations require of girlhood. These qualities are particularly those adults see themselves as having "lost" or outgrown, conscripting them mainly to the realm of girlhood as vehemently policed values, that are openly expected of girls. Innocence and purity, values associated both with being childlike and with feminine virtue, are standards of behavior that require absolutes; nothing can be generally innocent or mostly pure in a system that employs these kinds of "negative" valuations—those that require the absence (rather than the presence) of action and/or intention. The reading of that vacuousness onto children and the concurrent hegemonic attempts to discipline children into pre-conscripted realms of "acceptable" behavior become disrupted when real, violent, destabilizing childness enters the picture. All of these qualities share an emptiness, an ability to be over-written that is reproduced in cinema either as a photocopy of the "perfect" or desirable child—one that exhibits the above qualities and ultimately endorses the heteronormative narrative—or as a "monstrous" childness, one that actively rejects or performs against these expectations and is not able to be reabsorbed into a simplistic model of the childhood narrative.

The conscription of childness to these realms of inaction is often marked by the notable gendering of certain expectations. Hilary Neroni's *The Violent Woman* examines the violent woman in cinema as a destabilizing force against the heteronormative gender binary: "One powerful example—one that almost always acts as a nexus for concerns about gender identity—is the violent woman in film. If there is one characteristic that defines masculinity in the cultural imagination, it is violence. The depiction of a violent woman upsets this association of violence with masculinity."[13] Neroni lays out reasons provided by culture—protecting one's family, "boys will be boys," introducing lawful- or lawless-ness to the American landscape, and so forth—for the expected violence performed by men. But female violence is rationalized differently, on a more unstable and individually-determined footing, where the performance of violence itself often makes the female "monstrous." This kind of difference in the treatment of male and female violence extends to the child-versions of those performances, as well. As the aesthetic definition of little girls in Hollywood cinema is mostly concerned with appearance (i.e., fragile, small, high-pitched voice) and generic passive performance (i.e., vulnerable, easily frightened, physically weak/shrinking), it is particularly easy for filmic little girls—through the medium of violence, of behaving in a way that dramatically and directly contradicts the cultural expectations invested in them—to explode those boundaries.

Upsetting this binary/structural relationship also intrinsically upsets an understanding of the self, as the presumed concrete border between "childhood" and "adulthood" is shown to be similarly disturbable. Specifically for this inquiry, female child vampires and vigilantes are examined as sites of resistance to the hegemonic views of female and child performance that are encouraged in contemporary cultural definitions of "little girls." Vampirism has traditionally signified the fear of the intrusion of the Other—or, in many cases, appears as an iteration of Freud's "return of the repressed"—but here it specifically marks childhood as that which is Othered. Girlness, as a distinct and identifiable designation within childness, is such a rigidly socially-policed identity that its methods of rebellion are often enmeshed with its restrictive external signifiers. In monstrous children, the disruptive possibilities of childness become apparent, embodied in their empowered forms.

In a discussion of the filmic body—as either a rhetorical construct or a physical, sexed object—Judith Butler's *Gender Trouble* considers a necessary duality: "Is 'the body' or 'the sexed body' the firm foundation on which gender and systems of compulsory sexuality operate? Or is 'the body' itself shaped by political forces with strategic interests in keeping that body bounded and constituted by the markers of sex?"[14] To distinguish between the physical, sexed body and the constructed Butlerian body in a film—which is being consumed, necessarily, through a visual/aesthetic re-presentation of the physical body—helps establish semantic differences between discursive spaces, like those between "childhood" and "childness." While both of these conceptions of "the body" have philosophical weight, of particular interest is the consideration of how the body as a site of cultural inscription with certain acceptable spaces and performances is integral to both the formation of boundaries (i.e., taboos, self vs. Other) and the slippages thereof. Filmically, the body is one of the main sites of character identification; from costuming to lighting, it is paramount that the audience be able to see and read the character as intended. Foucault's body as "the inscribed surface of events"[15] is what these aesthetic artists try to create—a body that, aware of (at least some of) the values assigned to her by hegemonic discourse, finds a way to enact her agency more efficiently than any of the patriarchal powers around her. In the films under discussion, each little girl is consistently marked by two physical manifestations of her agency: violence, and the manipulative performance of the hegemonic construction of what child and female (particularly girl) bodies should be. Since violence is linked with acceptable masculine performance, its consistent coupling with outlandish, occasionally comical caricatures of "cute" or "desirable" girlness forcibly questions the "naturalness" of these provided (and rigidly enforced) standards of "sugar and spice" girl identity.

When examining the image of the violent child in cinema, looking specifically at prepubescent female vampires allows for a reading of the agency of the child-body as simultaneously controlled and controlling. For this reading, Eli of *Let the Right One In*,[16] Abby of *Let Me In*,[17] and Claudia from *Interview with the Vampire*[18] are primary examples of the complex treatment of vampiric girl bodies in cinema. In each of these films, the female child has not yet reached puberty when her aging process is stopped, and thus can still be concretely identified as having a child-body. Because the girls are forever girls (in that they are never women), they are afforded an interesting position: that of being simultaneously children and not-children, given their respective chronological ages. These girls' complicated position allows them and their particular childness to subvert Kincaid's point about the savage child, that "the energy in these figures would seem to work against the erotic emptiness of the [Romantic child ...], the hollow child whose innocence allowed for the inscription of all forms of desire. But those naughty figures are strangely innocent too, protected by their ignorance and their 'primitive' status from bearing any real responsibility for their misdeeds."[19] These girls have been consciously existing and performing this violence for years, in each instance, and are demonstrably more lethal than any of their male counterparts, so they can hardly be excused by the presumed ignorance or naivety that the "savage" moniker imparts. In fact, the performances of vulnerability and of "acceptable" girlness here have more in common with Kincaid's reading of Horatio Alger:

> Those favored by fortune and by Alger get what they get (which, incidentally, is never fame and fortune but just lower-middle-class security) because they are pretty and lucky. Alger may have felt he was inculcating a Protestant ethic, but he seems to have exploited instead a pedophilic fairy tale, a narrative that runs at least as deep in America as Puritanism. It's not hard work that brings success but being cute, cute in the presence of susceptible adults.[20]

The girls are consciously exploiting exactly that narrative, a deep-seated American phantasy that children need saving at all, that they are inherently vulnerable and always in need of adult help. Each character is aware of the emptiness of this expected performance (though in different ways, respectively), and so these children are able to deploy those cultural/adult oversimplifications of girlness as a powerful weapon against the dominant group.

Butler's observation about the possibility of fighting back against paternal law and its methods of repression outlines a possibility of these girls' unique positions: "If subversion is possible, it will be a subversion from within the terms of the law, through the possibilities that emerge when the law turns against itself and spawns unexpected permutations of itself."[21] This particular embodiment, then, explores possibilities for rebellion within the repressive hegemonic discourse of girlhood, specifically by having the characters in question enact their respective agencies through a masterful use of (1) a rhetoric of "natural" or feral violence that is inherently theirs, and (2) a performance/usurpation of the hegemonic construction of girlness. Perhaps the violence is a necessary component of this reaction precisely because of those constructions that restrict girl behavior. Kincaid asserts that the "Romantic child was largely figured as an inversion of Enlightenment virtues and was thus strangely hollow right from the start: uncorrupted, unsophisticated, unenlightened. The child was without a lot of things, things it was better off without, presumably, but still oddly dispossessed and eviscerated, without much substance."[22] The complete repression/exclusion of violence in any mainstream narrative about girlhood adds the quality of being unviolent to this specific set of values, so the return of violence (as a forbidden mode of discourse) to the performance of the girls is a direct way of engaging with that emptying out.

Children's bodies, particularly those of little girls, are constantly policed in terms of their signification. Smallness, frailty, helplessness, and naïveté typify misogynist images of both women and little girls in filmic culture: Shirley Temple, Little Orphan Annie, Dorothy Gale, and Alice (of Wonderland) immediately spring to mind. Michel Foucault's *Discipline and Punish* asserts that

> disciplinary power [...] is exercised through its invisibility; at the same time it imposes on those whom it subjects a principle of compulsory visibility. In discipline, it is the subjects who have to be seen. Their visibility assures the hold of power that is exercised over them. It is the fact of being constantly seen, of being able always to be seen, that maintains the disciplined individual in his subjection.[23]

The job of little girls, in many social and organized contexts, is to be seen; they are to maintain a particular appearance, and their "precociousness" and "cuteness" are qualities that remain accessible only through observation. Their behaviors are rigidly policed, much more so than their male counterparts;

there is no female equivalent, after all, of "boys will be boys." As numerous feminist theorists have outlined, the capability of women to speak back to a system in which they are embroiled is troubled by the presumed "always already there" nature of that hegemonic system. Girlness is given certain values, and so these violent girls will perform the song and dance, the trappings of those girlhoods, but only in their own certain contexts; the hyperbolic performances of helplessness and girlhood always intersect, just preceding and always facilitating moments of savage filmic violence. The performance of "proper" girlhood is used as a lure, preying on the projection of weakness onto girlness to ensnare adult prey. Girlness, particularly through the violent enacting of its agency, is a disruptive force that relies on the presumption of an inherent weakness or inefficacy of both the female and the child body, so most especially the girl-body.

Susan Bordo, while examining the need for "an effective political discourse about the female body," calls for

> a discourse that will enable us to account for the subversion of potential rebellion, a discourse that, while insisting on the necessity of objective analysis of power relations, social hierarchy, political backlash, and so forth, will nonetheless allow us to confront the mechanisms by which the subject at times becomes enmeshed in collusion with forces that sustain her own oppression.[24]

Childness, as a deconstructing force, attempts many of these discursive confrontations through its boundary-blurring, its inherent tendency to destabilize and blatantly question power with a "childlike" lack of subtlety. Horrific violence is the bodily expression, the physical rhetoric, through which girl bodies are here able to explode—or at least forcefully resist—the mapping onto themselves of both "child" and "girl" expectations and norms. If, as Mary Douglas's *Purity and Danger* suggests, the very limits of the body are established by the same discourses that police and mandate its performance, then the body itself can become a site of reading and reacting to hegemonic marginalization. She asserts that "the body is a model that can stand for any bounded system. Its boundaries can represent any boundaries which are threatened or precarious."[25] Boundaries that can be destabilized, that can be disrupted because of their constructedness (i.e., taboos), are coded as dangerous, threatening. Through violence, the girls this essay considers are able to expand the boundaries of possible girl performance and thus to forcibly demonstrate the permeability of those boundaries (adult/child, human/Other) that hegemonic patriarchal discourse asserts are natural and attempts to keep sacrosanct.

The vampire girls are also eternally young, inhabiting impossible (and abnormal, though visually human) bodies, permitting them a situation slightly outside the normative dominant structures dictating childhood and girlhood. This uniquely marginalized position allows the girls to be more operatively aware of the social positions they are always already expected to inhabit. As Butler notes, "the mark of gender appears to 'qualify' bodies as human bodies; the moment in which an infant becomes humanized is when the question, 'is it a boy or girl?' is answered." If these girls never reach other "natural" markers of gendered development, they become non-human, become "those bodily figures who do not fit into either gender" and who consequently "fall outside the human, indeed, constitute the domain of the dehumanized and the abject against which the human itself is constituted." Their visual association with stereotypically idealized expressions of little girlhood and their enshrinement as fetishistic objects for the protagonists in such context, however, belies their connection to the ways that gender, "the variable cultural construction of sex, the myriad and open possibilities of cultural meaning occasioned by a sexed body"[26] is not conscripted to the realm of "adulthood" but is expected to be absent in many ways from the expressions of children in order to maintain a particular positioning of the little girl as Othered, as non-threatening to the hegemonic discourse of gender. The liminal space that the girls physically inhabit—the void between (female) adulthood and childhood, as none of these subjects ever have or ever will reach puberty and have been trapped in that state for extended periods of time—is displayed within the vampire girl body, specifically and most notably that of Claudia (Kirsten Dunst). Her aesthetic engagement with the signifiers of "cuteness" and girlhood is singular among the vampire girls, as she is the most "appropriate"-appearing among them.

Interview with the Vampire follows the two protagonists—Lestat (Tom Cruise), a decadent vampiric partier, and Louis (Brad Pitt), his somewhat reluctant companion—who have created a vampire from a ten-year old, Claudia, whom they intend to raise as a daughter. Claudia's only action in the film before her re-creation as a vampire is to weep softly, calling "mama" and clinging to the corpse of her decaying mother, before she embraces Louis. Even in her creation scene, however, Claudia exhibits a talent for the aggressive; she ferociously latches onto Lestat's wrist, from which she imbibes his blood and her new life, and it is momentarily difficult for the much larger, stronger being to stop her. This is the first moment her intrinsic connection to violence becomes apparent in the film. This is a possibility for her only when she has been reimagined within a bodily identity that eschews the stereotypical role of the passive little girl. Later, Louis observes, "To me, she was a child. To Lestat, a pupil. An infant prodigy with a lust for killing that matched his own."

That same ferocity was earlier commented on as her being "now capable of the ruthless pursuit of blood with all a child's demanding." The rhetorical suggestion is that this monstrous manifestation of childness unites the willingness (childlike) and the physical ability (adultlike) to violently enact her own agency.

There is no surprise expressed in his observations that Claudia, as a child, would be naturally inclined to savagery; she is, in fact, the only character observed to kill in order to obtain a physical object (most often a doll). Kincaid's look at the assignation of erotic value to specific, childlike features perfectly encapsulates the paradigm of Claudia's situation: "We are told to look like children if we can and for as long as we can, to pine for that look. This imaginative dwarfing of cute adults into children suggests the extent to which 'the child' is both a fetish and a flexible construction that is, to a large extent, independent of outside standards like age."[27] During Claudia's transformation, she becomes less dirty and paler, but her hair also lightens to blonde and curls into perfect ringlets. She becomes the aesthetic ideal aligned with Shirley Temple, that of carelessly frolicking, always-happy, ever-young girlhood. She becomes the fetish, the perfect aesthetic construction of "desirable" or "appropriate" girlhood. Her porcelain dolls, which share her physical characteristics, are either given to her by Lestat on the anniversary of her "rebirth" or claimed by her as the goal of having slaughtered a shopkeeper; she only keeps dolls that are aesthetically similar to her, except for the body of a young Creole woman whom she slaughters and keeps on her bed. The juxtaposition of the images of her current (and permanent) childlike form—the ringleted and delicately frocked, easily breakable toys—and the reminder of the permanence of her physical childhood recalls the difficulty of her position, the liminality of her particular child body as well as the complicated relationship of a girl to girlness.

Claudia is a culturally unacceptable body. The union of her age and "innocence" is incompatible with the required violence of vampirism and her natural predilection thereto, and so she is killed by a group of vampires who cite that it is "illegal to make one so young" (because of the assumed innate innocence and helplessness of children). She is executed for her existence as a visible space of socially incompatible ideals, even to those with similar internal conflict. Claudia is an abomination even to vampiric adults, who see the union of violent/sexual performance and childhood as unacceptable in the social order.

These girl bodies do not themselves visually evoke disgust; it is not until Claudia is violent or presents her fangs that her victims ever react in any negative way to her, and they unequivocally do so with stunned disbelief at her presenting a threat. It is specifically her positioning as a child that makes her unacceptable, un-integratable into hegemonic (even non-human, but still similarly structured) society, but it is telling that her visible body count is higher than that of any other character in the film. Particularly, her innate talent for killing prey and the overt glee she takes in slaughter are unique to her character in this film. The "adult" vampires are less savage, less instinctually cruel, than Claudia. Her apparently innate predilection for violence is an interesting way in which she is put on even footing with her male counterparts. Her commission of so many of the instances of violent death in the film make her more performatively, visibly monstrous than any other single character—a particularly embodied response to the feminine association with the realm of the non-physical, as Elizabeth Grosz observes in *Volatile Bodies*:

> where patriarchs have used a fixed concept of the body to contain women, it is understandable that feminists would resist such conceptions and attempt to define themselves in non- or extracorporeal terms, seeking an equality on intellectual and conceptual grounds or in terms of an abstract universalism or humanism. The hostility that misogynist thought directs toward women and femininity has been commonly rationalized through the deprecation and derision of women's bodies.[28]

Here, however, the girl body is naturally more gifted, more able to function usefully, capable of amassing the highest body count of any character in the film; the filmic narrative in which powerful girl bodies can easily outperform the adult male company in a physical capacity is useful in that it engages exactly that arena that Grosz notes to be underexplored. The violent girls use the images and icons of the misogynist positioning of themselves—Claudia with her childlike, doll-like appearance and dress—in order to enact their will, their own primacy, through brutality. Perhaps the angle from which the corporeality of girl bodies can be usefully explored is one which necessarily must position their physical performance in direct opposition to all the social/patriarchal expectations of their bodies, non-violence primary among these expectations (and thus violence primary among the reactive expressions).

Interesting among vampire girls is the almost dissociative sense of identity that they display: bestial and calculating in one scene, then positionally and emotionally vulnerable in the next. The ability of the performer to enact consciously a masking performance of girlhood is tied to her physical embodiment of a particular set of signifiers of that girlhood. In *Interview*, Claudia's reading of institutional definitions of girlhood is illustrated quite plainly through the recurrence of dolls around and through her. When she sees a doll she wants, she takes it (by killing the shopkeeper, the guardian of the object she desires);

she is styled and dressed like her dolls, and she collects only those that reflect her new form. Her brightly-ringleted appearance, however, is not as consciously achieved as it would naturally have to be; Claudia is given the ultimate girl body as soon as she is transformed into a not-child, into a body that is monstrously incapable of aging out of the chronologically-defined category. Kincaid, in the passage quoted above, discusses the social trope of adult beauty standards being associated with traits of childhood in a way that reflects Claudia's interaction with her dolls: "This imaginative dwarfing of cute adults into children suggests the extent to which 'the child' is both a fetish and a flexible construction that is, to a large extent, independent of outside standards like age."[29] Claudia sees the constructedness of the childlike image she represents, and she uses the fetishized (and thus necessarily reductive) view of children to strike back violently against those adults who would minimize her childness into the "childlike." Her performances are carefully structured to make the best use of her physical form, as her body is the source of her power as well as her ability to enforce her will, which is—without her ability to violently resist—disregarded as that of a child. If not for her physical appearance (as the idealized blonde-ringleted, blue-eyed child), Claudia's body would not be able to hide so easily its capabilities. She also exerts control by manipulating her position as child—she pouts, throws tantrums, and acts particularly weak around Louis in order to exact submission from the ineffective father figure. In her interactions with humans, Claudia plays the endangered innocent, calling "mama" and crying softly until her victims embrace her, completely unaware of the threat. The cultural assumptions surrounding girl bodies—namely that they are unable to survive on their own, that they are never a source of physical threat—are what lend power to her hyperbolized enactment of those ideals. Not only do these exploitative performances of girlhood illustrate the metaphorical danger of making categorical assumptions about childhood and childness, but they are a way in which structurally conscripting individuals to a reductive collective identity is an underminable practice—that there is a way, through a violent narrative of body performance, to use that dominating gaze to one's own advantage.

Eli (Lina Leandersson) in *Let the Right One In* is violent in only five instances in the film, but the occurrences are (except for the merciful execution of her first companion) marked by a particularly bestial violence. She is a rabid killer, as demonstrated when she lures a man under a bridge with calls for help, draws him close with her performance of childlike innocence, and leaps preternaturally quickly to his neck, forcing him to the ground and killing him. After she finishes feeding and breaks his neck to prevent his infection with vampirism, she leans forward over the corpse, weeping. Abby (Chloë Moretz) of *Let Me In* performs this scene similarly, though she does not cry.[30] Without the image of her crying over the corpse, Eli's repentant, conflicted figure becomes Abby's less empathetic, more feral (and, perhaps not incidentally, more digitally-altered) personage. This is reinforced by Abby's having called out "Mommy!" at the distant approach of the stranger rather than waiting for him to enter her immediate presence; she lures him more consciously, using the "lost little girl" trope to both attract and capture her prey, knowing that he will hasten to her aid and take her into his arms with almost no provocation because of her social positioning. Because of the cultural investment in the construction of "little girl" as helpless object, neither man thinks twice before stooping to pick up the small vampire body in the snow, allowing that very assignation of value—of innocence and threatlessness—to cause his death directly.

Further complicating her position, Eli becomes, after the death of her older male companion (who hunts and kills for her), a surrogate mother figure for Oskar. He is shown to have an unsupportive, inattentive mother, emotionally absent and unable to perceive that her child is being mercilessly tortured at school, and Eli not only steps in to fill the role of a concerned, emotionally supportive parent, but also coaches the boy in his fulfillment of masculine social roles. After having been told the truth of Oskar's situation with bullies at school, she advises: "You have to hit back. Hard. Hit harder than you dare, then they'll stop." The vampire girl's ability to communicate the necessity of effective physical confrontation as a response within an existing social schema reinforces her existence in this capacity as a progenitor of violence. She does not seem interested, however, in creating a vampiric companion for herself— engaging in procreative sex/feeding with her new young male escort any more than she had with her previous accompaniment—but rather in passing on her knowledge of the transgressive capabilities of unexpected savagery and in being progenitive of a new discourse of power for Oskar and herself.

In order to embody the split between the child body and the chronologically-aged female identity, *Let the Right One In* substitutes an older actor for Lina Leandersson (Eli) twice in the film, once when she is speaking to Oskar about her past, and once when lapping some of the boy's spilled blood from the floor. By literally re-embodying Eli in the audience's eye as an adult, the concept of her as not-child is fairly cemented, fixing the audience with the idea of Eli's child body as an object, as a corporeal being that is apparently regularly divested from her "real" self. This specifically asks the audience to see Eli as a complicated physical being, one who has a "true" face that appears in moments of extreme violent performance, who is both a bestial ravager and a repentant child whose actions are regrettably necessary. Specifically, the scene in which she climbs into bed with Oskar, asking him not to look at her while she slowly and dejectedly removes her bloody clothes after the execution of her former human companion helps to reconfigure her as sympathetic. By establishing that this dichotomy—that of bestial or violent and childlike or innocent—is one which must be exploded, the film allows the audience to access a less reductive concept of childness, one that doesn't rely on the "emptying out" of children as signifiers. Rather than "corrupt versus innocent," all the realities of this child are bathed or born in violence, allowing the binary structuring of non-violent/violent and innocent/unapologetically experienced to break down and simultaneously to exist in a single body.

There is, of course, no reality for Eli, Abby, or Claudia in which they are completely adult or completely child, as the cultural distinctions between the two states begin to collapse when addressed with a non-normative performance, specifically a hyperviolent performance; this points again to the literal impossibility of this eternal-child who, by virtue of her performatively violent daily rituals (eating being a fairly nonviolent everyday ritual in normative viewing culture), is bodily coded also as not-child—specifically, as not girl-like. Some narratives offer an alternative to this necessarily impossible body; rather than invest their characters with a non-human identity, films featuring vigilante girls find their troubled understanding of girlhood in the human bodies themselves (and their potential, of course, for violence). Vigilante girls are significant because they embody violent girlness in a theoretically possible body. One of the two protagonists of *Kick-Ass*,[31] Hit-Girl (Chloë Moretz), is the human answer to the questions of embodiment raised by the vampiric girls. She is trained in gunplay, calls the massacres which she performs "a game," and never attacks an adult that she does not kill; she is not, however, invested with any particular super-human powers. She has been trained since she was five to affectionately produce violence and quite obviously enjoys committing murder, a curious difference from the vampiric girls, who often regret the butchery they commit. She uses her understanding of the cultural construction of girlhood to perform it almost as a kind of Butlerian drag: Hit-Girl's first costumed appearance in the film is in a plaid schoolgirl skirt and a purple bobbed wig, and her first line, spoken from behind the collapsing corpse of her first on-screen kill, is "Okay, you cunts. Let's see what you can do now." Her use of such a specifically offensive gendered insult precedes her playing "eeny, meeny, miny, moe" to select her next target and slaughtering everyone in the room—mocking their expectations of her as a child, as a girl, while her girlness violently rejects their reading onto her.

The violence of the vampire girls, because of their biological necessity and their need to drain their prey, is done in animalistic, close-quarters moments. They do, however, all share a predilection and passion for bloodshed that outpaces that of their adult contemporaries. Hit-Girl, however, has no such need to restrain herself—she chooses to kill and does so with aplomb, enthusiastically taunting her victims. Her violence is more far-reaching and performative than that of the vampire girls. She kills 41 people over the course of the film in much more gorily excessive ways than her immortal counterparts, and she openly taunts her victims both before and after their deaths. In all of these cases, their external projections of "appropriate" girlhood—which, for observers/targets, marked them as weak, unthreatening, and actively in need of assistance—enabled their violence. The girls exploit reductive and oversimplistic ideas of girlness to strike back at the hegemonic structure that constructed them, using violence as the bodily expression of that speaking back.

Mindy evolves as the ultimate mass murderer—Hit-Girl—because her father has trained her to do so; her predilection for violence, however, and ability to commit certain acrobatic feats of physics in order to slay her opponents are exclusive to her character, intrinsically hers. She is both the most sarcastic and the most vulgar character in the movie. Both her physical violence and her verbal ferocity specifically point to a different breed of the impossibly adult child—she is the ultimate vigilante child, embodying simultaneously a methodical and thoughtful killer (one who refuses even her own name in favor of her "super" alter-ego until the end of the film) and a monstrous (but, importantly, not bestial or feral) incarnation of a child's potential for performing and legitimately enjoying savage destructiveness.

The first time the audience sees Hit-Girl, it is as her everyday, alter-ego self: Mindy—a little blonde girl in a pink overcoat and hat, standing in an empty drainage ditch across from her father (Nicholas Cage), who is holding a gun at his side and intends to shoot her in the (armored) chest. Her first line is, "Daddy, I'm scared." The film immediately associates her character with the stereotypical color, rhetoric, and emotionality of girlhood, which makes her affection for violence and vulgarity a more jarring (and thus more effective) juxtaposition. The proposal of her father—that she take three bullets at close range so that she is prepared when the scenario arises in real life—is one she responds to with aplomb, asking to go bowling and get ice cream afterwards. Her interests, ultimately, are more invested in her violent performance than in seriously pursuing the prescribed "desires" of her hegemonically-defined identity.

Mary Douglas suggests that the body itself is not simply material, but that its boundaries are constituted by and simultaneously are the boundaries of the social, of the patriarchal hegemonic. They are partially constituted by definitions of what certain bodies can or can't do, couching the rhetoric in biological arguments; when an "impossible" body appears, then, it subverts the supposed concreteness of the limits placed upon it. Hit-Girl's ability to massacre on the scale that she does—neatly slaughtering eight large, armed, enraged men during the first two minutes she appears on-screen in costume— is her near-impossibility, though she is not inhumanly so. Hit-Girl's first image of the film is one of her capacity for violence, her appearance from behind the falling corpse of her first victim. Any time she (even out of costume) performs characteristics of stereotypical constructions of girlhood, she does so consciously, with a distinct purpose: to gain some kind of advantage, and always in the context of facilitating violence. This performativity rather plainly calls into question the legitimacy of such distinctions ("child" or "female," for example) since the conscious usurpation of the idealized image of girlhood is done so consistently and effortlessly by the ones who can monstrously enact their girlness as a practical component of their childness.

Importantly, all these images of the child-as-violent-performer commonly express, at one point or another, some level of desire to return to the normative social order. Claudia envies women and their ability to develop sexually, Eli and Abby show remorse for their killings and an apparently intractable need to bond with other like-aged children, and Hit-Girl ends the film happily ensconced in a public school environment. (Importantly, the last shot of her character leaves her an "acceptable" outlet for her violent expression: excitedly smiling and cracking her knuckles at the bullies who, buying into the hegemonic iconography of girlness as inherently weak, accost her. The vigilante girl has a place in society so long as her violence is surprising or comical; there is no place for her costumed alter-ego, the aesthetic iteration of her powerful girlness.) These girls are not irretrievably Othered in the language of the film; they are not operating completely outside of a discourse of sympathetic desires. These images of fragmented, impossible young girls' bodies are a discursive space wherein childness (and specifically girlness), as a hegemonically conscripted and policed identity, can be utilized as a useful tool of rebellion when consciously performed and paired with a "natural" appetite/aptitude for violence.

Perhaps the most "perfect" example of the vigilante girl is Hayley (Ellen Page) of *Hard Candy*,[32] because she is totemic, emblematic of "every little girl you ever watched, touched, hurt, screwed, killed" as she tells the pedophile, Geoff (Patrick Wilson), whom she has hunted before the start of the film and whom she drives to suicide by the end of it. Interestingly, she commits almost no real physical violence—her ability to damage her opponent psychologically, whose only constant companion seems to have been denial, is impressive, to say the least. One of her first accusatory statements to Geoff is that he found her on the internet, in a chat room, at that site of suburban parental panic about strangers preying on their children: "I went into other chat rooms using other screen names and watched as you'd get to know other women—then drop the chats when you realized they were older than me. You took your sweet time sniffing out someone my age." She was the predator in this situation; however, she took the time to make new profiles detailing different girls, at all different ages, until she hit the right categorical preference. She mocks her prey, allowing him moments of escape that, as the audience realizes only afterwards, are all premeditated. Though she claims to be getting specific revenge for the missing Donna Mauer, Hayley's violent girlness is not only a response to violence against girlhood but is a categorical vengeance, taken against a pedophile, a presumed predator of also presumably more impressive physical build. The toast during which Hayley poisons Geoff with a sedative (the action that kicks off her revenge plot) is "Carpe omnius"—as she translates it: "Take it all." That is what these girls can do; they can have a narrative that is outside the boundaries of what is hegemonically and heteronormatively "acceptable," can challenge why the definition of girlhood is necessarily such a reductive one that posits them as always already potential victims. Violent incarnations of girlhood in film allow for the performative upsetting of these kinds of structurally-embedded presumptions. More than that, they demand that we look at the presumptions—cute, weak, innocent, and the host of others—that we make culturally about girlhood as a whole.

Notes

1. James Kincaid, *Erotic Innocence: The Culture of Child Molesting* (Durham: Duke University Press, 1998), 20.
2. Kincaid, *Erotic Innocence*, 24.
3. Jacqueline Rose, *The Case of Peter Pan, or The Impossibility of Children's Fiction* (Philadelphia: University of Pennsylvania Press, 1993), 13.
4. Rose, *Peter Pan*, 12.
5. Kincaid notes that, in terms of the definition of childhood and the way it has changed over time, "innocence was filed down to mean little more than virginity coupled with ignorance; the child was, therefore, that which was innocent: the species incapable of practicing or inciting sex," with the attendant warning about this redefining that "the irony is not hard to miss: defining something entirely as a negation brings irresistibly before us that which we're trying to banish." The qualities identified as "childlike," therefore, are those that the adult has abjected from itself, has named Other and distinct from adulthood.
6. Many of these qualities are associated specifically with innocence/naïveté, two of the

most openly sexualized qualities that, as Kincaid points out, are also ascribed to the realm of the child.

7. When one is "being childish"—an extremely common phrase at the moment in pop culture—one is being selfish, petulant, unremittingly annoying, uncompromisingly stubborn. The host of ways in which this phrase is used to reference undesirable behavior is a testament to our rhetorical ability to assign value to both characteristics and to childhood simultaneously.

8. "Abjected" here refers to the general sense in which, according to Julia Kristeva, that which is abject does not "respect borders, positions, rules" while it "disturbs identity, system, order."

9. Kincaid, *Erotic Innocence*, 15.

10. Kristeva, *Powers of Horror*, 2.

11. The interesting problem with this terminology—that something is "childlike" when it occurs expectedly or desirably but is "childish" when it occurs outside of the approved disciplinary structures of childhood—indicates the way in which the language that structures child-performance relies on categorizing certain qualities as abject, fearing Freud's return of the ("childish") repressed.

12. Kincaid, *Erotic Innocence*, 14.

13. Hilary Neroni, *The Violent Woman: Femininity, Narrative, and Violence in Contemporary American Cinema* (Albany: SUNY Press, 2005), 19.

14. Judith Butler, *Gender Trouble: Feminism and the Subversion of Identity* (New York: Routledge, 1999), 164.

15. Michel Foucault, "Nietzsche, Genealogy, History," in *Language, Counter-Memory, Practice: Selected Essays and Interviews by Michel Foucault*, trans. Donald Bouchard and Sherry Simon, ed. Donald Bouchard (Ithaca: Cornell University Press, 1977), 148.

16. *Let the Right One In*, directed by Tomas Alfredson (2008; Magnolia Home Entertainment, 2009), DVD.

17. *Let Me In*, directed by Matt Reeves (2010; Anchor Bay, 2011), DVD.

18. *Interview with the Vampire*, directed by Neil Jordan (1994; Warner Home Video, 2010), DVD.

19. Kincaid, *Erotic Innocence*, 57.

20. Kincaid, *Erotic Innocence*, 66–67.

21. Butler, *Gender Trouble*, 119.

22. Kincaid, *Erotic Innocence*, 53.

23. Michel Foucault, *Discipline and Punish: The Birth of the Prison* (New York: Vintage, 1995), 187.

24. Susan Bordo, "The Body and the Reproduction of Femininity," in *Writing on the Body: Female Embodiment and Feminist Theory*, eds. Katie Conboy, Nadia Medina, and Sarah Stanbury (New York: Columbia, 1997), 92.

25. Mary Douglas, *Purity and Danger* (London: Routledge, 1969), 115.

26. Butler, *Gender Trouble*, 142.

27. Kincaid, *Erotic Innocence*, 18.

28. Elizabeth Grosz, *Volatile Bodies: Toward a Corporeal Feminism* (Bloomington: Indiana University Press, 1994), 14.

29. Kincaid, *Erotic Innocence*, 18.

30. Many of their scenes, in fact, are practically identical (as they are adaptations of the same character), and so Abby will only be discussed here in terms of her differences to Eli's character/performance.

31. *Kick-Ass*, directed by Matthew Vaughn (2010; Lionsgate, 2010), DVD.

32. *Hard Candy*, directed by David Slade (2005; Lionsgate, 2006), DVD.

PART V

Peek-a-boo: Future Monstrosities and Beyond

"Insects trapped in amber"
The Mutant Child Seer in Contemporary Spanish Horror Film

JESSICA BALANZATEGUI

The child has become a central recurring feature of contemporary Spanish horror film, functioning as the embodiment of a long repressed cultural trauma that has finally been unleashed. Because these child characters draw forth previously submerged horrors from the past, they disrupt the smooth progression of narrative time within the films, exposing fissures within teleological constructions of Spanish history. These child figures thus play a particularly important therapeutic function, allowing for recognition of previously elided collective trauma. In carrying out this role, the children of Spanish horror engage with the tension between "childhood" as a formative temporal stage of adulthood, and "the child" as highly charged social category integral to politico-historical structures. As a result, these characters come to embody the disconcerting nexus of "unfamiliar familiarity" at the heart of the uncanny, particularly as it relates to long repressed traumas that threaten to re-emerge. These uncanny creatures, who are typically ghosts or are caught in the process of becoming so, expose the temporal contortions inherent in constructions of childness[1]—a term introduced in this volume to overcome the monolithic use of the terms childhood and the child in describing representations of children and to avoid the loaded connotations surrounding the related terms "childlike" and "childish."

I suggest that the child-centered dislocations of linearity seen in Spanish horror are triggered by childhood's over-determined temporal relationship to models of socio-political progress. As Lee Edelman states, the child "remains the perpetual horizon of every acknowledged politics, the fantasmatic beneficiary of every political intervention."[2] Edelman suggests that "the pervasive invocation of the Child as the emblem of futurity's unquestioned value"[3] can best be overcome via queer theoretical frameworks that discompose structural binaries and "history as linear narrative ... in which meaning succeeds in revealing itself—*as itself*—through time."[4] However, if futurity is violently divorced from childhood—as is the case in most Spanish horror films—this linear narrative of historical progress is thrown into disarray, as the child disturbs instead the constrictive temporal structures with which it is usually intertwined. In Spain in particular, a fixation on futurity at the expense of assimilating the past has become a defining condition of modernity, as is particularly evidenced in the period directly following the Civil War (1936–39) and following the long-anticipated collapse of Francisco Franco's dictatorship after his death in 1975. Hereby, the uncanny child troubles fixations on futurity through (re)activating the past while simultaneously functioning as incubator for a future which will never eventuate. Such child characters expose the extent to which Spain's suppressed pasts co-exist with the present in ways that threaten ideologies of national progress, buttressed as they are by the vectors of "growing up" and "moving on."

The extent of the socio-cultural rupture evoked by the Spanish Civil War—in which an estimated 500,000 were killed, and the decmocratically elected Republicans overthrown and violently suppressed—was elided throughout Franco's rule in favor of triumphal discourse about Nationalist war heroes and the "return" of Imperial-era Spanish glory. Censorship laws were strict under Franco, who strived to control all cultural production in order to regulate national consciousness. Central to this process was the repression of the very recent past, both that of the Republican government and the Civil War, and the subsequent attempt to construct a smooth continuum between the post–Civil War present and pre–Republican Spain. This trend of obscuring cultural trauma continued, albeit in a different guise, during the transition to democracy from the late 1970s onwards, following Franco's death. The fragile new democratic government oversaw the deployment of extensive public relations campaigns from 1982 to 1996 aimed at projecting abroad "modern" Spanish cultural products—such as the films of Almodóvar—an impulse that Labanyi has described as the "promotion of an outrageous hypermodernity"[5] and that Aguilar has associated with the "deliberate turning-off of the collective memory."[6] As this period of "hypermodernity" drew to a close, the eerie child character began to emerge regularly in

Spanish horror, becoming a prevalent figure during the late 1990s and subsequent millennial turn—a transitional period in which narratives of progress seemed to waver. It is at this juncture that the figure of the child, typically the ultimate symbol of cultural futurity, appears to enforce a reconsideration of the interlacing of past and present.

The spectral children in the horror films discussed in this essay—*The Nameless* (Jaumé Balaguero, 1999),[7] *The Devil's Backbone* (Guillermo del Toro, 2001)[8] and *The Orphanage* (Juan Antonio Bayona, 2005)[9]—are caught between death and life, past and present. From this liminal position, they enact the resurgence of repressed collective memories from the traumatic post–Civil War period. They therefore extend the links between "childhood" and an adult's partly submerged personal past into the realm of the socio-cultural. As a passed stage before the advent of adulthood, simultaneously familiar and yet other to adult consciousness, childhood has become intertwined with the submerged traumas simmering beneath the fully-formed "present" represented by the adult. This is largely a result of Freud's influential claims that "we must insist on the great pathogenic importance of impressions from [childhood]," as there are "intimate links ... between the mental life of the child and the psychical material of [adult] neuroses."[10] Kincaid exposes the extent to which this ideological association of childhood with repressed personal pasts has reached epidemic proportions in the last few decades, most potently in the hysteric discourse of child sexual abuse, as childhood has become the arena upon which the obfuscated traumas of an adult's past are played out.[11] Yet this association of childhood with traumatic pasts sits in tension with the socio-cultural investment in "the child" as a symbol of "futurity's unquestioned value."[12] The a-temporal children of Spanish horror harness this symbolic splintering, traversing the gulf between personal and socio-cultural identities. They ostensibly embody Caruth's Freudian characterization of trauma as "a breach in the mind's experience of time, self, and the world" caused by an event that "is experienced too soon, too unexpectedly, to be fully known and is therefore not available to consciousness until it imposes itself ... repeatedly ... in ... nightmares and repetitive actions."[13] Yet these child characters come to relish this traumatic breach in homogenous time and meaning, in turn gaining a voice outside of linear norms and the constricting pressures of "futurity." Exigently bound up with the tragedies papered over in narratives of historical progress, the ghostly children of contemporary Spanish horror embody transgressions of spatio-temporal coherence, which are coded as both monstrous and powerful.

These child figures are monstrous in the Deleuzian sense, as outlined by Bohlmann and Moreland in the introduction to this volume: they become "the pure unformed,"[14] embodying a breakdown in accepted (adult) regimes of meaning to generate new ways of approaching disturbing situations. In the words of Deleuze, monstrosity is a "sense-producing machine, in which nonsense and sense are no longer found in simple opposition, but are rather co-present within a new discourse."[15] I will uncover the precise ways in which these ghostly children raise a "new discourse" by situating them as incarnations of the "child seer," a concept Deleuze outlines alongside his introduction of the time-image in *Cinema 2*. The seer[16] becomes trapped in the traumatic gap between perception, understanding and decisive action. Yet while entombed in this in-between state of physical and cognitive incapacity, the seer gains a powerful insight beyond the limits of homogenous temporality.[17] Through inhabiting the position of a seer, these children disrupt the flow of linear time, a particularly disconcerting act for a being defined according to the future-oriented process of growing up. Caught in the past while shaping the flow of the present, the child seers in the films discussed manifest a powerful "allegorical moment"—a term coined by Lowenstein to describe an intersection in certain horror films that exposes "our connection to historical trauma across the axes of text, context, and spectatorship … [through the mobilization of] the unpredictable and often painful juncture where the past and present collide."[18] Lowenstein draws on Benjamin's discussion of *Jetztzeit* to conceptualize this moment as a collision which "blast[s] open the continuum of history"[19] in a manner that is both confrontational and liberating.

By evoking an allegorical moment, the child characters under discussion unravel the narratives of national progress which previously worked to mask the cultural wounds of post–Civil War Spanish society. The uncanny children who populate these horror films have their roots in the enigmatic child characters featured in Spanish art films of the 1970s. Evoking a confrontation between past and present, which extends beyond the films' diegeses, the uncanny children in *The Nameless*, *The Devil's Backbone* and *The Orphanage* function as mutated incarnations of the child figures within iconic art films *The Spirit of the Beehive* (Victor Erice, 1973)[20] and *Raise Ravens* (Carlos Saura, 1976).[21] These "mutant" children thus figure a particularly layered instance of Lowenstein's allegorical moment. They continually drag viewers and protagonists back to a traumatic past, exposing that the apparently distinct relations between Spain's past and present are much more tangled than apparently undisturbed teleological conceptions of progress, themselves remnants of Francoist discourse, dare to acknowledge.

Seething Mutations in the Children of Franco: *The Spirit of the Beehive* and *Raise Ravens*

Before discussing the horror films, I will first turn to *Spirit of the Beehive* and *Raise Ravens,* as the quietly subversive child seer first emerges in these celebrated landmarks of Spanish cinema. Deleuze explains that the figure of the child seer surfaces when a powerless and confused child character experiences a disorienting breakdown in the sensory-motor schema, a condition he associates with the liminality of post-war periods. This sensory-motor collapse forces the child to experience a "purely optical or sound situation"[22] that is divorced from the relentless progression of linear time. Deleuze's theorization of the child seer is particularly fruitful in conjunction with my discussion of national trauma, as the jumbled temporal frameworks of the traumatized child express a re-imagining of narrative time. Through this process, the child seers of *Beehive* and *Ravens* foment a renegotiation of the rigid national narrative as promulgated by Franco—a particularly charged process at the moment of historical mutation in which the films were released. These children are not bound to the dominance of what Deleuze calls the movement-image, in which time is subordinated to movement and the physical actions of the characters determine the progression and rhythm of the film. Instead, they inhabit the realm of the time-image, resisting being tied to one linear timeline or coherent narrative.

The children of *Beehive* and *Ravens* are trapped within unsavory situations, which they are unable to physically change or interact with: confused and largely ignored in the liminal period that followed the Civil War in *Beehive* and that preceded the death of Franco in *Ravens*, they are continually forced to wait and watch rather than act. These arcane moments incarnate Caruth's "breach in the mind's experience of time, self, and the world"[23] outlined earlier. Yet the child characters' penetrative gaze upon these inscrutable situations—not a gaze that seeks to *master* the situations it confronts, as in Mulvey's seminal essay,[24] but to take in their fissures and opacity—comes to be the very source of their eerie yet generative power. As Martin-Jones explains, "the child seer encounters something 'intolerable and unbearable,' something ... beyond their power to act upon.... These are characters directly encountering contemporary social and political mutations, and who are mutating along with these historically shifting contexts."[25] Both *Beehive* and *Ravens* were made and released during a prolonged liminal moment saturated with anticipation and uncertainty towards the end of Franco's protracted period of illness, which lasted from 1962 until his death in 1975. As Pavlovic articulates, "Franco's slow and interminable dying and agony ... deeply marked the ... decade and were accompanied by the gradual and final decomposition of his regime."[26] Absorbing the agonizing sense of in-betweenness that permeated this cultural context through their contemplative gaze, the child characters in both *Beehive* and *Ravens* hover on the threshold of a mutation into something other.

The central motif of both *Ravens* and *Beehive* is the child's huge, staring eyes. The child character is played in both films by Ana Torrent, and her character is also called Ana in each, which solidifies her position as a metaphorical "every-child" around which the anxieties of the period constellate. The emphasis on Ana's huge eyes highlights her role as a seer whose watchful gaze penetrates the situations she encounters, and her stare serves as the core of each film's narrative and visual landscape. Yet in both films, Ana is markedly powerless to affect or to change her situation. She usually appears in the frame as a silent observer, unheeded by all but the camera. Ana is unable to act upon the situations she witnesses because many of the things she sees are too painful to synthesize in the present moment, a powerlessness reinforced by her status as a child. Deleuze claims that the child in particular is equipped to become a seer in traumatic conditions because "in the adult world, the child is affected by a certain motor helplessness, but one which makes him all the more capable

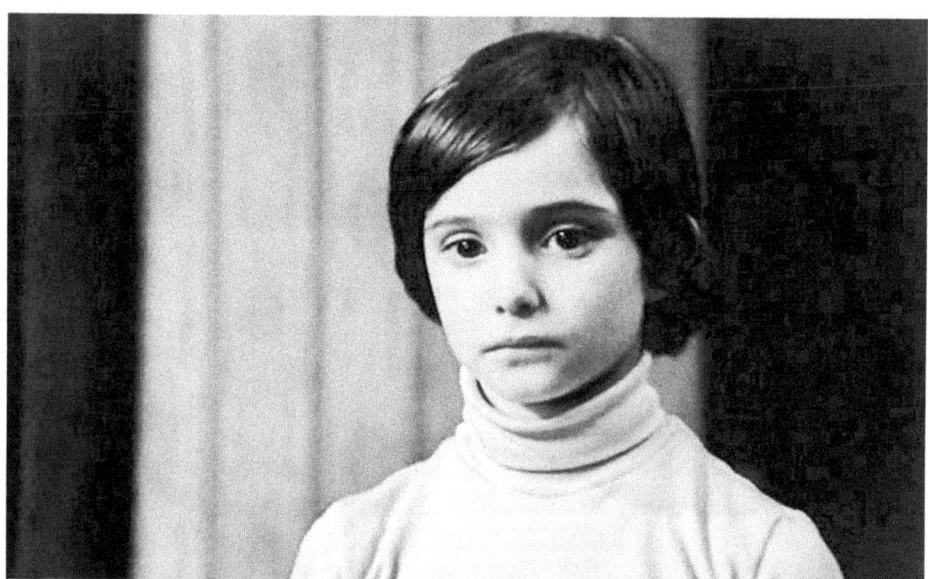

Figure 5. Ana (Ana Torrent) observes her dying mother suffer in *Raise Ravens* (Carlos Saura, 1976).

of seeing and hearing."[27] In Deleuze's conception, unendurable situations generate an extended gap between perception, understanding and action that the adult is wont to repress but which the child, being denied full access to context and information, is forced to accept, undermining the totalizing dominance of the sensory-motor chain. For instance, *Ravens* continually draws back to one of Ana's memories from her recent past in which Ana's mother lies on her death-bed, screaming and writhing in agony. Ana's only response is to stare at her mother in horror before silently backing away, an action that fails to vanquish the disturbing image of her agonized mother. This moment haunts the entire film, repeatedly invading the narrative in truncated form, signaling that Ana remains trapped in the gap between perception and decisive action evoked by the sight of her mother's suffering (see Figure 5).

Ana both literally and figuratively inhabits what Deleuze terms "any-spaces-whatever": liminal zones that he associates with derelict post–World War II spaces that could no longer be adequately understood or traversed. Deleuze characterizes such spaces as "deserted but inhabited, disused warehouses, waste grounds, cities in the course of demolition or reconstruction. And in these any-spaces-whatever a new race of characters was stirring, a kind of mutant: they saw rather than acted, they were seers."[28] The typical sensory-motor chain of action could not be used to effectively navigate these spaces. Both *Ravens* and *Beehive* inhabit the any-space-whatever through the liminal socio-political context in which they were developed, which is metaphorized within the diegesis by the child seer's willing engagement with deteriorating, liminal spaces.

Both films employ the child's confluence with these any-spaces-whatever to confront the cultural trauma laid bare at the time of their production, and as a means of resisting the linear metanarratives that enable its suppression. While the adult characters in both *Ravens* and *Beehive* attempt in vain to act upon their situations, the children choose to welcome these any-spaces-whatever. In *Ravens*, Ana appears happiest when she plays with her doll in a decaying, emptied out swimming pool, as her adult guardians watch on incredulously. In *Beehive*, Ana continually visits a disused barn where an exiled Republican soldier hides briefly until her father kills him. Ana is also drawn to an old well—at one point she calls into the well to summon the "spirit" of Frankenstein's monster, a figure she has become obsessed with after watching *Frankenstein* (James Whale, 1931).[29] Both the ex-soldier who attempts (and fails) to hide in the abandoned barn and the juddering, decaying monster evoke the adult's disintegration in the face of the post-war break down of the sensory-motor schema. The mindless, relentlessly forward-moving stagger of Frankenstein's monster crystallizes the manner in which the adult characters in *Beehive* cling to ideals of national progress: they utilize triumphal discourse about Nationalist war heroes (applied to Ana's father in both films) in order to elide the cultural rupture figured by the Civil War. While the adults flounder in their attempts at clutching the movement-image when confronted with the loss of encompassing meaning, Ana draws her power from the loss. This is particularly emphasized in the final scene of *Beehive*, in which Ana stands at an open window in a white night-dress, whispering repeatedly to the night sky "I am Ana." She appears like the mysterious specters which haunt later horror films, standing on the threshold of, and *summoning*, a new, unpredictable situation.

Further linking these child seers with their horror movie successors, in each film, Ana's consciousness is inextricably entwined with a supernatural other not perceived by the adult characters: in *Beehive*, the amorphous spirit of Frankenstein's monster, and in *Ravens*, the mysterious specter of Ana's dead mother. These ghostly figures crystallize Ana's disorienting relationship to linear temporality: both Anas actively invite the intrusion of specters from the past into the present. That they welcome the subsequent temporal disturbance raised by these specters foreshadows the children of contemporary Spanish horror films, in which disruptions of linear time and navigable space come to intrude upon the present in eerie and destructive ways. Ultimately, *Beehive* and *Ravens* use the child seer's affinity with the time-image to destabilize triumphalist narratives of the Civil War and conceptions of the teleological progress of Spain under Franco. Yet there is also a practical motivation behind Saura and Erice's use of non-linear time. As Saura points out, "for me and my compatriots, to make the stories we wanted to do, we had to use indirect methods. For example, we couldn't use a linear structure or the ideas would be too clear."[30] In *Ravens* and *Beehive*, the child seer's ability to access non-linear perspectives functions in coalition with the filmmakers' need to use "indirect methods" to evade censorship in their critiques of Francoist dogma.

The Mutant Child Seer

Of course, contemporary Spanish horror films no longer have to deal with such strict political censorship; thus, the child seer's ability to see beyond linear time is no longer intertwined with the films' methodological projects. As a result, their child seers no longer hover on the edge of mutation as Ana does: they are already mutants, no longer "growing up" but perpetually in the process of mutating. In the horror films discussed, the children's physical powerlessness to act upon their situations has been brought to its utmost conclusion and resulted in their demise. However, through their deaths, these child seers manage to escape the confining bounds of linear narrative time entirely. These spectral children expose awful secrets that, like the return of the repressed in Freud's uncanny, "ought to have remained hidden but have come to light."[31] Yet in so doing, they evoke Lowenstein's allegorical moment in which "an image of the past sparks a flash of unexpected recognition in the present."[32] This occurs within the diegesis of the films through the children's ghostly raising of the past, and also extra-diegetically as they recall the figures of '70s art films, engendering a rupture in the smooth continuum of Spanish historical discourse. In finally raising and acting out the unassimilated traumas of the Civil War and dictatorship, these children dismantle constricting visions of cultural identity, allowing space for their reformation from the rubble of a post-traumatic context.

The Devil's Backbone

Like its predecessor *Beehive*, *The Devil's Backbone* is set in the final years of the Civil War. However, unlike *Beehive*, *Backbone* is able to confront this period in a direct and retrospective way. The film is set in an orphanage for young boys from Republican families whose parents have been killed or captured in the Civil War. The orphanage itself is detached from civilization in the middle of the desert with an unexploded bomb sitting in the courtyard. The bomb has apparently been defused; however, the children are not fully convinced that this is true. As one of the oldest children, Jaime, says at one point, "They say it's switched off, but I don't believe them. Put your ear against her, you'll hear ticking." Constantly looming over the children, the bomb hypostatizes the adult's downplaying of the traumatic effects of the war upon the children, who are figured as vulnerable time-bombs that could mutate into something monstrous at any moment. Deterritorialized from society, this setting functions as the epitome of the any-space-whatever, injected with heightened urgency by the immobile bomb that constantly threatens to detonate.

As well as being haunted by this unexploded bomb, the orphanage is also haunted by a child ghost, Santi, a former inhabitant of the orphanage who disappeared on the same night that the bomb landed in the orphanage's grounds. As del Toro says of the bomb in the film's audio-commentary, "all the stories, occurrences are tied around the bomb, this constant looming reminder of a terrible past." The orphans, deserted products of a political movement all but vanquished by Franco and his Civil War, also exist as rem(a)inders of this past. Thus, through their very existence, these children trouble Franco's post-war efforts to suppress all remnants of the Republicans' cause and to set in place a triumphal national narrative. While figuring as a terrible past, the unexploded bomb and the ghost Santi simultaneously portend a disastrous future: just as the bomb constantly threatens to explode, virtually the only words Santi is heard uttering throughout the film are "Many of you will die." Santi and the bomb thus evoke an allegorical moment that comments on the way the past traumas represented by the film continue to seethe beneath the extra-diegetic present. While the children are able to see the ghost, Santi, the adults are not—a significant point of difference, as Santi's spectral realm displays the irrevocable contortions that afflict the process of "growing up" within children of wartime.

The scene of Santi's death, shown in full late in the film, figures as the apotheosis of the seer's physical incapacity, instigating his mutation. Santi is caught playing near the cistern in the orphanage's cellar late at night by the aggressive young janitor, Jacinto.[33] In his fury, Jacinto tosses Santi against the wall, injuring his head and rendering him unconscious. In a panic, Jacinto then places the motionless boy into the cistern of amber water. His body immobile, Santi drowns. This water, which appears like an infinite void as Santi is filmed sinking into its depths in slow motion, epitomizes the unnavigable qualities of the any-space-whatever. Through this death, the ultimate extreme of sensory-motor helplessness, Santi is transformed. He becomes what is described in the film as an "insect trapped in amber": a ghost whose consciousness is fused to the any-space-whatever represented by the seemingly endless depth of the amber water.

The amber that Santi becomes trapped within can also be likened to Deleuze's "crystal of time," a cinematic moment in which the sensory-motor link is severed, enforcing a collapse in the distinctions between the "actual" past as a specific point on a chronological line—a "dead" present which has already passed—and the "virtual" past which "coexists with the present that it was."[34] The crystal of time can be viewed as an aesthetic that mobilizes the allegorical moment, as meaning is formed between temporal and subjective boundaries rather than within them. Santi becomes forever welded to the moment of his drowning so that, through his presence, the past, present, and even the future fold into each other. This is enhanced by the fact that the shot of Santi drowning is shown multiple times throughout the film, including in

Figure 6. The ghost of Santi (Junio Valverde) attemps to establish contact with a fellow inhabitant of the orphanage in *The Devil's Backbone* (Guillermo del Toro, 2001).

the opening minutes. This allegorical moment ungrounds the linear progression of historical narratives that position the cultural rupture of the War as an ossified remnant of history. Santi's death refuses to remain lodged in an immobilized historical past—a present that has passed—but remains forever alongside the present as a past that "is." Wherever he goes, Santi appears to be underwater, with the blood from his head-wound constantly floating upwards. Sutured to the any-space-whatever of his death, Santi is caught forever as an expression of trauma, embodying the moment between perception and action. Thus, his abject presence impels other characters, and viewers, to experience the frisson of this previously repressed traumatic encounter (see Figure 6).

The Nameless

Unlike *Backbone*, *The Nameless* is set in the present and contains no overt references to the Civil War or Franco. However, like *Backbone*, through the mutant child seer, the film becomes fixated on the eruption of a formerly repressed past that overcomes the present. In the film, the uncanny child, Angela, personifies an amorphous, malevolent undercurrent seething beneath Spanish society that actively seeks to trap members of the general public in a perpetual traumatic encounter. Angela cannot be classified strictly as a ghost in the same way as Santi can: in fact, the film revolves around the impalpable enigma of her (non)presence. The opening scene suggests that young Angela has been murdered, depicting the excision of Angela's remains from a well in an abandoned factory. After this gruesome opening, the film jumps forward five years, demonstrating that Angela's grieving mother, Claudia, is moving forward with her life after enduring a period of intense mourning. Claudia has separated from her husband, Angela's father, and appears to be thriving in a successful career. However, in a sudden disruption to this proficient working through of trauma, Claudia starts to receive mysterious phone calls from a young girl claiming to be her daughter—in a small, desperate voice, the child utters "Mummy, it's me." In another call, the child impels her mother to come and rescue her from a derelict sanatorium on a beach where their family used to play.

Up until this point, Claudia has been shown repeatedly re-watching a home videotape of her former husband playing with little Angela on this very beach. The video has thus been a comfort for Claudia through its elision of the more recent past of Angela's gruesome death in favor of memorializing the child in a romanticized past—a mechanism that parallels Franco's post-War attempts to suppress depictions of Republican rule in favor of constructing a form of continuity with an idealized Imperial past. As Claudia receives this second phone call from the child, the videotape remains paused, flickering slightly, on a shot of Angela's face smiling at the camera. Looming in the background, behind the face of the "innocent" child, is the dark outline of the building in which she is supposedly currently trapped. This image of the child smiling out at both Claudia and the viewer from the screen invades the diegesis a number of times throughout the film, as the child's previously comforting look is rendered eerie. The videotape's continual replaying of a supposedly joyous moment from the past is thus injected with an uncanny power, suggesting that lurking beneath this sepia-hued image of carefree childhood is a sinister secret that has begun to re-emerge, as the past re-states itself within the present. The child is rendered disturbing for she is no longer "the emblem of futurity's unquestioned value"[35] in Edelman's sense; condensed within the figure of Angela is the realization that while the past may not be fully tangible, neither is it dead nor gone.

As a result, while Angela herself appears onscreen very little, she haunts the entire film. As implied by the images of the child on the videotape, Angela's power over her mother and the narrative is manifested by the uncanny penetration of her gaze. The film opens with a flurry of disorientating images, including shots of a child dressed in white staring directly at the camera. Such intercuts reoccur throughout the film at unexpected moments, composed of barely discernible images such as a "not dead" sign written in blood. These shots are accompanied by jarring sounds that meld a human scream and a camera shutter, aurally assaulting the viewer while highlighting that the omnipresent eye of the camera is intertwined with Angela's own gaze. Lazaro-Reboll aptly points out that these images "suggest the interminable replay of Claudia's traumatic loss."[36]

The child's mysterious phone calls set in motion a quasi-detective narrative, as Claudia discovers that Angela may not have been murdered after all, but abducted by a Satanic cult called "The Nameless" led by an institutionalized, Hannibal Lecter-esque madman called Santini. From his cell, Santini explains that he was a prisoner in a Nazi concentration camp while a child— a telling circumvention of Spain's own grisly past—an experience that damaged him beyond repair. He committed a series of child kidnappings in Spain in the early 1980s, a period that marked the final stages of the nation's transition to democracy, in turn heralding Spain's successful advancement from despotic regime to "modernity." The kidnapping of Spanish children, receptacles for the future, by a malevolent cult leader at this juncture thus destabilizes historical narratives that emphasize the rapid progress of this period. Santini suggests that he abducted children for his cult because they do not yet have a secure sense of identity and morality—members must "reject the idea of name. As long as they're the nameless ones they can reject human morality." The Nameless is thus the ghastly product of an unassimilated childhood trauma, which in turn threatens to engulf Spanish "childhood" wholesale: the mutant child seer is overtly figured as the vehicle for the release and perpetuation of a long-simmering trauma upon Spanish society.

In the final minutes of the film, Claudia finally thinks she has found her lost child at the cult's mysterious headquarters—a now abandoned hotel where Angela was conceived. Here Claudia is unexpectedly confronted with her ex-husband, who reveals that he has always been a member of the cult, for which he had claimed their daughter at birth: "a pure child to be perverted from the beginning." Thus, the film constructs a toxic vision of contemporary Spain in which from the moment of their birth, children are mutated by dogma force-fed to them by oppressive fathers. There is no escape for the child in this allegorical collapsing together of Spain's Franco-era past and the supposedly "liberated" present.

Despite this bleak twist, the film momentarily seems to have reached an exultant conclusion with the long anticipated reunion of mother and child.

Claudia's ex-husband introduces her to the now teenaged Angela and instructs the child to kill her mother. While it appears initially that Angela will comply, she suddenly breaks down in tears when her mother symbolically reinstates her identity by repeatedly calling her "Angela," and shoots her father instead. Yet just as it seems that the film has reached a cathartic resolution with the embracing of mother and child, Angela tells her mother to stop calling her Angela. She states, "I have no name," and suggests that she exists to perpetuate her mother's traumatic loss ("you'll suffer more this way") before putting a gun to her own mouth. The film then cuts to black and ends with the sound of a gunshot.

It is first signaled to the viewer that there may be something horribly wrong with the triumphant reuniting of mother and child when Angela opens her eyes while embracing her mother, focusing a cold stare directly at the camera, behind her mother's back. While portending her malevolent intent, Angela's gaze is threatening in that it appears to suddenly transgress the boundary between the "real" of the viewer and the fictional world of the film; as the other suddenly stares back, the viewer's imagined mastery over the film collapses (see Figure 7).

Before shooting herself, Angela says to her distraught mother, "I'll call you again sometime." Thus, in the final seconds, the neat resolution, and in fact the entire quest narrative established throughout the film, is overturned.

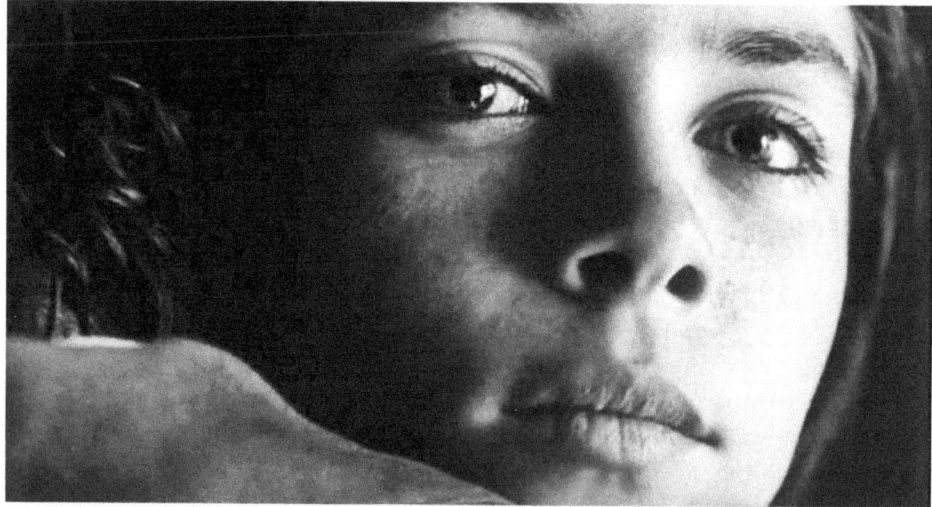

Figure 7. Angela (Jessica del Pozo) confronts the audience with a knowing look over her mother's shoulder in *The Nameless* (Balagueró, 1999).

It becomes impossible to discern if this girl truly was Claudia's daughter, and the film closes with the suggestion of a desolate future in which Claudia will endlessly be tormented by a chain of "nameless" children posing as Angela. At the end of the film, both Claudia and the viewer become trapped in a perceptual gap incarnated by the child's subversive ambiguity. This affect can be elucidated using Deleuze's conception of "indiscernibility": "we no longer know what is imaginary or real, physical or mental, in the situation, not because they are confused, but because ... there is no longer even a place from which to ask."[37] The child in *The Nameless* forces the adult to inhabit this position of indiscernibility, as the final scene suggests that Claudia will be forever entombed by the any-space-whatever of traumatic loss. Angela ultimately employs the aesthetics of trauma to co-mingle "nonsense and sense,"[38] setting in place a new discourse. By collapsing secure boundaries between the "real" space of the viewer and the fictional world of the film before abandoning both the protagonist and viewer in a position of narrative indiscernibility, this monstrous child enforces a new consideration of linear narrative structures, disallowing the suppression of trauma through teleological modes of progress.

The Orphanage

The child seers in *The Orphanage* are nowhere near as actively malevolent as Angela; however, they do engage the protagonist and viewer in the sensation of being fused to the any-space-whatever in their exposure of a gap between perception and action. The film in many ways functions like an echo of *Backbone*, and in fact del Toro produced the film. *The Orphanage* is set in the present in a building that was once an orphanage, but has become the home of a former inhabitant: the now middle-aged Laura and her family. By featuring a haunted former orphanage which is now an imperious house, the film suggests that the traumas of Franco-era Spain continue to reverberate beneath the façade of contemporary Spanish society—a construction heightened by the fact that Laura herself was once one of these orphans, and by the film's return to the "home" of her childhood, she remains unable to break with this past.

The seer of the film is Simón, Laura's adopted son. Young Simón is afflicted with HIV: he's the helpless victim of a disease passed down from the preceding generation, again evoking a vulnerability to adult malaise which comes to be figured as a threat. Like Santi, Simón's death is brought about by a situation of sensory-motor helplessness within an any-space-whatever. Laura unknowingly traps Simón in a cavernous cellar hidden beneath the house early in the film after placing some heavy bars against the cellar's door, which is concealed beneath new layers of wallpaper. Thus, the secrets of the orphanage's past have literally been papered over in the quest for a fresh start. Simón's parents do not hear his screams for help in the huge house, leaving him powerless to do anything but wait in the cellar to be found. Once Laura finally finds him, he is already dead.

Simón effectively shares the fate of a "friend" he has made within the orphanage: the ghost of Tomás, who was an inhabitant of the orphanage during the same period as Laura. An illegitimate child afflicted with a facial deformity, Tomás was concealed in the cellar by his mother, a nurse at the orphanage. One day, the other children (with the exception of Laura, who had recently been adopted) discovered Tomás, and lead him to a nearby cave by the ocean before running away. Tomás remained frightened and alone within the cave as the tide came in. Unable to comprehend his situation in time and thus physically powerless to escape it, echoing Santi, Tomás drowned. Tomás's grieving mother, traumatized and furious at the other orphaned children, placed poison in their food—they too were killed by a violent event before they were able to recognize it taking place, and like Tomás, they are now ghosts forever trapped in the any-space-whatever between perception, understanding and action. In a dramatic moment in which a medium[39] encounters these ghosts, the children cannot be seen but are heard shouting "we are sick! Please help us, why are we sick?"

Laura was not aware of Tomás's existence during her time at the orphanage, and she does not realize that all her childhood friends are dead until she uncovers their remains within a boatshed on the orphanage's grounds. She initially insists that Tomás is imaginary, and despite growing up in the building, she is oblivious to the existence of the cellar within which Simón is trapped. In a cyclic process, Simón's trauma is caused by his mother's inability to identify the concealed traumas of her own past. Although Laura ostensibly "solves" the mystery of Simón's disappearance at the film's climax, discovering Simón's body in the cellar, she is unable to act upon it, for he is already dead. Laura subsequently takes her own life: like Simón, she becomes a ghost, forever inhabiting the any-space-whatever.

Immediately prior to her discovery of Simón's body, Laura experiences a particularly uncanny moment of collision between her childhood past and her present, which is extended to the viewer via filmic repetition. The opening scene shows Laura as a child playing a game with her friends at the orphanage: Laura incants "one, two, knock on the wall" with her back to the other children, who quietly creep up behind her, freezing whenever she turns around. Even this opening scene, filmed in a bright wide shot on the orphanage grounds, seems eerie: the children, shrouded in shadow, stalk up to Laura from behind and stiffen like dolls whenever she attempts to catch them in the act. This childhood game metonymizes the ways in which suppressed pasts are mobilized by the figure of the child throughout the film. Stockton points out that while "childhood" is representative of the past of adulthood, "it is precisely who we are not and, in fact, never were. It is the act of adults looking back"[40]; in *The Orphanage* Laura's childhood friends trigger her own "looking back," forcing her to (re)experience a past she herself was not cognizant of during her own childhood.

Initially these dead children seem to be static remnants of recent history, figured through sepia-toned photographs of the children and through their dusty, aged porcelain dolls. However, through their ever-intensifying hauntings, this seemingly ossified past lurks ever closer to the present, threatening to engulf it—as crystallized in the scene immediately prior to that in which Laura finds Simón's body, which echoes the opening shot. Laura dresses in a replica of her old orphanage uniform and starts to play the game of her childhood in an attempt to compel the ghosts to materialize. This time, the game signals the impending conflation of Laura's childhood and her present. She nervously chants "one, two, knock on the wall" as the ghosts creep up behind her, the camera now depicting her obstructed view of the children through a tight close up on her face. The audience now shares the horrors of an unknown other just beyond our field of vision stalking ever closer, as the ghosts appear like fixed shadows whenever the camera whips around to catch them in motion. One of the film's final scenes shows Laura's own ghost sitting on a windowsill with all the other ghostly children—both Simón and the orphans—suggesting that Laura's childhood past and her adult present have now well and truly folded together, following the initial frisson of this collapse in subjective and temporal boundaries.

Similarly, the uncanny gaze of the child seer is marked by the lack of distinction between Simón, the lost child, and Tomás, the ghost from the past, who wore a mask while alive due to his facial deformity. Throughout the film, both children are seen wearing the sack mask, obscuring any ability by Laura or the viewer to differentiate them. Thus, the mask simultaneously erodes the boundaries between the two boys as singular identities and between past and present. Simón consciously invites this indiscernibility by dressing in the dead Tomás's clothing and dwelling in what he calls Tomás's "little house"—the cellar in which Tomás spent the majority of his short life.

Figure 8. Simón/Tómas (Roger/Príncep/Óscar Casas) disturb the boundary between their singular identities—and that between past and present—through the adornment of the dead child's mark in *The Orphanage* (J. A. Bayona, 2007).

Thus, the child is figured in *The Orphanage* as the locus for previously concealed traumas of the past, refusing to let the adult protagonist blindly paper over recent history. The surfacing of this trauma enforces a break-down in narrative progress, as both Laura and the viewer remain with the ghostly children in the any-space-whatever outside of linear development as the film draws to a close (see Figure 8).

Conclusion

Ultimately, Santi, Angela and Simón/Tomás are "insects trapped in amber," seemingly inconsequential, powerless beings who have been abused, murdered or mistreated in the recent past. As a result, they come to embody literally and allegorically the unassimilated traumas of post–Civil War Spanish society. The cultural rupture of the War has typically been uneasily patched over in the quest to maintain unified conceptions of national identity, a mechanism perfected and institutionalized by the Franco regime. Even in contemporary Spain, a time in which memorials are finally being constructed to recognize and to honor the Republican dead, the traumas of war and the oppression of Franco are neutralized through being positioned at specific points on the continuum of history: as tragic moments of the past, immobilized and defused by the progression of time. However, the uncanny child's over-determined relationship to temporality ensures that these spectral children resist being tied to a frozen past that is irretrievably distanced from the present. Instead, they raise allegorical moments that "blast open the continuum of history."[41] The uncanny child in these contexts points to the danger inherent in misrecognizing history as a present that has long-since "passed" instead of as a past that "is." Through their position of powerlessness, these child characters become fused to the any-spaces-whatever in which they died or disappeared, incorporating such fissures in spatio-temporal coherence into their beings and drawing supernatural agency from this fusion. Thus, through their deaths, Angela, Santi and Simón come to inhabit permanently the any-space-whatever, maintaining an existence outside the bounds of linear time. This process underlies their mutation from helpless children to powerful specters: it is these children's status as insects trapped in amber that ultimately lends them their uncanny force, as they escape the confining bounds of teleological progression and return to bring about its destruction.

Notes

1. Kathryn Bond Stockton also employs the figure of the ghost to discuss the potential children have to destabilize models of linear development. She uses the term "ghostliness" in her examination of the gay child's "sideways" growth, stating that there is "ghostliness surrounding children as figures in time.... Children grow sideways as well as up ... in part because they cannot, according to our concepts, advance to adulthood until we say it's time." *The Queer Child, or Growing Sideways in the 20th Century* (Durham: Duke University Press, 2009), 2–6.
2. Lee Edelman, *No Future: Queer Theory and the Death Drive* (Durham: Duke University Press, 2004), 3.
3. Edelman, 3–4.
4. Edelman, 4; emphasis in original.
5. Jo Labanyi, "Memory and Modernity in Democratic Spain: The Difficulty of Coming to Terms with the Spanish Civil War," *Poetics Today* 28.1 (Spring 2007): 95.
6. Paloma Aguilar, "Justice, Politics and Memory in the Spanish Transition," in *Memory: Transitional Justice in Democratizing Societies*, eds. Alexandra de Brito, Carmen Gonzaléz-Enríquez and Paloma Aguilar (Oxford: Oxford University Press, 2001), 11.
7. *The Nameless*, DVD, directed by Jaumé Balaguero (Madrid: Filmax SA, 1999).
8. *The Devil's Backbone*, DVD, directed by Guillermo del Toro (Madrid: El Deseo S.A., 2001).
9. *The Orphanage*, Blu-ray DVD, directed by Juan Antonio Bayona (Barcelona: Esta Vivo! Laboratorio de Nuevos Talentos, 2007).

10. Sigmund Freud, "Screen Memories," in *The Uncanny*, ed. and trans. David McLintock (London: Penguin Group, 2003), 3–8.
11. James Kincaid, *Erotic Innocence: The Culture of Child Molesting* (Durham: Duke University Press, 1998).
12. Edelman, *No Future*, 4.
13. Cathy Caruth, *Unclaimed Experience: Trauma, Narrative and History* (Baltimore: Johns Hopkins University Press, 1996), 4.
14. Gilles Deleuze, *The Logic of Sense* (New York: Columbia University Press, 1990), 107.
15. Deleuze, *The Logic of Sense*, 106.
16. Deleuze argues that the child seer character first emerged in Italian neo-realist films as a response to the massive cultural rupture of World War II.
17. Gilles Deleuze, *Cinema 2: The Time-Image*, trans. by Hugh Tomlinson and Robert Galeta (London: Continuum, 2005), xi–8.
18. Adam Lowenstein, *Shocking Representation: Historical Trauma, National Cinema and the Modern Horror Film* (New York: Columbia University Press, 2005), 9.
19. Walter Benjamin, cited in Lowenstein, 86.
20. *The Spirit of the Beehive*, DVD, directed by Victor Erice (Madrid: Elías Querejeta Producciones Cinematográficas S.L., 1973).
21. *Raise Ravens*, DVD, directed by Carlos Saura (Madrid: Elías Querejeta Producciones Cinematográficas S.L., 1976).
22. Deleuze, *Cinema 2*, 5.
23. Caruth, *Unclaimed Experience*, 4.
24. Laura Mulvey, "Visual Pleasure and Narrative Cinema," *Screen* 16.3 (1975): 6–18.
25. David Martin-Jones, *Deleuze and World Cinemas* (London: Continuum, 2011), 73.
26. Tatjana Pavlovic, *Despotic Bodies and Transgressive Bodies: Spanish Culture from Francisco Franco to Jesús Franco* (Albany: State University of New York Press, 2003), 70.
27. Deleuze, *Cinema 2*, 3.
28. Deleuze, *Cinema 2*, xi.
29. *Frankenstein*, DVD, directed by James Whale (Los Angeles: Universal Entertainment, 1931).
30. Carlos Saura, cited in Marsha Kinder, "Carlos Saura: The Political Development of Individual Consciousness," *Film Quarterly* 32.3 (1979): 16.
31. Sigmund Freud, "The Uncanny," in *The Uncanny*, ed. and trans. David McLintock (London: Penguin Group, 2003), 241.
32. Lowenstein, *Shocking Representation*, 14.
33. Jacinto is a former inhabitant of the orphanage who has been inexorably damaged by his experiences of war. He thus represents a parallel realist figuration of the child deformed by wartime turmoil.
34. Deleuze, *Cinema 2*, 79.
35. Edelman, *No Future*, 4.
36. Antonio Lazarro-Reboll, *Spanish Horror Film* (Edinburgh: Edinburgh University Press, 2012), 250.
37. Deleuze, *Cinema 2*, 7.
38. Deleuze, *The Logic of Sense*, 107.
39. The medium is played by Geraldine Chaplin, who also played both the adult Ana and Ana's dying mother in *Raise Ravens*. That Chaplin performed both roles in *Ravens* constitutes an often indiscernible folding together of the child's traumatic past and her future. Chaplin's role in *The Orphanage* thus establishes a conscious link to the earlier film, and echoes the depiction in *Ravens* of a woman eternally trapped by her childhood trauma.
40. Stockton, *The Queer Child*, 5.
41. Benjamin, cited in Lowenstein, *Shocking*.

Hanna

The Child as Monster Who Is Supposed to Believe

Tamas Nagypal

In many ways, Joe Wright's *Hanna* reads as a critique of both the post-apocalyptic morality tale *Children of Men* and Lee Edelman's somewhat heavy handed attack on it in his *No Future: Queer Theory and the Death Drive* for the novel/film's "reproductive futurist" propaganda that fetishizes a Child-messiah who is supposed to guarantee humanity's continuing existence. Where Edelman blasts out a space for queer resistance using rhetorical weapons of mass destruction, giving centuries old anarchist mantras a different twist ("Fuck the Child!"), Wright subtly changes the coordinates of this battlefield by focusing on the no-less-queer struggle of his androgynous, genetically engineered sociopathic teenage hero. Hanna is the posthuman obverse of the fetish-child that *Children of Men* presents with humanist pathos, but she *is* a child who neither can nor wants to escape the future her existence brings to this world with a vengeance. Thus, unlike Edelman, Wright doesn't draw the dividing line between the self-perpetuating force of the social-symbolic status quo and its queer ("sinthomosexual") disruption through an apocalyptic "No!" to our common future and to the Child who embodies it.[1] Instead, the film *Hanna* stages a dissensus about the place and role of resistance by setting up its two queer heroines, the "monstrous" child and her evil "lesbian" stepmother against each other in a struggle of life and death, restaging Andersen's "Snow White" for the posthuman epoch.

This essay argues that what can be called the *childness* of Hanna (as opposed to her childhood, her being the authentic Child-savior in Edelman's sense of the term) complicates the all too neat binary of socially included and excluded subject positions, the opposition between conformism and disruption, domination and victimhood. *Childness* as a third term arises precisely through the subjectivization of the hidden objectal supplement that unites these binarisms in a consensus; it is by turning the child qua fetish-for-others into a subject that the film constructs Hanna as both angelic and monstrous. This unwillingness to reduce her to established (queer or heteronormative) fantasies about childhood opens up a new discursive space, telling the story from her perspective, where a young girl's experiencing the world for the first time after years of isolation, her fascination with electricity coming into a light bulb or with the sound coming from the radio becomes indistinguishable from the quest for vengeance she has been programmed for. For this reason *Hanna* also reads as a modern techno-spy version of Andersen's "Little Mermaid" tale, as a spectacular yet disturbing fable about the magic of cinema and the strangely captivating effects it produces in the spectator, providing an allegory for the power of belief in the age of cynicism where, as Žižek claims, being the "subject supposed to believe," the infantilized supplement of others' disenchantment, means to occupy the place of the idiot.[2] Hanna's character is precisely in such a position, and she basically remains there throughout the film. This is where her apparent monstrosity comes from: not only does she blindly memorize like an automaton every important detail about the outside world before she even enters it, she also embraces this radically external dimension of her belief even when she realizes that there is no hidden purpose behind the symbolic order. Therefore, she is not simply naïve; she rather lacks a certain knee-jerk skepticism about the world of appearances that characterizes today's postmodern cynical attitude. She is a genetically engineered experiment of a subject in whose brain the fear of being duped was switched off, and who for that reason cannot but experience the entire world "magically," as a cinematic attraction. *Hanna* is thus an allegory for film spectatorship but also for our contemporary aesthetic experience of the world itself. Along the lines of Stanley Cavell, who talked about a skeptical crisis in modernity and cinema as a potential cure for it,[3] Wright's film is a reflection on a certain cynicism and discontent in the postmodern "distribution of the sensible"[4] which could be challenged by passing through the monstrous subjectivity of *childness*.

Sublime Accidents

The aesthetic consensus challenged by *Hanna* can be understood through Virilio's concept of the accident. He claims that while we used to think about the 20th century as the time of great discoveries in science and technology, by the new century the exponential acceleration of human civilization has shifted our perception, and all we see now is a series of disasters, the repetition of accidents one after the other. Or to put it differently, we live in a permanent state of emergency where the mediatized threat of natural disasters, financial crises, and civil unrest has turned into business as usual. As a result, human "consciousness only survives now as awareness of accidents."[5] What disappears, paradoxically, is our very consciousness about the *effects* of accidents: if there are only accidents, we lose the capacity to see them as abnormal, as an exception to the ordinary course of events. The consequence of this new perceptual blindness is what Virilio calls *philofolly* (as opposed to philosophy), "whereby the insane nature of our acts would not only stop consciously worrying us, but would thrill us and captivate us." Along these lines, he criticizes the contemporary tendency to glorify terror, torture and mutilation for artistic purposes and aesthetic pleasure, calling this trend the "academism of horror," the "conformism of abjection."[6] Contra Walter Benjamin's more optimistic account a century ago,[7] then, Virilio offers a cautionary tale about human perception in the age of the mechanical reproduction of images: the increasing speed and intensity of visual shocks the media bombards us with traps us in a never ending present, in a disoriented mode of existence that leads to the disappearance of humanity itself.[8]

The universe of Joe Wright's *Hanna* is properly posthuman in Virilio's sense of the term. At the beginning of the film, we find the young heroine in hiding from the American government, living with her father in an isolated land near the Arctic Circle, being trained to become the perfect killing machine. As the product of a discontinued CIA project to create genetically perfected assassins, she herself qualifies as an accident of science with monstrous consequences: she has a diminished capacity to feel fear and pity. In her repetitive daily routines, she also embodies the contemporary consciousness of accidents insofar as she is constantly alert, expecting the thrill of being surprised by the enemy she is hiding from at any minute; she kills animals for combat practice while remaining desensitized to their suffering. She illustrates perfectly Virilio's thesis that "a society that unthinkingly privileges the present, real time, to the detriment of the past and future, also privileges accidents. Since, at every moment, everything happens, most often unexpectedly, a civilization that implements immediacy, ubiquity and instantaneity, stages accidents and disasters."[9] The staging of accidents, consequences of the small mistakes in her performance of various tasks ordered by her father, is the most important part of Hanna's training; they re-produce her state of mind as the consciousness of accidents and purify it of anything else.

It is useful here to draw a parallel between such consciousness and Kant's aesthetic concept of the sublime. He argues that while the experience of beauty comes from the pleasure of imagining an object within the limits of its form, the sublime is linked to the object's lack of form and thus to a feeling of limitlessness.[10] Virilio's accidents also fall into this sublime domain; "there is no science of the accident" as he puts it,[11] that is, accidents always escape our faculty of imagination, blowing up the boundaries of any sensuous form we'd frame them with. The result is horrific rather than pleasurable, anxiety ridden rather than pacifying. How does then the sublime produce pleasure nonetheless, *indirectly*, as Kant suggests? How to account for Hanna's strange self-satisfaction and the zen-like quietude that accompanies her sublime-precarious situation? In the (Lacanian) reading of Alenka Zupancic, Kant distinguishes here two moments in the feeling of the sublime:

> At first the subject is fascinated by some spectacle of nature (for example, "the boundless ocean heaved up") and by the ineffable force that manifests itself therein. At this initial stage, the subject experiences only powerlessness and displeasure. Then, suddenly, an inversion takes place, an "echo" of this first feeling, which expresses itself as the feeling of the sublime: in his "physical" powerlessness the subject becomes aware of a power that he has as a rational being, capable of "elevating" himself above natural and phenomenal existence.[12]

When in the second moment the subject resolves the anxiety produced by the chaos of the sublime, she arrives to a strange split of her subjectivity; she overcomes the part of herself that is powerless, her ego, through a separation from it, by acting "contrary to her well-being, to renounce her interests, needs, pleasure" in the name of a higher moral agency: the superego.[13] The sublime terror of nature thus becomes metonymically linked to the infinite demands of the moral law that, as Žižek argues, pushes the subject towards the specter of *real* enjoyment (*jouissance*) by undermining/renouncing the more mundane pleasures of everyday life.[14]

This configuration allows us to explain the simultaneous presence of passivity and activity in Hanna's persona. On the one hand, she is trained to be able to "gain the upper hand" in an unexpected situation (she knows how to "neutralize" an accident). At the same time, however, her superhuman abilities come with the price of a self-instrumentalization. She is not fully present in her actions; it is as if part of her was "watching herself being subjected to the law."[15] Thus, the film *Hanna* is part of a long tradition in modern visual culture, from Caspar David Friedrich to Michelangelo Antonioni, that deals with the redoubling of the spectator in front of a sublime spectacle, where the passive spectator in the painting or film stands for our ego immobilized by forces bigger than her (like a natural disaster or a mysterious conspiracy). The fact that Hanna in her hyperactivity appears as the opposite of the modern passive heroes may signal a shift in our contemporary experience of the sublime. Much like accidents for Virilio, the sublime for us is not an exceptional state of mind anymore that we would seek out at the edges of our world; instead, it characterizes our everyday consciousness because, as Virilio would say, the frequency with which it occurs has accelerated. The ultra-mobile Hanna is thus today's postmodern accelerated version of the sublime's immobile spectator in modernity. She stands for a subjectivity created by the mechanical reproduction of the sublime as the accelerating repetition of accidents which for Virilio was a symptom of madness and the end of humanity. The film, however, complicates this apocalyptic take on the sublime by introducing, through Hanna's double, a split that cuts through this concept, undermining its homogeneity as a simple binary opposite of the beautiful.

Sublime, Which Sublime?

Hanna leaves her arctic isolation and enters the world through a life and death struggle with her "evil stepmother" Marissa, a CIA operative responsible for shutting down the genetic engineering project on government orders, ready to kill everyone who stands in her way. The film blows up their antagonism into mythical proportions, suggesting that the conflict between the two protagonists transcends the narrative framework of a secret service cover-up or even vengeance for Hanna's mother murdered by Marissa. The tagline for the movie might as well be "There Can Be Only One," as just like the *Highlander*, it belongs to a sub-genre of action films where the main character has to fight her own double to death, staging thus the conflict inherent in what psychoanalysis calls narcissism. For Lacan, the double is the product of the mirror stage in the child's development, that is, her fundamental self-alienation into an ideal image that introduces the first split into her subjectivity. From this, a narcissistic conflict arises, a rivalry with the double that can never fully overlap with who she is. Zupancic links this form of subjectivity to the experience of the sublime and the act of self-estimation that according to Kant emerges from it.[16] What for Kant meant our becoming aware of the power of the moral law gains here an additional meaning of self-overcoming by negating and destroying a part of ourselves that doesn't fit our ideal ego.

In the case of Hanna, such self-overcoming reaches a Nietzschean magnitude; she is the perfect *Übermensch*, combining total self-instrumentalization with a complete lack of ideological belief in (or even knowledge of) any particular guiding agency or god—there is even a dialogue where the neo-hippie woman whom she travels with asks her directly: "What do you believe in?"—Hanna: [silence]—woman: "Nothing!" Her convictions are always fully immanent to the situation (i.e., the accident) she finds herself in. There is, of course, the Oedipal authority of her father who had planned out his daughter's quest well in advance, preparing her, one might say, to carry out his own revenge for his lost lover, Hanna's mother. His daughter, however, is not vengeful in the same way. There is flatness not only to her way of accepting and carrying out her mission but also to her whole relationship to language, or languages rather, since she can shift between them without effort. She is angelic, beyond good and evil, as Nietzsche would put it, lacking any moral anchoring in a particular linguistic tradition or culture.[17] One might say that she was brought up by a post–Oedipal father in the sense that she wasn't pressured to develop any fixed identity including that of gender and sexuality (she is properly androgynous and bisexual, having brief romantic relations with both a girl and a boy); or to put it differently, the social role she was prepared for is how to transgress established boundaries, how to exist in a pure state of fluidity and movement without getting caught. The part of herself that she had learned to overcome, then, is precisely the gravity of her identity.

If Hanna stands for a queer form of life in its becoming, beyond all identities, her opponent, Marissa, is a disillusioned survivor of a more conventional lesbian identity politics, of a lost cause for which she is associated, somewhat problematically, with death. She is cold, single, childless (she has "made certain choices") but she is friends with a group of retired male assassins who are running a gay club in East Berlin and dress like neo–Nazis. As the ruthless executioner of the government's will, she is the obverse of Hanna's free spirit and elusiveness: she is fully anchored in a professionally successful, rather cynical postfeminist identity and she only occasionally allows herself to indulge melancholically in memories of happier, queerer times of her youth (her visit to the gay club is one of these rare moments).

Along these lines, the part of herself she wants to destroy is her own former queerness, something that Hanna reminds her of—the film even suggests that Marissa used to have feelings for Hanna's mother and that she killed her out of jealousy because she had betrayed her when she had left with *their* queer child to live with a man (the clue for this reading can be found in the scene when the otherwise cold and expressionless Marissa almost tears up when

Hanna's grandmother talks about the death of her daughter, claiming that the childless Marissa couldn't possibly imagine what such a loss feels like). Furthermore, the fact that the space of East Berlin (with some references to the formerly East-German Leipzig and Poland) serves as the site of this unrealized queer utopia, which the characters re-visit years after its traumatic loss, metonymically touches on the failure of another political project, that of Communism, which was also discontinued when nobody believed in it anymore. Summoning this specter of queer communism offers an alternative to the aesthetic consensus that, initially, both Hanna and Marissa seem to be equally caught within, each thrilled by the pursuit of the other, by their ultimate accident. In reality both of them are haunted by the same ghosts of the past that appears for them through the mediation of their double as the return of their own repressed loss in the form of the other's *childness*; what Hanna lacks as a child at the beginning is embodied in the Bond-villainesque infantile playfulness of Marissa while Hanna's childlike naivité, the rigid and humorlessness precision with which she executes her vengeance for her mother, reminds Marissa of her own youthful enthusiasm before she turned cynical.

The two heroines, then, are more intimately connected than it might appear at first, precisely through their shared trauma, their common inability to fully mourn the loss of their same sex other (mother/lover) which, as Judith Butler would argue, forms the lesbian configuration of their desire.[18] This failure is linked to the fact that their loss couldn't have been publicly, symbolically acknowledged; in this sense, they are queer versions of Antigone, whose dead brother the state refused to bury. Just like Antigone, the two occupy the place that Žižek calls the sublime domain between two deaths, actual and symbolic.[19] This conceptual space is based on the Lacanian distinction between the *symbolic*, our social order that we enter through the common language, and the *real*, defined as the impossible fullness of enjoyment that escapes symbolization, testifying to the incompleteness of every symbolic totalization. This libidinal excess of the real is kept at bay through the subject's symbolic castration, the partial substitution of the signifier for her being. Consequently, for a human being to die "properly," she has to die twice, both in the real and the symbolic, both as enjoying subject and as part of the social order (this is why we give those who die biologically funeral rites). The space between these two deaths opens up when someone dies only once, which is another way of saying that in her life the balance between real and symbolic has been disturbed. As Žižek explains, this can happen in two ways: "For a human being to be 'dead while alive' is to be colonized by the 'dead' symbolic order; to be 'alive while dead' is to give body to the remainder of Life-Substance which has escaped the symbolic colonization (lamella)."[20]

The more popular of these two categories is that of the "alive while dead," which Žižek associates with the "obscene immortality" of the undead in horror fiction as well as with the relentless and sublime figure of Antigone because of her identification with the persisting undead body of her brother, the body that is refused/refuses itself to be mourned, to be laid to rest under the conditions of the existing social order. We can add Virilio's subject of the accident to this series, as what worries him in the contemporary glorification of accidents is precisely the obscenity of the gaping hole of the sublime lacking a properly beautiful cover. Accordingly, the appeal of this concept is its usefulness in designating a site of resistance "in the real" to the normative symbolic, promising its revolutionary negation. This part of Žižek's theory is appropriated by Edelman in *No Future* for the purposes of queer theory, defining his own version of the sublime revolutionary, the *sinthomosexual*, precisely as the one embodying this obscene immortality against the totalizing attempts of the symbolic which uses the fantasy-figure of the Child to fill in its lack, guaranteeing its continuity in the future:

> Such immortality pertains to what the Symbolic constitutively forecloses: not reality, not the subject, not the future, not the Child, but the substance of jouissance itself, the Lacanian lamella, on which the sinthomosexual lives and against which social organization wields the weapon of futurity to keep the place of life empty—merely a hollow, inanimate form—the better to sustain the fantasy of its endurance in time to come. The death drive's "immortality," then, refers to a persistent negation that offers assurance of nothing at all: neither identity, nor survival, nor any promise of the future. Instead, it insists both on and as the impossibility of Symbolic closure, the absence of any Other to affirm the Symbolic order's truth, and hence the illusory status of meaning as defense against the self-negating substance of jouissance.[21]

Both the Child and the sinthomosexual occupy here the same place in the symbolic, that of its lack, that is, of *objet a*. In Edelman's reading the difference between these two figures, the Child is the fetishistic fiction that fills in the place of inconsistency symbolically prepared for her, emptied out of *jouissance* while the queer resister occupies the site of this gap with a different purpose, to keep it open for a continuous flow of enjoyment, or, in Virilio's terms, to seek out one accident after the other.

It is easy to discern the contours of the two protagonists of Wright's film in Edelman's theory. Hanna, not so surprisingly, would stand for the Child for whose survival her parents sacrifice themselves, while Marissa could represent the sinthomosexual, preventing the closure of the (heteronormative) symbolic by hunting down its fantasmatic support, Hanna (along with her mother, father and grandmother, for that matter). In Kantian terms, Edelman could say that the division between Child and sinthomosexual is also what distinguishes the subject of the beautiful from that of the sublime, the experience of well-ordained limits from that of boundless terror. What such a reading ignores is the dialectical interconnectedness of the two heroines outlined above (the fact that ultimately they are each other's doubles), for which reason it cannot but end up with a limited understanding of the sublime that glorifies horror and destruction while trying to eliminate the ideological closure that the Child represents. In Lacanian terms, the problem with taking Marissa as a queer revolutionary is that while she might stand for the force of the death drive destroying every meaning that would guarantee the temporary identity of the symbolic, this doesn't free her from serving the Law of the superego. In fact, she loses herself completely in her role as its executioner, in the *jouissance* of seeking out and neutralizing accidents—just like Hanna does at the beginning of the film. Being the agent of the CIA serves as a metaphor here for the obscene superego underside of ordinary reality, for the law that solicits its own transgression, suspending the law of the constitution, ordering the subject to "Obey!" without any positive content which, far from undermining the social-symbolic status quo, functions rather as its ultimate support, much like the way the actual CIA's unlawful tactics help the legal state apparatus function "normally" in the U.S.[22] No wonder, then, that in the end, it is Marissa who stands for a rather conservative, postfeminist, anti-queer identity politics, for the conformism that is formed out of her routine transgressions of social norms, what Virilio referred to as the "conformism of abjection."

For this reason, it may be more productive to read Hanna's position not simply as the beautiful, family-friendly obverse to Marissa's sublime sinthomosexual terrorist, but rather as a sublime figure herself, similarly entangled in the queer process of melancholic (unfinished) mourning with a different relation, however, to the symbolic order. She can be described as "dead while alive" (as opposed to "alive while dead"), as someone who is not "outside" the symbolic like the sinthomosexual, rather fully immersed in it, who appears to be taken over by the automatisms of language, seemingly unable produce a critical distance from them. Žižek's recurring example for this borderline psychotic subject is the idiot who upon being asked the question "How are you today?" takes it literally and starts recounting what happened to her that day, how is her health, etc.[23] This is exactly how Hanna is presented in the film. When she is asked: "What did your mum die of?," she answers: "Three bullets." The psychoanalytic category describing such a state of consciousness, often associated with children, is the "subject supposed to believe." For instance, as Žižek points out, adults of course don't believe Santa Claus really exists; they go through all the rituals to pretend they do for the sake of their children because they assume they do.[24] In Ranciere's terms, the practice of belief here defines a certain distribution of the sensible, the ideological splitting of the population in two parts. On the one hand, there are those who have the capacity to disbelieve, to dis-identify from symbolic fictions and those who are incapable to do so because they supposedly cannot understand the exceptions to the rules of language; they are the idiots who believe literally.[25] Žižek's point, in line with Ranciere's, is that the very assumption responsible for this split is fundamentally false; we project the fictional category of the idiot-who-really-believes on children not because they are unable to be skeptical but because they are the ones designated to believe *for* us, *instead of* us so that we don't have to.[26]

The Child/sinthomosexual opposition gets subverted when we consider how the former serves as the fetishized subject supposed to believe *for* the latter in her disbelief. *Hanna* demonstrates that, contrary to Edelman's claim, the dominant symbolic is not held together by its heteronormative subjects' belief in the Child; quite the opposite, it is those marked as Children who are supposed to believe *for* them, allowing them to dis-identify from their own publicly performed ideology. In the film, this dis-identification leads to a fundamental asymmetry between the two protagonists. True, Hanna and Marissa start out as each other's doubles, as two sides of the same coin of queerness understood as the accidental sublime of the "alive while dead," their place connected through a Moebius-strip where starting from one surface we eventually reach the opposite. This topological symmetry is subverted, however, with their different reactions to the return of their repressed *childness* which surprises them (as well as the spectator) through the film's form itself, as if to derail their straightforward quest for narcissistic vengeance through a series of cinematic distractions. Against their intentions, they keep finding themselves perplexed by the surreal fairy tale *mise-en-scene*, as part of the film's self-reflexive endeavor to become an audiovisual *Gesamtkustwerk* in the Romantic tradition, combining the trippy electro soundtrack of The Chemical Brothers with an arsenal of attractions selected from the over a century long history of cinematic techniques (the *camera obscura*, moving panoramas, the *mise-en-scene* of German Expressionist films as well as contemporary music video editing). While neither of the heroines believe in the real-impossible queer utopia of the past directly, it is Hanna who nonetheless embraces the insisting presence of its after-effects in the form of recurring sensual events while Marissa cynically rejects them, laughing at their fakeness—she ends up mocking the kitsch artifice of her old friend's gay club as if to insist that it's never going to be like the original (disavowed) queer event of her life was. By contrast, Hanna is able to keep an open mind because she has no preference for any original; she has learned neither to believe in such a thing nor to disavow such belief through a cynical distance (which is ultimately the same). We might say that she is open to the distraction of *childness* precisely because she is not bound by Marissa's childishness. *Childness* here should be understood as the subjectivity accompanying a fully artificial aesthetic experience of the world that one can only learn if she lets go of the melancholic attachment to her inner Child, the fetishistic remainder of some authentic childishness that, as Marissa's case shows, serves as the ultimate objectal supplement to the cynic's position.

Childness and Distraction

The aesthetic experience of *childness* as a third term destabilizing the Child/sinthomosexual binary parallels Lacan's discussion of the stain disrupting the dialectic between the eye and the gaze that constitutes a stable visual field. His first important claim regarding vision is that the zero level of our subjectivity is not simply the voyeuristic experience of looking at something but it always at the same time presupposes the condition of *being looked at*. In this setting the eye that is attached to the *seeing* subject is supplemented by the fantasmatic entity of the gaze that makes the subject *seen*. For Lacan, the gaze is both the product and the producer of castration anxiety insofar as it is related to the subject's "primal separation" from *objet a,* the origin of an irreducible lack, the founding trauma constitutive of the subject. Writes Lacan, "From the moment that this gaze appears, the subject tries to adapt himself to it, he becomes that punctiform object, that point of vanishing being with which the subject confuses his own failure."[27] The inapprehensible nature of the gaze is a consequence of the subject's structural inability to reach completeness, the fullness of enjoyment. But because of her confusion, she tries to do so nonetheless; this is how the gaze appears in her visual field as an object that cannot be captured through the power of vision: it appears as the stain in the picture. However, it is crucial to emphasize the difference between the gaze and the stain. As Žižek explains: "*objet petit a* [...] is not the stain itself but rather the gaze in the precise sense of the point of view from which the stain can be perceived in its 'true meaning,' the point from which, instead of the anamorphic distortion, it would be possible to discern the true contours of what the subject perceives as a formless stain." The fantasmatic gaze as *objet a* is all seeing; in the analytic context, it is the analyst as the *subject supposed to know* who is falsely assumed to be able to see the patient in her impossible fullness, who's supposed to know the secrets of her unconscious without any stain to block his view.[28] What, then, is the Edelmanian sinthomosexual's strategy towards the gaze as *objet a* ? At first, it seems to be the occupation of its place and thereby the destruction of the myth of the panoptic gaze, the withdrawal of belief in the hidden knowledge it supposedly has about her. For this reason, insofar as the film's two sublime subjects, Hanna and Marissa, are playing the role of a materialized *objet a* for each other, they both effectively act as sinthomosexuals trying to push the other out of the place of knowledge about themselves, about their past trauma. Upon closer look, however, it becomes clear that this sublime strategy to eliminate *objet a* in its concrete appearances (as distracting stains of *childness*) in fact keeps alive the myth of a hidden truth at the core of the subject, and betrays a belief in one's lost childhood as real-impossible. In the case of Marissa, this leads to the melancholic fidelity to her lost object (Hanna's mother) by killing (the stain of) anyone who tries to take her place or even reminds her of the loss.

By contrast, Hanna's relation to the gaze and her stain is more ambiguous here than Marissa's purely sinthomosexual strategy. On the one hand, at the beginning of her journey, there are numerous scenes where she is shooting surveillance cameras or agents who try to capture and interrogate her, which goes in line with fighting the panoptic aspect of the gaze. On the other hand, she also encounters the gaze (stain) as a source of light, the experience of which she takes rather positively. For instance, after escaping from a CIA holding facility through underground tunnels, she climbs up a ladder of a manhole the punctured cover of which lets small streams of light shine through its holes. When Hanna removes the cover she finds herself overwhelmed by the scorching sunlight outside. As Lacan emphasized, the "gaze is always a play of light and opacity."[29] From the perspective of the sinthomosexual (Marissa) this would mean that the gaze, while it appears all seeing, is in fact fundamentally blind (it's always "just" a stain)—a realization that can lead to the subject's self-instrumentalization in front of a *blind*, that is, ultimately arbitrary force of law (the law as nothing but a series of accidents, i.e., the law of the superego) as opposed to the "ideological" belief in this or that particular set of rules.

Lacan's point about the blindness of the gaze is, however, something different; in Seminar XI he tells the story of his youthful endeavor to find his true self by working as a fisherman in a poor seaside town of Brittany. One day, while engaged in hard labor on a boat, one of his fellow fishermen pointed at a sardine can floating in the water: "It floated there in the sun, a witness to the canning industry, which we, in fact, were supposed to supply. It glittered in the sun. And Petit-Jean said to me—You see that can? Do you see it? Well, it doesn't see you!" Lacan describes his feeling after the encounter as "rather out of place in the picture." In what picture? In the fantasmatic one that positioned him as a manual laborer, the "supposed supplier" of belief for the panoptic gaze of the Other that in exchange had knowledge about his true, raw, authentic self. This fantasy scenario about identification was, of course, properly unconscious until the encounter; until that point, he was convinced that his attempt at self-discovery among "common people" was a form of dis-identification from the routines of academic life, distance from the normative symbolic he tried to escape through exploring the sublime, raw forces of nature on that fishing boat. The light reflecting on the sardine can reveals to him the futility and ridiculousness of this enterprise insofar as the Other appears now as the rather banal object of the fishing industry, a stain on the picture. It is this gleam of light that distracts the subject at the precise moment when she becomes aware that her fundamental fantasy of full enjoyment cannot be realized[30]; it reveals, in Hegelian terms, the speculative identity of the naïve belief of the Child and the sublime disbelief of the sinthomosexual, sublating/synthesizing their opposition into a new mode of subjectivity that can be called *childness*.

The term "distraction" was used by Walter Benjamin for the aesthetic experience of modernity where the intensifying overload of our senses leads to the loss of aura in natural and man-made objects, that is, to the perception of shock-effects without any intentionality. In Wright's film, there's a scene that illustrates this quite adequately, brutally realizing Hanna's dream for a childhood she never had through the disorientating shocks of *childness*. It's about her encounter with the technological advances of human civilization for the first time in her life when she is left alone in a hotel room, full of electronic devices. At first, she is fascinated by the effects of the light switch or the TV's remote control; soon, however, she becomes overwhelmed by all the lights and noises and runs out of the room in panic. This defining experience is her "sardine can moment." The fact that, despite the initial anxiety, she embraces the radical externality of such sense-events makes it possible for her to remain captivated by moving images, music and other forms of distractions that the film, as an obvious love letter to the powers of cinema, simply calls "magic."

Such an understanding of distraction also sheds a different light on the Kantian formula of the beautiful as "purposiveness without a purpose." In beauty, according to Kant, nature appears as a system organized by laws that we don't have in our intellect; the ground of nature's "sense-ful form" is outside of us.[31] The obvious danger here is to attribute some kind of hidden knowledge to Nature that would serve as the guarantor of our meaningful place in a totality bigger than us and that would thus hold the knowledge about our true self.[32] However, this type of beauty, according to Benjamin, is linked to contemplation, the subjective practice that supports the distanced aesthetics of the aura that he diametrically opposes to the tactility of distraction.[33] By contrast, the beautiful as distraction appears as the *byproduct* of the sublime subject's accelerated endeavor to construct melancholically the gaze as her *objet a*, as a pure void while always negating any particular manifestations of it. Distraction brings out the unexpected surplus of the closed, cynical dialectic of disbelief and belief, disidentification and identification. It marks the necessary failure of this enterprise, the failure of cynicism that is accompanied by the emergence of *childness*. Distraction occurs when the stain floats into the picture, causing the subject's falling out of it, that is, out of her own fundamental fantasy about an impossible, authentic, sublime childhood.

Childness, then, is produced by the stain of beauty that unexpectedly appears where one anticipates the void of sublime terror, when even the sublime object of pure nothingness, the substance of the accident that serves as the last ideological support of the subject's fantasmatic true selfhood, evaporates in a Hegelian negation of negation. For Lacan, the stain prevents the subject from becoming the screen, from becoming complete even through an impossible-real fantasy scenario; in return, it is a beautiful stain, a purposiveness without a purpose, that is screened in front of her. The machine of such beauty (the machine of the stain), the film suggests, that is producing the subjectivity of *childness* is cinema itself. Along these lines the aesthetic state Hanna reaches in the film can be called cinematic: a captivation with the "magical" purposiveness of music and moving images, which lacks any apparent purpose, combined with a latent anxiety coming from, to paraphrase Cavell, the awareness that she doesn't know what her conviction in their reality turns upon.[34] This anxiety of a *childness* intruding from the outside may be an alternative to today's accelerated melancholic search for the sublime core of the self, that is, one's inner Child.

Notes

1. Lee Edelman, *No Future: Queer Theory and the Death Drive* (Durham: Duke University Press, 2004), 29.
2. Slavoj Žižek, *How to Read Lacan* (New York: W.W. Norton, 2006), 29.

3. Stanley Cavell, *The World Viewed: Reflections on the Ontology of Film* (Cambridge, MA: Harvard University Press, 1979).
4. Jacques Ranciere, *The Politics of Aesthetics* (New York: Continuum, 2004).
5. Paul Valery quoted in Paul Virilio, *The Original Accident* (Cambridge: Polity Press, 2007), 5.
6. Virilio, *The Original Accident*, 6–8; Paul Virilio, *Art and Fear* (New York: Continuum, 2003), 37.
7. Walter Benjamin, "The Work of Art in the Age of Mechanical Reproduction," in *Media and Cultural Studes Key Works*, eds. M. J. Durham and D. Kellner (Oxford: Blackwell, 2006), 33.
8. Virilio, *Art and Fear*, 46.
9. Virilio, *The Original Accident*, 23.
10. Immanuel Kant, "Selections from Critique of Judgment" in *Basic Writings of Kant* (New York: Random House, 2001), 306–307.
11. Virilio, *The Original Accident*, 10.
12. Alenka Zupancic, *Ethics of the Real: Kant, Lacan* (New York: Verso, 2000), 149.
13. Zupancic, 154.
14. Slavoj Žižek, *The Sublime Object of Ideology* (New York: Verso, 2008), 89.
15. Zupancic, *Ethics of the Real*, 158.
16. Zupancic, 153.
17. See Friedrich Nietzsche, *Beyond Good and Evil: Prelude to a Philosophy of the Future*, trans. Judith Norman (Cambridge: Cambridge University Press, 2001).
18. See Judith Butler, *The Psychic Life of Power: Theories in Subjection* (Stanford: Stanford University Press, 1997).
19. Slavoj Žižek, *Looking Awry: An Introduction to Jacques Lacan Through Popular Culture* (Cambridge MIT Press, 1992), 22–23.
20. Slavoj Žižek, *The Plague of Fantasies* (London: Verso, 1997), 89.
21. Edelman, *No Future*, 48.
22. Žižek, *The Sublime Object*, 88–89.
23. Žižek, *How to Read Lacan*, 31.
24. Žižek, *How to Read Lacan*, 30.
25. See Ranciere, *The Emancipated Spectator*, 12.
26. Žižek, *How To Read Lacan*, 29.
27. Jacques Lacan, "Of the Gaze as Objet Petit a" in *The Four Fundamental Concepts of Psychoanalysis, The Seminars of Jacques Lacan, Book XI*, trans. Alan Sheridan (New York: W.W. Norton, 1981), 72, 83.
28. Slavoj Žižek, *Tarrying with the Negative: Kant, Hegel and the Critique of Ideology* (Durham: Duke University Press, 1993), 65–66.
29. Lacan, *Of the Gaze*, 96.
30. Lacan, *Of the Gaze*, 95–96.
31. Kant, *Critique of Judgment*, 308.
32. Zupancic, *Ethics of the Real*, 157.
33. Benjamin, "Work of Art," 33.
34. Benjamin, "Work of Art," 71–72.

Afterword

Monstrously Yours?

Kathryn Bond Stockton

Was it just me, or does every child who is growing queerly, sliding liquidly, twisting, falling, feel she is a monster? I was this metaphor. This simile. This referent. That was how it felt. To be more specific, I thought I was (like) Barnabas Collins, that congenial vampire. A great guy, really, with a propensity he couldn't help. He could not *not* bite women along the alluring length of their necks, opalescent pearl of any colored flesh apt to reveal his own wound: his own tendency to pursue an action which made women, in the last analysis, sadly unavailable to him. Talk about no future. He was never going to get the girl, I felt. Nor was I. We were monsters. Shadowy figures with shadowy secrets surrounding women.

If only someone would have told me I had company, so much company, as I know in the wake of this book. Mothers, pregnant women, babies, fat girls (all crush-worthy, except the babies). Kids of color, warrior-creatures, even teachers. Surrounded by these comrades, I might have noticed the monstrous forces arrayed against us—monstrous forces stacked against monsters, for a juicy paradox—monstrous in the sense of "outrageously wrong."

Naïve reading, incuriosity, sometimes the police. These are a few of the forces against us, we charming monsters. Indeed, this volume has reminded me that the monster figure arises in the midst of non-best-practices, to put it mildly (and a bit facetiously), practiced by the general culture. Let me leave us now with a few to contemplate, in tribute to this thoughtful book. Oscar Wilde's Dorian Gray—giving rise to several cinematic adaptations of this "monster"—is a queer youth attacked by his own unsophisticated reading. He's not evil due to hedonism. He's not corrupted by pursuing pleasure. He's not a monster of monstrous desire. He's a naïve reader. Make that even a virginal reader, with no condom on. He lacks a condom stretched upon his head. What do I mean? He can't handle unprotected reading. He naively believes that art's about him and forgets that reading makes a fertile mess—leads to "childness."[1] He's a Gothic reader, prone to Gothic fright. His understanding of metaphor says as much: "[In the yellow book, Dorian thinks] there were ... metaphors as monstrous as orchids, and as subtle in colour.... One hardly knew at times whether one was reading the spiritual ecstasies of some medieval saint or the morbid confessions of a modern sinner. It was a poisonous book. The heavy odour of incense seemed to cling about its pages and to trouble the brain."[2]

Dorian's monstrosity is not a sign of pederasty. Of his being touched or opened by a man. It is the face of the general public's naïve reading, their own fright over new sensations, over forms of influence they take inside, a fright afflicting *Dorian*, paradoxically enough. Wilde's novel thematizes this very problem, though it eludes the cinema screen. Dorian drinking in Lord Henry Wotton's musical words, in a garden, no less; taking in the portrait of himself through his eye, before he makes his Faustian pact. Thus penetrated in his eyes and his ears, throbbing with the signifiers he takes inside, Dorian goes Gothic in the way he gleans meaning from different surface-signs. Henry, by contrast, a master of childness, a monster of childness, becomes a master of artful decay. By his forgetting exactly what he's said, letting signs decay, tripping on metaphors as monstrous as orchids, Henry slips inside the genre of a play. Wilde thus shows them as two different readers who have kissed the same surface to different effects. Childness is the inverse of naïveté.

No less monstrous of a force against us monsters is incuriosity. The force this volume is crafted to battle. Readers are used to thinking of Humbert Humbert in *Lolita* as the novel's monster. He deems himself such along the way, after all. In a famous scene, possibly too scandalous to appear in cinema —in either Stanley Kubrick's or Adrian Lyne's filmic renderings of *Lolita*— Humbert tries to climax via Lolita's movements in his lap, all while she remains blissfully unaware, so he imagines, of his bliss. Here Nabokov plants his first detective clue to the mystery of Lolita's childhood sexuality and its motive forces—a competing monster (sexual childhood seen as frightening, daunting, unnatural, even mutant, by the general culture) that runs along a sidetrack Humbert fails to notice.

In fact, in the moment just before climax, Nabokov has Humbert running his hand up Lolita's leg to pause at "a yellowish-violet bruise on her lovely ... thigh"—before "I crushed out against her left buttock the last throb of the longest ecstasy man or monster had ever known."[3] It seems as if Lolita, abused without her knowing it, some might say, has been made to cause effects in which she has no share: "Blessed be the Lord," Humbert narrates, "she had noticed nothing!"[4] Can we be so sure? "'Oh, it's nothing at all,' she cried with a sudden shrill note in her voice," as Humbert's thumb presses past the bruise to the "hollow of her groin," "and she wiggled, and squirmed, and threw her head back, and her teeth rested on her glistening underlip as she half-turned away."[5] Actually, the clues themselves surround the bruise in the form of motions—squirming, wiggling, even half-turning—we struggle to read. Read with *curiosity*.

Not so, he. Humbert, in fact, may drive Lolita all over the country—both films certainly do show this—but, as the novel in a thousand ways indicates, Dolly, as Humbert often calls her, is driving Humbert strangely from behind, as she sits beside him. Communicating constantly with Quilty who follows their every move a few lengths back, she is wrapped up in Quilty and the car that's chasing Humbert. For it's the great joke of the plot to have Humbert's "pet" be in league with Mr. Quilty, her *preferred* pedophile, who with Lolita's knowledge and help steers sad Humbert to a predetermined terminus in the state of Utah, where both Dolly and her Quilty disappear. Crafty little monster with sexual motives....

The girl-child's childness in *Lolita* is, by definition, a detective fiction that reveals a monster (child sexuality) that defeats a monstrousness (incuriosity). This way of answering a mystery with a mystery—children's motives appear in the hieroglyphics of their motions—makes the more compelling twin of Humbert Humbert not Clare Quilty but the law itself. *Like Nabokov's pedophile*, who is himself shockingly incurious about Lolita's wishes, American legal constructions of the child rob children of their motives. To the motions of the child and the wish of children to move in certain ways, sexual ways our culture deems monstrous still to this day, justice has been blind.

Speaking of the law, police from time to time are their own monstrosity, as they claim to be catching monsters. Not surprisingly, Jean Genet offers these complexities, which become progeny, which Rainer Fassbinder puts on the screen. (Each man, of course, an *enfant terrible*.) In both the novel and film *Querelle*, the title character is both a fantasy man and a monster. A beautiful sailor who murders men. Such is his splendor, he seems unreal: more of a projection of what a "homosexual" might be seeking if he were seeking a straight-acting man. Why would such a glorious figure be a monster? Because, on some level, when Genet is writing in the 1950's and Fassbinder is filming in the early 80's, the manly straight man is likely to harbor murderous thoughts about homosexuals. This is how he appears so manly, strange to say (or not). The man who is my fantasy, *Querelle* implies, wants to murder me. Stranger still, he is my child. How can this be? Simply, he is birthed by "gay" desires. The invert narrators of *Querelle* figure their desire as a monstrous child. Hear them speak of their desires: "Little by little, we saw how Querelle—already contained in our flesh—was beginning to grow in our soul, to feed on what is best in us, above all on our despair at not being in any way inside him, while having him inside ourselves. After this discovery of Querelle we want him to become the Hero, even to those who may despise him....[He is the] fruit of our secret loves."[6] Hear them speak of this monstrous child, a magnificent child, a majestic child, an empress child, if you can believe it:

> Querelle was not used to the idea ... that he was a monster.... Thus might a young boy ... who has been metamorphosed into an alligator, even if he were not fully conscious of his horrendous head and jaws, consider his scaly body ... with which he strikes the water or the beach or brushes against that of other monsters, and which extends him with the same touching, heart-rending and indestructible majesty as the train of a robe, adorned with lace, with crests, with battles, with a thousand crimes, worn by a Child Empress, extends her.[7]

S/he grows sideways. And so does this paean. Metaphors as monstrous as orchids, anyone? They convey the ache of this dream to be touched by a man you've birthed as a child-you'll-never-hold.

The police, evidently, are there to stop this dream. To be more precise, to snatch this dream. *Catch* this dream. Genet, in a beautiful line, informs us: "Charged with the drainage of dreams, the police catch them in their filters. And that explains why policemen bear such resemblance to those they pursue."[8] Truly to stop crime, they must prevent crime; but to prevent crime, they must foresee crime; thus to foresee crime, they must see as.... Ah, they are monsters? No, not exactly. They are stopped-monsters, or in *Querelle* stopped-homosexuals, stopped-child-empresses. They must stop from going where they dearly would. Cops, then, stop what the law forbids: their own wish to pursue our dreams. Our most cherished progeny.

For Genet and Fassbinder and, I'm guessing, the authors of this book, progeny-stoppage of this variety is precisely monstrous. This is naïve reading. Incuriosity. However, these are things that monsters, volumes exploring monsters, this fine book analyzing monsters, and the childness-monster will redress.

Monster though I am, I am not monstrously yours.

Notes

1. As defined by Markus Bohlmann and Sean Moreland in the introduction.
2. Oscar Wilde, *The Picture of Dorian Gray* (New York: Penguin, 1985), 156.

3. Vladimir Nabokov, *Lolita* (New York: Vintage, 1997), 60–61.
4. Nabokov, *Lolita*, 61.
5. Nabokov, *Lolita*, 61.
6. Jean Genet, *Querelle*, trans. Anselm Hollo (New York: Grove, 1974), 17–18.
7. Genet, *Querelle*, 14.
8. Genet, *Querelle*, 78.

Kathryn Bond Stockton is a distinguished professor of English and associate vice president for equity and diversity at the University of Utah. Her most recent books, Beautiful Bottom, Beautiful Shame: Where "Black" Meets "Queer" and The Queer Child, or Growing Sideways in the Twentieth Century, *both were finalists for the Lambda Literary Award in LGBT studies. In 2013, she was awarded the Rosenblatt Prize for Excellence, the highest honor granted by the University of Utah.*

Afterword

Harry M. Benshoff

Whether or not the 21st-century horror film is going through a renaissance or a retrogression (and in many ways perhaps it is doing both), it does seem that in this newest century horror film criticism is reaching something of a golden age. Perhaps it is the fall out of 9/11, and the public's newfound awareness of how the horror genre always has and continues to reflect social conditions, that makes this era so ripe for horror film commentary of all sorts. Among scholars, horror films have always been thought to be expressive of the cultures and contexts that produce and consume them, whether those contexts be two World Wars, the Great Depression, the Cold War, the rise of the 1960s counterculture, (backlash to) feminism, and/or the AIDS crisis of the 1980s. But since 9/11 we have witnessed even more finely nuanced horror subgenres exploring extreme rendition and enhanced interrogation techniques (torture porn), surveillance culture (found footage horror films), and survival itself in a world whose infrastructure is allegedly crumbling (the proliferation of zombie apocalypse texts across all aspects of the media landscape). We have also seen an interest in horror films as vehicles for teen romance (*Twilight*, et al.), and a surge in both films and film criticism that speak to the various fears surrounding birth and childhood (or as this fine volume would posit, *childness*). The history of monstrous children has been ably explored by the authors in this volume, who trace its development through key literary texts such as *Beowulf*, *Frankenstein*, *The Turn of the Screw*, and *Les Enfants Terrible* to its first cinematic boom in the 1960s, where it was tied to—among other things—new birth control techniques and the upheaval of traditional gender roles wrought by the counterculture. And as reproductive technologies continue to evolve beyond science fiction narratives, and as new understandings of gender and sexuality continue to rewrite "the rules" for men, women, and (hetero)sexuality, so too it seems the interest in monstrous children in the mass media has only continued to grow.

Rather than speak to one or all of the essays in this volume, I would like to take this brief opportunity to draw attention to two other "monstrous child" texts not mentioned herein: the Italian-American horror film *The Visitor* (1979), and *Extant* (2014-), a new mini-series from CBS starring Halle Berry as an astronaut who returns to earth after a year in space carrying a mysterious fetus. Both speak to many of the concerns and issues raised throughout this volume, albeit in very different ways.

The Visitor is one of those outrageously campy cinematic mash-ups that only non–American filmmakers seem to get away with (in this case director Giulio Paradisi and writer-producer Ovidio G. Assonitis). Its 1970s American stars—who were apparently eager for a paycheck—include Shelley Winters, Mel Ferrer, Glenn Ford, Lance Henriksen, Kareem Abdul-Jabbar, and Sam Peckinpah. Old, white-bearded John Huston more or less plays God, herein figured as an intergalactic crusader following in the tradition of "Commander Yahweh"—or so a blond and blue-eyed Jesus figure played by an uncredited Franco Nero tells us—dedicated to stopping the evil descendants of a fallen alien being named "Sateen" (I am guessing at the correct spelling of this name). True to the sexist conventions of 1960s/1970s evil child tropes, a tainted mother (Joanne Nail) and her bratty telekinetic daughter (Paige Conner) are mostly to blame for much of the mayhem, although her husband and a corporate mogul played by Mel Ferrer also seem to have some interest in abetting Sateen's spawn. Along the way we have rape, abortion, mean bird attacks, a shooting that results in paralysis, and much ice skating and gymnastics as the Devil-Girl shows off her superior physical skills. *The Visitor* is perhaps best appreciated for the way it combines apparently devout Christian theology with the tropes of horror and science fiction, liberally cribbing ideas and even visuals from well-known films as diverse as *The Birds* (1963), *Rosemary's Baby* (1968), *The Exorcist* (1973), *The Omen* (1976), *Demon Seed* (1977), *Star Wars* (1977), *Close Encounters on the Third Kind* (1977), and *The Fury* (1978). And as such a genre mash-up, *The Visitor* might rightly be called a culmination of its era's child horror tropes. Needless to say, John Huston's "God" character eventually gets the Devil-Girl to succumb to his benevolent control.

Extant, on the other hand, has Halle Berry and Steven Spielberg on board as executive producers; it aims to be intelligent quality television for today's hungry genre consumers. Still, many of the same themes of the 1960s-1970s monster child narrative are present. So far—and as of this writing only a few episodes have aired—*Extant* focuses on a confused (if not hysterical) astronaut played by Halle Berry, whose unexplained pregnancy may or may not give rise to some sort of alien monster child. (Call it *I Married a Monster from Outer*

Space [1958] for the new millennium.) However, *Extant* has another potential monster child lurking in the wings, a robotic boy created by the Berry character's husband (Goran Visnjic). Curiously enough, this other potential monster child also has a thing for birds, as did the Devil-Girl from *The Visitor*.

So far, *Extant* eschews the overt Christian morality of *The Visitor* (and much monstrous child cinema of its era) in favor of less controversial science fiction tropes: will the greatest threat to humankind come from an alien species housed in Berry's womb, some sort of man-made robot created by her scientist husband, or some hybrid combination of both? Only time will tell, but it will be interesting to see how the usual canonical tropes of "the monstrous child" will play out across this newest media landscape. Doubtless we will have monstrous children as long as we have not-so-monstrous children, and scholars such as those contained in this volume will continue to help us understand what such children have to say about the fears and anxieties they engender.

Harry M. Benshoff is a professor of radio, television, and film at the University of North Texas. He is the author of Monsters in the Closet: Homosexuality and the Horror Film *and* Dark Shadows, *and he is the editor of* A Companion to the Horror Film. *His other publications include essays on blaxploitation horror films, Hollywood LSD films,* The Talented Mr. Ripley, Brokeback Mountain, *and* Twilight.

About the Contributors

Jessica **Balanzategui** is a PhD candidate at the University of Melbourne, Australia. She has taught film, literature and media studies at James Cook University and the University of Melbourne. Her doctoral thesis explores uncanny child characters in recent transnational horror films. She has published work on the uncanny child, madness and asylums in the horror film in *Etropic* and *Refractory: A Journal of Entertainment Media*, and reviews for *Media International Australia*.

Markus P.J. **Bohlmann** is a professor of English at Seneca College, Toronto. His research and teaching interests include American literature and film, queer literature and theory, childhood studies, and Deleuze studies. He has published in venues such as *Post Script: Essays in Film and the Humanities* and *Children's Literature Association Quarterly*, and he is on the editorial boards for *Red Feather Journal* and *Children and Youth in Popular Culture*, a Lexington Book Series.

Rebecca A. **Brown** completed a PhD in English at the University of Florida. She teaches composition and developmental reading and writing courses at North Seattle College. Her research focuses on picture books, horror films, and Gothic graphic novels. She is coeditor of a forthcoming collection of essays concerning the gothic monster from the fin de siècle to the millennium.

John Edgar **Browning** is a Marion L. Brittain Postdoctoral Fellow at the Georgia Institute of Technology. He has over ten published or forthcoming books, including *Speaking of Monsters: A Teratological Anthology* (2012) and *The Forgotten Writings of Bram Stoker* (2012), as well as over 45 published or forthcoming articles, book chapters, and reviews.

Lisa **Cunningham** is a PhD candidate at Georgia State University. Her theoretical focus is on feminist body work and film, and her research interests also include Frank Henenlotter and exploitation film. She has given presentations at Film & History and SCMS.

Brooke W. **Edge** is a doctoral candidate in media studies at the University of Colorado, Boulder. She earned an MA from New York University in cinema studies, and a BA in English from Davidson College, and previously wrote dance criticism and features for *The Prague Post* and other publications. Her dissertation focuses on infertility in popular culture, notably film, television, and celebrity media.

Dustin **Freeley** is an independent scholar and writer. He has taught in the English departments of Hunter College, the College of New Rochelle, and Berkeley College.

He is the cofounder and editor of the film-criticism site MoviesAboutGladiators.com and a member of the Online Film Critics Society.

Danny **Gorny** has a PhD from the University of Ottawa. His primary research examines how fifteenth-century popular fiction absorbed and responded to the development of English nationalism around the end of the Hundred Years' War. Other research interests include codicology, relationships between narrative and identity, and formulations of nationhood.

Kristine **Larsen** is an astronomy professor at Central Connecticut State University. She is the author of *Cosmology 101* and *Stephen Hawking: A Biography* and co-editor of *The Mythological Dimensions of Doctor Who* and *The Mythological Dimensions of Neil Gaiman*. Her scholarship focuses on the intersections between science and society, including science and ethics, women in science, and science and popular culture.

Sarah **Leventer** is a PhD candidate in the American and New England studies program and a graduate writing fellow in the College of Arts and Sciences at Boston University. She holds an MFA in film studies from Boston University. Her dissertation explores representations of the South, Southern literature, race, gender, and trauma in American film.

Sean **Moreland** teaches horror fiction and film, American literature, literature and psychology and literary theory at the University of Ottawa. His essays have appeared in a number of collections, including *Terror of the Soul: Essays on Canadian Horror Film*, *Deciphering Poe*, *Generation Zombie*, and *A History of Evil in American Popular Culture*. He coedited the essay collection *Fear and Learning: Essays on the Pedagogy of Horror* (McFarland, 2013).

Tamas **Nagypal** is a PhD candidate in cinema and media studies at York University, Toronto. His research focuses on cynicism and capitalist realism in contemporary neo-noir. He has published in *Žižek and Media Studies: A Reader* and the *Journal for Cultural and Religious Theory*.

Debbie **Olson** is a lecturer at University of Texas at Arlington. Her research interests include West African film, images of African and African American children in film and popular media, transnationalism, cultural studies, and new Hollywood cinema. She is the editor-in-chief of *Red Feather Journal*, series editor of *Children and Youth in Popular Culture*, and coeditor of *Lost and Othered Children in Contemporary Cinema* and *Portrayals of Children in Popular Culture: Fleeting Images*.

Sharon **Packer**, MD, is a New York–based psychiatrist and assistant professor of psychiatry at Icahn School of Medicine at Mount Sinai. She is the author of *Dreams in Myth, Medicine & Movies*, *Movies and the Modern Psyche*, *Superheroes & Superegos: The Minds behind the Myths*, *Cinema's Sinister Psychiatrists*, and *Neuroscience in Science Fiction Film*, and she is co-editor of *A History of Evil in Popular Culture*.

Karen J. **Renner** is a lecturer at Northern Arizona University, where she teaches American literature and popular culture. She has published essays on ghost-hunting reality television, the apocalypse, and the antichrist-as-child narrative. She is the editor of *The "Evil" Child in Film, Literature and Popular Culture*. Her research on this topic continues.

About the Contributors

Fredrik **Tydal** received a PhD in American literature from Uppsala University, Sweden. He has combined teaching with research in different capacities, most recently as visiting assistant professor at Södertörn University in Stockholm, and conducting postdoctoral research at the University of Virginia.

Colin **Yeo** is a doctoral candidate in English and cultural studies at the University of Western Australia. His doctoral research looks at the connections between the concept of the Gothic and the literature of the early modern period. His scholarly interests include Gothic literature, literary works of the English Renaissance and film studies.

Index

Abortion 49, 53–4, 63, 66–71, 74, 268
Acromegaly 183
Adaptation 10, 22, 125–130, 137–9, 143, 146, 149, 153, 261
Adoption 22, 43, 48, 53
"Adult Child" killer 129, 178–186
Agamben, Giorgio 19
Agency 8, 86–9, 103–4, 113, 116–9, 133, 146, 164–7, 210–5, 243, 248–50
Alien (film series) 44, 48, 57, 88, 96–8, 103–5
Almond, Barbara 74
Ariès, Philippe 11, 128, 140
Assisted Reproductive Technology (ART) 45, 54–57, 63–5, 71, 74

Baartman, Saartjie 188–90, 193, 203
Balaguero, Jaumé 227, 238
Battaglia, Debbora 63
Bayona, Juan Antonio 227, 243
Benjamin, Walter 244, 247, 257–9
Benshoff, Harry 16, 42, 47, 55
Benzedrine 174–6
Beowulf (character) 126–39
Beowulf (poem) 125–31
Beowulf and Grendel (film) 125–139
Berland, Elaine 2, 49
Big Pharma 175–6
Birth 15, 18, 21, 28, 32, 39, 43, 46, 48, 51, 53–6, 61–74, 79–81, 84–90, 97–102, 128, 186, 202, 237, 264
Birth of a Nation 191–2, 195
Black Bodies, White Gazes see Yancy, George
Blade Runner 96–103
Blum, Virginia L. 12, 82
"body genre" *see* Williams, Linda
Bond Stockton, Kathryn 16, 19, 164, 241
Bordo, Susan 213
Bradbury, Mary 61
Brain death 69
Brains (novel) 70
Breast-feeding 38, 63
Breathers (novel) 65, 70
Browning, John Edgar 3, 23, 128–9
Browning, Tod 177
Bruhm, Steven 15, 18, 19, 119–21
Burcar, Jillian 64

Carpenter, John 180–1
Carroll, Noël 17, 29, 32, 38, 49–52, 62
Caruth, Cathy 227, 229
Castañeda, Claudia 156–7
Central Park 82–3
Century of the Child *see* Key, Ellen
child-savage analogy 156–7
Childhood 4, 10–16, 19–24, 30, 82, 166, 116–118, 127–9, 133–4, 137, 139, 149–50, 156–7, 170, 179–81, 190–1, 195, 197–8, 203, 206–10, 214–17, 225–7, 236–41, 245–6, 257–8, 262, 267; and innocence 4, 10–12, 30; and monstrosity 128, 137; as performance 116–118; and secrecy 22, 149–50, 156–7
Childishness 14–16, 19, 24n17, 111, 129, 135, 150, 208, 223n7, 225, 255
"Childlike" 15, 24n17, 111, 130, 135, 140n32, 190, 203, 208–9, 213–19, 222n5, 223n11, 225, 251
"Childness" 4, 9–10, 13–23, 79–80, 85, 92n2, 97, 105, 119, 161, 185–6, 206–221, 225, 245–6, 251, 254–8, 262–4, 268
Children of Men 245
Christine (film) 185
Clayton, Jack 114, 143, 146–54
Clomid 45, 54
Clover, Carol J. 179–80, 186
Cocteau, Jean 9–10
Cohen, Jeffrey Jerome 11, 18, 29, 32, 46–7, 87, 108, 128–9, 143, 177
Cohen, Larry 28, 31–3
Corea, Gena 102
Corpse 33, 35, 61–2, 72, 90, 137, 182, 214, 218, 221
Count Dracula (character) 177, 185
Creed, Barbara 16, 52–4, 56–9, 62
Cronenberg, David 39
The Cultural Contradictions of Motherhood see Hays, Sharon

Dark Romance 80–4, 91
Darwin, Charles 156
Dawn of the Dead (1978) 66–8
Dawn of the Dead (2004) 71–2
Dead Alive 65, 70, 73
Dead baby jokes 61, 75 n.1

275

276 INDEX

Death 23, 33–6, 50, 61–5, 69–71, 74, 80–1, 84, 96, 99–105, 112, 115, 130, 135, 145, 148, 155, 161, 164, 183, 216, 218, 220, 226–39, 243, 245, 249–53
Death Wish 186
Deleuze, Gilles 13, 18, 22, 81, 86, 92, 168–9, 188, 228–31, 234, 239
del Toro, Guillermo 227, 233–5, 239
Demon Seed 88, 268
The Devil's Backbone 227, 233–43
The Dialectic of Sex see Firestone, Shulamith
Dirt 61, 66, 72, 215
Disability 23, 175, 177–81, 186
Dr. Frankenstein (Victor) 2, 8, 20, 35, 79, 80, 84–5, 87, 90–1, 96–7, 102–4
Don't Answer the Phone! 182
Don't Go in the House 182
Douglas, Mary 61, 66–7, 74, 213, 220
Dracula (novel) 3, 144
Dracula (1931 film) 177
DTC (Direct-To-Consumer) advertising 175–6
Du Bois, W.E.B. 189, 202

Edelman, Lee 2, 4, 12, 23, 47, 162–3, 226, 236, 245, 252–6
Embryo (film) 88
Les Enfants Terribles (film) 10
Les Enfants Terribles (novel) 9–10, 15, 267
Enfreakment 191
Enlightenment 21, 79–87, 212
Eraserhead 21, 79–82, 88–92
Erice, Victor 4, 228, 232
Exorcism 118–9, 173
The Exorcist (film) 2, 11, 23, 158, 173–6, 268
Extant 268–9

Fassbinder, Rainer Werner 263–4
Fatal Attraction 49–50
Fertility/infertility 21, 42–59, 63, 65, 71, 74
Fetal container 67–70
Fetus 45, 51, 55, 57, 66–72, 104, 268
Filmic Body 210
Firestone, Shulamith 54, 57
Foucault, Michel 50, 51, 55, 210, 212
Frankenstein (novel) 2, 21–2, 64, 66, 79–92, 96, 100, 267 (1931 film) 101, 231, 35, 56
Frankenstein's Monster 3, 79, 80, 86, 88, 96–7, 99, 231–2
Freaks (film) 177
Freeland, Cynthia 48
Friday the 13th (1980) 3, 40n4, 178, 181–2
Friedkin, William 23, 175
The Funhouse (1981) 182

Genet, Jean 263–4
Girlhood 207–222
"Girlness" 23, 207, 210–22
Godwin, William 84
Goethe, Johann Wolfgang von 9
Goffman, Erving 46
Gork 182

Gothic 1–4, 15, 21–2, 8–4, 91, 111, 114–19, 142, 262
Grace 28, 31, 35–40, 44, 50–1, 71–5
Greil, Arthur 45
Grendel 126–139
Greven, David 179
Grosz, Elisabeth 216
Gunnarson, Sturla 126–139

Haeckel, Ernst 156
Halberstam, Judith/Jack 11, 111, 116
Hallenbeck, Bruce 107
Halloween (1978) 3, 178, 180–1
Halloween II (1981) 180–1
The Hand That Rocks the Cradle 47
handicapped see disability
Hanna 245–58
Hard Candy 221
Hays, Sharon 27–8
Hell Night (1981) 182
Henderson, Carol E. 191–2
Heywood, Colin 11
Hill, Debra 180–1
Hills, Matt 29, 38
Hitchcock, Alfred 18, 178–9
Holt, Seth 107–109, 114, 119
Holy terror(s) 9–11
The Holy Terrors see *Les Enfants Terribles*
Homosexuality 42, 47, 163
Honeyman, Susan 16–17
Hooper, Tobe 177
Horror (affect/emotion) 84–5, 87, 91–2, 142–58, 164, 169, 202, 251–3
Horror (film genre) 42–58, 62–3, 70–1, 107, 108–10, 117, 129, 116, 166, 168, 177–86, 191, 225–33, 241, 267–8
Hottentot Venus see Baartman, Sartije
Huckvale, David 107, 116
Humongous 183–4
Hutcheon, Linda 125
Hutchings, Peter 107, 109
Hyperactive 173–4
Hyperkinetic 173

Imagining the Black Female Body: Reconciling Image in Print and Visual Culture see fertility
In Vitro Fertilization (IVF) 63, 65
The Innocents 10, 109, 114, 118, 143, 145, 149–58
Intensive motherhood 31, 39
Interview with the Vampire (film) 211, 214, 216
It's Alive (1974) 31–2, 39–40, 44, 54–5, 88
It's Alive (2008) 28, 31–2, 35–9

Jackson, Peter 65
JAMA (*Journal of the American Medical Association*) 175–6
Jason Voorhees see *Friday the 13th*
Jaws (film 1977) 185
Just Before Dawn (1981) 182–3

Kant, Immanuel 248–9, 253, 257–8
Keathley, Christian 86, 89
Key, Ellen 11–12
Kick-Ass (film) 219
Kincaid, James 13, 16, 19–20, 206, 208–12, 215–17, 222–3, 227
King, Stephen 14, 169–70
Knock Me Up, Knock Me Down see Oliver, Kelly
Kristeva, Julia 15, 44, 52, 58, 61–2, 67, 70
Kubrick, Stanley 79, 160–3, 168–70, 262

Lacan, Jacques 12–3, 23, 164–7, 248–258
Let Me In 211, 218
Let the Right One In (film) 211, 217–8
Lewy Body Dementia (LBD) 174
Liminality 22, 97, 101, 127–31, 138, 195, 202, 215, 217, 229, 231
Lolita (film) 160
Lolita (novel) 20, 262–3
Losey, Joseph 107–9
Lowenstein, Adam 228, 233
Lynch, David 79–82, 88–92

MacCormack, Patricia 99
Marsh, Margaret 46
Mask Maker 183
May, Elaine Tyler 51
MBD *see* Minimal Brain Dysfunction
McGowan, Todd 88–9
Medicalization 44–5, 51
Melville, Jean-Pierre 10
Methylphenidate 174
Michael Myers *see Halloween*
Midgley, Mary 73
Minimal Brain Dysfunction (MBD) 173, 175
Mitchell, David T. 178–9, 185–6
Mittman, Asa 29, 38
mongoloid (pathology) 182, 191
Monsters in the Closet see Benshoff, Harry
Monstrosity 3, 9,-11, 14, 17, 19–23, 38, 43, 46–56, 73, 99, 107–12, 116, 119, 128–34, 139, 143–4, 149, 158, 161, 167, 202, 228, 246, 262–3, 185; incidental or physical 30–1, 33, 35, 36, 98, 116, 128, 185; moral, intentional or performative 29–30, 32, 35, 39, 116–18, 161, 185
Monstrous-childness 9–10, 17–18, 21–22, 29, 31, 85, 89, 105, 108, 119, 161, 185, 264, 267
Motherhood mandate 47–8, 52
Mrs. (Angela) Voorhees *see Friday the 13th*
"My hideous progeny" 21, 79

Nabokov, Vladimir 20, 262–3
The Nameless 227–8, 235, 237–9
Narcolepsy 174
Neroni, Hilary 209
The New England Journal of Medicine 175
Newman, Kim 114–5
Night of the Dead: Leben Tod 69, 72
The Nightcomers 143, 145, 151–8
Norman Bates *see Psycho*

"Obsessive Avenger" *see* Sutton, Travis
O'Keefe, Katherine O'Brien 131, 133
Old Testament 130–1
Oliver, Kelly 53, 55
The Omen 2, 53, 166, 268
Oneroid 174
Orphan (film) 109
The Orphanage 227, 228, 239–243
Osborn, Marijane 126

Paganism 130–4, 138
Parkinson's disease (PD) 174
Peck, M. Scott 176
Pediatrics 173–4
Pedophilia/pedophile 8, 20, 211, 221–2, 263
Peeping Tom 178–80
Performance: childhood as 20, 23, 116, 117–19, 157, 206, 208, 209, 254; of girlhood/girlness 23, 206, 212–13, 215–222; of monstrosity *see* monstrosity as performance; newborn narratives as 30; sexual and/or gender 35–6, 201, 210–11; of violence: 108, 209, 211, 212, 216–222
Pirie, David 107
Polanski, Roman 79–89
Prometheus (film) 57, 96–104
Pro-natalism 2, 43, 46, 49, 58–9
Psycho (1960 film) 178–9

Raise Ravens 228–30
Rancière, Jacques 254
Religious preoccupations 174
REM behavioral disorder 174
Rilke, Rainer Maria 9
The Ring 2, 44, 48, 53
Ritalin 174–5
Romantic child 7, 212
Romanticism 9, 17, 19, 20, 30, 80–1, 83–8, 91, 113, 188, 236, 254
Rosemary's Baby (film) 2, 10, 21, 79–92, 185, 268
Rousseau, Jean-Jacques 119, 92, 49, 150, 157
Rusnak, Joseph 28, 32, 37

Sanger, Margaret 51, 202
Sargent, John Singer 142
Saura, Carlos 228, 230, 232
Scott, Ridley 22, 57, 96, 100–5
Sedgwick, Eve Kosofsky 3, 150, 157
Seizure 88, 90, 174; temporal lobe seizure 174
Shakespeare, William 9, 13, 117
Shelley, Mary 2–3, 21–2, 64, 79–81, 84–7, 90, 96–7, 100
The Shining (film) 22, 79, 92, 160–170
Slasher films 23, 177–187, 191
Sleep specialist 174
Sleepaway Camp 182
Sleeping Beauty (fairytale) 18
Smith, Klein & French 174
Snyder, Sharon L. 178–9, 185–6
Sobchack, Vivian 56, 58

278 INDEX

Solet, Paul 28, 38, 71, 74
The Spirit of the Beehive 228–9
Splice 48, 56
Springer, Claudia 103
Stigma 42–8, 52–5, 58
Stimulant 173–6
Still-birth 53, 71, 74
Sulzbacher, S.I. 175
Sutton, Travis 186

Teras, teratology 46, 80, 128, 179, 185
Transgression 52–3, 62–70, 73–5, 91, 101–5, 108, 112, 130, 177–8, 181, 185–6, 218, 227, 238, 250, 253
Trauma 4, 23, 43, 84, 86, 89, 114, 119, 133–4, 139, 167, 178, 185–6, 197, 225–44, 251, 255–6

Ussher, Jane 44

Vampire 23, 33, 36, 207, 210–20, 261
Victorian 4, 9, 11, 15, 93, 110, 115, 144, 156

Vigilantism 23, 130, 178, 186, 206–10, 219–21
Virilio, Paul 246–53
The Visitor 268–9

Waldeman, Diane 83
Wechter, Marilyn 2, 49
Williams, Linda 81, 185
Wojik-Andrews, Ian 14
Wood, Robin 11, 14, 39, 42
Woodson, Stephani Etheridge 108, 116
Wordsworth, William 19
Wright, Joe 245–7, 252, 257

Yancy, George 189

Zemeckis, Robert 126–7
Žižek, Slavoj 23, 246, 248, 251–5, 258
Zombie 21, 36, 61–74, 111, 267
Zombie Babies (film) 67, 70
Zupancic, Alenka 248–9

www.ingramcontent.com/pod-product-compliance
Ingram Content Group UK Ltd.
Pitfield, Milton Keynes, MK11 3LW, UK
UKHW041929140426
5217IPUK00014B/384